60 HIKES WITHIN 60 MILES

3RD Edition

ALBUQUERQUE

Including Santa Fe, Mount Taylor, and San Lorenzo Canyon

60 HIKES WITHIN 60 MILES: ALBUQUERQUE

Printed in China
Published by Menasha Ridge Press
Distributed by Publishers Group West
Third edition, second printing 2020

Library of Congress Cataloging-in-Publication Data
Names: Ryan, David, author.
Title: 60 hikes within 60 miles : Albuquerque, including Santa Fe, Mount Taylor, and San Lorenzo Canyon / David Ryan.
Description: Third Edition. | Birmingham, Alabama : Menasha Ridge Press, [2019] | "Distributed by Publishers Group West"—T.p. verso.
Identifiers: LCCN 2018029633| ISBN 9781634041546 (paperback) | ISBN 9781634041553 (ebook) ISBN 9781634042567 (hardcover)
Subjects: LCSH: Hiking—New Mexico—Albuquerque Region—Guidebooks. | Walking—New Mexico—Albuquerque Region—Guidebooks. | Backpacking—New Mexico—Albuquerque Region—Guidebooks. | Mountaineering—New Mexico—Albuquerque Region—Guidebooks. | Trails—New Mexico—Albuquerque Region—Guidebooks. | Outdoor recreation—New Mexico—Albuquerque Region—Guidebooks. | Albuquerque Region (N.M.)—Guidebooks. | New Mexico—Guidebooks.
Classification: LCC GV199.42.N62 A434 2019 | DDC 796.5109791—dc23
LC record available at https://lccn.loc.gov/2018029633

Cover and text design by Jonathan Norberg
Cover and interior photos by David Ryan
Cartography and elevation profiles by Scott McGrew, Tim Kissell, and David Ryan
Index by Rich Carlson

MENASHA RIDGE PRESS
An imprint of AdventureKEEN
2204 First Ave. S, Ste. 102
Birmingham, Alabama 35233
menasharidge.com

Dedication

This book is dedicated to Teddy and to those who love to hike with dogs.

60 HIKES WITHIN 60 MILES

3RD Edition

ALBUQUERQUE

Including Santa Fe, Mount Taylor, and San Lorenzo Canyon

David Ryan and Stephen Ausherman

60 Hikes Within 60 Miles: Albuquerque

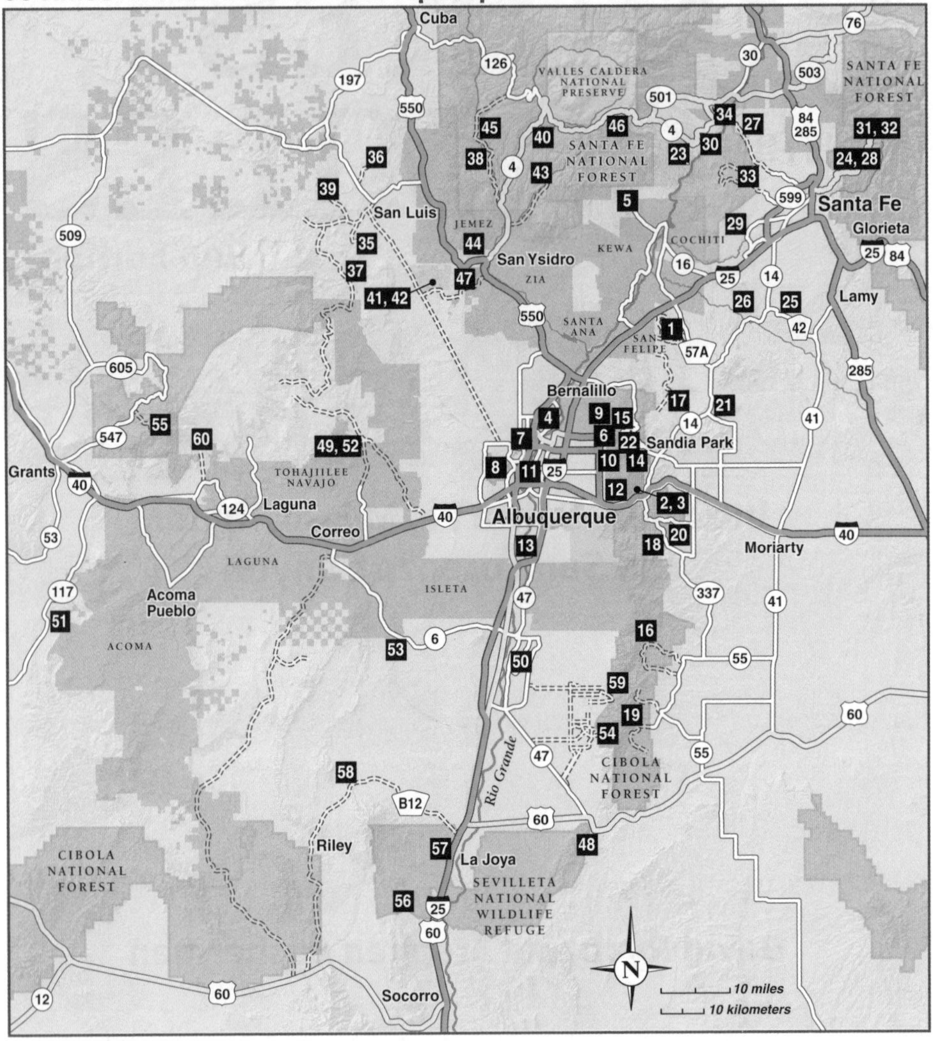

Cuba
VALLES CALDERA NATIONAL PRESERVE
SANTA FE NATIONAL FOREST
SANTA FE NATIONAL FOREST
Santa Fe
Glorieta
Lamy
San Luis
JEMEZ
San Ysidro
ZIA
KEWA
COCHITI
SANTA ANA
SAN FELIPE
Bernalillo
Sandia Park
Grants
Laguna
TOHAJIILEE NAVAJO
Correo
Albuquerque
Moriarty
LAGUNA
Acoma Pueblo
ACOMA
ISLETA
CIBOLA NATIONAL FOREST
Rio Grande
Riley
La Joya
SEVILLETA NATIONAL WILDLIFE REFUGE
CIBOLA NATIONAL FOREST
Socorro
N
10 miles
10 kilometers

TABLE OF CONTENTS

Overview Map iv
Map Legend vii
Acknowledgments ix
Foreword x
Preface xi
60 Hikes by Category xiii
Introduction 1

GREATER ALBUQUERQUE 21

1 Ball Ranch 22
2 Canyon Estates–Faulty Trails 26
3 Carlito Springs 31
4 Corrales Acequias and Bosque Preserve 36
5 Kasha-Katuwe Tent Rocks National Monument 41
6 La Luz Trail to the Crest and Tram 45
7 Petroglyph National Monument: *Piedras Marcadas* . . . 50
8 Petroglyph National Monument: *The Volcanoes* 54
9 Piedra Lisa Trailhead Options 59
10 Pino Trail 64
11 Rio Grande Nature Center–Bosque/Ditch Walk 69
12 Three Gun–Embudo Trails: *Up-and-Over-the-Sandias Adventure* . . . 74
13 Valle de Oro National Wildlife Refuge 79

EAST OF THE MOUNTAINS 85

14 Armijo Trail–Cienega Spring 86
15 Del Agua Overlook 91
16 Fourth of July Canyon–Cerro Blanco 95
17 Golden Open Space 100
18 Mars Court Trailhead–David Canyon 105
19 Red Canyon 110
20 Sabino Canyon and Juan Tomas Open Spaces 115
21 San Pedro Mountains Mining Area 120
22 Tree Spring–Crest Trail 125

GREATER SANTA FE 131

23 Bandelier National Monument: *Falls Trail* 132

24 Borrego Trail 137

25 Cañada de la Cueva 141

26 Cerrillos Hills State Park 146

27 Diablo Canyon–Buckman. 151

28 Hyde Memorial State Park 156

29 La Cieneguilla Petroglyph Site and Cañon 161

30 Lower Water Canyon–Lion Cave Trails 166

31 Nambe Lake. 171

32 Puerto Nambe–Santa Fe Baldy 176

33 Twin Hills 180

34 White Rock Canyon: *Red Dot/Blue Dot Trails* 185

NORTHWEST OF ALBUQUERQUE 191

35 Cabezon Peak 192

36 Continental Divide Trail (CDT): *Deadman Peaks* 196

37 Guadalupe Outlier 200

38 Holiday Mesa 204

39 La Leña WSA: *Empedrado Ridge–CDT* 209

40 McCauley Hot Springs 213

41 Ojito Wilderness: *Hoodoo Trail*. 218

42 Ojito Wilderness: *Seismosaurus Trail*. 222

43 Paliza Canyon Goblin Colony 227

44 San Ysidro Trials Area 232

45 Stable Mesa 237

46 Valles Caldera National Preserve 242

47 White Ridge Bike Trails Area 247

SOUTH AND WEST OF ALBUQUERQUE 253

48 Abó Pass Area 254

49 Cañada del Ojo 259

50 El Cerro Tomé. 264

51 El Malpais National Monument: *Sandstone Bluffs* 269
52 Herrera Mesa 274
53 Hidden Mountain. 278
54 Monte Largo Canyon 283
55 Mount Taylor: *Gooseberry Spring* 288
56 San Lorenzo Canyon 293
57 Sevilleta National Wildlife Refuge 298
58 Sierra Ladrones 303
59 Trigo Canyon 307
60 Water Canyon Wildlife Area 312

Appendix A: Public Lands 316

Appendix B: Everything Else You Need to Know About New Mexico 319

Index 321

About the Authors 327

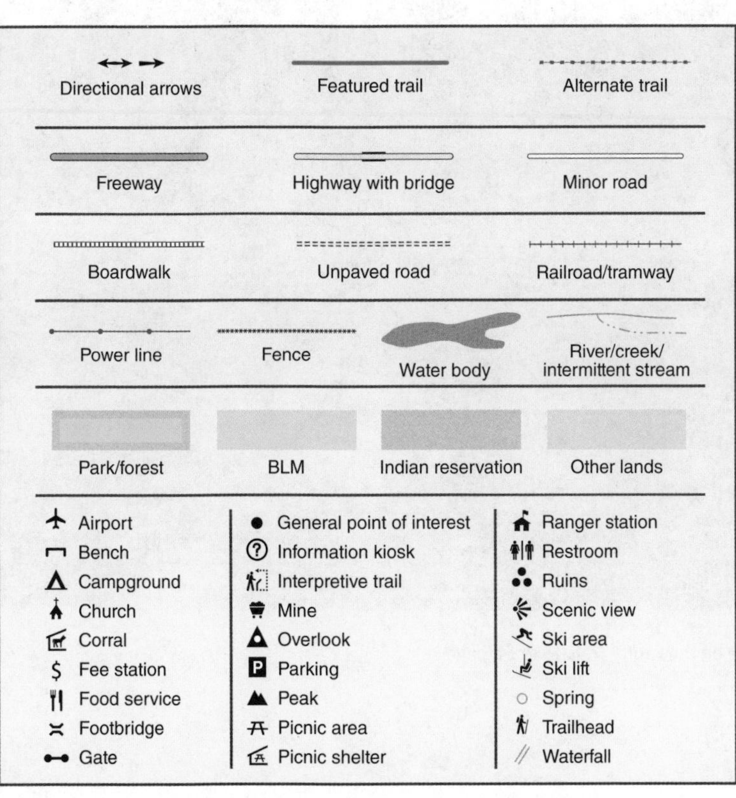

Thong tree on the Faulty Trail (Hike 14, page 86)

ACKNOWLEDGMENTS

First and foremost, I would like to thank Stephen Ausherman for inviting me to participate in this third edition of *60 Hikes Within 60 Miles: Albuquerque.* Without his previous body of work and continuing guidance, this project would have been very hard to complete in a reasonable time frame. I especially want to thank Michael Woodruff for accompanying me on many of the hikes and for introducing me to new ones that are now part of this book. I also want to give special thanks to Bob Julyan and Phil Neils for coming up with ideas for new hikes to add to the book. And I want to thank the team at Menasha Ridge Press and all of those who accompanied me on hikes or provided information related to this book, including Claudia, Jennifer, Amy, Ralph, Carolyn, Ivan, Bart, Henry, Dana, Matt, Doug, Rebecca, Gretchen, Jim, Brian, Jess, Maria, Tammy, Colleen, Katie, Dean, Bobby, and others whom I may have forgotten to mention.

But most of all I would like to thank Paddy, Petey, and Sparky, who came on all of the hikes where they were allowed. And I would also like to thank Fletcher, Beau, Barney, Lucky, Wesley, Pokey, and Teddy, who would have come if they were still here.

FOREWORD

Welcome to Menasha Ridge Press's 60 Hikes Within 60 Miles, a series designed to provide hikers with the information they need to find and hike the very best trails surrounding metropolitan areas.

Our strategy is simple: First, find a hiker who knows the area and loves to hike. Second, ask that person to spend a year researching the most popular and very best trails around. And third, have that person describe each trail in terms of difficulty, scenery, condition, elevation change, and other categories of information that are important to hikers. "Pretend you've just completed a hike and met up with other hikers at the trailhead," we told each author. "Imagine their questions; be clear in your answers."

As experienced hikers and writers, authors David Ryan and Stephen Ausherman have selected 60 of the best hikes in and around the Albuquerque metropolitan area. This third edition includes new hikes, as well as additional sections and new routes for some of the existing hikes. Ausherman and Ryan provide hikers (and walkers) with a great variety of hikes—all within roughly 60 miles of Albuquerque—from strolls along the Rio Grande to aerobic outings in mountains over 11,000 feet in altitude.

You'll get more out of this book if you take a moment to read the introduction, which explains how to read the trail listings. The "Maps" section will help you understand how useful topos are on a hike and will also tell you where to get them. And though this is a where-to, not a how-to, guide, readers who have not hiked extensively will find the introduction of particular value.

As much for the opportunity to free the spirit as to free the body, let these hikes elevate you above the urban hurry.

All the best,
The Editors at Menasha Ridge Press

PREFACE

I was honored when Stephen Ausherman asked me to participate in developing the third edition of *60 Hikes Within 60 Miles: Albuquerque.* We both knew at the time that we had to replace several of the hikes in the second edition because of access and other issues. And between the two of us, we knew of some better hikes that would be good additions to the book. After all, a new edition of any book should reflect what the authors have learned since the previous edition was written to make the book more useful to the reader.

As a result, the third edition has 19 brand-new hikes. Seventeen of the retained hikes have been significantly revised with new routings to make them fresh and better. And we have added seven new secondary or bonus hikes to the book. The remaining hikes have all been updated to reflect changes in signage, trail conditions, access rules, and the like. In most we have added options for making a trip shorter or longer. So please don't let the length of a hike deter you from considering it. Our hope is that you will find every hike in the book worth doing and worth the drive it takes to get there.

For me personally, developing this edition has been a transformative experience in realizing how lucky we are to be in New Mexico. It's very easy to get caught up in one's daily life and forget that we live in a remarkable and wonderful state. If you are fortunate enough to go on every one of these hikes, you'll encounter the most beautiful landscapes in the country. You'll go from high-country mountains

Santa Fe Baldy (Hike 32, page 176)

and alpine lakes to the most twisted sandstone formations in the desert that you can imagine. You'll pass through remarkable canyons, find amazing rock art, and encounter things that you can find only in New Mexico. You'll find some hikes right around the corner and others in areas so remote that you'll have a hard time believing that you are within 60 miles of anything, let alone Albuquerque. You'll find dozens of hikes on lands that would be national parks if they were in another state. There is so much out there for you to discover!

In addition to its extraordinary landscape, Albuquerque is a city that was meant for hiking. You can hike in all four seasons. When the mountains are snowed in, you can hike in the deserts. When the deserts and the city are blistering hot, you can cool off in the mountains. You can hike almost every day of the year in comfortable weather. I personally cannot think of any other city in the country that has the same access to remarkable and diverse landscapes and perfect hiking weather as Albuquerque. Again, we are fortunate to have so much available to us.

I have been asked many times which hike I like the best. All I can say is that they are all good and have something to offer in their own special way. One thing I've learned from hiking with dogs is that the best hike is the one that you're on, or as my dog Lucky (1997–2011) often said to me:

All walks are good.
I don't know how long this walk is going to be,
But I do know one thing:
This is the best walk I have ever been on
Because this is the walk I am on right now.

60 HIKES BY CATEGORY

REGION Hike Number/Hike Name		page #	Mileage	Difficulty	Kid Friendly	Dog Friendly	Mountain Bikes	Equestrians	Running
GREATER ALBUQUERQUE									
1	Ball Ranch	22	4.8	M		✓			
2	Canyon Estates–Faulty Trails	26	5.7	M	✓	✓			✓
3	Carlito Springs	31	2.0	M	✓	✓			
4	Corrales Acequias and Bosque Preserve	36	7.4	E	✓	✓	✓	✓	✓
5	Kasha-Katuwe Tent Rocks National Monument	41	3.4	M	✓				
6	La Luz Trail to the Crest and Tram	45	9.0	S					✓
7	Petroglyph National Monument: Piedras Marcadas	50	1.8	E	✓	✓			✓
8	Petroglyph National Monument: The Volcanoes	54	1.0/2.0/6.3 options	E/M	✓	✓			✓
9	Piedra Lisa Trailhead Options	59	4.2	M	✓	✓			✓
10	Pino Trail	64	9.0	M	✓	✓			✓
11	Rio Grande Nature Center–Bosque/Ditch Walk	69	3.7	E	✓	✓	✓	✓	✓
12	Three Gun–Embudo Trails: Up-and-Over-the-Sandias Adventure	74	5.6	M		✓			✓
13	Valle de Oro National Wildlife Refuge	79	2.5	E	✓	✓	✓		✓
EAST OF THE MOUNTAINS									
14	Armijo Trail–Cienega Spring	86	4.5/6.5	M	✓	✓	✓	✓	✓
15	Del Agua Overlook	91	4.4	M	✓	✓			✓
16	Fourth of July Canyon–Cerro Blanco	95	6.4	M	✓	✓		✓	
17	Golden Open Space	100	7.2	M		✓	✓	✓	✓
18	Mars Court Trailhead–David Canyon	105	4.8/6.8	M	✓	✓	✓	✓	✓
19	Red Canyon	110	5.5/8.6	M/S		✓		✓	
20	Sabino Canyon and Juan Tomas Open Spaces	115	2.0/3.7	E/M	✓	✓	✓	✓	✓
21	San Pedro Mountains Mining Area	120	3.2	M		✓			
22	Tree Spring–Crest Trail	125	4.0/7.2	M/M–S	✓	✓		✓	✓
GREATER SANTA FE									
23	Bandelier National Monument: Falls Trail	132	3.0	M	✓				
24	Borrego Trail	137	4.0	E–M	✓	✓	✓	✓	✓
25	Cañada de la Cueva	141	7.4	M		✓		✓	✓
26	Cerrillos Hills State Park	146	4.5/5.0	M	✓	✓		✓	✓
27	Diablo Canyon–Buckman	151	2.0/6.0	E/M		✓			
28	Hyde Memorial State Park	156	3.3	M–S	✓	✓			

DIFFICULTY RATINGS		
E = Easy	M = Moderate	S = Strenuous

REGION Hike Number/Hike Name		page #	Mileage	Difficulty	Kid Friendly	Dog Friendly	Mountain Bikes	Equestrians	Running
GREATER SANTA FE *(continued)*									
29	La Cieneguilla Petroglyph Site and Cañon	161	2.0–3.0/3.5	M	✓	✓			
30	Lower Water Canyon–Lion Cave Trails	166	2.2/5.0	M	✓	✓			
31	Nambe Lake	171	7.0	S		✓			
32	Puerto Nambe–Santa Fe Baldy	176	8.4	M	✓	✓		✓	
33	Twin Hills	180	6.9	E–S		✓			
34	White Rock Canyon: Red Dot/Blue Dot Trails	185	6.5	S		✓			
NORTHWEST OF ALBUQUERQUE									
35	Cabezon Peak	192	2.5	M–S		✓			
36	Continental Divide Trail (CDT): Deadman Peaks	196	2.8/4.9	E	✓	✓			
37	Guadalupe Outlier	200	0.5	E	✓	✓			
38	Holiday Mesa	204	4.6/8.5	E–S		✓			
39	La Leña WSA: Empedrado Ridge–CDT	209	5.5/6.0	M		✓			
40	McCauley Hot Springs	213	3.2/3.4	M	✓	✓			
41	Ojito Wilderness: Hoodoo Trail	218	4.0	E	✓	✓			
42	Ojito Wilderness: Seismosaurus Trail	222	2.25	E	✓	✓			
43	Paliza Canyon Goblin Colony	227	3.6/5.25	E–M	✓	✓			
44	San Ysidro Trials Area	232	3.0/5.4	E–M	✓	✓			
45	Stable Mesa	237	6.6	M–S		✓			
46	Valles Caldera National Preserve	242	2.0/2.9	E	✓	✓			
47	White Ridge Bike Trails Area	247	5.5	M		✓	✓		
SOUTH AND WEST OF ALBUQUERQUE									
48	Abó Pass Area	254	4.1	E–M	✓	✓			
49	Cañada del Ojo	259	4.5	M	✓	✓			
50	El Cerro Tomé	264	1.7	M–S	✓				
51	El Malpais National Monument: Sandstone Bluffs	269	5.5/4.0–6.0	M	✓	✓			
52	Herrera Mesa	274	4.0–5.0	M		✓			
53	Hidden Mountain	278	1.6/3.3	E/M	✓	✓			
54	Monte Largo Canyon	283	5.0	M		✓			
55	Mount Taylor: Gooseberry Spring	288	6.0	M–S		✓			✓
56	San Lorenzo Canyon	293	4.0	E	✓	✓			
57	Sevilleta National Wildlife Refuge	298	5.5	E–M	✓	✓			
58	Sierra Ladrones	303	7.0	M–S		✓			
59	Trigo Canyon	307	5.2	M–S		✓			
60	Water Canyon Wildlife Area	312	2.5–3.5	M–S		✓			

Hikes by Category
(continued)

REGION Hike Number/Hike Name		page #	Solitude	Bird-watching	Reptiles	Rock Formations	Water Features	Wildflowers	Vistas
GREATER ALBUQUERQUE									
1	Ball Ranch	22	✓	✓	✓	✓		✓	✓
2	Canyon Estates–Faulty Trails	26		✓	✓	✓	✓	✓	✓
3	Carlito Springs	31		✓	✓	✓	✓	✓	✓
4	Corrales Acequias and Bosque Preserve	36		✓	✓		✓	✓	✓
5	Kasha-Katuwe Tent Rocks National Monument	41		✓	✓	✓		✓	✓
6	La Luz Trail to the Crest and Tram	45		✓	✓	✓		✓	✓
7	Petroglyph National Monument: Piedras Marcadas	50		✓	✓	✓		✓	✓
8	Petroglyph National Monument: The Volcanoes	54		✓	✓	✓		✓	✓
9	Piedra Lisa Trailhead Options	59		✓	✓	✓	✓	✓	✓
10	Pino Trail	64		✓	✓	✓	✓	✓	✓
11	Rio Grande Nature Center–Bosque/Ditch Walk	69		✓	✓		✓	✓	
12	Three Gun–Embudo Trails: Up-and-Over-the-Sandias Adventure	74		✓	✓	✓		✓	✓
13	Valle de Oro National Wildlife Refuge	79		✓	✓		✓	✓	✓
EAST OF THE MOUNTAINS									
14	Armijo Trail–Cienega Spring	86		✓	✓		✓	✓	✓
15	Del Agua Overlook	91		✓		✓		✓	✓
16	Fourth of July Canyon–Cerro Blanco	95	✓	✓		✓	✓	✓	✓
17	Golden Open Space	100		✓	✓	✓		✓	✓
18	Mars Court Trailhead–David Canyon	105	✓	✓	✓			✓	✓
19	Red Canyon	110	✓	✓		✓	✓	✓	✓
20	Sabino Canyon and Juan Tomas Open Spaces	115		✓	✓			✓	
21	San Pedro Mountains Mining Area	120	✓	✓	✓				✓
22	Tree Spring–Crest Trail	125		✓				✓	✓
GREATER SANTA FE									
23	Bandelier National Monument: Falls Trail	132		✓		✓	✓	✓	✓
24	Borrego Trail	137		✓			✓	✓	✓
25	Cañada de la Cueva	141	✓	✓	✓	✓			✓
26	Cerrillos Hills State Park	146		✓	✓			✓	✓
27	Diablo Canyon–Buckman	151	✓	✓	✓	✓	✓	✓	✓
28	Hyde Memorial State Park	156		✓			✓	✓	✓
29	La Cieneguilla Petroglyph Site and Cañon	161		✓	✓		✓	✓	✓
30	Lower Water Canyon–Lion Cave Trails	166		✓		✓		✓	✓

Hikes by Category *(continued)* **REGION** Hike Number/Hike Name		page #	Solitude	Bird-watching	Reptiles	Rock Formations	Water Features	Wildflowers	Vistas
GREATER SANTA FE *(continued)*									
31	Nambe Lake	171		✓		✓	✓	✓	✓
32	Puerto Nambe–Santa Fe Baldy	176		✓			✓	✓	✓
33	Twin Hills	180	✓	✓	✓	✓		✓	✓
34	White Rock Canyon: Red Dot/Blue Dot Trails	185		✓	✓	✓	✓	✓	✓
NORTHWEST OF ALBUQUERQUE									
35	Cabezon Peak	192		✓	✓	✓		✓	✓
36	Continental Divide Trail (CDT): Deadman Peaks	196	✓	✓	✓	✓		✓	✓
37	Guadalupe Outlier	200	✓	✓	✓	✓		✓	✓
38	Holiday Mesa	204	✓	✓		✓	✓	✓	✓
39	La Leña WSA: Empedrado Ridge–CDT	209	✓	✓	✓	✓		✓	✓
40	McCauley Hot Springs	213		✓		✓	✓	✓	✓
41	Ojito Wilderness: Hoodoo Trail	218		✓	✓	✓		✓	✓
42	Ojito Wilderness: Seismosaurus Trail	222		✓	✓	✓		✓	✓
43	Paliza Canyon Goblin Colony	227		✓	✓	✓		✓	✓
44	San Ysidro Trials Area	232	✓	✓	✓	✓	✓	✓	✓
45	Stable Mesa	237	✓	✓		✓	✓	✓	✓
46	Valles Caldera National Preserve	242		✓		✓		✓	✓
47	White Ridge Bike Trails Area	247		✓	✓	✓	✓	✓	✓
SOUTH AND WEST OF ALBUQUERQUE									
48	Abó Pass Area	254	✓	✓	✓	✓		✓	✓
49	Cañada del Ojo	259	✓	✓	✓	✓		✓	✓
50	El Cerro Tomé	264		✓	✓			✓	✓
51	El Malpais National Monument: Sandstone Bluffs	269		✓	✓	✓		✓	✓
52	Herrera Mesa	274	✓	✓	✓	✓		✓	✓
53	Hidden Mountain	278		✓	✓	✓		✓	✓
54	Monte Largo Canyon	283	✓	✓	✓			✓	✓
55	Mount Taylor: Gooseberry Spring	288	✓	✓				✓	✓
56	San Lorenzo Canyon	293		✓	✓	✓	✓	✓	✓
57	Sevilleta National Wildlife Refuge	298		✓	✓	✓		✓	✓
58	Sierra Ladrones	303	✓	✓	✓	✓		✓	✓
59	Trigo Canyon	307	✓	✓	✓	✓	✓	✓	✓
60	Water Canyon Wildlife Area	312	✓	✓	✓	✓	✓	✓	✓

INTRODUCTION

Welcome to *60 Hikes Within 60 Miles: Albuquerque*. If you're new to hiking or even if you're a seasoned trekker, take a few minutes to read the following introduction. We'll explain how this book is organized and how to get the best use of it.

About This Book

Sitting in the middle of the nation's fifth-largest state, Albuquerque has many options for a fantastic hike. They range from high-country hikes in the mountains to quiet strolls along the Rio Grande to wandering through amazing landscapes in the backcountry. If you're looking for a hike with a lot of climbing, you can find it here in this book. If you're looking for a hike with a more horizontal component, you can find that too. And if you want to make amazing discoveries, we have hikes for you.

With so much to choose from, we wanted to make sure that every hike in this book was more than just a nice place to walk your dog and that it was worth your time and effort to get there. Our criteria for selecting the hikes is that they should

- **have a sense of adventure or accomplishment**
- **inspire a sense of awe or have a wow factor**
- **offer an opportunity for discovery, learning, or exploring**
- **provide a serene place for peace and contemplation**

We believe that all 60 hikes meet most, if not all, of the above criteria. The 60 hikes are organized as follows:

GREATER ALBUQUERQUE

We feature 13 hikes in the greater Albuquerque area. Six are in the Sandia Mountains on the east side of town, two are at Petroglyph National Monument on the west side, three are along the Rio Grande in the bosque (wooded area), and two are north of town, including the must-see, world-class destination of Tent Rocks. If you have an out-of-town guest, Tent Rocks is the place to go. If your guest would rather do a mountain hike, the Pino Trail is hard to beat. For something easier, there is always a walk in the bosque, and Piedras Marcadas is good for something cultural. Hiking to Sandia Crest on the La Luz Trail and taking the tram back to the bottom is a world-class adventure right in our own backyard.

EAST OF THE MOUNTAINS

Nine hikes are located on the other side of the mountains from Albuquerque. Four of them are south of Tijeras in the Manzanita and Manzano Mountains. The Mars Court Trailhead provides access to David Canyon for one of the best hikes fairly close to Albuquerque. Fourth of July Canyon offers great fall colors, and Red Canyon has amazing landforms. North of Tijeras are three hikes on the east side of the Sandias. Armijo-Cienega in the lower Sandias is full of surprises. Tree Spring farther up the mountain is a family-friendly hike that provides easy access to the top of the mountain, and Del Agua at the top of the mountain has the best fall colors in the Sandias. Two more hikes are farther north, near the ghost town of Golden. The colors of the eroded canyon at Golden Open Space will remind you of a smaller Grand Canyon. The hike in the San Pedros allows you to explore an old mining area that had been off-limits to the public for years.

GREATER SANTA FE

Twelve hikes are featured in the greater Santa Fe area. Three trips south of town include hiking in the Cerrillos Hills mining area, an exploration of a seldom-visited canyon, and a visit to a world-class petroglyph site. A companion hike of the petroglyph site includes a walk to a peaceful corner of the Santa Fe River. Two hikes explore the volcanic features of the Caja del Rio west of Santa Fe. Twin Hills has a volcanic vent that doesn't seem to have a bottom. The setting at Diablo Canyon is so spectacular that it has been used in several movies. Four hikes are east of town in the Sangre de Cristo Mountains. Hyde Park and Borrego are close in to town for a quick mountain getaway. Puerto Nambe and Nambe Lake are farther up the mountain and allow you to explore the world-famous Pecos Wilderness for two wonderful high-country adventures. Nambe Lake may have the most spectacular setting in the entire book! Three more hikes are northwest of town on the Pajarito Plateau. Bandelier National Monument is a must-see destination. A visit there is like dropping into Shangri-La. Lower Water Canyon has the same scenery as Bandelier without the fees and allows dogs. White Rock Canyon offers you an adventure that you'll never forget.

NORTHWEST OF ALBUQUERQUE

We include 13 hikes northwest of Albuquerque. This area can be broken down into three separate sections: the Ojito, the Upper Rio Puerco, and the Jemez Mountains. The Ojito, Albuquerque's close-in backcountry playground, features four hikes (White Ridge, Seismosaurus, Hoodoo, and San Ysidro). All four hikes feature unforgettable scenery and should be on your must-do list. The Upper Rio Puerco with four hikes has national park–quality scenery with views that will take your breath away. The drive to Guadalupe Outlier rivals California Highway 1 in scenic beauty. It has to be the nation's least visited scenic drive. With five hikes, the Jemez Mountains are another close-to-Albuquerque playground. The hikes feature fabulous landforms, ancient ruins, incredible views, and a hike to a remote hot spring. Our hike at Valles Caldera doesn't require a permit and allows dogs. The caldera is worth a trip across the country to see.

SOUTH AND WEST OF ALBUQUERQUE

Thirteen hikes are located south and west of Albuquerque. The eight hikes to the south of Albuquerque include a mysterious rock, the destination of a Good Friday pilgrimage, exploration of the west side of the Manzano Mountains, interesting fossils, quality time with birds, an amazing canyon, and a view of the "big empty" from high up in the Sierra Ladrones. To the west we have two close-in backcountry hikes. The hike at Cañada del Ojo features a hoodoo village and two abandoned homesteads. Farther west at Water Canyon we visit an isolated tract of publicly accessible land. And even farther west we have two of the best hikes in the book. The sandstone bluffs at El Malpais are, in a word, spectacular. The open meadows at the top of Mount Taylor will remind you of the opening scene in the movie *The Sound of Music.* It's a hike guaranteed to make you feel wonderful.

In fact, we hope that all of the hikes in the book will make you feel wonderful!

How to Use This Guidebook

The following information walks you through this guidebook's organization to make it easy and convenient for planning great hikes.

OVERVIEW MAP AND MAP LEGEND

Use the overview map on page iv to assess the general location of each hike's primary trailhead. Each hike's number appears on the overview map and in the table of contents. As you flip through the book, a hike's full profile is easy to locate by watching for the hike number at the top of each page. A map legend that details the symbols found on trail maps appears on page vii.

REGIONAL MAPS

The book is divided into regions, and prefacing each regional section is a regional overview map. The regional maps provide more detail than the overview map, bringing you closer to the hikes.

TRAIL MAPS

A detailed map of each hike's route appears with its profile. On each of these maps, symbols indicate the trailhead, the complete route, significant features, facilities, and topographic landmarks such as creeks, overlooks, and peaks.

To produce the highly accurate maps in this book, the author used a handheld GPS unit to gather data while hiking each route, and then sent that data to the publisher's expert cartographers. However, your GPS is not really a substitute for sound, sensible navigation that takes into account the conditions that you observe while hiking.

Further, despite the high quality of the maps in this guidebook, the publisher and author strongly recommend that you always carry an additional map, such as the ones noted in each entry's listing for "Maps."

ELEVATION PROFILES (DIAGRAM)

For trails with any significant elevation changes, the hike description *will* include this profile graph. Entries for fairly flat routes, such as along the Rio Grande, will *not* display an elevation profile.

For hike descriptions where the elevation profile is included, this diagram represents the rises and falls of the trail as viewed from the side, over the complete distance (in miles) of that trail. On the diagram's vertical axis, or height scale, the number of feet indicated between each tick mark lets you visualize the climb. To avoid making flat hikes look steep and steep hikes appear flat, varying height scales provide an accurate image of each hike's climbing challenge. For example, one hike's scale might rise to 6,000 feet, while another goes to 11,000 feet.

THE HIKE PROFILE

Each hike contains a brief overview of the trail, a description of the route from start to finish, key at-a-glance information—from the trail's distance and configuration to contacts for local information—GPS trailhead coordinates, and directions for driving to the trailhead area. Each profile also includes a map (see "Trail Maps," on the previous page) and elevation profile (if the elevation gain is 100 feet or more). Many hike profiles also include notes on nearby activities.

KEY INFORMATION

The information in this box gives you a quick idea of the statistics and specifics of each hike.

DISTANCE & CONFIGURATION *Distance* notes the length of the hike round-trip, from start to finish. If the hike description includes options to shorten or extend the hike, those round-trip distances will also be factored here. *Configuration* defines the trail as a loop, an out-and-back (taking you in and out via the same route), a figure eight, or a balloon.

DIFFICULTY The degree of effort that a typical hiker should expect on a given route. For simplicity, the trails are rated as *easy, moderate,* or *strenuous.*

SCENERY A short summary of the attractions offered by the hike and what to expect in terms of plant life, wildlife, natural wonders, and historic features.

EXPOSURE A quick check of how much sun you can expect on your shoulders during the hike.

TRAIL TRAFFIC Indicates how busy the trail might be on an average day. Trail traffic, of course, varies from day to day and season to season. Weekend days typically see the most visitors. Other trail users that may be encountered on the trail are also noted here.

TRAIL SURFACE Indicates whether the trail surface is paved, rocky, gravel, dirt, boardwalk, or a mixture of elements.

HIKING TIME How long it takes to hike the trail. A slow but steady hiker will average 2–3 miles an hour, depending on the terrain.

DRIVING DISTANCE Listed in miles from the "Big I" (I-25/I-40 interchange).

ELEVATION GAIN Lists elevation at the trailhead and another figure for the highest or lowest altitude on the route. If there is no significant gain, that is also noted.

ACCESS Fees or permits required to hike the trail are detailed here—and noted if there are none. Trail access hours are also shown here.

WHEELCHAIR ACCESS At a glance, you'll see if there are paved sections or other areas for safely using a wheelchair.

MAPS Resources for maps, in addition to those in this guidebook, are listed here. (As previously noted, the publisher and author recommend that you carry more than one map—and that you consult those maps before heading out on the trail in order to resolve any confusion or discrepancy.)

FACILITIES This item alerts you to restrooms, water, picnic tables, and other basics at or near the trailhead.

CONTACT Listed here are phone numbers and website addresses for checking trail conditions and gleaning other day-to-day information.

LOCATION The city (or nearby community) in which the trail is located.

COMMENTS Here you will find assorted nuggets of information, such as whether or not dogs are allowed on the trails.

LAST-CHANCE FOOD/GAS This section identifies where to get food or gas when away from Albuquerque or Santa Fe.

IN BRIEF

Think of this section as a taste of the trail, a snapshot focused on the historical landmarks, beautiful vistas, and other sights you may encounter on the hike.

DESCRIPTION

The heart of each hike. Here, the author provides a summary of the trail's essence and highlights any special traits the hike has to offer. The route is clearly outlined, including landmarks, side trips, and possible alternate routes along the way. Ultimately, the hike description will help you choose which hikes are best for you.

NEARBY ACTIVITIES

Look here for information on things to do or points of interest: nearby parks, museums, restaurants, and the like. Note that not every hike has a listing.

DIRECTIONS

Used in conjunction with the GPS coordinates, the driving directions will help you locate each trailhead. Once at the trailhead, park only in designated areas.

GPS TRAILHEAD COORDINATES

As noted in "Trail Maps," page 3, the author used a handheld GPS unit to obtain geographic data and sent the information to the publisher's cartographers. The trailhead coordinates—the intersection of the latitude (north) and longitude (west)—will orient you from the trailhead. In some cases, you can drive within viewing distance of a trailhead. Other hiking routes require a short walk to the trailhead from a parking area.

You will also note that this guidebook uses the degree–decimal minute format for presenting the latitude and longitude GPS coordinates.

N35° 23.372' W106° 18.116'

The latitude and longitude grid system is likely quite familiar to you, but here is a refresher, pertinent to visualizing the GPS coordinates:

Imaginary lines of latitude—called parallels and approximately 69 miles apart from each other—run horizontally around the globe. The equator is established to be 0°, and each parallel is indicated by degrees from the equator: up to 90°N at the North Pole, and down to 90°S at the South Pole.

Imaginary lines of longitude—called meridians—run perpendicular to latitude lines. Longitude lines are likewise indicated by degrees. Starting from 0° at the Prime Meridian in Greenwich, England, they continue to the east and west until they meet 180° later at the International Date Line in the Pacific Ocean. At the equator, longitude lines are also approximately 69 miles apart, but that distance narrows as the meridians converge toward the North and South Poles.

To convert GPS coordinates given in degrees, minutes, and seconds to the above degrees and decimal minutes, the seconds are divided by 60. For more information on GPS technology, visit usgs.gov.

TOPOGRAPHIC MAPS

The maps in this book have been produced with great care and, used with the hike text, will direct you to the trail and help you stay on course. However, you'll find superior detail and valuable information in the U.S. Geological Survey's 7.5-minute-series topographic maps. At mytopo.com, for example, you can view and print free USGS topos of the entire United States. Online services such as Trails.com charge annual fees for additional features such as shaded relief, which makes the topography stand out more. If you expect to print out many topo maps each year, it might be worth paying for such extras. The downside to USGS maps is that most are outdated, having been created 20–30 years ago; nevertheless, they provide excellent topographic detail. Of course, Google Earth (earth.google.com) does away with topo maps and their inaccuracies . . . replacing them with satellite imagery and its inaccuracies. Regardless, what one lacks, the other augments. Google Earth is an excellent tool whether you have difficulty with topos or not.

If you're new to hiking, you might be wondering, "What's a topo map?" In short, it indicates not only linear distance but elevation as well, using contour lines. These lines spread across the map like dozens of intricate spiderwebs. Each line represents a particular elevation, and at the base of each topo a contour's interval designation is given. If, for example, the contour interval is 20 feet, then the distance between each contour line is 20 feet. Follow five contour lines up on the same map, and the elevation has increased by 100 feet. In addition to the sources listed previously, you'll find topos at major universities, outdoors shops, and some public libraries, as well as online at nationalmap.gov and store.usgs.gov.

Weather

With a base elevation of 5,000 feet, Albuquerque usually enjoys a high-desert climate. Think of it as the happy medium between the extremes of Denver and Phoenix. Days are generally sunny and warm, but as the sun sets, the temperature falls. The city experiences an average change of 24 degrees from day to night all year. An average year here includes 310 days of sunshine and about 9 inches of rain, with relative humidity normally around 44%.

Summer is hot, of course, but low humidity helps keep it cooler than just about anywhere else south of the 36th parallel. And even when daytime temperatures soar into triple digits, you can always count on cool nights. In July and August, afternoon monsoons break the heat with sudden and furious thunderstorms.

Autumn can bring sunshine, thunderstorms, snow, or all of the above at once. Generally, warm temperatures still linger in September and early October, with sweater days firmly established by November.

Winter requires extra layers, though a light jacket often suffices on sunny days. Snow seldom lasts more than a day or two in town. However, deep canyons, north-facing slopes, and elevations above 8,000 feet can take weeks or months to fully defrost.

Spring often begins with high winds that can blow for days. Whether gusting off the West Mesa or howling through Tijeras Canyon, they create miserable conditions for outdoor recreation. On the plus side, it's a sure sign that perfect weather is right around the corner.

Before you go out, check the forecast with the National Weather Service: 505-821-1111 or weather.gov/abq.

And no matter what they say, be prepared for anything.

The following chart lists average temperatures and precipitation by month for the Albuquerque region. For each month, "High" temp is the average daytime high, "Low" temp is the average nighttime low.

AVERAGE DAILY TEMPERATURES						
	JAN	FEB	MARCH	APRIL	MAY	JUNE
High	46.8°F	52.5°F	60.5°F	69.0°F	78.8°F	88.3°F
Low	26.1°F	30.3°F	35.7°F	43.0°F	52.5°F	61.6°F
	JULY	AUG	SEPT	OCT	NOV	DEC
High	90.1°F	87.2°F	80.7°F	69.0°F	55.8°F	46.1°F
Low	66.4°F	65.1°F	57.9°F	46.1°F	34.1°F	26.5°F

AVERAGE PRECIPITATION					
JAN	FEB	MARCH	APRIL	MAY	JUNE
0.38"	0.48"	0.57"	0.61"	0.50"	0.66"
JULY	AUG	SEPT	OCT	NOV	DEC
1.50"	1.58"	1.08"	1.02"	0.57"	0.50"

Water

How much is enough? Well, one simple physiological fact should convince you to err on the side of excess when deciding how much water to pack: a hiker walking steadily in 90°F heat needs approximately 10 quarts of fluid per day. That's 2.5 gallons. A good rule of thumb is to hydrate prior to your hike, carry (and drink) 6 ounces of water for every mile you plan to hike, and hydrate again after the hike. For most people, the pleasures of hiking make carrying water a relatively minor price to pay to remain safe and healthy. So pack more water than you anticipate needing even for short hikes.

If you are tempted to drink "found" water, do so with extreme caution. Many ponds and lakes encountered by hikers are fairly stagnant and the water tastes terrible. Drinking such water presents inherent risks for thirsty trekkers. Giardia parasites contaminate many water sources and cause the dreaded intestinal giardiasis that can last for weeks after ingestion. For information, visit the Centers for Disease Control and Prevention website at cdc.gov/parasites/giardia.

In any case, effective treatment is essential before using any water source found along the trail. Boiling water for 2–3 minutes is always a safe measure for camping, but day hikers can consider iodine tablets, approved chemical mixes, filtration units rated for giardia, and UV filtration. Some of these methods (for example, filtration with an added carbon filter) remove bad tastes typical in stagnant water, while others add their own taste. As a precaution, carry a means of water purification to help in a pinch and if you realize you have underestimated your consumption needs.

Clothing

Weather, unexpected trail conditions, fatigue, extended hiking duration, and wrong turns can individually or collectively turn a great outing into a very uncomfortable one at best—and a life-threatening one at worst. Thus, proper attire plays a key role in staying comfortable and, sometimes, in staying alive. Here are some helpful guidelines:

- **Choose silk, wool, or synthetics for maximum comfort in all of your hiking attire**—from hats to socks and in between. Cotton is fine if the weather remains dry and stable, but you won't be happy if that material gets wet.
- **Always wear a hat, or at least tuck one into your day pack or hitch it to your belt.** Hats offer all-weather sun and wind protection as well as warmth if it turns cold.
- **Be ready to layer up or down as the day progresses and the mercury rises or falls.** Today's outdoor wear makes layering easy, with such designs as jackets that convert to vests and zip-off or button-up legs.
- **Wear hiking boots or sturdy hiking sandals with toe protection.** Flip-flopping along a paved urban greenway is one thing, but never hike a trail in open sandals or casual sneakers. Your bones and arches need support, and your skin needs protection.
- **Pair that footwear with good socks!** If you prefer not to sheathe your feet when wearing hiking sandals, tuck the socks into your day pack; you may need them if the weather plummets or if you hit rocky turf and pebbles begin to irritate your feet. And, in an emergency, if you have lost your gloves, you can adapt the socks into mittens.
- **Unless you are certain that it is not going to rain or snow, don't leave rainwear behind, even if the day dawns clear and sunny.** Tuck into your day pack, or tie around your waist, a jacket that is breathable and either water-resistant or waterproof. Investigate different choices at your local outdoors retailer. If you are a frequent hiker, ideally you'll have more than one rainwear weight, material, and style in your closet to protect you in all seasons in your regional climate and hiking microclimates.

Essential Gear

Today you can buy outdoor vests that have up to 20 pockets shaped and sized to carry everything from toothpicks to binoculars. Or, if you don't aspire to feel like a burro, you can neatly stow all of these items in your day pack or backpack. The following list showcases never-hike-without-them items, in alphabetical order, as all are important:

- **Extra clothes** (Raingear, warm hat, gloves, and change of socks and shirt)
- **Extra food** (Trail mix, granola bars, or other high-energy foods)
- **Flashlight or headlamp with extra bulb and batteries**
- **Insect repellent** (For some areas and seasons, this is extremely vital.)
- **Maps and a high-quality compass** (Even if you know the terrain from previous hikes, don't leave home without these tools. And, as previously noted, bring maps in addition to those in this guidebook, and consult your maps prior to the hike. If you are versed in GPS usage, bring that device too, but don't rely on it as your sole navigational tool, as battery life can dwindle or die, and be sure to compare its guidance with that of your maps.)
- **Pocketknife and/or multitool**
- **Sunscreen** (Note the expiration date on the tube or bottle; it's usually embossed on the top.)
- **Water** (As emphasized more than once in this book, bring more than you think you will drink. Depending on your destination, you may want to bring a container and iodine or a filter for purifying water in case you run out.)
- **Whistle** (This little gadget will be your best friend in an emergency.)
- **Windproof matches and/or a lighter, as well as a fire starter**

FIRST AID KIT

In addition to the aforementioned items, those below may appear overwhelming for a day hike. But any paramedic will tell you that the products listed here—in alphabetical order, because all are important—are just the basics. The reality of hiking is that you can be out for a week of backpacking and acquire only a mosquito bite. Or you can hike for an hour, slip, and suffer a bleeding abrasion or broken bone. Fortunately, these listed items will collapse into a very small space. You also may purchase convenient, prepackaged kits at your pharmacy or online.

- **Adhesive bandages**
- **Antibiotic ointment** (Neosporin or the generic equivalent)
- **Athletic tape**
- **Benadryl** or the generic equivalent, diphenhydramine (in case of allergic reactions)
- **Blister kit** (such as Moleskin/Spenco 2nd Skin)

- **Butterfly-closure bandages**
- **Elastic bandages or joint wraps**
- **Epinephrine in a prefilled syringe** (typically by prescription only, and for people known to have severe allergic reactions to hiking occurrences such as bee stings)
- **Gauze** (one roll and a half dozen 4-by-4-inch pads)
- **Hydrogen peroxide** or iodine
- **Ibuprofen** or acetaminophen

Note: Consider your intended terrain and the number of hikers in your party before you exclude any article cited above. A botanical garden stroll may not inspire you to carry a complete kit, but anything beyond that warrants precaution. When hiking alone, you should always be prepared for a medical need. And if you are a twosome or with a group, one or more people in your party should be equipped with first aid material.

General Safety

The following tips may have the familiar ring of your mother's voice as you take note of them.

- **Always let someone know where you will be hiking and how long you expect to be gone.** It's a good idea to give that person a copy of your route, particularly if you are headed into any isolated area. Let them know when you return.
- **Always sign in and out of any trail registers provided.** Don't hesitate to comment on the trail condition if space is provided; that's your opportunity to alert others to any problems you encounter.
- **Do not count on a cell phone for your safety.** Reception may be spotty or nonexistent on the trail, even on an urban walk—especially if it is embraced by towering trees.
- **Always carry food and water, even for a short hike.** And bring more water than you think you will need. (That cannot be said often enough!)
- **Ask questions.** Land management agency and park employees are there to help. It's a lot easier to solicit advice before a problem occurs, and it will help you avoid a mishap away from civilization when it's too late to amend an error.
- **Stay on designated trails.** Even on the most clearly marked trails, there is usually a point where you have to stop and consider in which direction to head. If you become disoriented, don't panic. As soon as you think you may be off track, stop, assess your current direction, and then retrace your steps to the point where you went astray. Using a map, a compass, and this book, and

keeping in mind what you have passed thus far, reorient yourself, and trust your judgment on which way to continue. If you become absolutely unsure of how to continue, return to your vehicle the way you came in. Should you become completely lost and have no idea how to find the trailhead, remaining in place along the trail and waiting for help is most often the best option for adults and always the best option for children.

- **Always carry a whistle, another precaution that cannot be overemphasized.** It may be a lifesaver if you do become lost or sustain an injury.
- **Be especially careful when crossing streams.** Whether you are fording the stream or crossing on a log, make every step count. If you have any doubt about maintaining your balance on a log, ford the stream instead: use a trekking pole or stout stick for balance *and face upstream as you cross.* If a stream seems too deep to ford, turn back. Whatever is on the other side is not worth risking your life.
- **Be careful at overlooks.** While these areas may provide spectacular views, they are potentially hazardous. Stay back from the edge of outcrops, and make absolutely sure of your footing; a misstep can mean a nasty and possibly fatal fall.
- **Standing dead trees and storm-damaged living trees pose a significant hazard to hikers.** These trees may have loose or broken limbs that could fall at any time. While walking beneath trees, and when choosing a spot to rest or enjoy your snack, look up.
- **Know the symptoms of subnormal body temperature known as hypothermia.** Shivering and forgetfulness are the two most common indicators of this stealthy killer. Hypothermia can occur at any elevation, even in the summer, especially when the hiker is wearing lightweight cotton clothing. If symptoms present themselves, get to shelter, hot liquids, and dry clothes as soon as possible.
- **Know the symptoms of heat exhaustion (hyperthermia).** Light-headedness and loss of energy are two indicators. If you feel these symptoms, find some shade, drink your water, remove as many layers of clothing as practical, and stay put until you cool down. Marching through heat exhaustion leads to heatstroke—which can be fatal. If you should be sweating and you're not, that's the signature warning sign. Your hike is over at that point—heatstroke is a life-threatening condition that can cause seizures, convulsions, and eventually death. If you or a companion reaches that point, do whatever can be done to cool the victim down and seek medical attention immediately.
- **Most important of all, take along your brain.** A cool, calculating mind is the single-most important asset on the trail. It allows you to think before you act.
- **In summary: Plan ahead.** Watch your step. Avoid accidents before they happen. Enjoy a rewarding and relaxing hike.

Safety Advice for Hikers in the Southwest

The trails are generally safer than the roads you'll drive to reach them, provided of course that you adhere to common sense. Unfortunately, even experienced hikers suffer an occasional lapse in judgment. Suffice it to say one of the biggest potential hazards on the trail is gravity. Many hiking injuries result from falling rocks, but even more result from falling hikers. Use caution near cliff edges, whether you're above or beneath them. New Mexico is the fifth-highest state, with five peaks of more than 13,000 feet—so there's no shortage of opportunities for a spectacular fall.

ALTITUDE SICKNESS

Elevations for hikes in this book range from 4,700 to 12,600 feet. A serious case of altitude sickness is unlikely, though lowlanders do occasionally experience shortness of breath, headaches, dizziness, and nausea. Take a day or two to acclimatize before attempting a strenuous hike.

EXPOSURE

Most of these hikes occur in the high desert, where there's precious little shade and less atmosphere to shield you from the sun. Protective clothing and sunscreen are essential. Also be prepared for sudden drops in temperature. Lost hikers have been known to suffer from heat exhaustion and hypothermia in the same day. Of the two extremes, cold weather is by far the greater danger in New Mexico.

DEHYDRATION

In 1944 several German sailors almost perished from dehydration as they hauled their makeshift raft 20 miles down a dry streambed in the Sonoran Desert. These Nazi prisoners of war had made a potentially fatal mistake in an otherwise flawless escape plan when they assumed that they'd find water in rivers they'd seen on a map. Sure, it sounds hilarious now, but it's not so funny when it happens to you. Always bring enough drinking water for the entire hike, and save your great rafting escape for snowmelt season.

THUNDERSTORMS AND LIGHTNING

Rain is rare, but it can come with a fury. Many of these hikes follow canyon routes and drainages, where flash flooding can be a serious hazard. Areas burned in wildfires and downhill of burn zones are susceptible to flooding.

If you see storm clouds building or hear distant thunder, turn around and get back to your car as soon as possible. If you drove on a dirt road to get to your hike, don't mess around; you want to be off the dirt road before the storm rolls in. Driving on a dirt road in a storm can be a nightmare.

If you are caught on an exposed ridge when lightning strikes, get off the ridge as fast as you can. You do not want to be the tallest object or be standing next to the tallest object on the ridge. If you can't get off the ridge, squat down with two feet on the ground (do not sit). Stand on your pack or something else to insulate yourself from lightning traveling along the ground. Shallow caves or depressions will not protect you from a ground current.

Your best bet is to be off the mountain or an exposed area before the storm rolls in. With storms usually building in the afternoon, do your hiking in the morning during the summer monsoon season (July and August). If you're uncertain about the weather, check the forecast before heading out.

Watchwords for Flora and Fauna

BLACK BEARS

Though attacks by black bears are uncommon, the sight or approach of a bear can give anyone a start. If you encounter a bear while hiking, remain calm and avoid running in any direction. Make loud noises to scare off the bear and back away slowly. In primitive and remote areas, assume bears are present; in more developed sites, check on the current bear situation prior to hiking. Most encounters are food related, as bears have an exceptional sense of smell and not particularly discriminating tastes. While this is of greater concern to backpackers and campers, on a day hike, you may plan a lunchtime picnic or munch on an energy bar or other snack from time to time. So remain aware and alert.

HAZARD TREES

Drought, disease, and insect infestation have taken a toll on New Mexico forests in recent years. Recreation areas occasionally close for hazard-tree removal and cleanup. In wilderness areas, snags (standing dead trees) are often left to fall naturally in order to preserve and protect wilderness character, as required by the Wilderness Act of 1964. Stay alert, especially when entering damaged areas. Risk of death or serious injury increases in windy conditions.

LIVESTOCK

Cows encountered on the trail are generally skittish, but there are a few exceptions. If it doesn't run away, steer clear.

MOSQUITOES

Ward off these pests with insect repellent and/or repellent-impregnated clothing. In some areas, mosquitoes are known to carry the West Nile virus, so all due caution should be taken to avoid their bites.

MOUNTAIN LIONS

It's unlikely that you'll see a mountain lion (or a bear) on the trail, but to be on the safe side, there are a few things you should know, just in case. Mountain lions are the largest cats found in North America, but your chances of seeing one are extremely small (most hikers are content to simply look for the cat's four-toed print on the trail). Sometimes called cougars or pumas, they are shy, solitary creatures that hunt (mostly deer) alone and are masters at camouflage with their tawny coats and preference for wooded cover. They can grow up to 8 feet in length, including their distinctively long tails. In the unlikely instance that you should come across a mountain lion, you should make eye contact, try to appear larger by spreading your arms, and make noise. Do not run from a mountain lion as this may trigger its natural instinct to chase you.

Here are a few guidelines for handling potential mountain lion encounters:

- **Keep kids close to you.** Observed in captivity, mountain lions seem especially drawn to small children.
- **Do not run from a mountain lion.** Running may stimulate the animal's instinct to chase.
- **Don't approach a mountain lion**—give him room to get away.
- **Try to make yourself look larger** by raising your arms and/or opening your jacket if you're wearing one.
- **Do not crouch or kneel.** These movements could make you look smaller and more like the mountain lion's prey.
- **Try to persuade the mountain lion you are dangerous**—not prey. Without crouching, gather nearby stones or branches and toss them at the animal. Slowly wave your arms above your head and speak in a firm voice.
- **If all fails and you are attacked, fight back.** People have successfully fought off attacking mountain lions with rocks and sticks. Try to remain facing the animal, and fend off its attempts to bite your head or neck—the lion's typical aim.

All of this may sound a bit alarmist in nature to some people, but it's always best to be prepared just in case. That said, you probably will never see a mountain lion on any of these hikes.

PLAGUE AND HANTAVIRUS

Bubonic plague can be transmitted from infected rodents to humans via fleas. Pets that are allowed to roam may become infected or carry infected fleas, leading to plague transmission to people. Incidents are rare but can be fatal if untreated. From 1949 to 2017, a total of 283 human plague cases, more than 30 of them fatal, were reported in New Mexico.

Deer mice are the primary carriers of the viruses that cause hantavirus pulmonary syndrome, a rare but often fatal infection. Rodents shed the virus in their urine, droppings, and saliva. The virus is mainly transmitted to people when they breathe in contaminated air. From 1975 to 2016, 109 cases (47 fatal) were reported in New Mexico.

Hikers should take precautions to reduce the likelihood of their exposure to infectious materials. Avoid coming into contact with rodents and rodent burrows, or disturbing dens such as pack-rat nests. Also avoid confined spaces such as caves and abandoned structures that contain evidence of rodent activity. Always keep kids and pets a safe distance from wild animals.

For more information, check with the New Mexico Department of Health at nmhealth.org.

Photo: Tom Watson

POISON IVY

Recognizing and avoiding poison ivy is the most effective way to prevent the painful, itchy rashes associated with this plant. Poison ivy (left) occurs as a vine or ground cover, three leaflets to a leaf. Urushiol, the oil in the sap of these plants, is responsible for the rash. Within 14 hours of exposure, raised lines and/or blisters will appear on the affected area, accompanied by a terrible itch. Refrain from scratching because bacteria under your fingernails can cause an infection. Wash and dry the affected area thoroughly, applying a calamine lotion to help dry out the rash. If itching or blistering is severe, seek medical attention. If you do come into contact with poison ivy, remember that oil-contaminated clothes, hiking gear, and pets can easily cause an irritating rash on you or someone else, so wash not only any exposed parts of your body but also any exposed clothes, gear, and pets.

SCORPIONS

You probably won't find any scorpions unless you look at night. As many desert ravers have learned, scorpions glow under black light. Though a sting from most scorpions is painful, none of the dangerous species, such as the bark scorpion, commonly range within 60 miles of Albuquerque. (The last scorpion-related death in the United States was reported from Arizona in 1968.) If camping, shake out your shoes, sleeping bags, and any clothes left on the ground. If stung, gently cleanse and elevate the wound, and apply a cold compress to reduce swelling.

SNAKES

Photo: Jane Huber

Rattlesnakes are the only poisonous snakes in the Albuquerque area. It is unlikely that you'll run into one, but the most important preventative measure is to watch your step. Don't hike during times of peak rattlesnake activity, which is usually at night. Wear high-top hiking boots and long pants for additional protection. If bitten, gently cleanse the area and apply a clean dressing. If bitten on the arm or hand, splint the limb. Do not use pressure dressings or tourniquets or make incisions. Remain calm and seek transport to a medical facility. If you need to walk to reach help, do so as soon as possible. Severe reactions from a venomous snakebite may not occur for several hours. Rattlesnakes rarely strike hikers, and when they do it's usually a dry bite. They don't want to kill you. They just want you to leave them alone.

TICKS

Ticks like to hang out in the brush that grows along trails. Though they're rare in this region, you should be tick aware during all months of the year. Ticks need a host to feast on in order to reproduce. The ticks that alight on you while hiking will be very small, sometimes so tiny that you won't be able to spot them. Primarily of two varieties, deer ticks and dog ticks, these arthropods (not insects) need a few hours of actual attachment before they can transmit any disease they may harbor. Ticks may settle in shoes, socks, and hats, and they may take several hours to actually latch on. The best strategy is to visually check every half hour or so while hiking, do a thorough check before you get in your car, and then, when you take a posthike shower, do an even more thorough check of your entire body. Ticks that haven't attached are easily removed but not easily killed. If you pick off a tick in the woods, just toss it aside. If you find one on your body at home, dispatch it and then send it down the toilet. For ticks that have embedded, removal with tweezers is best.

YUCCA AND CACTI

Steer clear of spiny plants. A casual bump against a yucca hurts worse than a flu shot. Cactus needles easily penetrate canvas shoes. Sturdy footwear is essential. For more drastic encounters, use tweezers to pluck thick needles, then remove the finer ones with careful applications of adhesive tape or school glue.

Hunting

Seasonal hunting is permitted on most public lands. Wear bright colors if hiking in active areas. For more specifics on where and when hunting is permitted, consult the annual game proclamations, which are available free from most sporting goods retailers and from the New Mexico Department of Game and Fish: 505-476-8000, wildlife.state.nm.us.

Trail Etiquette

Always treat the trail, wildlife, and fellow hikers with respect. Here are some reminders.

- **Plan ahead in order to be self-sufficient at all times.** For example, carry necessary supplies for changes in weather or other conditions. A well-planned trip brings satisfaction to you and to others.
- **Hike on open trails only.**
- **In seasons or construction areas where road or trail closures may be a possibility,** use the website addresses or phone numbers shown in the "Contacts" line for each of this guidebook's hikes to check conditions prior to heading out for your hike. And do not attempt to circumvent such closures.
- **Avoid trespassing on private land,** and obtain all permits and authorization as required. Also, leave gates as you found them or as directed by signage.
- **Be courteous to other hikers,** bikers, equestrians, and others you encounter on the trails.
- **Never spook wild animals or pets.** An unannounced approach, a sudden movement, or a loud noise startles most critters, and a surprised animal can be dangerous to you, to others, and to itself. Give animals plenty of space.
- **Observe the yield signs around the region's trailheads and backcountry.** Typically they advise hikers to yield to horses, and bikers yield to both horses and hikers. By common courtesy on hills, hikers and bikers yield to any uphill traffic. When encountering mounted riders or horsepackers, hikers can courteously step off the trail, on the downhill side if possible. So the horse can see and hear you, calmly greet the riders before they reach you and do not dart behind trees. Also resist the urge to pet horses unless you are invited to do so.
- **Stay on the existing trail** and do not blaze any new trails.
- **Be sure to pack out what you pack in,** leaving only your footprints. No one likes to see the trash someone else has left behind.

Looking north from Herrera Mesa (Hike 52, page 274)

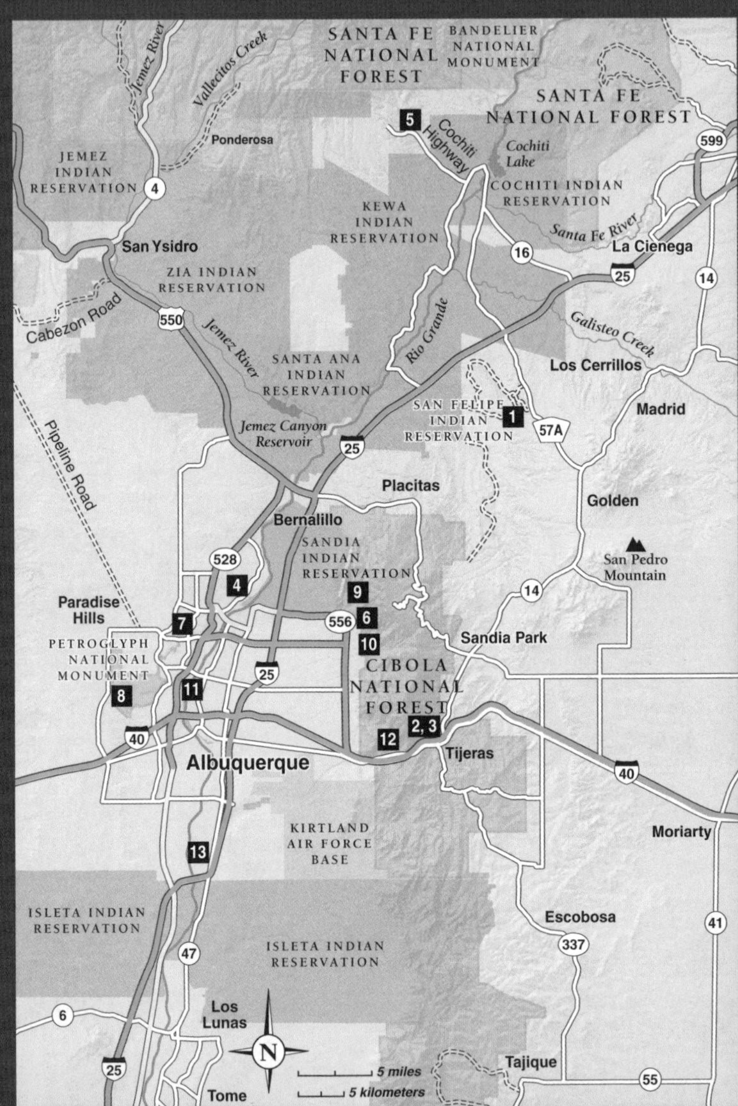

SANTA FE NATIONAL FOREST
BANDELIER NATIONAL MONUMENT
SANTA FE NATIONAL FOREST
Jemez River
Vallecitos Creek
Ponderosa
Cochiti Highway
Cochiti Lake
JEMEZ INDIAN RESERVATION
COCHITI INDIAN RESERVATION
KEWA INDIAN RESERVATION
Santa Fe River
San Ysidro
La Cienega
ZIA INDIAN RESERVATION
Cabezon Road
Jemez River
Rio Grande
Galisteo Creek
SANTA ANA INDIAN RESERVATION
Los Cerrillos
Madrid
SAN FELIPE INDIAN RESERVATION
Jemez Canyon Reservoir
Pipeline Road
Placitas
Golden
Bernalillo
SANDIA INDIAN RESERVATION
San Pedro Mountain
Paradise Hills
Sandia Park
PETROGLYPH NATIONAL MONUMENT
CIBOLA NATIONAL FOREST
Tijeras
Albuquerque
Moriarty
KIRTLAND AIR FORCE BASE
ISLETA INDIAN RESERVATION
Escobosa
ISLETA INDIAN RESERVATION
Los Lunas
Tajique
Tome
5 miles
5 kilometers

GREATER ALBUQUERQUE

1 Ball Ranch 22

2 Canyon Estates–Faulty Trails 26

3 Carlito Springs 31

4 Corrales Acequias and Bosque Preserve 36

5 Kasha-Katuwe Tent Rocks National Monument 41

6 La Luz Trail to the Crest and Tram 45

7 Petroglyph National Monument: Piedras Marcadas 50

8 Petroglyph National Monument: The Volcanoes 54

9 Piedra Lisa Trailhead Options 59

10 Pino Trail 64

11 Rio Grande Nature Center–Bosque/Ditch Walk 69

12 Three Gun–Embudo Trails: Up-and-Over the Sandias Adventure 74

13 Valle de Oro National Wildlife Refuge 79

1 BALL RANCH

You'll follow red rock walls along portions of this hike.

SURROUNDED BY TRIBAL LANDS and accessed by an unpaved easement road behind locked gates, the trailhead can be a challenge to reach—but it's worth the extra effort. This hike follows arroyos and old ranch roads from the lowest canyon to the highest ridge to give you the full flavor of this seldom-visited public land.

DESCRIPTION

Part of the mystique of Ball Ranch is that you need a key to reach it. The Bureau of Land Management (BLM) only has a few keys, so you are assured of having the place to yourself. The other attraction is that Ball Ranch may have the best petrified wood in the Albuquerque area.

When you reach the access road, make sure you lock the gate behind you. As for the dirt access road, it is fine in dry weather, but stay away from it when it is wet. The road is easy to navigate, as there are fences on both sides to keep you on the right track. And for those few places where you could venture astray, there are NO TRESPASSING signs to guide you back on the right path.

You'll see a wire drop gate when you reach the BLM boundary. Just open the gate and close it behind you. Park just inside the gate.

DISTANCE & CONFIGURATION: 4.8-mile loop

DIFFICULTY: Moderate

SCENERY: Winding canyon, petrified wood, red mesas, hilltop overlook

EXPOSURE: Some canyon shade

TRAIL TRAFFIC: Low

TRAIL SURFACE: Sand, dirt

HIKING TIME: 2.5–3 hours

DRIVING DISTANCE: 41 miles from the Big I

ELEVATION GAIN: 5,886' at trailhead; 5,656' at lowest point; 6,048' at high point

ACCESS: Year-round; no fees, but do need to pick up a gate key from the Bureau of Land Management (BLM) (see Comments)

WHEELCHAIR ACCESS: No

MAPS: USGS *San Felipe Pueblo NE*

FACILITIES: None

CONTACT: BLM–Rio Puerco Field Office, blm.gov/office/rio-puerco-field-office, 505-761-8700

LOCATION: Southeast of Kewa Pueblo (formerly Santo Domingo Pueblo) and east of San Felipe Pueblo

COMMENTS: Pick up a gate key from the BLM office at 100 Sun Ave. NE, Pan American Building, Suite 330 in Albuquerque. Leashed dogs are allowed on trails.

LAST-CHANCE FOOD/GAS: Convenience store, food, gas at Exit 259

There are a hundred different ways to explore this little BLM venue known as Ball Ranch, and twice as many ways to get lost or inadvertently trespass on tribal land. To keep things simple, this hike is confined to the southeast portion of BLM land.

Begin the hike by walking west (away from the gate) a few hundred feet to the first dirt doubletrack going left (south) and heading downhill. Turn left and go down to the windmill. From the windmill, head straight into the Arroyo del Tuerto. Turn to the right (southwest) and follow the arroyo into the canyon ahead, keeping in mind the usual precaution about traveling in arroyos: beware of flash flooding. You can also walk on one of the many cow paths following the arroyo.

The canyon soon narrows, running deep and sinuous as it squeezes between two hills. Look for birds' nests in the pocked walls. Keep an eye on the ground as well, as you are likely to see plenty of animal tracks.

After walking about 1 mile down the streambed, you'll notice that the canyon shallows and the arroyo straightens. At the top of the last sharp bend, the wall on the right reveals tan, pink, and green striations. Meanwhile, on the left, the wall shrinks down to a low bank. Exit the arroyo there, and pick up a doubletrack running south.

About 0.2 mile from the arroyo, shortly after crossing a wash, the road splits. Take a sharp left and follow the road as it crooks southward. The road and wash soon merge and diverge. It's a mess, really, but just continue south, keeping the wash on your right.

About 0.2 mile from the sharp left, the wash shallows down to a sandy bed. You'll see it in a distinct clearing through the juniper on your right. This is where you'll exit the path for a short detour.

Cross straight over the wash and continue west about 200 feet until you see a hillside littered with strange dark rocks, some with a brilliant patchwork of lichen. Closer inspection reveals a woody grain in the stone surface. It doesn't take an expert

Ball Ranch

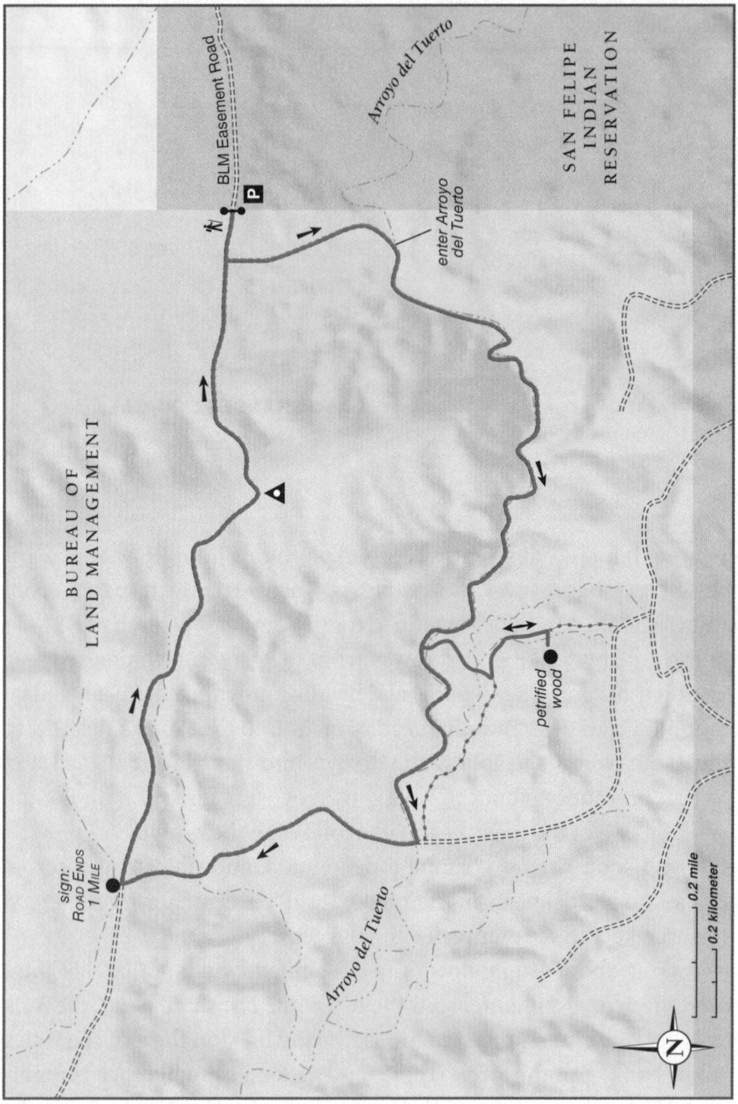

BLM Easement Road
P
Arroyo del Tuerto
SAN FELIPE
INDIAN
RESERVATION
enter Arroyo
del Tuerto
BUREAU OF
LAND MANAGEMENT
petrified
wood
sign:
ROAD ENDS
1 MILE
Arroyo del Tuerto
0.2 mile
0.2 kilometer
N

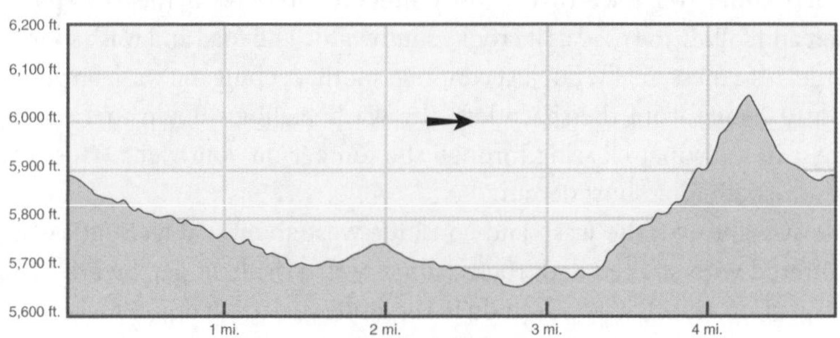
6,200 ft.
6,100 ft.
6,000 ft.
5,900 ft.
5,800 ft.
5,700 ft.
5,600 ft.
1 mi.
2 mi.
3 mi.
4 mi.

eye to see they were once trees, albeit several million years ago. (The GPS coordinates for the petrified wood area are N35° 22.865' W106° 18.962').

Feel free to wander around this area, as there seems to be petrified wood in all directions. Some of the pieces of petrified wood are bigger than you and have fantastic colors. Some of them look like logs and still have a bit of branch sticking out. Others have grain so well preserved that you could mistake it for actual wood. Running into a patch of petrified wood like this is what makes this hike special.

When you've had your fill of petrified wood, return to the Arroyo del Tuerto and continue downstream about a half mile to an intersecting road. There may even be some wet areas where water beneath the arroyo reaches the surface. You can also continue looking for other patches of petrified wood, but please keep the intersection of the arroyo and road in mind as it provides a good boundary for keeping you on BLM land and from getting lost.

When you are ready to continue with the hike, turn right (north) at the intersection and follow the road north 0.6 mile to the BLM easement road. There is a beautiful layer of red rock all along the way. When you arrive at the T-junction, you'll see the back side of a sign that states ROAD ENDS 1 MILE (referring, of course, to the road you just traveled). Turn right (east) and follow the easement road about 0.8 mile to the top of the hill. The views are gorgeous in all directions. It's even better at night, when Santa Fe glimmers to the northeast while the Sandias shield the glow of Albuquerque in the southwest. You may even see some stakes for an old mining claim as you climb to the top of the ridge.

To finish the loop, go straight ahead to your car. As you drive out of Ball Ranch, secure both gates behind you. And don't forget to return the key to the BLM so someone else can go on this great hike.

Trivia: Ball Ranch shares its namesake with the Indiana-based Ball Corporation (manufacturers of Ball canning jars) and Ball State University.

• •

GPS TRAILHEAD COORDINATES N35° 23.372' W106° 18.116'

DIRECTIONS From I-25 North, take Exit 259 and turn right on County Road 52A (formerly NM 22; some maps show CR 57A or CR 252A). Measuring from the top of the northbound exit ramp, go south 5.9 miles to the second gate on the right, marked BALL RANCH. (GPS coordinates for the gate are N35° 23.490' W106° 16.214'). If you have the key, unlock the gate. Drive through and lock the gate behind you. Follow the BLM signs 2.2 miles to the drop gate. (See "Description" for more details.) Unlatch the gate, drive through, and close it behind you. Park just beyond the gate.

2 CANYON ESTATES–FAULTY TRAILS

These wooded trails just minutes east of Albuquerque are perfect for casual hikes most of the year.

A SHORT STROLL up Hondo Canyon leads to a waterfall spilling over a travertine formation. Continue up the Crest Trail to join the Faulty trails for a pennant-shaped loop on gentle terrain through cool pine wilderness.

DESCRIPTION

This popular hike begins at the southern terminus of the Crest Trail (130) at the Canyon Estates Trailhead just outside Tijeras. The Crest Trail runs 26 miles to span the length of the Sandia Mountain Range. Many of the Sandia Mountain hikes in this book end at or follow part of the Crest Trail. The Pino Trail (Hike 10, page 64) ends at the Crest Trail; the Tree Spring hike (Hike 22, page 125) follows the Crest Trail to the upper tram terminal; the hiking portion of the La Luz–Tram adventure (Hike 6, page 45) ends at the Crest Trail; and the Del Agua Overlook walk (Hike 15, page 91) follows the Crest Trail for 2 miles.

A map on a signboard illustrates all of that at the Canyon Estates Trailhead. A sign posted ahead indicates distances to Sandia Spring (5 miles) and Sandia Crest (16 miles). The three trails used on this hike are well marked with wooden signs at every turn; carefully placed rocks, logs, and limbs help keep you from wandering down countless informal paths and shortcuts between switchbacks. The extra maintenance simplifies navigation. You can help further by sticking to designated trails.

DISTANCE & CONFIGURATION: 5.7-mile balloon

DIFFICULTY: Moderate

SCENERY: Travertine grotto, waterfall, seasonal wildflowers, wooded canyons

EXPOSURE: Mostly shaded

TRAIL TRAFFIC: Popular

TRAIL SURFACE: Packed dirt, rock

HIKING TIME: 3 hours

DRIVING DISTANCE: 15 miles from the Big I

ELEVATION GAIN: 6,546' at trailhead; 7,688' at high point

ACCESS: Trailhead area open 6 a.m.–10 p.m., year-round; no fees or permits required

WHEELCHAIR ACCESS: No

MAPS: Sandia Ranger District; USGS *Tijeras*

FACILITIES: None

CONTACT: Cibola National Forest–Sandia Mountain Wilderness, fs.usda.gov/cibola, 505-281-3304

LOCATION: Tijeras

COMMENTS: Leashed dogs are allowed on trails.

LAST-CHANCE FOOD/GAS: All services at Exit 167 (Tramway Boulevard and Central Avenue)

The hike begins alongside a mostly dry creek, which you'll cross a few times throughout the route. The lower trail lacks shade, but tree cover increases intermittently as you gain elevation. It also passes in the shadow of a stone cliff that seems ideal for impromptu climbing practice, provided you don't cause any rocks to fall on hikers below. If you look closely, you might spot a faint informal trail going off to the left (N35° 05.396' W106° 23.542'). This trail gets stronger on the other side of the dry creek and in 0.25 mile it connects with the loop trail at Carlito Springs (Hike 3, page 31).

Less than 0.4 mile up the trail, a sign marks the 100-yard spur to Travertine Falls. A popular destination for families, the falls are situated in an alcove. By late spring, it becomes a cool, green oasis, thanks in large part to box elder and its little twin, poison ivy. The falls are usually just a trickle, but through eons of depositing dissolved limestone, they've created impressive travertine grottoes. A cruciform etched at the cave entrance appears to be the handiwork of modern teen goths, though local lore suggests that it's a centuries-old display of Franciscan devotion.

From the falls, return to the Crest Trail and continue uphill on the designated switchback. A vista opens to the south, across Tijeras Canyon, to reveal the industrial side of the Manzanita Mountains. Although it may not be the view you'd hope for in a national forest, the factory and quarries you see there fulfill much of Albuquerque's demand for cement. The quarries pass out of view as you approach the top of the waterfall.

Just before you cross the small stream that feeds the waterfall, you might want to take a moment to examine the limestone face to your right. The limestone is full of marine fossils. You might also want to check out the unusual shapes of travertine rock below your feet along this portion of the trail. On the other side of the stream, to the left, there is a trail leading back down to the base of the falls. Our hike turns to the right and continues uphill on the main trail.

One mile into the hike, you will arrive at the junction with Faulty Trail (195), so named because it roughly follows a fracture in the Earth's crust known as the Flatiron

Canyon Estates–Faulty Trails

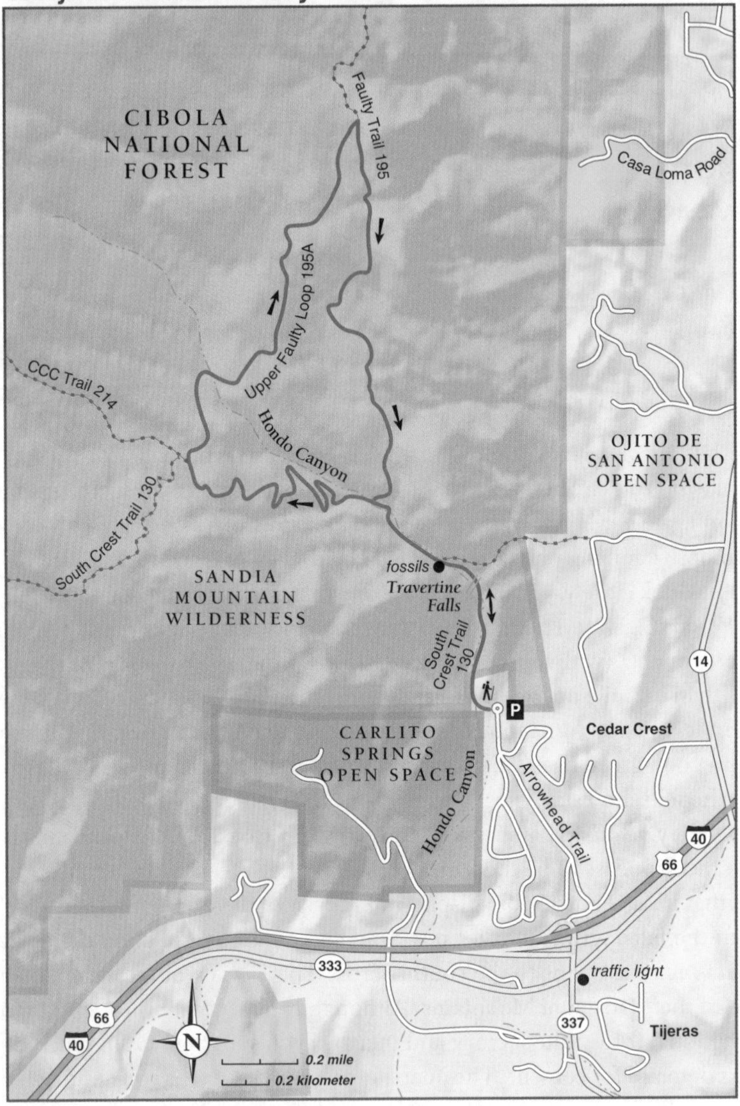

CIBOLA NATIONAL FOREST
Faulty Trail 195
Casa Loma Road
Upper Faulty Loop 195A
CCC Trail 214
Hondo Canyon
South Crest Trail 130
OJITO DE SAN ANTONIO OPEN SPACE
SANDIA MOUNTAIN WILDERNESS
fossils
Travertine Falls
South Crest Trail 130
14
P
Cedar Crest
CARLITO SPRINGS OPEN SPACE
Hondo Canyon
Arrowhead Trail
40
66
333
traffic light
66
40
337
Tijeras
N
0.2 mile
0.2 kilometer

8,000 ft.
7,500 ft.
7,000 ft.
6,500 ft.
6,000 ft.
5,500 ft.
5,000 ft.
1 mi.
2 mi.
3 mi.
4 mi.
5 mi.

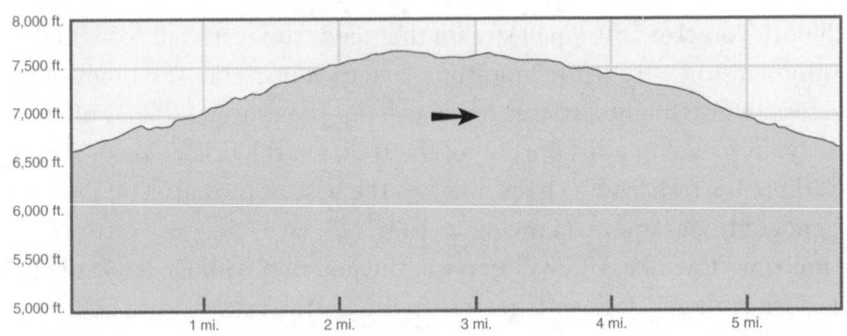

South Mountain and the San Pedro Mountains from the Faulty Trail

Fault. You'll use this trail on the return route, so stay on the Crest Trail for now. (If you turn here, you can do this hike in reverse.) The south end of Upper Faulty Trail is another 0.5 mile up, but multiple switchbacks more than double the hiking distance. With an elevation gain of 600 feet, this segment is the most strenuous mile in the hike.

When you reach the clearing at the top, take a breather. A nearby marker indicates that the Crest Trail continues to the west. It turns north to meet Embudito Trail (192) at a junction 4.1 miles ahead. Also, although there's no indication of it here at the clearing, the seldom-used CCC Trail (214) starts nearby to the northwest at the enormous cairn on a more direct 1.8-mile route to the same junction. From there, a short spur leads to South Sandia Peak. Anyone bent on bagging it can set off in either direction, but take a detailed map and be advised of the 1,200-foot elevation gain.

To stick with this more relaxing route, head north past the CCC Trail cairn on Upper Faulty Trail (195A). This 1.3-mile segment gently undulates between 7,540 and 7,650 feet, where ponderosa, oak, and Rocky Mountain juniper flourish. Much of this trail is a quiet walk on a bed of pine needles.

The sign marking the junction with Faulty Trail stands 3.5 miles into the hike. You can pad on a few easy miles by continuing north along the shaded Faulty Trail and returning to this point at your leisure, or you can pull a U-turn now to head south on Faulty Trail, back down to the Crest Trail.

If you're lucky, you might spot one of the several Sandia Mountain Medallion Trees along this stretch of the trail. The Medallion Trees are the creation of an unknown person who took a core sample from the tree to determine its germination date and then mounted a small medallion named for an event that occurred near its germination date. For example, "Coronado Expedition Tree, GD-1541, #32."

This segment is not quite as flat as the one above. Turn a rocky corner ahead, and you'll find yourself even with the tops of trees growing from the canyon below. The trail drops to the bottom and quickly climbs out the other side. The mile that follows is a fairly tame descent that ends with a stunning view over Hondo Canyon. If the reason for the name hasn't already become apparent, it should be now—*hondo* is Spanish for "deep."

The remaining bit of Faulty Trail proves to be the most challenging. It's steep, with plenty of loose rock to test your balance. Take it slowly. When you reach the Crest Trail below, turn left and backtrack 1 mile to the trailhead.

NEARBY ACTIVITIES

The 88-acre **Ojito de San Antonio Open Space** features a meadow, an apple orchard, and piñon–juniper forest on the surrounding slopes. Spend a lazy afternoon in the shade of an ancient willow by the side of a historic acequia. Two natural springs have provided drinking water for wildlife and the nearby community for centuries. To get there from Canyon Estates, return to I-40 and continue to a traffic light. Turn left onto NM 333 (Historic Route 66) and go east to NM 14. Go north on NM 14 for about 1 mile to San Antonio Drive. A parking lot and access to the open space are hidden behind the San Antonio de Padua Church. For more information, call Bernalillo Open Space at 505-314-0400 or visit bernco.gov/openspace.

• •

GPS TRAILHEAD COORDINATES N35° 05.373' W106° 23.479'

DIRECTIONS From I-40 East, take Exit 175 and aim for Tijeras, but turn left before you reach the traffic light at the bottom of the ramp. Drive north under the interstate and bear right on Arrowhead Trail ahead. Follow it 0.6 mile to its end at the Canyon Estates Trailhead. The hike begins on the west side of the parking circle.

3 CARLITO SPRINGS

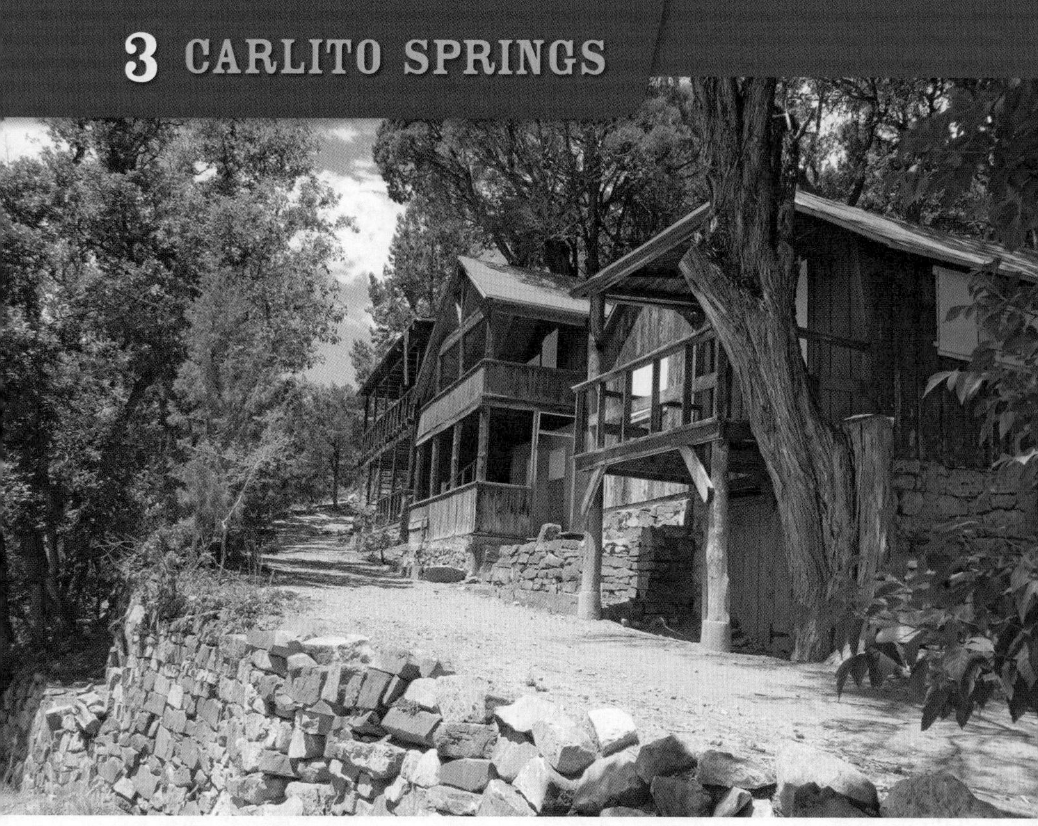

Some of the historic buildings at Carlito Springs

THIS HIKE VISITS the jewel of the Bernalillo County Open Space properties. Long hidden behind locked gates, the old resort and spring, including a 2-mile loop trail, is now open to the public. This is a popular and fabulous place to visit.

DESCRIPTION

Carlito Springs Open Space, overlooking the village of Tijeras, is a true oasis on the south slope of the Sandia Mountains. It is a special place only minutes from Albuquerque. The 179-acre site formerly served as an ancestral Puebloan camp, a Union veteran's homestead, a camp, a school, a tuberculosis sanitorium, and a residence. It features a 2-mile loop hike, spring-fed ponds, old resort buildings, lush riparian habitats, ornamental gardens, and orchards. The combination of historic buildings and lush surroundings makes it a very cool place to visit.

Bernalillo County acquired Carlito Springs in 2000. Up until August 2014, the site remained behind a locked gate and was only open for special occasions. The county used that time to perform required environmental clearances, determine how best to use the property, stabilize the site, repair infrastructure, and build a 2-mile loop hiking trail. Work is still being done, and there is always the possibility

DISTANCE & CONFIGURATION: 2-mile loop hike with options for exploring

DIFFICULTY: Moderate

SCENERY: Natural springs, ponds, historic buildings, orchards, mountain views, great overlooks

EXPOSURE: Mostly shaded

TRAIL TRAFFIC: Popular

TRAIL SURFACE: Packed dirt, rock

HIKING TIME: 1–1.5 hours

DRIVING DISTANCE: 16 miles from the Big I

ELEVATION GAIN: 6,422' at trailhead; 6,755' at high point

ACCESS: Bernalillo County Open Space is open sunrise–sunset and is subject to closures for construction and bear activity

WHEELCHAIR ACCESS: No

MAPS: Sandia Ranger District; USGS *Tijeras*

FACILITIES: Portable toilet at parking lot

CONTACT: Bernalillo County Open Space, bernco.gov/openspace, 505-314-0400

LOCATION: Tijeras

COMMENTS: Leashed dogs are allowed on trail.

LAST-CHANCE FOOD/GAS: All services at Exit 167 (Tramway Boulevard and Central Avenue)

of temporary closures in the future. Temporary closures can also occur when bear activity increases at the end of the summer and early fall. You should check with Bernalillo County Open Space before going (see Contact information above).

When you visit Carlito Springs, you'll see a sign off to your right for the open space as soon as you pass under I-40 on Carlito Springs Road. Turn right and drive a couple hundred feet until you see another open space sign and a gravel road with a gate (N35° 04.863' W106° 23.726') on the left side of the road. The open space is open from sunrise to sunset. Turn left onto the gravel road to reach the parking area. The road is fenced on both sides as it passes through private land. Please respect the speed limit of 10 miles per hour.

The trailhead is across from the parking area. The trail begins with a small drop into a lush riparian environment. There are even a couple of ponderosa pines. As soon as you cross the small arroyo, which is almost immediately, you'll have a choice of going left or right. If you turn left you'll cross two bridges and climb 75 steps as you follow the arroyo up to the spring and old resort. You'll gain 300 feet in 0.5 mile.

If you turn right, you'll follow the arroyo down for a few feet before beginning a gentle climb through piñon–juniper woodland to the northeast. You'll have nice views to the south of the Manzano Mountains and the large limestone quarry in Tijeras. The trail cuts back to the southwest when it approaches the Canyon Estates subdivision. The trail will soon cut again back to the northeast.

After 1 mile of walking, the trail will turn west. You may notice an informal trail (N35° 05.388' W106° 23.550') at the turn heading off to your right. The informal trail joins the Crest Trail in 0.25 mile very close to the Canyon Estates Trailhead, the starting point of Hike 2 (page 26). The connecting trail is difficult to spot from the Crest Trail. It's almost a secret connection. The main trail reaches the spring and resort area in less than 0.5 mile after making the turn west. The trail continues back down to the parking area for a very nice 2-mile loop hike.

Carlito Springs

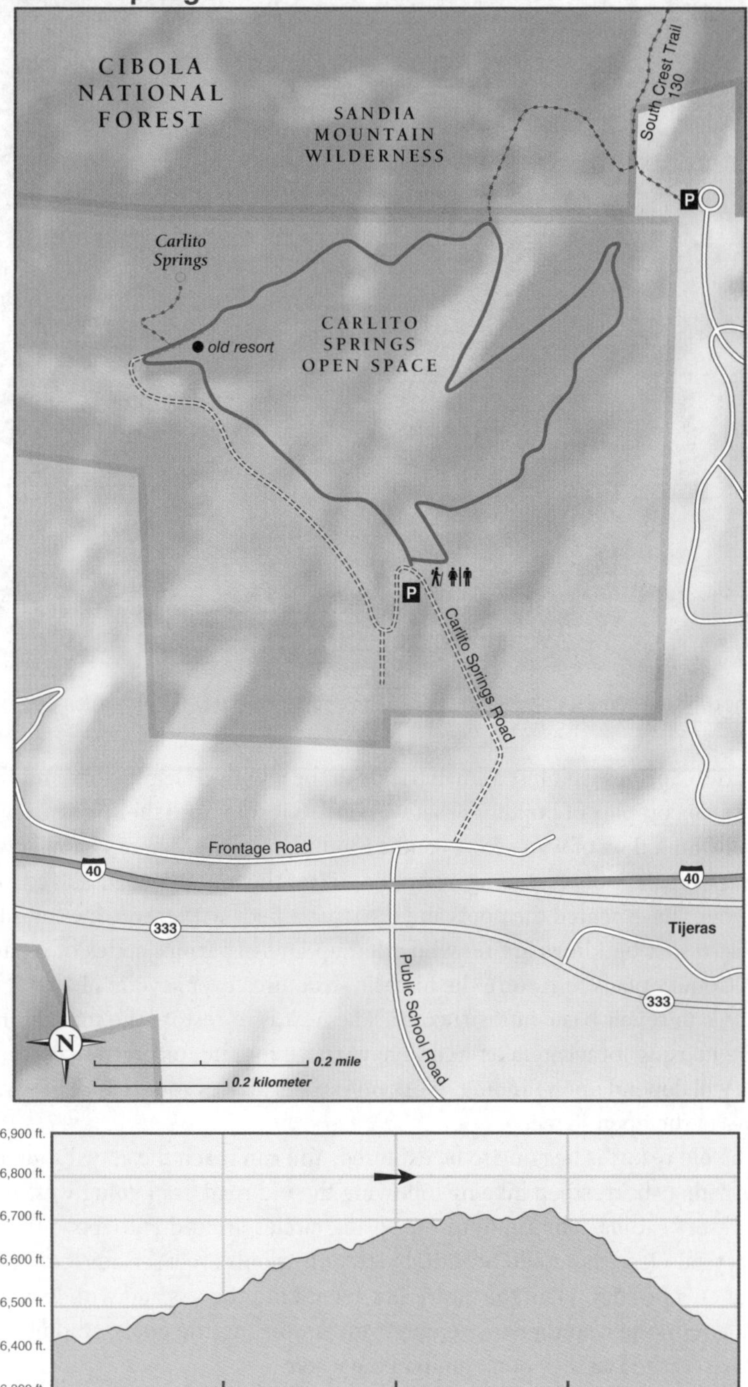

The many pools fed by the spring here are tempting on a hot summer day, but please don't get in the water—this site is still a work in progress.

Carlito Springs isn't just a small trickle in the woods. It has history and is a truly remarkable complex of buildings that was once a resort. And the spring itself has an unusually high flow of water for a Sandia Mountain spring. There's enough water to fill several small pools cascading down the side of the mountain. Dissolved minerals in the water have coated the pools and the stream beds with travertine (or tufa).

The resort buildings are now boarded up and in various states of repair. Bernalillo County plans to restore the historic structures over several phases. The first priority is to repair basic infrastructure. The next is to restore the main building to provide housing for a caretaker and to have space for an interpretive center. Future phases will depend upon funding. Work on various phases could result in temporary closures of the open space.

The old resort is begging to be explored. You can reach the actual source of the spring with a short, steep hike by following the old road/trail going west from the green resort cabins. The route to the spring circles around and above the cabins. With crystal-clear water and beautiful views, the pools are a serious temptation for soaking on a hot day. With the entire site a work in progress and with local wildlife dependent on the water, please refrain from jumping in the pools. And please keep your dogs leashed so they don't jump in the water.

The trail back down to the parking area is well marked. Keep an eye out for several old stone retaining walls as you go down. They were built to provide flat terraces for orchard trees and other plants. If you come in the summer, you'll see that many of the trees are still bearing fruit. The fruit is also a natural magnet for bears when it ripens. As a result the county will close down the open space if bears become too active.

The bottom line is that Carlito Springs is a perfect place for a quick getaway close to Albuquerque. Because of this, it is very popular and can be crowded, especially on weekends.

NEARBY ACTIVITIES

The Musical Highway is a little more than a mile west of Carlito Springs Road on the eastbound lane of NM 333 (Historic Route 66) between mile markers 4 and 5. If you line up your car properly on the rumble strip and drive at 45 miles per hour, your tires will play "America the Beautiful." The musical rumble strip was built in 2014 to encourage driving at the speed limit and to add a bit of pizzazz to the drive. The project was a joint effort of the New Mexico Department of Transportation and the National Geographic Channel. There are signs along the road identifying where the Musical Highway begins.

GPS TRAILHEAD COORDINATES N35° 05.057' W106° 23.761'

DIRECTIONS From I-40 East, take Exit 175 and aim for Tijeras. Turn right on NM 333 (Historic Route 66) and go around 0.5 mile to Carlito Springs Road. Turn right and go under I-40. Turn right again and go to the open space sign; turn left on the gravel road. The parking lot will be on your left in 0.3 mile. The trailhead will be on the right.

4 CORRALES ACEQUIAS AND BOSQUE PRESERVE

The Sandias from the Corrales bosque

FOLLOW THE WATERWAYS around the village of Corrales for a display of eclectic architecture from the past and present. Groves of cottonwood and Siberian elm and plentiful waterfowl also highlight the route. And you may spot riparian creatures such as beavers, muskrats, and pocket gophers.

DESCRIPTION

Stepping into the community of Corrales is almost like taking a short vacation. With only one main street, there are plenty of cars, but what's missing is the sense of suburban sprawl. There are no big box stores, or malls, or continuous housing developments. Instead you'll find a unique mixture of adobe homes, small farms, horses, and wildlife. The planned walk passes all of them and more by following acequias to the bosque, continuing through the bosque, and returning to our starting point with a short road walk. If you take this walk in the winter, you'll see plenty of cranes chowing down in the fields.

Acequias (3.3 miles): Begin by crossing the soccer field behind the rec center. The line of trees on the far side indicates where the Corrales Lateral flows. This prominent acequia, or irrigation ditch, has been channeling water to local farm fields since the early 18th century. The system has since been enhanced. Currently about 17 miles

DISTANCE & CONFIGURATION: 7.4-mile loop

DIFFICULTY: Easy

SCENERY: Vineyards, historic buildings, deciduous forest, mountain views

EXPOSURE: Half shaded

TRAIL TRAFFIC: Popular

TRAIL SURFACE: Dirt, some asphalt

HIKING TIME: 4 hours, longer with optional detours

DRIVING DISTANCE: 13 miles from the Big I

ELEVATION GAIN: 5,006' at trailhead, with no significant rise

ACCESS: Daily, 5 a.m.–10 p.m.; no fees or permits required

WHEELCHAIR ACCESS: No

MAPS: USGS *Alameda* and *Bernalillo*

FACILITIES: Portable toilets outside the rec center

CONTACT: Village of Corrales, corrales-nm.org; Middle Rio Grande Conservancy District, 505-247-0234

LOCATION: Corrales

COMMENTS: Village Hall at 4234 Corrales Road (0.3 mile past Jones Road) has brochures for touring Corrales. Interpretive information is also posted on their display boards.

of canals and ditches course through Corrales. The ditch rider, or system administrator, maintains the flow of water from early March through early November.

Service roads run along both sides of the acequia. Turn right (north) after the gate and take the one with the least mud. Dams allow for frequent crossings in case you change your mind. You can simply follow the ditch for the first 3 miles of the loop or take a few detours for a closer look at nearby historic buildings.

Often you can identify an architectural style by the roof alone. Red tiles suggest Spanish Revival. Rounded corners are indicative of the Pueblo style. Flat roofs with stepped parapets and exposed vigas (ceiling beams) indicate Spanish-Pueblo Revival, more popularly known as Santa Fe style, which in turn developed into a craze for incorporating multiple styles into a single structure for no apparent reason. You'll find numerous examples of that in Corrales.

About a mile into the hike you'll see the new San Ysidro Church over on Corrales Road on the right. Ahead and a little ways off to the left are the pitched tin roofs of the Old San Ysidro Church's twin bell towers. The towers function as buttresses to support the old adobe walls, which are nearly 3 feet thick. You may have trouble spotting them if the foliage is thick.

The Gutiérrez-Minge House, also known as Casa San Ysidro, is across the street from the old church. This extension of the Albuquerque Museum features a replica of a 19th-century rancho and offers tours for a small fee. To visit the San Ysidro complex, turn left (west) at the next crossroad, Old Church Road. This detour adds less than 0.4 mile to the hike.

To keep track of your pace, note that Old Church Road is 1.2 miles into the hike. Stella Lane marks the end of the second mile. Ahead you'll pass by Sandia View Adventist Academy on the left and, soon after, the Corrales Winery on the right (see Nearby Activities for more information). At the end of the third mile, you arrive at

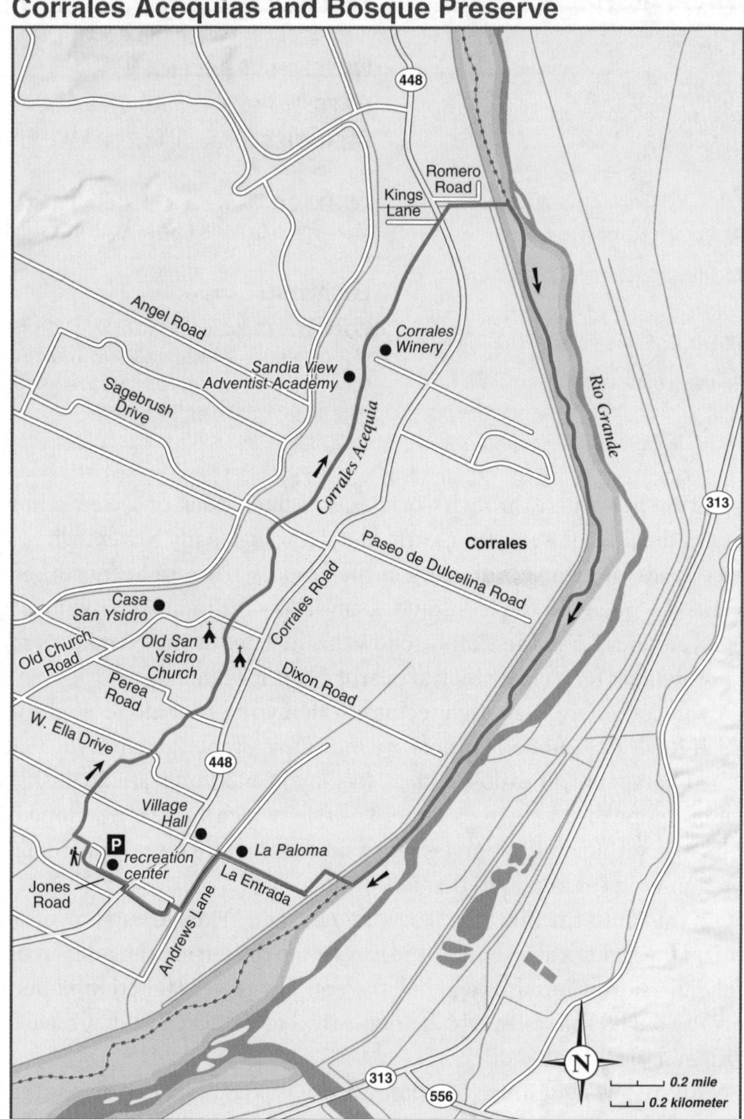

the intersection of Kings Lane and Corrales Road. The latter is often busy, so use care in crossing it.

Soon the Corrales Lateral merges into the Sandoval Lateral. Turn right (east), heading toward the mountains. The mature Rio Grande Valley cottonwoods closer ahead mark the western edge of the Corrales Bosque Preserve.

There is a small parking area on the near side of a green pipe gate. The Sandoval Lateral turns right and flows south. Shady service roads running alongside it present an enticing alternate route on hot days.

Bosque Preserve (3.1 miles): To stick with the planned route, go through the gate, cross the wide Corrales Riverside Drain (also called the Clear Ditch), and climb up the levee. Turn right and follow the high road (also known as the Clear Ditch road and the dike road).

But before setting off in that direction, note two footpaths continuing down the east side of the levee. Both lead to the Rio Grande, less than 500 feet ahead. These, too, are shaded alternatives to the planned route and are part of an informal path system that spiderwebs between the road and the river throughout the cool deciduous woods.

The paths often break up or disappear under weeds and fallen trees, but this dense floodplain habitat makes for a more interesting hike than does the linear dike road. Though rare, black bears occasionally raid nearby apple orchards and leave evidence along these trails. Getting lost may look effortless in places; just remember to keep the river on your left and the levee on your right. Detours along these trails can add a few hundred feet or a couple of miles to the hike, depending on how much you want to explore the bosque.

Of course, the dike road has the advantage of being remarkably easy to follow, and its elevation affords more expansive views. Overlooking the bosque, the drain, and nearby farm fields, you're more likely to spot wildlife, such as cottontails, porcupines, and any one of approximately 180 bird species—from ruby-crowned kinglets to yellow-rumped warblers. Hawks, owls, herons, and woodpeckers are also common in the area. During the winter there will be plenty of sandhill cranes for the entire walk. The Audubon Society has identified the Bosque Preserve as an Important Bird Area.

This stretch also has the advantage of built-in mile markers. Those vertical galvanized steel pipes at the base of the dike are part of the irrigation and flood-control system. They are spaced 0.1 mile apart and are labeled with their distance north of Alameda Bridge. The planned hike joins the dike road between markers 5.6 and 5.5.

Opportunities to cross back over the riverside drain are few. About 1.5 miles downstream from your first crossing, the river and the road bend westward. Another mile past the bend, you'll see a single-lane bridge that leads to Dixon Road. Continue on the dike road another 0.6 mile, rounding a slight bend, to a wooden bridge (marker 2.6 is just south of the bridge). Cross that one and proceed up to the parallel ditch just to the west. Turn right (west) and cross the ditch at your first chance. Turn left (south). About 200 yards ahead, turn right (west) and exit through the green gate.

Bosque access gate to Rec Center (1 mile): You're now on East La Entrada Road. It goes straight to Corrales Road, which is not what you'd call pedestrian friendly. So instead, go one block west, just past La Paloma Greenhouse, and turn left (south) on a ditchbank road marked LINDERO DEL DRENAJE. Follow it south about 0.25 mile, then turn right (west) at the fourth crossroad, Bernaval Place (paved, but missing signage). About 200 feet ahead it ends at a T-junction with Priestly Place. Turn left (south) and follow it around to the right (west), where it becomes Coroval Road. Follow that to its end at Corrales Road; Territorial Plaza is across the street. To the immediate right is Jones Road. Follow it back to the rec center.

NEARBY ACTIVITIES

Corrales Winery is open for free tours and wine tastings Wednesday–Sunday, noon–5 p.m. Its entrance is on Corrales Road, 2.2 miles north of Jones Road. Call 505-898-5165 or visit corraleswinery.com for more information.

GPS TRAILHEAD COORDINATES N35° 13.279' W106° 37.354'

DIRECTIONS From I-25 North, take Exit 233 at Alameda Boulevard (NM 528). Turn left (west) on Alameda Boulevard and go 4.2 miles. Turn right (north) on Corrales Road (NM 448—notorious for speed traps) and drive 2 miles. Turn left on Jones Road (immediately after Territorial Plaza). Go 0.2 mile and park near the Corrales Recreation Center.

5 KASHA-KATUWE TENT ROCKS NATIONAL MONUMENT

Hundreds of towering tent rocks create a bizarre landscape that you won't find anywhere else in the US.

IF YOU HAVE out-of-town guests, this is the place to bring them. There is no place quite like Tent Rocks with its 90-foot-tall hoodoos. Enter a sinuous slot canyon to admire them from below, and then climb high up to a ridge to gaze down upon them. In warm seasons, wildlife comes in furred, feathered, and spiked varieties, and wildflower identification can turn into a full-day affair.

DESCRIPTION

Since Tent Rocks was designated a national monument in 2001, crowds in the lower Peralta Canyon have increased steadily. Although you could arrive to find it virtually deserted, particularly in winter or on a midweek morning, you're almost as likely to find a camera safari or a busload of schoolchildren around every corner. But if you haven't yet seen the jaw-dropping spectacle in the lower canyon, make it your top priority. This is a must-do hike!

The National Recreation Trail is composed of two segments: Cave Loop Trail and its spur, Canyon Trail. Both segments are well groomed and clearly marked. An information kiosk at the trailhead will further help keep you on the right track.

The big attraction here is Kasha-Katuwe, but there's more to it than the words imply. Meaning "white cliffs" in the traditional language of the Cochiti people,

DISTANCE & CONFIGURATION: 3.4-mile loop and spur

DIFFICULTY: Moderate

SCENERY: Tent rock formations, birds and wildlife, seasonal wildflowers, wonderful views

EXPOSURE: Some canyon shade

TRAIL TRAFFIC: Popular

TRAIL SURFACE: Packed sand and gravel, bedrock

HIKING TIME: 2 hours

DRIVING DISTANCE: 55 miles from the Big I

ELEVATION GAIN: 5,720' at trailhead; 6,329' at high point

ACCESS: November 1–March 10: 8 a.m.–5 p.m.; March 11–October 31: 7 a.m.–7 p.m. Visitors must be out by closing time. On-site fee is $5/noncommercial vehicle. Federal Land Recreation Passes are accepted.

WHEELCHAIR ACCESS: Cave Loop Trail is wheelchair accessible.

MAPS: Brochure map available at park entrance station; USGS *Canada*

FACILITIES: Picnic area, restrooms; no water

CONTACT: BLM–Rio Puerco, blm.gov/office/rio-puerco-field-office, 505-761-8700; Cochiti Pueblo, 505-465-2234

LOCATION: West of Cochiti Pueblo

COMMENTS: No dogs allowed. Monument subject to closures due to inclement weather and by order of the Pueblo de Cochiti governor (call first).

LAST-CHANCE FOOD/GAS: Convenience store–gas station in the town of Cochiti Lake (see Nearby Activities)

Kasha-Katuwe is packed with fascinating formations. To summarize the complex geologic processes at work: When the Jemez volcanic field erupted 6–7 million years ago, it piled 1,000 feet of pumice, ash, and tuff upon the Pajarito Plateau. Over the ensuing millennia, wind and rain cut into the soft rock layers, eventually carving deep canyons. But in places where durable caprock withstood erosion, it protected the soft rock directly beneath it. The result: hundreds of towering conical spires known as tent rocks, each donning a boulder for a hat. Their shapes resemble tepees and castle towers. When covered in snow, they evoke the soft-serve creations of Tastee Freez. It's a bizarre landscape, to say the least. To see another one like it, you'd need to travel to Cappadocia in central Turkey.

Cave Loop Trail begins at the kiosk north of the parking area and soon splits in two. Take the left path for the long way to Canyon Trail—it leads you through a small party of tent rocks, with the tallest among them standing no higher than a streetlight. These hoodoos have lost their caps and are gradually melting.

As the lesser-traveled of the two trails, Cave Loop is where you're more likely to spot animal life. Ground squirrels, chipmunks, coyotes, and rabbits are prevalent. Also keep an eye out for horned lizards, or "horny toads." A member of the iguana family, the short-horned lizard is common throughout much of New Mexico. Colored and patterned to match their environment, these spiked reptiles are difficult to spot unless they're moving, and they often stay perfectly still until they're a step away from getting trampled. In addition to using camouflage and their spiny heads, they can defend themselves by squirting a noxious dose of blood into a predator's eyes and mouth.

Located at the top of the loop, the cave is a scooped-out hole in the wall. Its ceiling is charred from ancient wood fires. The trail follows the wall down to a drainage. After 0.7 mile on the loop, you arrive at a T-junction. Turn left into the canyon.

Kasha-Katuwe Tent Rocks National Monument

KASHA-KATUWE TENT ROCKS NATIONAL MONUMENT

Tent Rocks

Canyon Trail

cave

Cave Loop

Tribal Road 92

To 22

N

0.2 mile

0.2 kilometer

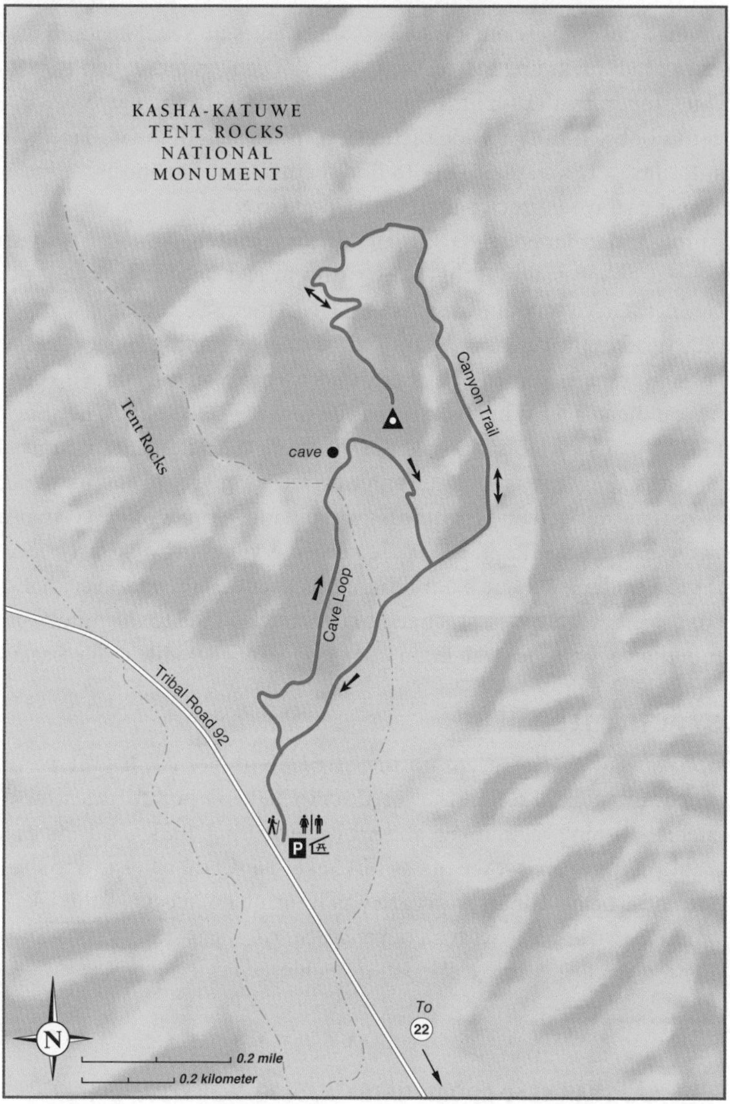

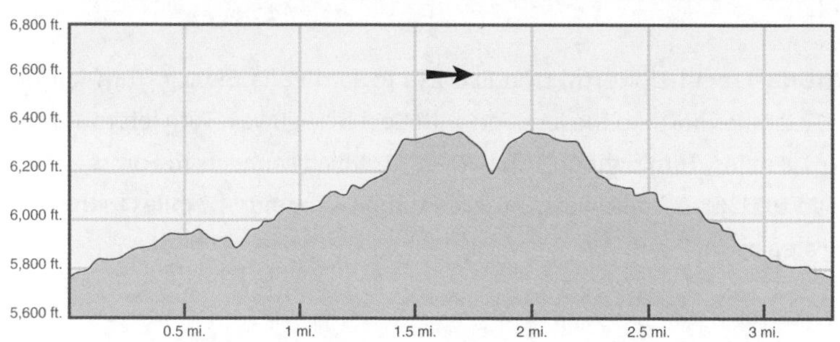

Canyon Trail is easily one of the best short hikes in New Mexico. This 1.1-mile spur features tent rocks up to 90 feet tall and a slot canyon more than 1,000 feet long. Mind your step in winter—a little snow and ice can turn the narrow, winding segments into a bobsled run. In wide sections, scan the base of the wall for petroglyphs and handprints. It takes a sharp eye to find them. (*Hint:* Pay special attention to the left wall near a stray tent rock paired with a ponderosa.)

In spring and summer, white-throated swifts spend their days careening through the canyon. Unlike swallows, they won't stop to rest until the sun goes down. At night they roost in cantaloupe-size niches high in the rock walls.

At the head of the canyon, the trail turns steep, climbing 200 feet in 0.3 mile. A couple of steps require some upper-body effort, but if you can climb up on a kitchen counter, you'll manage. When you reach the top, the trail splits. The short spur on the left leads to an overlook. The right branch runs 0.3 mile. Refrain from exploring informal paths along the way. They enter private property to the immediate west. The designated trail descends southeast, culminating with a brief, vertigo-inducing ridge traverse to the overlook. There are gorgeous views in every direction. You can also spot the trailhead about 0.5 mile southwest and 500 feet lower than the vista point. To get there, however, you need to backtrack a mile to the mouth of the canyon. From there, continue straight on Cave Loop Trail 0.4 mile to the parking lot.

NEARBY ACTIVITIES

No doubt you saw Cochiti Dam on the east side of NM 22. It's the world's 13th-largest earth-filled dam. Behind it lies **Cochiti Lake,** a popular area for camping, bird-watching, fishing, swimming, and no-wake boating. Basic food and gas services are available in the nearby town of Cochiti Lake. To get there, return to the junction of NM 22 and Cochiti Highway, where you'll turn left. Access to the lake is 1 mile north on the right. A plaza with a convenience store–gas station is 0.4 mile farther north. For more information, call Cochiti Pueblo.

GPS TRAILHEAD COORDINATES N35° 39.452' W106° 24.717'

DIRECTIONS From I-25 North, take Exit 259 toward Peña Blanca. Turn left on NM 22 and go 12.2 miles north to the junction with Cochiti Highway. Turn left to stay on NM 22 another 1.8 miles. Turn right on Tribal Road 92, which connects to Forest Road 266 and BLM Road 1011. Go 0.5 mile west to the fee station. Continue 4.7 miles to the designated parking area on the right.

6 LA LUZ TRAIL TO THE CREST AND TRAM

With fantastic views coming and going, this is a hike you should do at least once.

FOR THIS WONDERFUL ADVENTURE, you'll park your car at the base of the tram, hike 9 miles and climb 3,700 feet to the top, and then ride back in style on the longest tram in the country.

DESCRIPTION

The 7.5-mile **La Luz Trail (137)** climbing from the base of Sandia Crest to the top is probably Albuquerque's best-known trail. It is a true adventure hike right in our own backyard. Along the lines of adventure, it is also where 400 dedicated trail runners race from the bottom to the top every August in the grueling 9-mile La Luz Trail Run.

You can hike the La Luz Trail out and back for a 15-mile hike. But for our hike, we'll be hiking up and then taking the tram down. Because the tram has a policy of no dogs, you won't be able to take your dog on this hike. If you have two cars, you could spot one car at the base of the tram and then drive over to the La Luz Trailhead to start your walk from there.

Our hike is 9 miles. It begins at the base of the tram and follows the **Tramway Trail (82)** north to where it joins the La Luz Trail. The hike continues on the La Luz to where the trail ends at the tram and concludes with a spectacular 15-minute tram ride back down to the car.

DISTANCE & CONFIGURATION: 9-mile hike one way, return on tram

DIFFICULTY: Strenuous

SCENERY: Fantastic views, mixed forest, mountain scenery

EXPOSURE: Mostly shaded

TRAIL TRAFFIC: Popular

TRAIL SURFACE: Dirt, rock

HIKING TIME: 6–7 hours

DRIVING DISTANCE: 15 miles from the Big I

ELEVATION GAIN: 6,540' at trailhead; 10,256' at summit

ACCESS: Year-round, hike may be difficult to do in winter; $2 parking fee at tram base; tram is subject to shutdowns for maintenance

WHEELCHAIR ACCESS: No

MAPS: Sandia Ranger District; USGS *Sandia Crest*

FACILITIES: Restaurant and restroom at base; restroom and exhibits at top; a new restaurant on top is expected to open in 2019

CONTACT: Cibola National Forest–Sandia Mountain Wilderness, fs.usda.gov/cibola, 505-281-3304; Sandia Tram, sandiapeak.com, 505-856-7325

LOCATION: Albuquerque

COMMENTS: No dogs are allowed on tram.

This is a good hike for most of the year. During the winter the La Luz can have too much ice and snow for a safe hike. Except for maintenance shutdowns in April and November, the tram is open year-round. There are, however, reduced hours on Tuesdays, so you might want to check the tram's website (sandiapeak.com) to make sure it's running on the day you plan to hike. At the time of this writing, parking at the base of the tram is $2 and a one-way trip on the tram costs $15.

Riding the tram is worth doing on its own. At 2.7 miles, it was the world's longest aerial tramway until 2011. The ride is amazing. At one point the tramcar is 900 feet above the ground, and the views looking down on the mountains are unbelievable.

With the hike passing through four climatic zones (piñon–juniper, ponderosa, Douglas-fir–aspen, and spruce–fir), you'll need to be prepared for multiple weather conditions. It will be cooler at the top. There is no food or water along the way, so make sure you start out with enough.

The hike begins at the trailhead of the Tramway Trail at the northeast corner of the tram parking lot and heads north in a circuitous route through eroded Sandia Mountain granite formations. With little shade, this part of the hike can become hot in the afternoon.

There is a nice residential area off to the left and down below at the base of the mountains. Being above a neighborhood gives you the opportunity to be a distant observer of everyday life from afar while enjoying a fantastic hike. If you start early in the day, you're likely to see the neighborhood wake up. If it's a little later in the morning, you may hear the sounds of delivery trucks straining to climb the hilly streets.

The houses become distant as you continue north. There will still be granite formations and several casual trails leading back to the houses. Just stay with the main trail and in about 1 mile from the trailhead you'll see a sign saying TO SPRING CREEK. If you want to do some exploring, you can follow the side trail to the foundation of the old Jaral Ranger Station.

La Luz Trail to the Crest and Tram

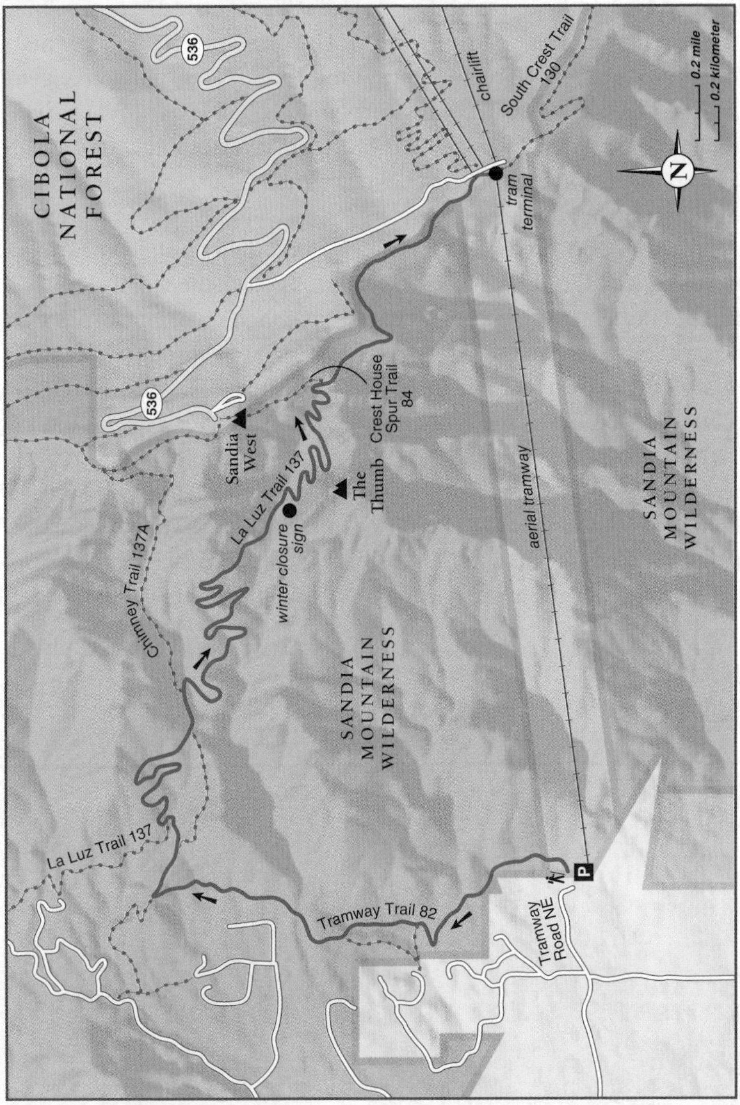

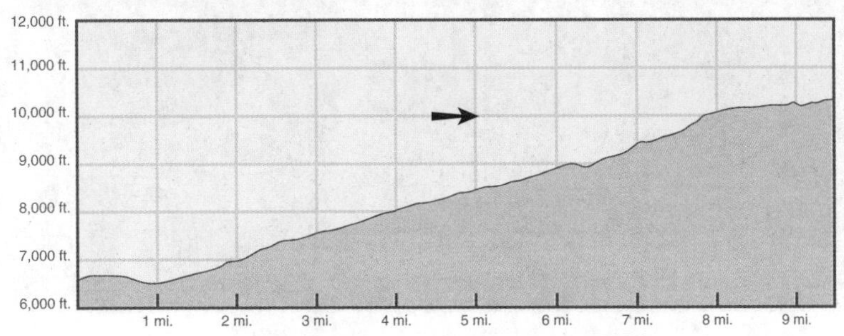

At around 2.2 miles into the hike, the trail will make a sharp turn to the right and start heading east on a ridge above a canyon. The vegetation is decidedly thicker at this point with more shade. You're not quite at the La Luz Trail, but you're getting close. The La Luz is on the other side of the canyon. Keep going east. When the trail starts descending toward the bottom of the canyon, there will be another trail going off to the right and up. Keep going straight; you'll reach the La Luz, when the trail crosses the bottom of the canyon, 2.5 miles into the hike. The La Luz Trailhead is 1 mile downhill.

The hike on the Tramway Trail is much better than most people expect, but the La Luz Trail is wonderful. The broad switchbacks make the uphill climb much easier than it could be. The stone retaining walls along the trail are great places to rest, to grab a snack, or to take in the views. And the views are absolutely fantastic in every direction. With the crest looming to the east, you can see all types of stone formations, the radio towers on top of the crest, and the thicker woods ahead. To the west, you can see the trail below and the Rio Grande Valley beyond. It just doesn't get better.

As you push toward the crest, the views intensify. There will be sheer granite walls around you, prominent formations, and more trees. You are now in the Douglas-fir–aspen zone. Just as you enter a dark corner full of trees 6.7 miles into the hike, you'll see a caution sign saying that the trail beyond here may be impassible in the

You'll experience amazing scenery all along La Luz Trail.

winter. And it is here where the hike becomes hard. Many people doing an out-and-back day hike will turn around here.

The next 1.5 miles of the hike are one switchback after another through a narrow chimney of scree and rock slides. Although the trail is well defined through the rocky portions, the uneven footing on the rocks tends to slow many people down. Every now and then a switchback will leave the rocks to reenter the forest, and you'll say to yourself that maybe this is the end of the rocks. But then the trail will make a cutback to cross the rocks again. For many, the 1.5-mile stretch through the rocks is harder than the rest of the hike combined! Fortunately, there are fantastic views to soften the blow of the rocks.

But like everything, the switchbacks come to an end, and the hike returns to normal. Even though the remaining 1.4 miles of the trail are above 10,000 feet in altitude, they're a breeze compared to the rocks. You'll run into the junction with Crest Spur Trail (84) right after the switchbacks. It is, as its name implies, a 0.6-mile connector going off to the left to the Sandia Crest high point. Before you reach the tram, you'll be hiking on a ledge below the ridge above. In some places the ledge will get narrow and have a very steep drop-off to your right, so keep paying attention during these last moments of the hike.

Before you know it you'll be above the ridge and at the tram. You can buy a ticket for the ride down at the Upper Tram Terminal. There is usually a tram running (called *Flights*) every 20 or 30 minutes. The actual ride down is about 15 minutes. That's a good time to reflect on the sense of adventure and accomplishment that this hike offers.

NEARBY ACTIVITIES

If you didn't bring enough food or water for the hike and are famished, you might want to grab a bite to eat at Sandiago's Grill in the Lower Tram Terminal Building. It serves very good New Mexican food and has great views looking across Albuquerque from the dining room. For more information visit sandiagos.com or call 505-856-6692.

GPS TRAILHEAD COORDINATES N35° 11.496' W106° 28.744'

DIRECTIONS From I-25 North, take Exit 234 and go 5 miles east on NM 556/Tramway Boulevard. Turn east on Tramway Road and go 1 mile to the tram at the end of the road. Or from I-40 East, take Exit 167 and go 8.5 miles north to Tramway Road and go east to the tram.

7 PETROGLYPH NATIONAL MONUMENT: Piedras Marcadas

Half the fun at Piedras Marcadas is finding petroglyphs between trail markers, so look closely.

HIDDEN IN WEST SIDE suburbia, the northernmost outpost of this national monument contains an estimated 5,000 petroglyphs. Any hunt for images carved into the basalt lava escarpment will yield fascinating finds.

DESCRIPTION

Albuquerque's escarpment is a product of the volcanoes described in Hike 8 (page 54). This 17-mile ribbon of basalt lava winds along the base of the West Mesa, forming points, alcoves, and canyons. The flat surfaces of boulders found here are shiny and smooth, with a sheen known as desert varnish. People figured out long ago that by pecking through this patina, they could create pictures that were, if nothing else, durable. The oldest of their squiggly lines date back to around 1000 B.C.

Most works seen in Piedras Marcadas ("marked rocks") Canyon feature the elaborate designs from what was likely the largest pueblo in the Rio Grande Valley during the Pueblo IV period (A.D. 1300–1600). The pueblo flourished with more than 1,000 rooms before expeditionary forces under Francisco Vasquez de Coronado arrived. Though largely unexcavated today, the Piedras Marcadas Pueblo ruins are at the Open Space Visitor Center (see Nearby Activities).

The canyon contains about a fourth of the monument's petroglyphs, yet only 3% of the 124,000 annual visitors venture into this area. Suburban sprawl is the chief

DISTANCE & CONFIGURATION: 1.8 miles of interconnected loops

DIFFICULTY: Easy

SCENERY: Ancient etchings on volcanic rock; city views

EXPOSURE: No shade

TRAIL TRAFFIC: Popular

TRAIL SURFACE: Sand

HIKING TIME: 1 hour

DRIVING DISTANCE: 12 miles from the Big I

ELEVATION GAIN: 5,209', with no significant rise

ACCESS: Year-round, sunrise–sunset; no fees or permits required

WHEELCHAIR ACCESS: No

MAPS: Basic trail map posted at trailhead and available at visitor centers; USGS *Los Griegos*

FACILITIES: Picnic shelter, playground

CONTACT: National Park Service, nps.gov/petr; Albuquerque Open Space, cabq.gov/openspace, 505-987-8831

LOCATION: Albuquerque

COMMENTS: Leashed dogs are permitted on trails. See Nearby Activities for more information on the petroglyphs.

deterrent. Residential developments over the past decade have nearly sealed off this area of the park, which you'll no doubt notice as you begin your hike up a concrete alley between two houses wedged into a corner behind a gas station.

It's not the classic Richard Attenborough expedition. Instead, Piedras Marcadas Canyon might be best appreciated as a study in contrasts. For better or worse, few places in America present such an immediate juxtaposition of ancient and modern worlds. And though you'll be reminded in every piece of tourist literature, it bears repeating: the land is a living shrine that continues to have a sacred role in contemporary Pueblo cultures.

A sign at the top end of the walkway shows a basic trail map. However, the canyon contains far more trails than indicated. In fact, for every mile of designated trails within the monument, local wanderers have blazed 5 miles of social trails.

From the sign, follow the trail to your left past a barrier gate. Bypass any little shortcuts angling toward the south side of the escarpment. At the Y ahead, turn right on a wide path. **Marker 1,** a subtle gray post about knee high, is just around the bend. Now look up at the escarpment to find faces staring back at you.

First-time visitors share a tendency to climb up for a closer look. Park regulations aside, your time is better spent at the petroglyphs ahead, which are not only closer to the trail but also represent finer craftsmanship in terms of detail and definition. The most-revered designs include full-bodied kachina iconography and crosses and cattle brands from the Spanish colonial era.

As you follow the trail deeper into the alcove, the views and sounds of the city diminish, and it's easy to forget for a moment that just outside the walls of this basalt fortress, the suburban hordes are mustering in golf carts and SUVs. **Markers 2** and **3** are set off the main trail. Side trails allow for a closer look at nearby petroglyphs. Also keep an eye out for petroglyphs between markers. Half the fun is finding one without the assistance of trail markers.

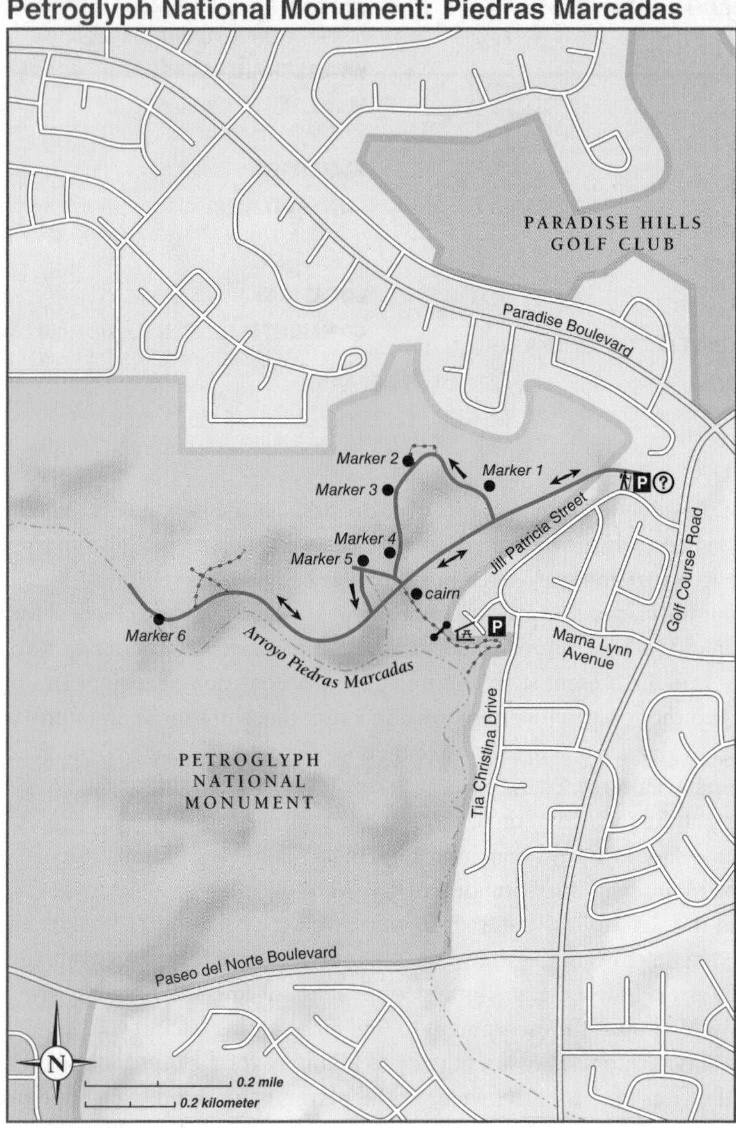

After Marker 3, you will cross a dry wash and head downhill. The trail points directly toward a prominent cluster of buildings about 8 miles to the southeast. The tall one is U.S. Eagle Plaza on the downtown Civic Plaza. Also dead ahead, **Marker 4** indicates the location of five handprints, three of which are riddled with bullet holes.

Turnoffs for the trail into the second alcove, where you'll find **Marker 5,** start about 80 feet ahead on the right. Access to this smaller trail is sometimes obscured under dense vegetation. If you stumble across a large cairn, you've gone too far. Go back and follow the trail nearest the escarpment wall. The trail heading out of the alcove is easy to lose, but it runs parallel to the wash and stays close to the escarpment. Once out of the alcove, you'll find a perpendicular trail. Turn right and follow it around the basalt outcropping.

Unlike the trails in previous alcoves, this one bends in only slightly en route to the next marker on the far side. However, at least one park official has hinted that the path skirting the base of the escarpment is the best of the social trails. This detour into the canyon's deepest alcove meets up with the main trail at **Marker 6** and adds less than 0.25 mile to the overall hike.

If you continue straight ahead, the trail soon becomes more of a trench, with devil's claw growing from the edges as though reaching for a handout. Park maps show this trail ending about 200 feet past Marker 6, but there it arrives at another trail. To the right it climbs through a gap in the escarpment. From there the canyon widens, exposing developments along Paradise Boulevard to the north.

To return to the parking lot, follow the trail that crosses in front of the last alcove. Or, if you packed a lunch and the kids, visit the sheltered picnic table and playground 250 yards east of the outcropping. The picnic table is in a small city park at an entrance south of where the hike began.

NEARBY ACTIVITIES

To learn more about petroglyphs and the monument, visit the **Petroglyph National Monument Visitor Center, Las Imágenes.** It is best reached en route from I-40 west. Take Exit 155 and go 1.8 miles north on Coors Boulevard. Turn left on Western Trail, and go west about 1 mile. Open all year, 8 a.m.–5 p.m.; closed January 1, Thanksgiving, and December 25. Call 505-899-0205 or visit nps.gov/petr.

The ruins of Piedras Marcadas Pueblo are located at the **Open Space Visitor Center.** The visitor center is at 6500 Coors Blvd. and is open Tuesday–Saturday, 9 a.m.–5 p.m.; call 505-897-8831 or visit cabq.gov/openspace.

• •

GPS TRAILHEAD COORDINATES N35° 11.324' W106° 41.161'

DIRECTIONS From I-40 West, take Exit 155 and go 5.8 miles north on Coors Boulevard. Turn left on Paseo del Norte and go west 1.2 miles. (Alternate directions: From I-25 North, take Exit 232 on Paseo del Norte and go west 5.9 miles.) Turn right on Golf Course Road and go 0.6 mile north. Turn left on Jill Patricia Street. The parking lot entrance is about 100 yards ahead on the right. The trail begins on the sidewalk on the west side at the sign for Piedras Marcadas.

8 PETROGLYPH NATIONAL MONUMENT: The Volcanoes

Vulcan Volcano is the largest of the volcanoes here.

WALK THE FLANKS of four scoria cones and look for lizards in the lava rock. The Albuquerque Volcanoes also boast the West Side's best views of both the city and the Sandia Mountains.

DESCRIPTION

Try counting every volcano within 60 miles of Albuquerque, and you should come up with a tally in the neighborhood of 270. They range in size from scorched dents in the earth to the towering peak of Mount Taylor.

Ten volcanoes reside within Albuquerque's city limits, with five blistering the otherwise flat western horizon. Compared to the Sandia granite that dominates the eastern vista, the spatter cones are mere babes, born in the final throes of a fissure eruption just 140,000 years ago.

Lava spilled primarily east into the Rio Grande Valley. Concealed beneath the sand and sage of Albuquerque's West Mesa, a lava crust (basalt caprock) rests upon older layers of sediments. Thousands of years of erosion undermined the eastern edges of the caprock, causing it to break apart and collapse. The result is an exposed volcanic escarpment that appears from a distance as a fairly uniform black cliff.

Pueblo Indians have long considered this a sacred landscape. Later cultures developed their own interpretations, with each new generation finding unique ways

DISTANCE & CONFIGURATION: 1-, 2-, and 6.3-mile loop options

DIFFICULTY: Easy–moderate

SCENERY: Cinder cones, city views, birds, reptiles

EXPOSURE: Full sun

TRAIL TRAFFIC: Popular

TRAIL SURFACE: Packed dirt, sand, loose rock

HIKING TIME: 20 minutes–3 hours

DRIVING DISTANCE: 15 miles from the Big I

ELEVATION GAIN: 5,788' at trailhead; 5,976 at the top of Black Volcano

ACCESS: Daily, sunrise–sunset; parking lot, 9 a.m.–5 p.m.; no fees or permits required

WHEELCHAIR ACCESS: Limited wheelchair access to trails; wheelchair-accessible restrooms

MAPS: Trail map at nps.gov/petr; USGS *The Volcanoes*

FACILITIES: Shade shelters, interpretive signage, no water

CONTACT: National Park Service, nps.gov/petr; Albuquerque Open Space, cabq.gov/openspace, 505-897-8831

LOCATION: Albuquerque

COMMENTS: Leashed dogs are permitted on trails. See Nearby Activities in Hike 7 (page 50) for information about the Petroglyph National Monument Visitor Center.

to express its fondness for the volcanoes. During World War II the Army Air Corps had several bomb targets in the area for training bomber crews.

On a quiet morning in 1947, Albuquerque residents seemed to gain a new appreciation for their volcanoes when they woke to find thick black smoke billowing from the biggest cone. Citywide panic naturally ensued. A brave crew eventually assessed the fuming crater and returned to announce that the smoke was coming from strategically placed car tires, soaked in gasoline and set ablaze. The prank would be repeated over successive years with considerably less impact.

When you approach the volcanoes from the south, you'll see three volcanoes rising above the flat grassland in front of you and become more apparent as you get closer. When you turn in the entry road, you'll see an overflow parking lot just outside the gate. The park is open from sunrise to sunset, while the gate is open from 9 a.m. to 5 p.m. If you're planning to hike outside of the gate's hours, you'll want to park in the overflow area. Otherwise, continue to the main parking area and trailhead.

Navigating the wide-open space in the volcanoes area is easy. For orientation, the three volcanoes from south to north are JA Volcano, Black Volcano, and Vulcan Volcano. There are well-defined trails with signage to all of the volcanoes. There are old trails that are now closed. You'll want to avoid those trails to allow vegetation to recover. Also, although climbing to the top of the volcanoes is not expressly prohibited, it is considered an act of desecration to many Pueblo peoples.

Most volcano visitors tend to dash to the scenic overlook at JA Volcano for a gawk before rushing back to the interstate. The scenic overlook has fantastic unobstructed views of the entire Albuquerque basin. You'll see the grassland immediately in front of you and the spread of Albuquerque all the way to the Sandia Mountains. Downtown will be a bit off to the right. The 1-mile out-and-back to the overlook takes about 20 or 30 minutes.

Petroglyph National Monument: The Volcanoes

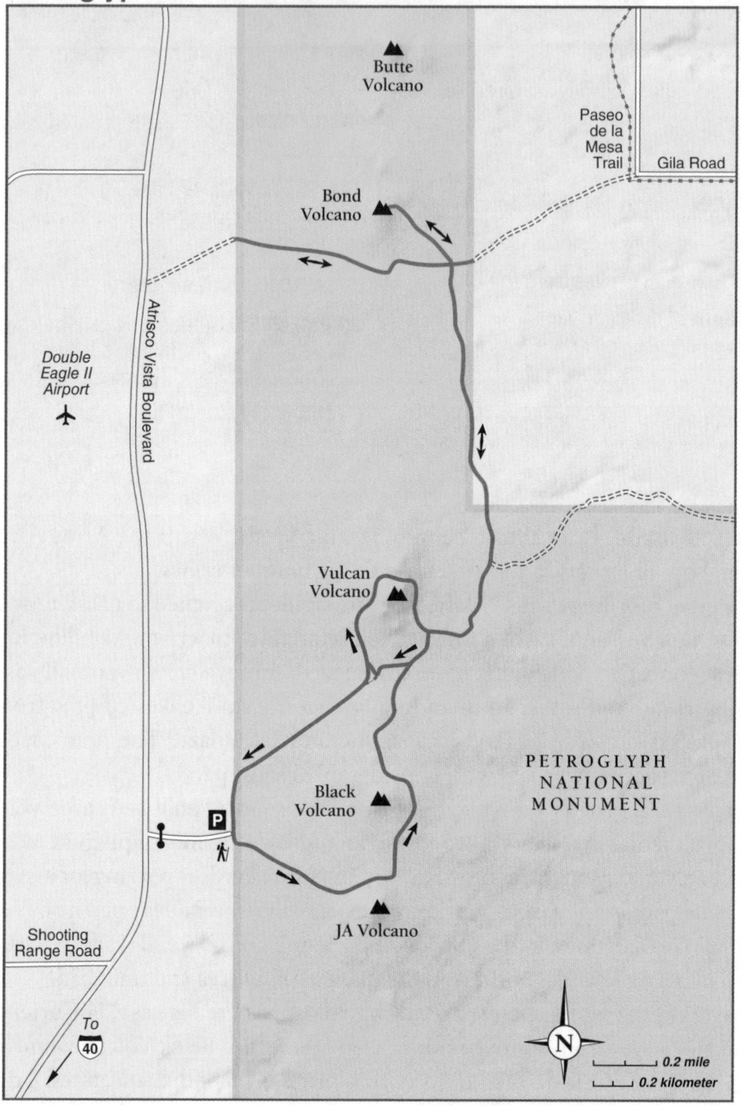

Butte Volcano
Paseo de la Mesa Trail
Gila Road
Bond Volcano
Atrisco Vista Boulevard
Double Eagle II Airport
Vulcan Volcano
PETROGLYPH NATIONAL MONUMENT
Black Volcano
P
JA Volcano
Shooting Range Road
To
40
N
0.2 mile
0.2 kilometer

6,200 ft.
6,100 ft.
6,000 ft.
5,900 ft.
5,800 ft.
5,700 ft.
5,600 ft.
1 mi.
2 mi.
3 mi.
4 mi.
5 mi.
6 mi.

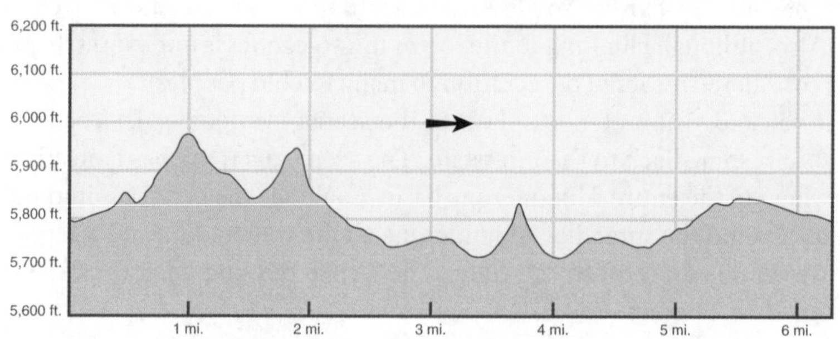

Looking east after a summer rain

With the volcanoes so close to Albuquerque, you can come out here often to try out other options. You can start the hike from the gate at the southeast corner of the parking lot, take a moment to read the interpretive displays at the trailhead, and then proceed out to JA Volcano. There is good signage all the way to keep you on the right path.

JA Volcano gets its name from a pair of initials painted long ago on its eastern face. They've since faded, but those who know where to look claim the letters are still visible from 8 miles away. These tend to be the same people who claim to see gases rising from the cones and insist that the city's Technicolor sunsets are due to the filtering effect of volcanic vapors.

From the overlook, turn left and head north on the main trail. It skirts around east sides of Black and Cinder Volcanoes—or what's left of them. (There is a side trail to the top of Black Volcano if you're interested.) Some Burqueños still remember when six robust cones stood out here, before miners cut Black down to a stump and reduced Cinder to a pit.

About 1.4 miles into the hike, you'll arrive at the junction with the return path at the base of Vulcan Volcano. Named for the Roman god of fire, this cone is the biggest in the group. The old parking area was here, which helps explain the remnants of roads and several footpaths. Stay on the main path going up the south side of the cone; it will angle to the left and circle the volcano. The trail crosses over a saddle between the main volcano and a baby cone. Continuing clockwise, it passes by a half-domed outcrop. From here the path tends to fade as it rounds the steepest flank. Stick to the base of Vulcan until you reach the hollowed-out area of a former quarry. From here you can finish the loop and head back to the parking lot via the old access road, which runs southwest to a fence, and then straight south. The Vulcan loop totals 2 miles and takes about an hour.

To visit Bond Volcano, follow the road south-southeast from the Vulcan quarry. This hike is a good way to get a taste of backcountry hiking without having to travel far from Albuquerque. It is a very peaceful walk with fabulous views. Please refrain from taking any shortcuts, as you may disturb birds and snakes nesting in the grassy areas. The trail soon curves left and goes roughly north about 1.2 miles to the remains of an old corral at the junction of five roads. Take the road heading northwest about 0.25 mile to Bond's southern flank. There you'll find a cave that sometimes smells ripe with musk, depending on the season.

About halfway between the corral and Bond Volcano, you'll pass under a power line. If you turn left and follow the power line service road west, you'll come to a backdoor entrance to park in a little more than a 0.5 mile. If you turn right and follow the service road east, you'll start running into practice-bomb fragments in around 300 feet. The center of a World War II bomb target is just to the north of here. Please leave the bomb fragments as you found them. They are cultural artifacts and are protected by law.

Return to Vulcan the same way you came. From there you can return to the parking lot via the old access road.

NEARBY ACTIVITIES

Shooting Range Park is a public facility for target practice and skeet shooting. It is a much better place to practice shooting than our public lands. Open Wednesday–Sunday, 9 a.m.–5 p.m. To get there from the Volcanoes area, turn left (south) onto Atrisco Vista and go 0.4 mile to Shooting Range Road. Turn right (west) and follow the signs 3 miles to the park. For more information, call 505-836-8785 or visit cabq.gov/openspace/shootingrange.html.

Paseo de la Mesa Trail is open to bicyclists, walkers, persons in wheelchairs, in-line skaters, and equestrians. Highlights include a 4.2-mile paved trail uninterrupted by roadways, side paths to geologic windows, probable encounters with West Mesa wildlife, and 360-degree views encompassing mountain ranges. For an exhilarating downhill ride, start at the dirt access lot off Atrisco Vista, near Paseo del Norte, and finish at the paved lot off 81st Street near Unser Boulevard. Overall, it's a 400-foot drop in elevation, with some steep sections and sharp curves. For more information, call Albuquerque Open Space at 505-897-8831 or visit cabq.gov/openspace.

GPS TRAILHEAD COORDINATES N35° 07.819' W106° 46.821'

DIRECTIONS From I-40 West, take Exit 149 and go 4.8 miles north on Atrisco Vista Boulevard. Turn right on the access road and follow it east 0.25 mile to the parking lot. The trailhead is near the southeastern corner of the lot.

9 PIEDRA LISA TRAILHEAD OPTIONS

Views from the Piedra Lisa Trail are some of the best in the Sandias.

THE PIEDRA LISA Trailhead provides access to one of the prettiest corners of the Sandias. Options from the trailhead lead to great views and, on one option, to a relatively unknown niche of paradise. Whatever option(s) you choose will be worth the effort.

DESCRIPTION

The most dramatic landforms in the Sandia Mountains are at the north end of Albuquerque. When you turn onto Forest Road 333 from Tramway Boulevard for the Piedra Lisa Trailhead, you'll be overwhelmed by the view of the crest looming over you. When you reach the top of the ridge, you'll be looking into Juan Tabo Canyon. The canyon is gorgeous! This is a good place to get the lay of the land.

You'll clearly see the crest to the east. But you might start noticing how the face and the area in front of the crest is broken up into several dramatic landforms with the Needle, the Prow, and the Shield being the most prominent. As you continue looking, you'll notice how there is almost an arm coming out from the crest to encircle the canyon in front of you. The east–west part of the arm is the Rincon. You'll probably also notice some very nice houses in the canyon, but not too many. And

DISTANCE & CONFIGURATION: 4.2-mile out-and-back; longer and shorter options

DIFFICULTY: Moderate; some options can get strenuous

SCENERY: Wooded canyons, granite formations, waterfalls

EXPOSURE: Mostly shaded

TRAIL TRAFFIC: Popular on Piedra Lisa, low on the options

TRAIL SURFACE: Dirt, rock

HIKING TIME: 2–4 hours

DRIVING DISTANCE: 15 miles from the Big I

ELEVATION GAIN: 6,936' at trailhead; 8,165' at the Rincon

ACCESS: Year-round; no fees or permits required; the parking fee station has been removed (for now)

WHEELCHAIR ACCESS: No

MAPS: Sandia Ranger District; USGS *Sandia Crest*

FACILITIES: None (seasonal restrooms at nearby Juan Tabo Picnic Area)

CONTACT: Cibola National Forest–Sandia Mountain Wilderness, fs.usda.gov/cibola, 505-281-3304

LOCATION: Albuquerque

COMMENTS: Leashed dogs are allowed on trails. Mountain lion tracks are common in Waterfall Canyon, so keep little hikers close at hand.

then if you look behind you, you'll have dramatic views of most of Albuquerque. From here it is a 0.4-mile stretch of unpaved road to the parking area.

At press time, the fee station in the parking area has been removed. The trailhead and information signs are at the far end of the parking area. The **Piedra Lisa Trail** is the starting point for four different hiking options. The trail leads up from the parking lot to the road and continues on the other side of the road.

The trail on the other side of the road was recently built by the U.S. Forest Service to eliminate a 0.4-mile road walk. The new trail was designed to enhance the views in all directions and has greatly improved the quality of hiking along this stretch. The trail becomes lusher as you walk north. You'll pass a connector trail to the La Luz Trail almost as soon as you cross the road. Our hike stays on the main trail.

The new section of trail joins the original trail in around 0.6 mile at the top of a ridge. As you can see, this part of the trail was once a road. We'll angle to the right to follow the trail down to the drainage. Just before reaching the bottom there will be a Sandia Mountain Wilderness sign. There will also be a gray post with a trail behind it. That trail is a shortcut to Waterfall Canyon. For now we'll continue to the center of the drainage.

At this point you've hiked 0.75 mile, and this is where your options begin. From north to south, they are continuing on the Piedra Lisa Trail or choosing the Fletcher Trail, the Movie Trail, or Waterfall Canyon. Piedra Lisa goes uphill to the north. Fletcher follows the drainage going off to the northeast. Waterfall Canyon follows the drainage going off to the southeast. The Movie Trail follows the ridge between the two drainages.

Piedra Lisa Trail is the most obvious and by far the most popular of the four options. With it being one of the prettiest trails in the Sandias, it is a good one. It climbs a shady ridge that separates two drainages to gain around 1,100 feet in the

Piedra Lisa Trailhead Options

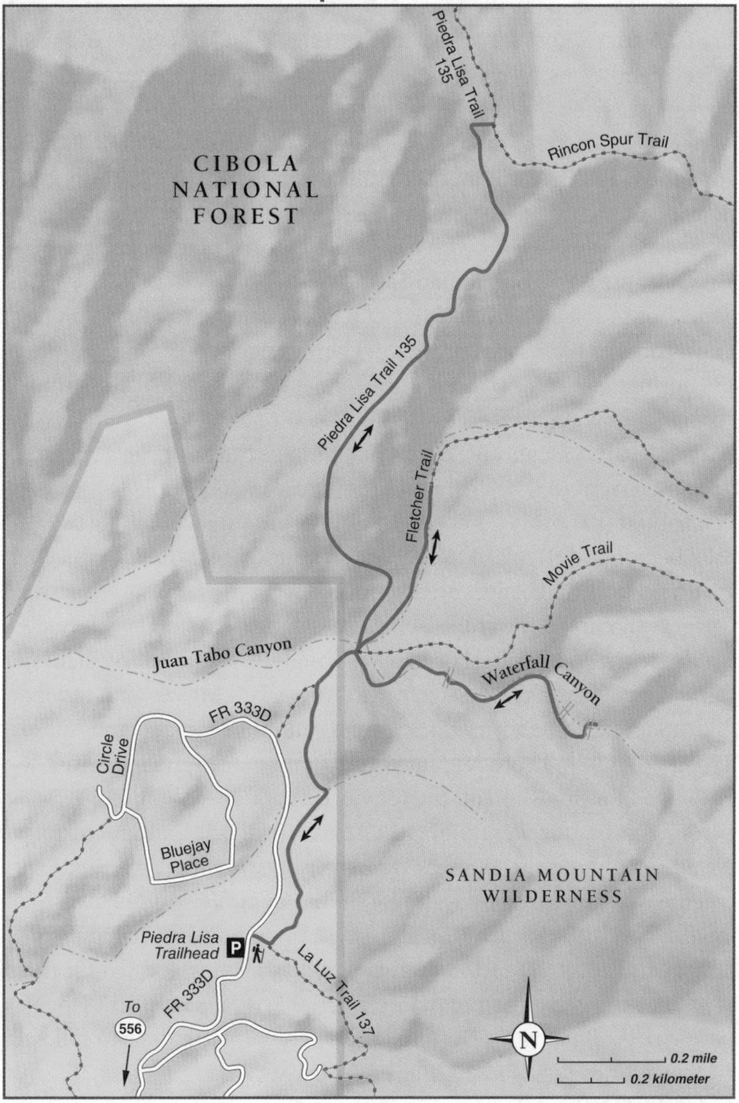

Piedra Lisa Trail 135
Rincon Spur Trail
CIBOLA NATIONAL FOREST
Piedra Lisa Trail 135
Fletcher Trail
Movie Trail
Juan Tabo Canyon
Waterfall Canyon
FR 333D
Circle Drive
Bluejay Place
SANDIA MOUNTAIN WILDERNESS
Piedra Lisa Trailhead
La Luz Trail 137
FR 333D
To 556
N
0.2 mile
0.2 kilometer

9,000 ft.
8,500 ft.
8,000 ft.
7,500 ft.
7,000 ft.
6,500 ft.
6,000 ft.
0.5 mi.
1 mi.
1.5 mi.
2 mi.

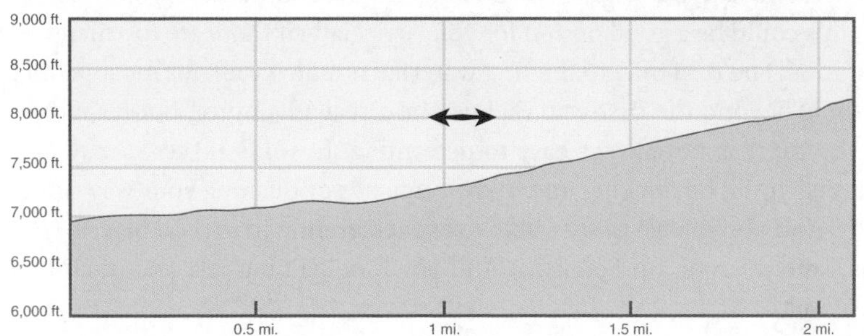

next 1.3 miles. The trail is well defined, so there is no chance of getting lost, and the views are fantastic. It goes through a lush forest and still has views of the spectacular Sandia Crest landforms. When you reach the top, you'll be on top of Rincon Ridge and have fantastic views to the north.

There is a sign post at the top marking the Rincon Spur Trail. It runs east and west along the ridge. The Piedra Lisa Trail continues north for another 3.5 miles on the other side of the ridge. So when you reach the top you'll have plenty of options. You can return to your car for a nice 4.2-mile hike, or hike along the top of Rincon Ridge, or continue north on Piedra Lisa.

If you choose to extend your hike, you won't be able to hike east on the Rincon Spur Trail from March 1 to August 15. The drainage to the east of Piedra Lisa is off-limits during that time for wildlife and endangered species protection. There are plenty of signs showing where it's off-limits.

Fletcher Trail is an unofficial trail that follows the drainage going to the northeast. This option is closed from March 1 to August 15. The trail is a nice walk through a riparian habitat that provides access to various mountain climbing routes. The trail eventually becomes difficult to follow and, if you're not climbing, this might be the time to turn around. The colors are beautiful during the fall.

Movie Trail climbs the ridge between Fletcher Trail and Waterfall Canyon. It starts on the left side of Waterfall Canyon about 20 yards east of Piedra Lisa Trail. This trail is also off-limits from March 1 to August 15. Movie Trail is very steep and severely eroded. It can be a very difficult and sometimes treacherous hike, especially when going downhill. There are, however, some nice views along the way. Unless you have a need for punishment, the Movie Trail is not worth doing.

The only reason for mentioning the Movie Trail is its cultural history. The trail was created for filming the 1962 movie *Lonely Are the Brave*, starring Kirk Douglas. The screenplay was written by Dalton Trumbo of Hollywood blacklist fame and is based on Edward Abbey's novel *The Brave Cowboy*. Abbey, a University of New Mexico graduate and sometime Albuquerque resident, is best known for the novel *The Monkey Wrench Gang* and the nonfiction work *Desert Solitaire*. Kirk Douglas has said that *Lonely Are the Brave* is his favorite movie. The movie still has a following, and it is fun to get a glimpse of Albuquerque in the early 1960s.

Waterfall Canyon follows the drainage to the southeast. If you're up for a challenge, this could be a good option for you, especially if there are too many people on Piedra Lisa. The 0.25 mile to the first waterfall is a nice walk for most people.

Going beyond the first waterfall can be a real adventure, but it's not for everyone. The route is not always easy to determine. In some places it may be so overgrown that you'll be ducking under low branches or pushing your way through tight growth. And you'll have to scramble over slick granite in several places. (*Piedra Lisa* means "smooth rock" in Spanish.) And you'll be gaining 300 feet of altitude in the next 0.3 mile.

But if you're OK with these types of challenges and like to explore, this can be a cool hike. The special landforms of the Sandias will be right on top of you. The eroded granite formations of the canyon walls are exceptionally neat. And unless it's been a long drought, you'll have running water for the rest of the hike. In many places water will be running over granite ledges and forming small pools at the bottom. The land is so wild that it's hard to believe that 500,000-plus people live down below. And you might even make it to the upper falls. Again, this option is not for everyone, but if it's for you, it can be well worth the effort.

Regardless of what option you choose, they are all great ways to explore this beautiful corner of the Sandias.

GPS TRAILHEAD COORDINATES N35° 13.364' W106° 29.003'

DIRECTIONS From I-25 North, take Exit 234 and turn right on Tramway Boulevard/NM 556. Go 4 miles east to Forest Road 333. Turn left and go 2.2 miles northwest to the Piedra Lisa parking area. Note the last 0.4 mile (FR 333D) is not paved and can be icy in winter.

A typical eroded granite formation found in the Sandias

10 PINO TRAIL

The vistas from near the top of the Pino Trail make the extra climbing worthwhile.

PINO TRAIL (140) is the perfect hike. Its trailhead at Elena Gallegos makes it a quick and easy drive from almost anywhere in Albuquerque. The stunning and dominating scenery of Sandia Crest is outstanding. The diversity of life zones and changing texture of the land keep the hike interesting from beginning to end. And best yet, you can follow the well-defined and well-maintained trail for as long or as short a distance as you want and still have a wonderful hike.

DESCRIPTION

Pino Trail is never a disappointment and is one that you can feel confident in recommending to a friend or taking an out-of-town guest to experience. If you want a hike with a lot of elevation gain and the potential for long miles, you can find it here. If you would like a hike with possible extensions to make it an all-day affair, the Pino has three different options for doing this. One of those is good for an up-and-over-the-Sandias adventure. And if you're looking for a very nice, pretty, and shorter walk that won't wear you out, you can also find it on the Pino. For all of these reasons, Pino is a perfect hike.

DISTANCE & CONFIGURATION: 9-mile out-and-back with shorter and longer options

DIFFICULTY: Moderate

SCENERY: Continuous mountain views, mixed forest, open views to the west

EXPOSURE: Mostly shaded

TRAIL TRAFFIC: Popular

TRAIL SURFACE: Decomposed granite, packed dirt, some rocks

HIKING TIME: 5–6 hours if you go to the top

DRIVING DISTANCE: 17 miles from the Big I

ELEVATION GAIN: 6,450' at trailhead; 9,250' at summit

ACCESS: April–October, 7 a.m.– 9 p.m., and November–March, 7 a.m.–7 p.m.; $1/car weekdays, $2 weekends; free with Open Space annual pass

WHEELCHAIR ACCESS: No

MAPS: Sandia Ranger District; USGS *Sandia Crest*

FACILITIES: Restroom and picnic areas at trailhead

CONTACT: Cibola National Forest–Sandia Mountain Wilderness, fs.usda.gov/cibola, 505-281-3304; Albuquerque Open Space, 505-987-8831

LOCATION: Albuquerque

COMMENTS: Leashed dogs are allowed on trail.

The trail starts in the Elena Gallegos Picnic Area at Albert G. Simms Park. The park is a unit of the Albuquerque Open Space Division and was once part of the Elena Gallegos Land Grant that ran from the Rio Grande to the top of the Sandia Mountains.

The first thing that you'll notice at Elena Gallegos are the awesome views of Sandia Crest to the east and being able to see all the way to Mount Taylor to the west. The Pino Trail begins in high-desert juniper grassland on the east side of the road.

There are a couple of paths in the picnic area, but it doesn't matter which one you take, as they eventually converge east of the picnic tables. In around 0.3 mile the trail will cross a wide bike path; just keep going east on the Pino Trail. In another 0.5 mile the trail will reach the boundary of the open space and the Sandia Mountain Wilderness. The balance of the hike will be in the wilderness.

The trail is now about to get very interesting. In many places the mountain slopes will look like a pile of rocks. Someone new to Albuquerque may wonder if the rocks are going to tumble down. They won't. The rocks are all part of the same granite bedrock mass. The unusual shapes of the rock are a product of erosion and may be the identifying characteristic of the west face of the Sandias.

If you look toward the ground, the composition of the tan-colored trail is decomposed granite. Later on, where there is more organic material from decaying leaves, the ground and trail will have more black soil. And if you look around, you'll notice that piñon trees have joined the mix and that the trail has more shade.

The trail proceeds through rolling terrain but continuously trends up. And if you look in the drainage courses to your right, you'll see that there are ponderosa pine trees where cooler air travels down the side of the mountain. You might notice that the high-desert grassland has been replaced by piñons with some junipers and Gambel oak.

There are enough openings in the forest canopy to provide great views of the face of Sandia Crest to left. Every now and then you might catch a glimpse of the tram. With the trail on the south side of Pino Canyon the crest is always in view on

Pino Trail

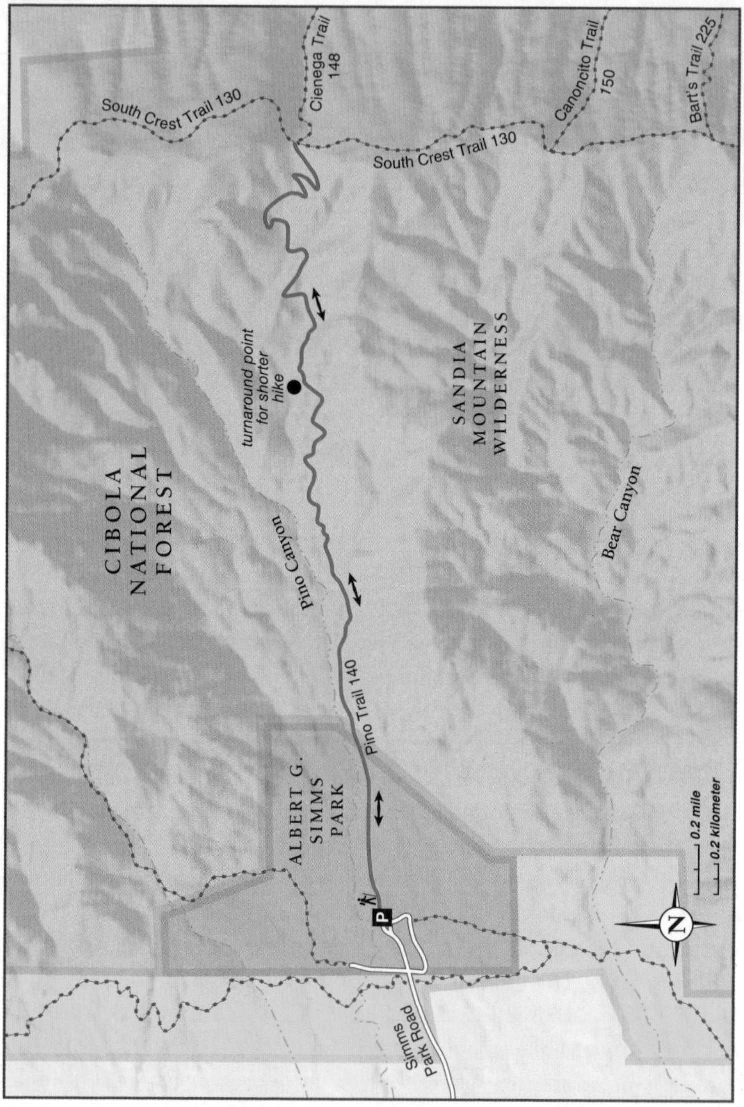

South Crest Trail 130
Cienega Trail 148
Canoncito Trail 150
Bart's Trail 225
South Crest Trail 130
turnaround point for shorter hike
SANDIA MOUNTAIN WILDERNESS
CIBOLA NATIONAL FOREST
Pino Canyon
Bear Canyon
Pino Trail 140
ALBERT G. SIMMS PARK
P
Simms Park Road
N
0.2 mile
0.2 kilometer

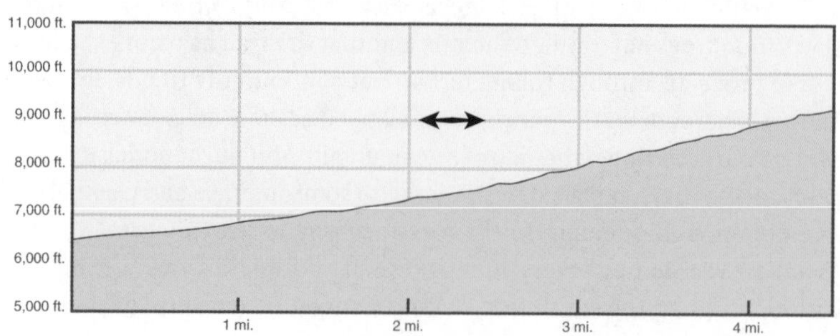
11,000 ft.
10,000 ft.
9,000 ft.
8,000 ft.
7,000 ft.
6,000 ft.
5,000 ft.
1 mi.
2 mi.
3 mi.
4 mi.

A popular turnaround point for a shorter hike, this spot is also great for a snack break.

the left and on the shadier and cooler side of the canyon. This hike is tolerable when it is very hot outside.

As you continue hiking into higher elevations, the ponderosa pine trees begin to dominate, and you'll start seeing fir trees in drainage courses where you first saw the ponderosa pines. At 2.5 miles or so into the hike you'll reach a flat spot with a great overlook (N35° 10.113' W106° 25.886'). There are even some nice rocks for sitting, so this is a good place to stop for a snack. At 7,700 feet, you have gained 1,200 feet from the trailhead.

So far this has been a nice moderate hike, and many people use this as a turnaround point for a nice 5-mile hike. If you continue, the trail becomes a bit steeper but not overly steep. But as you gain elevation the hike will become harder because of the higher altitude. The increase in difficulty is easily offset by the views of not only the crest but also of the views of Albuquerque far down below to the west.

If you decide to continue, you'll pass the trickling water of two small springs in the next 0.5 mile. The fir trees will become more pronounced, and you'll start to see some aspen. You are definitely getting into higher country, and as the elevation gets higher the vegetation gets denser. There will be flowers, ferns, and wild raspberries mixed in with the fir trees and aspen.

You'll also notice that many of the fir trees in the higher elevations have succumbed to the bark beetle. It will be interesting to see how long it will take for the forest to come back. In many cases, an opening in a forest is an opportunity for aspen to thrive. On many of the hikes in this book you'll see plenty of young trees coming in to take the place of the trees that were lost.

After 4.5 miles hiking and a steady climb to 9,200 feet (2,700 feet higher than the trailhead) you'll reach the terminus of the Pino Trail when it joins the Crest Trail (130) at the top of the mountain. You might also notice that you have left the granite and are now on limestone. The limestone is eroded, so the surface is irregular. The vegetation on top is a dense chaparral of oak and other shrubs.

From here you can turn around and have a great 9-mile hike, or you can continue. If you turn left, you can follow the Crest Trail north to the tram (about 3.5 miles north) or even to Sandia Crest (another 1.5 miles north). If you turn right, you can follow the Crest Trail south to Sandia Peak (about 5 miles south) or all the way to the Canyon Estates trailhead (Hike 2, page 26) (another 6 miles south).

But the best option for continuing your hike is to take the Cienega Trail (148) 2.2 miles (and a descent of 1,500 feet) to the Cienega Picnic Ground. The Cienega Trail comes up from the east side of the Sandias and joins the Crest Trail at the same place as the Pino Trail coming up from the west. If you have someone picking you up on the other side, the top of the crest is a good place to make a call to let them know that you'll be at the picnic ground in around an hour and a half. Because the Cienega Picnic Ground is subject to fire, bear, and winter closures, you may want to check with the Sandia Ranger Station before planning on this option.

This hike will be great no matter how you do it.

NEARBY ACTIVITIES

Elena Gallegos is worth visiting on its own, as it has a wetland, nature trail, rock sculptures, regular talks during the summer, and other trails to explore. It's a great place to hang out. Contact the open space at 505-281-3304 or visit cabq.gov/openspace/elenagallegos.html for more information on activities.

• •

GPS TRAILHEAD COORDINATES N35° 09.749' W106° 28.203'

DIRECTIONS From I-40, take Exit 167 and go 6 miles north on Tramway Boulevard. (Or from I-25, take Exit 234 and go 7.5 miles east and then south on Tramway Boulevard.) Turn east on Simms Park Road and go 1.5 miles to the fee station at Elena Gallegos Picnic Area/Albert G. Simms Park. Follow the one-way road from the entrance around the parking area on the east side.

11 RIO GRANDE NATURE CENTER–BOSQUE/DITCH WALK

In late fall and winter, look for migratory birds along this route.

FIND PEACE AND TRANQUILITY in the middle of an urban oasis. The bosque and ditch network offers miles of cottonwood-shaded trails that can extend your hike for as long as you want. This 3.2-mile loop with optional extensions of up to a 5.6-mile loop is a good introduction to this true Albuquerque gem.

DESCRIPTION

At 1,885 miles, the Rio Grande is the third-longest river in the United States. The 175-mile stretch from Cochiti Dam to Elephant Butte is known as the Middle Rio Grande. Here the river supports a cottonwood forest called the bosque and 1,200 miles of acequias (irrigation ditches) managed by the Middle Rio Grande Conservancy District. They provide a thin strip of shaded relief in our 60-hike area.

The bosque and ditches are interesting to explore any time of the year. In spring, there are nesting birds, including owls. Along the river you can see where beavers have gnawed small trees down to the nub. Look closely and you might see a porcupine rustling in the leaves or hanging in a branch. You might even see a murder of crows chasing a hawk or an eagle.

When it gets warm in the summer, you can still take a cool, shaded walk in the morning. In fall the bosque becomes a blaze of color and starts to fill with cranes and

DISTANCE & CONFIGURATION: 3.7-mile loop; with optional 5.2-mile and 5.6-mile loops

DIFFICULTY: Easy

SCENERY: Riparian habitat, cottonwood forest, acequias

EXPOSURE: Mostly shaded

TRAIL TRAFFIC: Popular

TRAIL SURFACE: Packed dirt, crusher fines, gravel, pavement

HIKING TIME: 1–3 hours

DRIVING DISTANCE: 4 miles from the Big I

ELEVATION GAIN: 4,965' at trailhead, with no significant rise

ACCESS: Trails open year-round; no fees or permits required for trails; nature center building open 10 a.m.– 5 p.m. daily, except Thanksgiving, Christmas, and New Year's Days; $3 parking fee if you park at the nature center; free parking available nearby

WHEELCHAIR ACCESS: Limited; the nature center and the crusher fines and paved trails in the bosque are wheelchair accessible.

MAPS: USGS *Los Griegos*

FACILITIES: Wildlife blinds, picnic areas, visitor center

CONTACT: Nature center, 505-344-7240, rgnc.org; Albuquerque Open Space, 505-897-8831; Middle Rio Grande Conservancy District, 505-247-0234

LOCATION: Albuquerque

COMMENTS: Dogs are allowed on trails, but not on the nature center grounds. Check with the nature center for tours and special events.

other migratory birds. And on any day of the year you'll have Canada geese honking and flying low overhead and might meet a coyote or two on your walk. We are lucky to have the bosque and ditches right in the heart of Albuquerque.

This hike begins at the Rio Grande Nature Center and explores both the bosque and ditches. The nature center itself is a popular attraction with its wetlands and wildlife viewing platforms. If you like turtles, this is the place to see them.

There are two ways to reach the trailhead. If the nature center gate is closed or if you have a dog, take the Candelaria Access Trail, a narrow corridor that begins at the yellow pylons at the end of Candelaria Road. Turn right (north) at the far end and follow the path to the wooden footbridge.

Otherwise, start down the path on the west side of the nature center parking lot. The left fork leads straight to the footbridge. The right one detours into what appears to be a half-buried drainage pipe. This is the entrance to the visitor center. Inside, you'll find natural history exhibits and restrooms. Exit through the back door and proceed to the aforementioned footbridge.

The bridge spans the Albuquerque Riverside Drain. Stairs ahead and a ramp to the right climb the levee. The trail atop the levee is Paseo del Bosque. This paved 16-mile recreation route crosses the city without traffic interruption from Alameda Bridge to south of the Rio Bravo Bridge. There is even some talk of extending the bike path to Valle del Oro National Wildlife Refuge (Hike 13, page 79).

The ramp leads to the Aldo Leopold Trail, which is paved for the first 0.5 mile. Turn right and head north on the trail. You'll see a tangle of flood-control fences, or jetty jacks, that were installed by the U.S. Army Corps of Engineers to protect

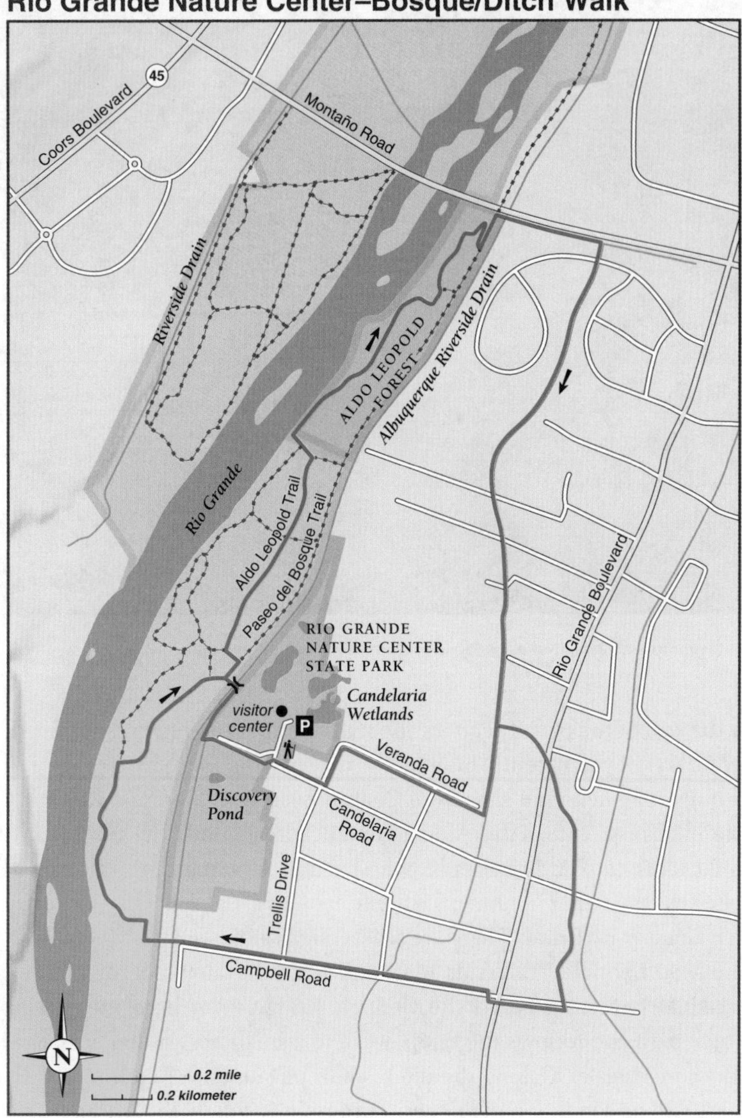

the levee from flood debris when you enter the bosque. Upriver damming has since rendered them obsolete.

As you walk along the trail, the Silvery Minnow Channel will be on your left. During high flows in the Rio Grande, the channel fills with water to provide habitat for this federally endangered species.

Acequias (irrigation ditches) make the Rio Grande valley a lush green oasis.

At the end of the paved section, the trail continues as tan crusher fines. The tan crusher fines trail was recently built by the City of Albuquerque to replace a network of user trails. The new trail runs from Central Avenue to Montaño Road.

The hike now enters the Aldo Leopold Forest. Both the forest and trail are named for local hero Aldo Leopold, who lived in Albuquerque 100 years ago. He is often cited as "the father of modern wildlife ecology," and was a key player in protecting the bosque as parkland. There are several signs along the trail depicting his life.

The Aldo Leopold Trail ends at around 1.25 miles north of the nature center at the paved bike path just south of the Montaño Bridge. From here, the hike crosses the paved bike path and follows the ramp down to a small bridge that crosses the drain. The hike continues east along the ditch south of Montaño Road. In less than 1,000 feet, there will be a junction of ditches. Turn right to follow the Duranes ditch south.

The ditch has a great walking path for the entire route and is fantastic any time of the year. When the ditches are flowing from early March to the end of October, you'll see mallards, wood ducks, coots, and other fowl swimming in the ditches. If you look closely at the bottom, you can see crawfish crawling around. When the water in the ditch is low, you'll see small fish congregating in small pools of water waiting for more water to come. Cranes and other migratory birds arrive just as the ditches dry out in late October and November and leave before they fill with water again in March. It is a never-ending cycle that guarantees that every walk along the ditch will be special regardless of the season.

The Duranes ditch passes several small farm fields and many nice homes. In 1 mile another ditch will branch off to the left. If you wish to extend your walk, you can follow that ditch as it crosses both Rio Grande Boulevard and Candelaria Road. The next crossing is Campbell Road. You can turn right at Campbell and follow it back to the bosque. The north side of Campbell has a nice crusher fines path. You can then follow bosque paths back to the nature center for a 5.6-mile loop.

For the planned hike, keep heading south. A city nursery will be on the left and Candelaria Farm will be on the right. The farm is a city-owned open space that is managed as a wildlife refuge. It is filled with cranes and Canada geese during the winter. At the southern end of the farm, turn right (west) onto Veranda Road. The hike continues on Veranda along the southern boundary of Candelaria Farm.

If you missed the turn at Veranda, that's OK. The next road crossing is Candelaria. You can turn right and take Candelaria back to your car. If you wish to extend your walk, you can cross Candelaria and follow the ditch to Campbell Road. (Campbell is the second street.) There you can turn right to follow Campbell west to the bosque and take bosque trails north to the nature center for a 5.2-mile loop.

Returning to the hike, Veranda ends at Trellis Drive, which is just east of the nature center. Turn left (south) and follow Trellis one block south to Candelaria. Turn right (west) and follow Candelaria back to your car to complete the 3.7-mile loop. No matter how often you walk in the bosque and along the ditches, you'll always find something to make the walk wonderful.

NEARBY ACTIVITIES

There are paths and ditches on both sides of the river. When you reach Montaño, you can walk on the protected pedestrian and bicycle lane to the other side. The bridge has viewing platforms for watching wildlife in the river. In addition to trails you can find a collection of chainsaw sculptures on the other side of the bridge.

GPS TRAILHEAD COORDINATES N35° 07.671' W106° 40.895'

DIRECTIONS From I-40 West, take Exit 157A to Rio Grande Boulevard. Drive north 1.4 miles and turn left onto Candelaria Road. Go west 0.6 mile and turn right at the park entrance. Note that if you park your car inside, the 5 p.m. gate closure can force you to rush an otherwise leisurely hike. To avoid the worry (and the $3 parking fee), go back one block and park on Trellis Drive.

12 THREE GUN-EMBUDO TRAILS: Up-and-Over-the-Sandias Adventure

With its different textures and vegetation, South Sandia Peak bursts with colors.

SATISFYING, PRETTY, AND DOABLE in a few hours, this one-way hike up and over the southern end of the Sandia Mountains is an opportunity for an adventure right here in Albuquerque.

DESCRIPTION

The idea of stepping onto a trail and getting off elsewhere has a certain allure to many people. If you do not have the time for a long-distance hike, you can do a very nice one-way hike right here in Albuquerque.

Our up-and-over-the-Sandias adventure is only 5.6 miles long and can be done in a few hours. It assumes that you'll have two cars. One car will be spotted at the open space parking area at the end of Indian School Road (open 7 a.m.–7 p.m., November–March, and 7 a.m.–9 p.m., April–October). If those hours don't work, there is parking just outside the gate. The hike begins from the Three Gun parking area, where there is no gate. When you turn off of Old Route 66 (NM 333) to drive up to the Three Gun parking area, South Sandia Peak dominates the view and will remain in your sight for the entire hike.

DISTANCE & CONFIGURATION: 5.6-mile point-to-point

DIFFICULTY: Moderate with a few tricky sections

SCENERY: Open views of the South Sandia Peak

EXPOSURE: Open with some shade

TRAIL TRAFFIC: Moderate; heavy in some places

TRAIL SURFACE: Decomposed granite

HIKING TIME: 4 hours

DRIVING DISTANCE: 11 miles from the Big I to the Embudo Trailhead

ELEVATION GAIN: 6,331' at Three Gun Trailhead; 7,889' at the top of the mountain

ACCESS: Year-round; no fees or permits required

WHEELCHAIR ACCESS: No

MAPS: Sandia Ranger District; USGS *Tijeras*

FACILITIES: None

CONTACT: Cibola National Forest–Sandia Mountain Wilderness, fs.usda.gov/cibola, 505-281-3304; Albuquerque Open Space, 505-987-8831

LOCATION: Albuquerque

COMMENTS: Leashed dogs are allowed on trails.

Three Gun Spring Trail (194) begins at the north end of the parking area and has the usual map and information signs at the trailhead. There are several little trails in the area, but just stay on the well-defined main path with the decomposed granite surface. As you hike, you'll see an abundance of eroded granite formations that compete with South Peak to grab your attention. The trail here is stunning.

After around 0.5 mile of walking, you'll reach the Sandia Mountain Wilderness. The wilderness boundary is marked by a metal sign and a wooden pole fence. Immediately after the fence the Hawk Watch Trail goes off to the right. That trail was built to support Hawk Watch International's efforts to observe, study, and band hawks. Those activities have moved elsewhere, but the trail still offers a vigorous hike with beautiful views.

Three Gun Trail continues north, more or less parallel with the base of South Peak. After around 1.5 miles into the hike, there will be a gray post marking a side trail to Three Gun Spring. Up to this point we've been walking generally to the north and have climbed almost 800 feet. Starting from here, the trail will become a series of switchbacks up to the summit. Very soon, we'll pass another gray post marking a different route to the spring.

The vegetation becomes lusher near the summit, and we'll get glimpses of Albuquerque on the other side of the mountain. The summit is 0.9 mile after the first gray post, with another 800 feet of gain. There is another gray post at the summit marking the junction with the **Embudo Trail.**

Three Gun Trail continues north for another 1.5 miles to Oso Pass. There are several options to extend a hike from Oso. Our hike follows Embudo Trail down the other side of the mountain to our other car. So far we have walked around 2.4 miles and have climbed 1,600 feet to reach the summit. This is a good time to take a break and take in all of the wonderful views and check out the eroded granite formations.

Embudo Trail starts in a thick piñon forest and winds its way down through a nest of eroded granite formations. In some places the eroded granite looks like a huge pile of boulders. Even though the rounded edges make them look like separate

Three Gun–Embudo Trails: Up-and-Over-the-Sandias Adventure

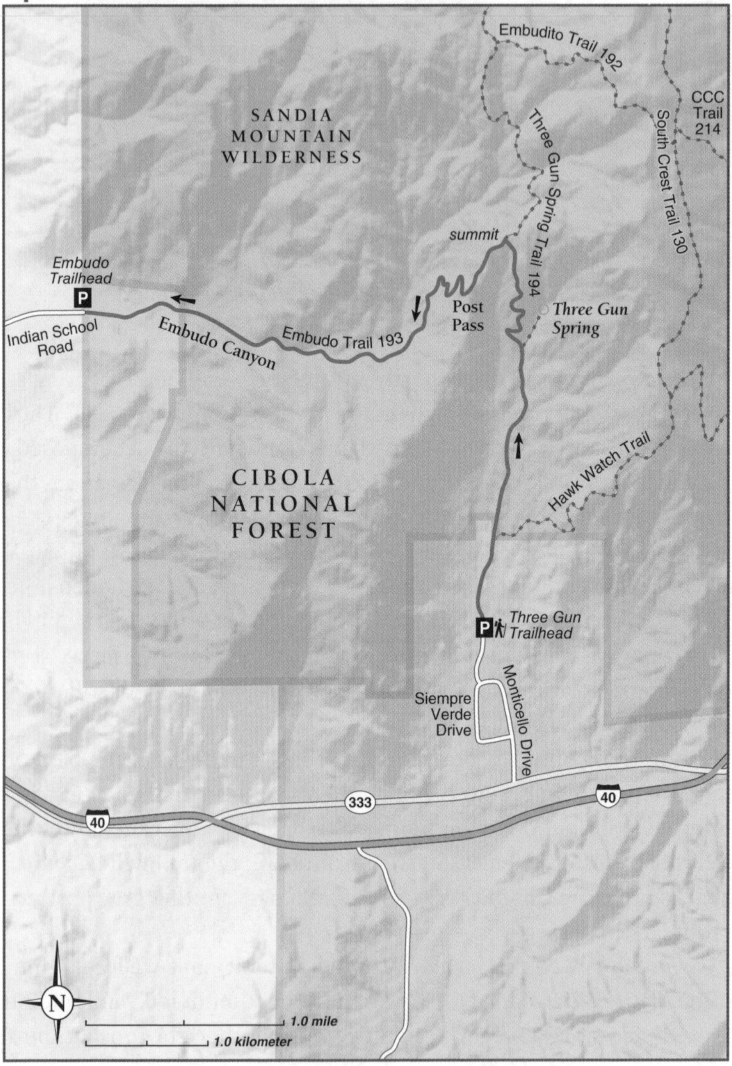

Embudito Trail 192
CCC Trail 214
SANDIA MOUNTAIN WILDERNESS
Three Gun Spring Trail 194
South Crest Trail 130
summit
Embudo Trailhead
Post Pass
Three Gun Spring
Indian School Road
Embudo Canyon
Embudo Trail 193
Hawk Watch Trail
CIBOLA NATIONAL FOREST
Three Gun Trailhead
Siempre Verde Drive
Monticello Drive
333
40
40
N
1.0 mile
1.0 kilometer

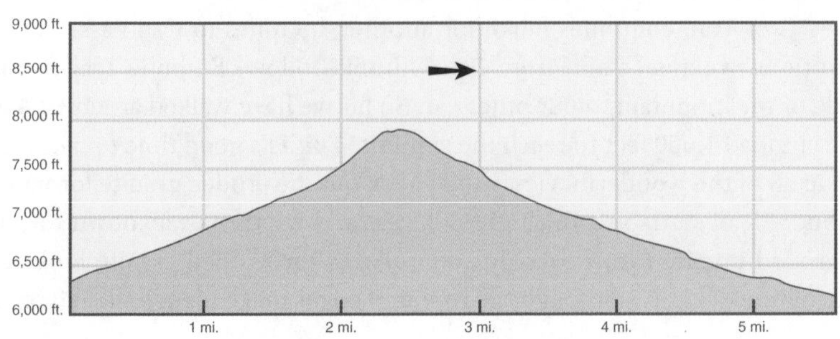

You can see Albuquerque and points west from the high point of this hike.

rocks, they are all part of one massive piece of granite. If you're inclined to climb boulders, this is the place to be.

In 0.35 mile from the summit, you'll reach Post Pass. It is an open ridge with views to both sides. If you look to the right (west) you'll see all of Albuquerque and Mount Taylor on the far horizon. If you look to the left (east) you'll see our starting point and I-40 in Tijeras Canyon. You'll also see a lesser trail continuing straight ahead on top of the ridge. Post Pass is a good turnaround point for a hike starting from the Embudo Trailhead. For our hike we'll be continuing downhill on the Embudo Trail with around 2.7 miles to go.

There are a few places the trail goes over boulders to jump down to a lower level. A few of them can be tricky to navigate, but none of them is truly hard. In some cases it might be easier just to climb down backward. Fortunately this stretch of the trail is not long. There are a couple of places where the trail makes a sharp switchback. When you come upon one, just look around to make sure you're following the trail. If you find yourself at a dead end, look behind you and you'll probably see that the trail made a turn that you missed. The trail is well defined the entire way.

Once the trail clears the switchbacks it becomes a gentle slope in an open piñon–juniper grassland bowl surrounded by mountainous ridges. The trail follows a drainage to a funnel-like outlet. (The Spanish word for funnel is *embudo.*)

When the trail reaches a gravel bottom drainage, there are two choices. One is to go up around the funnel (Embudo Canyon); the other is go through it. Our route goes through it. For this, turn right and follow the drainage downstream. It will join the main arroyo within a few feet. Turn left and follow the main arroyo downstream into the canyon. The canyon is choked with willow and other riparian brush. You might even start to see water flowing. Once in the canyon you will start picking up trails. Keep to the trail on the right side of the arroyo.

In addition to going through thick shrub, the trail through Embudo Canyon winds in, out, and over smooth granite obstacles. None of them is too difficult, but again you might find it easier to climb down backward on some of them. Before you know it, you'll be out of the canyon and in a normal rain year will see water flowing over an old concrete dam like a little waterfall.

Once out of the canyon, you're almost done. There are a few paths leading away from the waterfall. As long as you head downstream, you'll be OK, as the paths eventually converge into a wide path that at one time was a road. You'll soon reach a fence that marks the boundary of the Sandia Mountain Wilderness. There will be a flood retention dam immediately after the wilderness boundary and several trail options. You'll see plenty of people, as this area is popular for mountain biking and neighborhood walks.

Follow a trail going along the right (north) side of the retention basin to the top of the dam. When you reach the top of the dam, you'll see a large water tank and a wide path leading to the parking area. When you get to the car, you will have walked around 5.6 miles, and the only thing left to finish your adventure is to pick up the other car.

• •

GPS TRAILHEAD COORDINATES N35° 04.575' W106° 26.638'

DIRECTIONS To reach the Embudo Trailhead: From I-40 East, take Exit 167 and go 1.8 miles north on Tramway Boulevard to Indian School Road. Turn east on Indian School and go 1.1 miles all the way to the open space parking area.

To reach the Three Gun Trailhead: Take Indian School 1.1 miles back to Tramway. Turn south on Tramway and go 1.2 miles to Central Avenue/NM 333. Turn east on Central/NM 333 and go 2.7 miles east to Monticello Drive. (There is an orange barrel in the median to mark Monticello.) Turn north and jog right to remain on Monticello. Continue north on Monticello 0.9 mile to Allegre Street. (There is a sign saying TRAIL.) Turn west on Allegre and go 0.2 mile to Siempre Verde. (There is another sign saying TRAIL.) Turn north and drive to the trailhead at the end of the road.

13 VALLE DE ORO NATIONAL WILDLIFE REFUGE

On the right day you might see young foals chasing Canada geese feeding in their fields.

VALLE DE ORO in Albuquerque's south valley is an urban oasis in the making. Here you can walk through the bosque, spend quality time with wildlife, and see how a former farm is being turned into various wildlife habitats.

DESCRIPTION

Tucked between the Rio Grande bosque and the BNSF Railway, the 570-acre Valle de Oro National Wildlife Refuge, located 6 miles or so south of downtown Albuquerque, is the Southwest's first urban wildlife refuge. Several local, state, and federal agencies cooperated to help the U.S. Fish and Wildlife Service acquire the former location of Price's Valley Gold Dairies in 2012. Although the refuge is very much a work in progress, it still offers the opportunity for a nice hike close to Albuquerque.

For the first few years of its existence the refuge pretty much looked like and to some extent was a big farm. At the time of this writing work has begun in transforming the property into several different wetland and upland habitats. With the refuge under the glide path of the airport and with some of the military aircraft flying at low altitudes at high speeds, refuge managers have decided to develop habitats that attract smaller animals and low-flying waterfowl, such as ducks. The goal is to reduce the refuge's number of high-flying migratory birds (such as cranes and snow

DISTANCE & CONFIGURATION: 2.5-mile loop with options to extend the hike

DIFFICULTY: Easy

SCENERY: Riparian habitat, cottonwood forest, farm fields, wildlife, migratory birds

EXPOSURE: Mostly shaded

TRAIL TRAFFIC: Light

TRAIL SURFACE: Packed dirt, sand, gravel

HIKING TIME: 1–2 hours

DRIVING DISTANCE: 11 miles from the Big I

ELEVATION GAIN: 4,905' at trailhead, with no significant rise

ACCESS: Refuge is open daily, 8 a.m.–5 p.m.; no fees or permits required for trails

WHEELCHAIR ACCESS: No

MAPS: USGS *Isleta*

FACILITIES: Information kiosk at main entrance, portable toilets

CONTACT: Valle de Oro NWR, fws.gov/refuge/valle_de_oro, 505-248-6667

LOCATION: Albuquerque

COMMENTS: Leashed dogs are allowed on trails. The wildlife refuge is a work in progress and subject to changes.

geese). However, as long as the river is nearby, there will always be some migratory birds in the neighborhood.

There are many options for hiking at Valle de Oro today. One option is to park at the information kiosk near the entrance and walk on the roads through the farm fields. If you take this walk in the winter, you are likely to see cranes and geese spending the day eating in the fields. This obviously will change when the fields are replaced by the new habitats.

A better hiking option is to drive through the farm fields on the farm roads (see map) to the parking lot at the southwest corner of the refuge (N34° 58.289' W106° 41.092'). By doing this, you'll get a good look at any birds that happen to be visiting the refuge on that particular day and will then have a 2.5-mile walk in the bosque. The adjacent bosque is within the boundaries of Rio Grande Valley State Park. There is an ongoing effort between the Army Corps of Engineers, State Land Office, and the wildlife refuge to improve habitat and add trails in the bosque. In a sense, the combined area is being developed into a natural oasis close to the heart of Albuquerque.

Whereas many hikes are measured by their miles and elevation gain, this hike in the refuge and bosque has no elevation gain and can be better measured in the sounds you hear and its peacefulness. With the combination of bosque trails and ditches, you can make this walk as long or as short as you want. Over time the length of the walk will be extended when the wildlife refuge relocates the parking area to accommodate the new habitats.

The hike begins by walking west from the parking area toward the bosque. The hike passes through the gate and goes over the bridge. Cross both ditches to reach the ditch road. Turn left onto the ditch road and walk south along the ditch.

In late fall and winter there will be plenty of Canada geese, sandhill cranes, and maybe even snow geese feeding in the fields and flying overhead. Even after

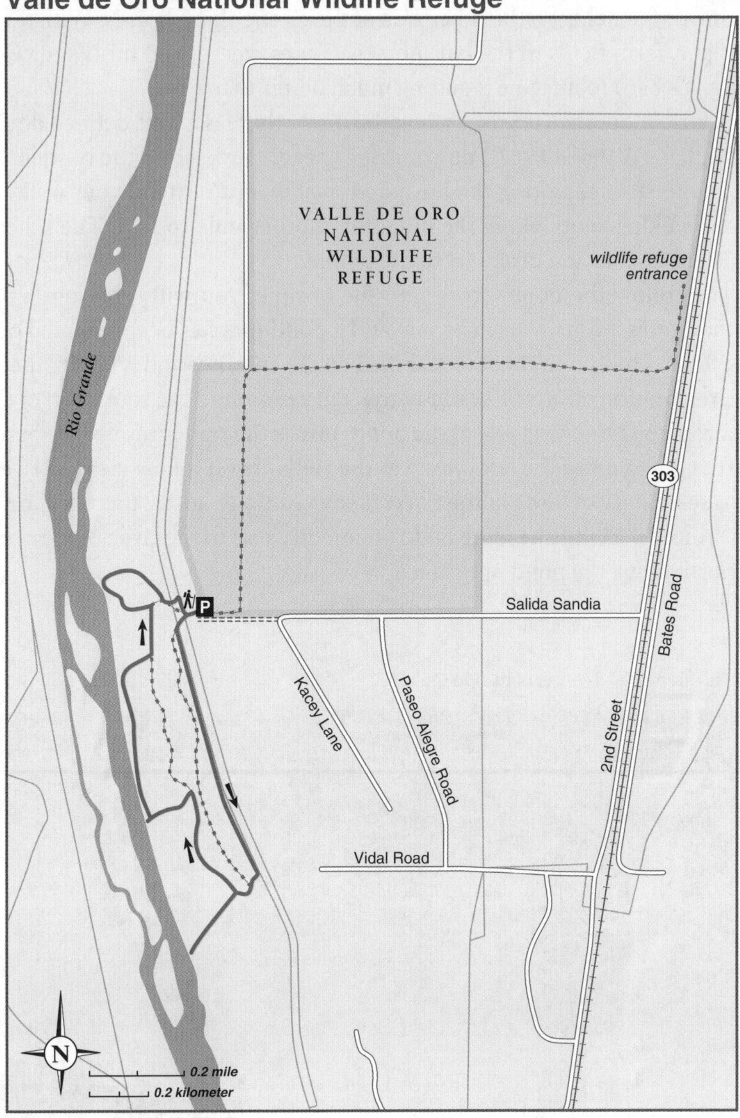

the refuge replaces its farm fields with new habitats, there will still be other nearby farm fields and the river to attract the migratory birds. In late February and early March, there will be huge groups of cranes flying high overhead on their northern migration. On certain days, it will be one group after another. Sometimes they'll be circling overhead to gain altitude and to give stragglers time to catch up before continuing north. And the sounds they make will be wonderful.

Some of the fields on the other side of the ditches have horses. With the bosque to the right, farm fields to the left, horses, cranes, geese, and birds squawking and clucking, it's hard to imagine it getting much better than this.

In a little more than 0.5 mile along the ditch, there is a well-defined doubletrack (N34° 57.820' W106° 40.967') on your right heading west into the bosque. This is a good time to start exploring the bosque. If you want to extend your walk, you can continue walking south along the ditch for another mile to I-25. The other side of I-25 is Isleta Pueblo and off-limits to the public.

If you follow the doubletrack into the bosque, you will soon join a path that circumnavigates a usually dry channel and a pond that has been sculpted out of the bosque floor. The "pond" begins near the bosque entrance and is part of the ongoing bosque restoration efforts. The sandy trail curves around the south end of the pond to go north along the west side of the pond. Just as the trail turns north, there will be a side trail going off to the left (west) to the river. If you follow it to the river you're likely to see plenty of birds in the river. If you continue north, there will be another trail in around 0.25 mile heading off to your left (west) to the river. You can continue going north along the pond or turn left.

Don't miss this peaceful corner of the Rio Grande.

If you turn left, you'll reach the river in a little over 600 feet and find another doubletrack heading north along the river. In a little more than 0.3 mile the main route will curve back to the east. A lesser route will continue along the river. The bottom line is that there are several routes through the bosque. All are wonderful and peaceful, especially with the birds flying overhead. If you stay with the main route going east, you'll soon rejoin the pond trail. From here you can continue north along the pond and return to where you entered the bosque. Or you can take one of the many trails you'll see along the way to explore other parts of the bosque and river. All of the routes are good. You can also continue your hike by going north along the ditch. In 3 miles the ditch will join the 16-mile paved bike path going north all the way to Alameda Bridge. At the time of this writing, there is some discussion on extending the bike path south to the refuge.

Whether you come to Valle de Oro by car or bike, it is nice to have special places like the refuge so close to Albuquerque.

NEARBY ACTIVITIES

If you want a change of pace, you might want to consider taking Second Street back to Albuquerque rather than I-25. In some ways Second Street is like having a chance to see the backyard of our community. Second Street parallels the BNSF Railway the entire way and passes through a diverse array of urban landscapes. There are farm fields, different types of houses, municipal infrastructure, industrial sites, scrap metal sites, and others. Some of it may appear unattractive to you, but even the most unattractive industrial site plays a role in the community.

Regardless of your opinion of Second Street, we can all agree that a stop at **El Modelo** at 1715 Second St. SW for some very tasty New Mexican/Mexican food is a good idea. It's takeout only, so you won't have to worry about wearing hiking clothes into a restaurant. And with picnic tables by the parking lot you can continue your outdoor adventure.

And when you're done eating, you can go around the corner to check the **National Hispanic Cultural Center**. For hours, fees, and event schedules, call 505-246-2261 or visit nhccnm.org.

• •

GPS COORDINATES FOR MAIN ENTRANCE N34° 58.856' W106° 40.028'

DIRECTIONS From I-25 South, take Exit 220 and go 1.1 miles west on Rio Bravo Boulevard to Second Street. Turn left on Second Street and go 3.1 miles south to the refuge entrance.

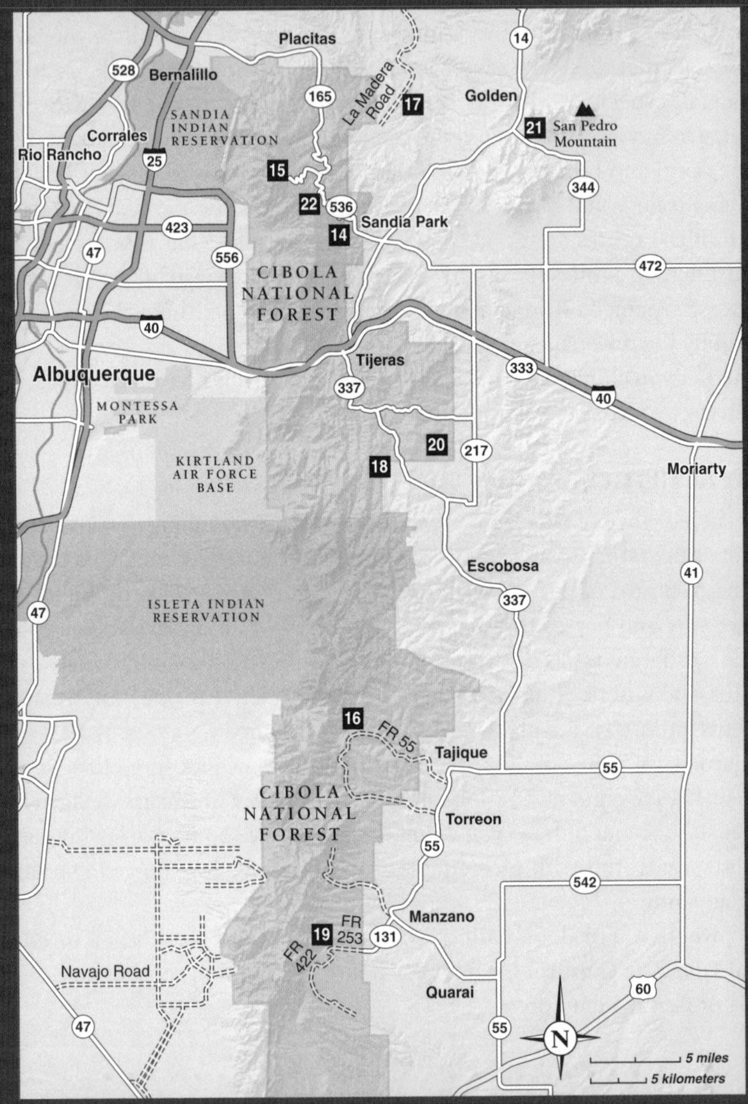

Placitas
528
Bernalillo
165
La Madera Road
17
Golden
14
21
San Pedro Mountain
SANDIA INDIAN RESERVATION
Corrales
Rio Rancho
25
15
22
536
Sandia Park
344
423
47
556
14
472
CIBOLA NATIONAL FOREST
40
Tijeras
Albuquerque
333
337
40
MONTESSA PARK
20
217
KIRTLAND AIR FORCE BASE
18
Moriarty
Escobosa
41
337
47
ISLETA INDIAN RESERVATION
16
FR 55
Tajique
55
CIBOLA NATIONAL FOREST
Torreon
55
542
Manzano
19
FR 253
131
FR 422
Navajo Road
Quarai
60
47
55
N
5 miles
5 kilometers

EAST OF THE MOUNTAINS

14 Armijo Trail–Cienega Spring 86
15 Del Agua Overlook 91
16 Fourth of July Canyon–Cerro Blanco 95
17 Golden Open Space 100
18 Mars Court Trailhead–David Canyon 105
19 Red Canyon 110
20 Sabino Canyon and Juan Tomas Open Spaces 115
21 San Pedro Mountains Mining Area 120
22 Tree Spring–Crest Trail 125

14 ARMIJO TRAIL–CIENEGA SPRING

Wooded trails on the lower slopes of the Sandias' east side provide welcome shade to hikers.

THIS PEACEFUL WALK through the forest has it all: beautiful overlooks, a medallion tree, a thong tree, a travertine spring, and many other surprises.

DESCRIPTION

The wonderful wooded trails on the lower east side of the Sandias are easy to follow, have very nice grades, and are perfect for engaging in the Japanese practice of *Shinrin-Yoku,* or "forest bathing." A forest bath is not a quick dip in a creek. It is more along the lines of breathing in the scents of the forest, being present, and walking quietly through the woods. Studies in Japan have shown that *Shinrin-Yoku* has significant health benefits.

To reach the lower Sandia trails, turn left from Sandia Crest Scenic Byway (NM 536) into the first U.S. Forest Service picnic grounds (Sulphur Canyon/Cienega) that you see. (With bears sometimes active in late summer and fall you might want to call first to see if the area is open.) You'll see a gate right after the turn for Sulphur Canyon. There is a second gate farther up the road just after the Horse Bypass parking area. If both gates are open, you can drive all the way to the end of the road and park at the Cienega Trailhead. The hike description begins from there.

As for the gates, the Horse Bypass gate is usually closed at the end of the picnic season. In that case you can join the hike en route from the bypass parking lot. The

DISTANCE & CONFIGURATION: 6.5- or 4.5-mile loop hike with an optional 2-mile spur

DIFFICULTY: Moderate

SCENERY: Mountain pine forest, springs, other surprises

EXPOSURE: Mostly shaded

TRAIL TRAFFIC: Moderate; heavy on weekends

TRAIL SURFACE: Dirt

HIKING TIME: 3–4 hours

DRIVING DISTANCE: 24 miles from the Big I

ELEVATION GAIN: 7,522' at trailhead; 7,871' at high point; 7,076' at low point

ACCESS: Year-round (see Description regarding seasonal access); day-use fee $3/car; free with Sandia Mountain Annual Permit or National Parks and Federal Recreation Lands Annual Pass

WHEELCHAIR ACCESS: No; wheelchair access in picnic area

MAPS: Sandia Ranger District; USGS *Sandia Crest* and *Sandia Park*

FACILITIES: Picnic shelters, restrooms, nature trail

CONTACT: Cibola National Forest–Sandia Ranger District, fs.usda.gov/cibola, 505-281-3304

LOCATION: Sandia Park

COMMENTS: Leashed dogs are allowed on trails.

LAST-CHANCE FOOD/GAS: Convenience store–gas station at the junction of NM 14 and NM 536

Sulphur Canyon gate is usually closed after the first snow. If that gate is closed, you can park there and take the Sulphur Canyon trail up to the hike route.

The hike begins at the Cienega Trailhead at the end of the road. The trails are well marked and have new signs. The hike is very simple: go up (west) Cienega (148); turn left (south) on Faulty (195); turn left (east) on Armijo (222); follow Cienega Horse Bypass (266) west until it ends at Faulty; turn left (south) onto Faulty; take Faulty to Cienega; and turn left (east) onto Cienega back to your car.

As for the details of the hike, you'll pass some picnic tables before reaching the U.S. Forest Service information sign with a map of the Sandias. The trail continues uphill (west) behind the sign and soon passes Cienega Spring. In around 0.5 mile the trail will reach the junction with the Faulty Trail and the Sandia Mountain Wilderness boundary.

You could continue up Cienega to the top of the mountain to where it joins the Pino Trail (Hike 10, page 64) coming up from the other side. Our hike follows Faulty out of the canyon and then south through a ponderosa forest. Along the way you may notice many cone-shaped piles of wood. They are part of the U.S. Forest Service's ongoing tree thinning efforts in this area. The cones will eventually be burned or cleared away.

This is a perfect place to start your forest bathing experiment by breathing in the pine scented air and letting the shade and the quiet stimulation in the forest dial down your mind. This will help you to be present and get closer to the forest around you. And if you can let your arms hang naturally and hands relax, you may notice your face relaxing as stress leaves your body.

Within 1.25 miles you'll reach the junction with Armijo. The trail sign at the junction also points to the Medallion Tree. The Sandias have several dozen Medallion Trees that were made by someone who drilled core samples from the trees, determined the germination date by counting the rings, and then placed a silver color medallion over

Armijo Trail–Cienega Spring

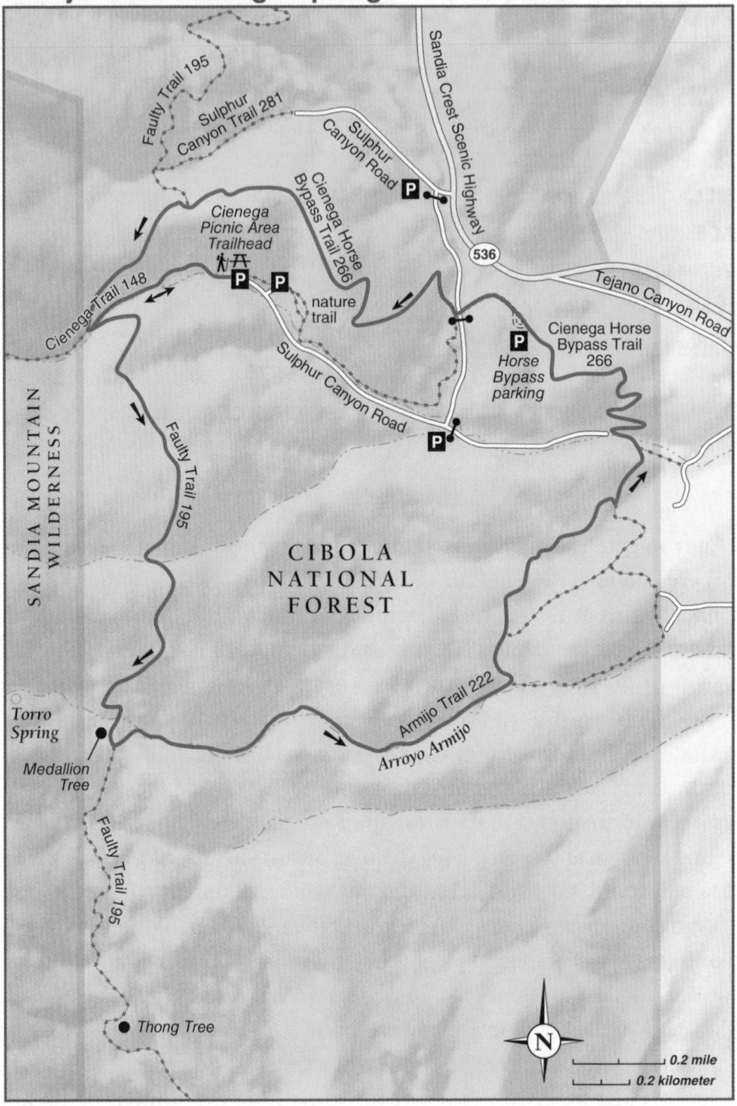

Faulty Trail 195
Sulphur Canyon Trail 281
Sulphur Canyon Road
Sandia Crest Scenic Highway
Cienega Horse Bypass Trail 266
Cienega Picnic Area Trailhead
536
Tejano Canyon Road
Cienega Trail 148
nature trail
Horse Bypass parking
Cienega Horse Bypass Trail 266
Sulphur Canyon Road
SANDIA MOUNTAIN WILDERNESS
Faulty Trail 195
CIBOLA NATIONAL FOREST
Torro Spring
Medallion Tree
Armijo Trail 222
Arroyo Armijo
Faulty Trail 195
Thong Tree
N
0.2 mile
0.2 kilometer

8,200 ft.
8,000 ft.
7,800 ft.
7,600 ft.
7,400 ft.
7,200 ft.
7,000 ft.
1 mi.
2 mi.
3 mi.
4 mi.
5 mi.
6 mi.

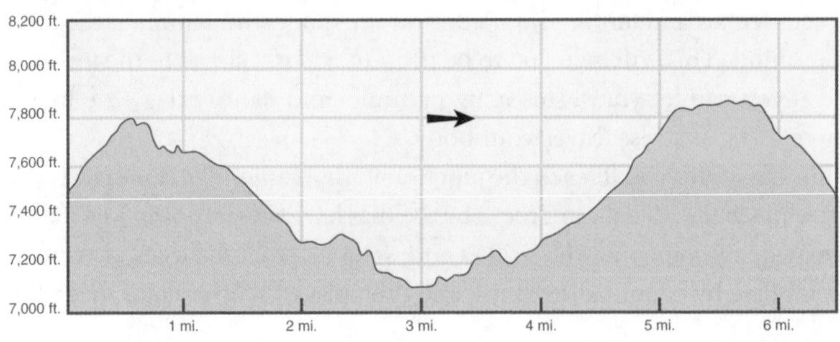

One of many great vistas along the route

the core holes. Each medallion is named for an event that took place near the germination date. This medallion is named SANTA FE TRAIL-1821. The tree is located on an older section of the Faulty Trail that was abandoned when the trail was rerouted.

From here, turn left to follow Armijo east. If you enjoyed discovering the Medallion Tree, you can make a detour by going south on Faulty for another 1 mile. There you can find a Native American thong tree (N35° 08.805' W106° 23.314') and an amazing stair-stepped travertine spring. Both are near the junction of the Faulty and Cañoncito Trails.

Thong trees are made by tying the branch of a young sapling back onto itself with a leather thong. This creates a loop in the tree to use as a pointer (to Cañoncito Spring). The thong will eventually break as the tree grows, but the branch will retain its distorted shape.

Dissolved minerals in the water at Cañoncito Spring have created several stair-stepped pools made out of travertine. Both the Cañoncito and Faulty Trails have been rerouted to protect the spring from being trampled by horses. Fortunately for us, the U.S. Forest Service has built a small connector trail to access the spring.

Returning to the planned hike, Armijo heads east down a canyon and eventually turns left to head generally north. The U.S. Forest Service has done some reroutes in this area. In less than 2 miles the trail will reach a road that is no longer used. This is the end of the Armijo Trail and the beginning of the Horse Bypass Trail.

Our hike continues on Horse Bypass. If you are running out of time, you can turn left (west) and follow the road back to the car. The U.S. Forest Service has recently built trails along the north side of the road. If you take the shortcut, your hike will be around a 4.5-mile loop.

The Horse Bypass Trail continues uphill to the bypass parking lot. (This is where you'll start the hike if gate closures force you to park in this lot.) When you reach the parking lot in 0.7 mile, you will be generally heading northwest. The hike continues through the parking lot and reaches the main road in 0.2 mile. Cross the main road, turn right, and follow the trail uphill.

The U.S. Forest Service has done major thinning in this area. This has increased the amount of forage for wildlife and has also revealed a large population of alligator juniper trees. For many years it was thought that alligator junipers were rare in the Sandias. It turns out that they were just hiding behind other trees.

In 1 mile, Horse Bypass will reach the Faulty Trail. Turn left (south) onto Faulty to complete the loop. The trail heads down into Cienega Canyon and will reach Cienega Trail in 0.5 mile. Turn left (east) onto Cienega to finish the hike in another 0.5 mile for a 6.5-mile loop hike.

Sulphur Canyon Option: If the Sulphur Canyon gate is closed, you can park your car at the Sulphur Canyon parking lot and follow the road uphill to the Sulphur Canyon Trail (281). The canyon itself is very interesting as it has trees (aspen and Douglas-fir) that are normally found at much higher elevations. The trail goes up the canyon and ends at the Faulty Trail. Turn left (south) to join the route of this hike. This option adds about 1 mile in each direction, so you may want to vary the route rather than do the entire loop.

NEARBY ACTIVITIES

Tinkertown Museum is on the south side of the Sandia Crest National Scenic Byway. No doubt you saw the sign en route to the Cienega Spring turnoff. Within the walls of this ramshackle compound lies the labyrinthine *Wunderkammer* of Ross J. Ward, a creator and curator of unusual things. Open daily, 9 a.m.–6 p.m., April–October. For more information, call 505-281-5233 or visit tinkertown.com.

• •

GPS TRAILHEAD COORDINATES N35° 10.181' W106° 23.027'

DIRECTIONS From I-40 East, take Exit 175 toward Cedar Crest. From the I-40 overpass, go north 5.9 miles on NM 14. Turn left on NM 536 (Sandia Crest Scenic Byway) and drive 1.8 miles west. Turn left at the Sulphur Canyon/Cienega Spring picnic areas. See "Description" regarding gate closure options.

15 DEL AGUA OVERLOOK

For a sense of peace, look up at the sunlight filtering through the aspen leaves.

THE DEL AGUA CANYON overlook is the best place to see fall colors in the Sandias. If you do this 4.4-mile round-trip hike in late September or early October, you'll be swimming in a sea of yellow-gold aspen leaves. The scene will leave you breathless. If you come in the summer, the quaking green aspen leaves will sound like a light rain. And no matter when you come, the views will be fabulous.

DESCRIPTION

Aspens are not only the most widespread tree in North America; they are probably the most unusual. It is unlikely that the aspens we see in New Mexico grew from a seed. They most likely grew from a root or a shoot already in the ground. The aspen grove on this hike is probably one organism rather than several individual trees. When thought of as one body, aspens may be one of the largest organisms on Earth. And their lives have a cycle of life, death, and resurrection.

Aspens need sunlight to thrive and are not likely to get enough sun in a mixed forest and will eventually die down. But when a fire comes through that same forest to open it to sunlight, the aspens will start putting out shoots from roots already in place. If aspen roots are present, they are usually the first trees to come back after

DISTANCE & CONFIGURATION: 4.4-mile out-and-back with options to extend the hike

DIFFICULTY: Moderate

SCENERY: Amazing fall colors, mountain scenery, aspen and fir, wildflowers, fantastic unobstructed views

EXPOSURE: Mostly shaded

TRAIL TRAFFIC: Popular

TRAIL SURFACE: Dirt, rock

HIKING TIME: 2–2.5 hours

DRIVING DISTANCE: 36 miles from the Big I

ELEVATION GAIN: 10,574' at trailhead; 9,910' at overlook

ACCESS: Year-round; day-use fee $3/car; free with Sandia Mountain Annual Pass or National Parks and Federal Recreation Lands Annual Pass; the crest has snow in the winter; no permits required

WHEELCHAIR ACCESS: No

MAPS: Sandia Ranger District; USGS *Sandia Crest;* trail maps of the area are sometimes available at Crest House

FACILITIES: Sandia Crest House; gifts, food, information, restrooms; hours vary by season; for more information call 505-243-0605 or visit sandiacresthouse.com

CONTACT: Cibola National Forest–Sandia Ranger District, fs.usda.gov/cibola, 505-281-3304

LOCATION: Sandia Park

COMMENTS: Leashed dogs are allowed on trails.

LAST-CHANCE FOOD/GAS: Food at Crest House; convenience store–gas station at the junction of NM 14 and NM 536

a fire. As the aspens get taller their shade keeps the soil below cool and moist. This makes it possible for young conifers to start growing. Eventually the conifers will become taller than the aspens, and their shade in turn will deny aspens the sunlight they need to thrive. Over time the aspens will die out, but their roots will remain for the next opportunity for resurrection and a new cycle.

What this means for our hike is that future generations may have a completely different experience than we. Where we see a sea of yellow-gold, they may see a sea of green. There are already conifers poking out of this aspen grove, and who knows how long the transition will take. In the meantime, the scene we have today is there to take our breath away.

When you reach the parking area at the top of the crest, the trailhead will be at the north end of the parking area by the radio towers. The Crest House is at the south end of the parking lot. And if you want to stand on the highest point in Bernalillo County, the top of Sandia Crest at 10,678 feet is right in front of you a few yards to the west. Before leaving the car, you might want to check your car door opener to make sure that the towers are not interfering with the opener's signal.

The trailhead for the north Crest Trail (130) is at the southeast corner of the towers. The hike is pretty straightforward. Just follow the Crest Trail north for 2.2 miles to the stone bench at the Del Agua overlook and return the same way you went out for a 4.4-mile hike. The hike starts at 10,574 feet and descends almost 700 feet to 9,910 feet. There are a few subtle ups and downs along the way, but the trend is definitely downhill.

The hike begins by following the east fenceline of the towers. The humming from the towers will end as soon as you pass them and enter the Sandia Mountain Wilderness.

Del Agua Overlook

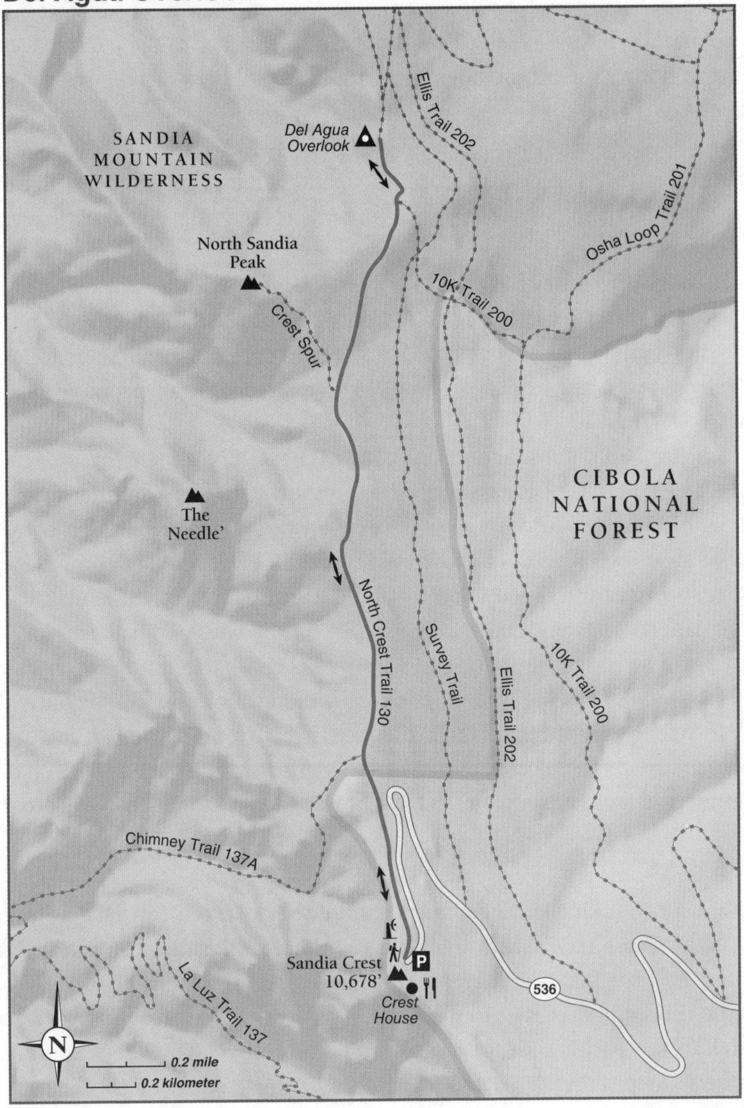

SANDIA MOUNTAIN WILDERNESS
Del Agua Overlook
Ellis Trail 202
Osha Loop Trail 201
North Sandia Peak
Crest Spur
10K Trail 200
CIBOLA NATIONAL FOREST
The Needle'
North Crest Trail 130
Survey Trail
Ellis Trail 202
10K Trail 200
Chimney Trail 137A
La Luz Trail 137
Sandia Crest 10,678'
P
Crest House
536
N
0.2 mile
0.2 kilometer

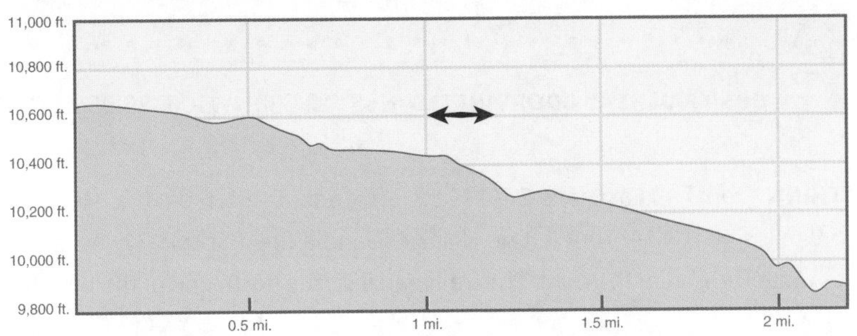

Once past the towers, you'll be walking through a dense fir tree forest sprinkled with aspens. You'll soon reach a trail sign saying 1.5 miles to the overlook. From this point on you'll have periodic openings with beautiful views to the west. The jagged formations of the Sandias below are amazing. And when you look across Rio Grande Valley you'll see across Albuquerque and all the way to Mount Taylor far to the west.

The aspens increase as you move north and you'll even pass a recent burn zone. Now is a good chance to see how the forest is recovering. And you'll keep having great views to the west.

Just short of 2 miles into the hike, you'll reach the junction with the western terminus of the 10K Trail (200). The eastern terminus of the 10K is at the terminus of Tree Spring Trail (Hike 22, page 125). You could extend your hike by following the 10K Trail, but with the overlook only 0.25 mile farther, you'll probably want to stay on the Crest Trail.

From the 10K Trail junction on, you will have wide-open views of the mountain, the trees, and the Rio Grande Valley to the west. The farm fields down below are at Sandia Pueblo. And if you're here when the leaves are turning colors, you'll be blown away by the sea of yellow-gold. Fortunately, there is a stone bench at the overlook so you can sit down to take it all in. This is what you came for!

You can, if you want, continue your hike on the Crest Trail all the way to Placitas, but it will be a long way back and a strenuous climb to get to your car. If you have a need for some exploring, the junction with the Osha Loop Trail is only 120 yards ahead. Just keep in mind that you'll still have to return the same way you came in.

If you're ready to go back, just return the same way you came. With all the leaves and wonderful views again, you'll hardly notice the 700-foot climb back to the car.

BONUS HIKE

There are more hiking options when you get back to the car. One is to continue south on the Crest Trail. The trail resumes on the south side of the Crest House and is about a 1.5-mile hike to the tram. You can pick up the La Luz Trail (Hike 6, page 45) at the tram and take that to the Crest Spur Trail. The Crest Spur Trail will take you back to the parking lot for a nice 3-mile loop hike. The Crest Spur Trail does have a very steep staircase, so you may not want to take dogs on this hike.

• •

GPS TRAILHEAD COORDINATES N35° 12.680' W106° 26.955'

DIRECTIONS From I-40 East, take Exit 175 toward Cedar Crest. From the I-40 overpass, go north 5.9 miles on NM 14. Turn left on NM 536 (Sandia Crest Scenic Byway) and follow it 14 miles up to the end of the road. The trailhead is at the north end of the parking area.

16 FOURTH OF JULY CANYON–CERRO BLANCO

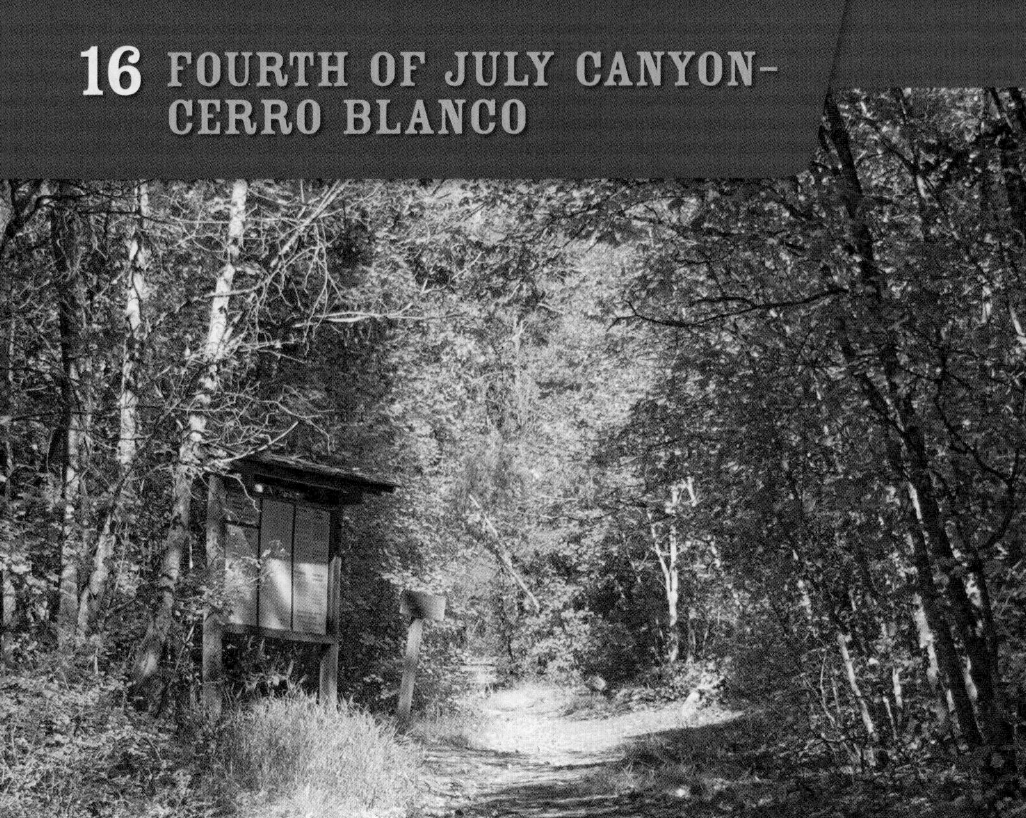

This area has multiple loop options for exploring, so check out the sheltered bulletin board along the way for a comprehensive map.

CROWDS TURN OUT each autumn to gawk at leaves, but you can find solitude here throughout most of the year. Meander along established trails from a popular picnic area to the crest of the Manzano Mountains. Clearings on the ridgeline reveal vistas that seem to stretch halfway to the next state.

DESCRIPTION

New Mexico is blessed with two Fourth of July Canyons. One is on the border of Colfax and Taos Counties, while the more famous one is in Torrance County. Each fall, hikers mob the latter's trails to witness a pyrotechnic display of foliage. This Fourth of July Canyon contains concentrations of bigtooth and Rocky Mountain maples to rival any autumnal clump in New England.

If the crowds are too dense, take heart in the fact that most will turn back within the first mile and won't return for another year because what they don't seem to understand is that the trails are just as colorful in other seasons.

Spring and summer bring neotropical migrants—Central and South American birds of brilliant plumage, such as orange-crowned warblers. Dense clusters of seep-spring monkeyflowers bloom from March to October. Like snapdragons, they can be manipulated to resemble their namesake. A healthy population of Abert's squirrels

DISTANCE & CONFIGURATION: 6.4-mile loop and spur

DIFFICULTY: Moderate

SCENERY: Seasonal wildflowers and foliage, wooded canyons, eastern and western vistas

EXPOSURE: Mostly shaded

TRAIL TRAFFIC: Heavy when leaves are in color

TRAIL SURFACE: Gravel forest roads, dirt trails

HIKING TIME: 4 hours

DRIVING DISTANCE: 54 miles from the Big I

ELEVATION GAIN: 7,531' at trailhead; 8,708' feet on crest

ACCESS: Year-round, snow in winter may make it difficult to reach crest; no fees or permits required

WHEELCHAIR ACCESS: No, but restrooms, picnic area, and campground are wheelchair accessible

MAPS: Mountainair Ranger District–Manzano Division; Manzano Mountain Wilderness; USGS *Bosque Peak*

FACILITIES: Campsites (April–October), picnic area, and restrooms (no water)

CONTACT: Cibola National Forest–Mountainair Ranger District, fs.usda.gov/cibola, 505-847-2990

LOCATION: Tajique

COMMENTS: Leashed dogs are allowed on trails.

LAST-CHANCE FOOD/GAS: Ray's One Stop at 8572 NM 337 in Tajique

stays active year-round. Named after the U.S. Army lieutenant who cataloged them during a New Mexico expedition in the 1840s, these tassel-eared arboreal rodents were released into the Manzano Mountains in 1929 and have thrived here since.

As you get closer to Fourth of July Canyon on Forest Road 55, it will seem like you've left New Mexico and have been transported to someplace back east. The deciduous trees and density of vegetation seem out of place, and there is definitely more moisture in the air and ground. And on a warm day it may even seem steamy. And if you come during the summer, you may be the only person here. With the overgrown grass in the campground, you may even wonder if it has been abandoned. It's almost eerie.

But if you come in late September and October when the colors are out, you'll have plenty of company. Regardless of when you come, you will have a great hike. If you're not staying in the campground, you can save some money by parking in the free hiker parking area. Once you've parked, you can head uphill toward the campground for the trailhead.

Hikers can choose from multiple loop options to explore the area. No two maps agree exactly on where all these trails go. So although the route described below is fairly simple, keep in mind that, like many U.S. Forest Service trails, the designated ways are subject to alteration.

You can start your hike with a detour along the Crimson Maple and the Spring Loop Trails, with their interpretive signs for some background information on the vegetation. Or you can keep going to the end of the campground toward the **Fourth of July Trail (173)**. The sheltered bulletin board along the way has a comprehensive map of the area.

Fourth of July Canyon–Cerro Blanco

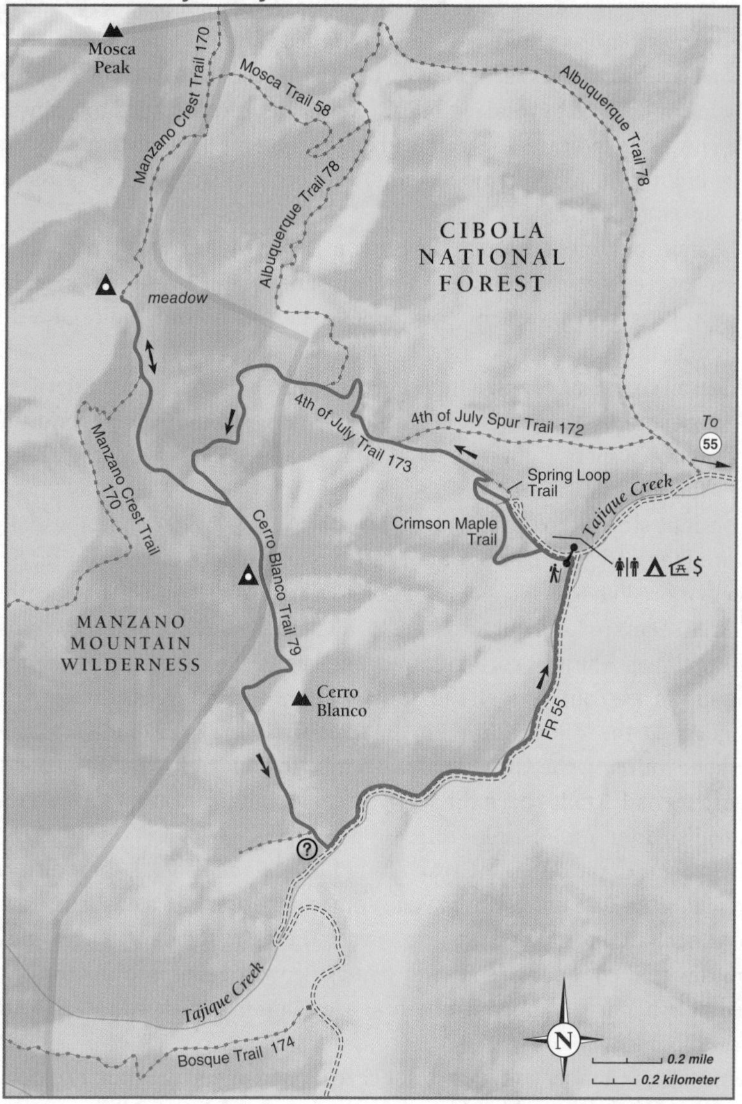

Mosca Peak
Manzano Crest Trail 170
Mosca Trail 58
Albuquerque Trail 78
Albuquerque Trail 78
CIBOLA NATIONAL FOREST
meadow
4th of July Trail 173
4th of July Spur Trail 172
To
55
Spring Loop Trail
Tajique Creek
Crimson Maple Trail
Manzano Crest Trail 170
Cerro Blanco Trail 79
MANZANO MOUNTAIN WILDERNESS
Cerro Blanco
FR 55
Tajique Creek
Bosque Trail 174
N
0.2 mile
0.2 kilometer

10,000 ft.
9,500 ft.
9,000 ft.
8,500 ft.
8,000 ft.
7,500 ft.
7,000 ft.
1 mi.
2 mi.
3 mi.
4 mi.
5 mi.
6 mi.

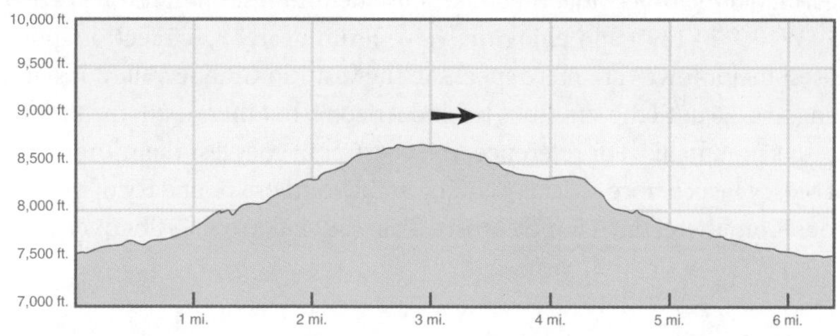

After passing through a gate, note the wooden sign pointing ways and distances to nearby trails. Similar signs have been positioned along trails throughout the Manzanos. However, black bears seem bent on destroying them, so don't be surprised if any are missing or defaced beyond legibility. (New signs are scheduled to be installed.)

The next sign indicates the trailhead on the right for the Fourth of July Trail Spur, a 1-mile link to the Albuquerque Trail (78). Continue straight and cross through a pedestrian gateway ahead.

The trail goes uphill through the canyon. Along the way you'll pass old concrete water enclosures that provide water for cattle and wildlife. And see several varieties of flowers, horsetail, and plenty of maples. There is nothing quite like this moist ecosystem in the Albuquerque area.

The trail soon passes a sign marking the Manzano Mountain Wilderness boundary, as indicated by the icons that forbid bicycles and mopeds beyond this point. (For reference, a sharp right here would put you on a 3.5-mile course back to FR 55 via the Albuquerque Trail.)

Continue straight to the end of the Fourth of July Trail, 0.6 mile ahead. Pine needles soften the path as it climbs out of the canyon and into mixed-conifer forest that will seem more like New Mexico. But don't worry; you'll soon be back with maples. As the trail seems to level out, crossing through rocky outcroppings, the crest comes into view above. These absorbent limestone bands allow rainwater to sink into the mountain and seep out through the canyons below to support the diverse vegetation.

Signage at the T-junction with **Cerro Blanco Trail (79)** indicates that FR 55 is 1 mile to your left, the Crest Trail is 0.5 mile to your right, and the Fourth of July Campground is 1.5 miles back the way you came. But if you also followed the nature trails, you've done a solid 2-plus miles so far.

Turn right to pick up the **Crest Trail (170)** 0.5 mile ahead, then turn right and follow it another 0.25 mile. Mosca Peak comes into dramatic view before a meadow, where you might find grazing cattle, opens on the right. Incidentally, bovine encounters on this trail commonly end with panicky cows fleeing into the forest. To fully appreciate a heifer stampede in the upper-mountain forest, you must witness the spectacle yourself.

Thickets of Gambel oak start to squeeze in, narrowing the trail. Press through to the clearing on the other side, then take a moment to rest on the stone bench (N34° 48.035' W106° 24.139') and enjoy the view. From nearly 8,700 feet, it appears that the closest major towns are mere specks in the vast Rio Grande Valley. It's more than tempting to gaze until the sun sinks behind Arizona, but there's still the matter of getting off this mountain. (For reference, the Crest Trail goes less than 1 mile to the east side of Mosca Peak before officially ending at the southern boundary of the Isleta Reservation. From there, the 0.8-mile Mosca Trail (58) links to the Albuquerque Trail.)

To continue on this hike, backtrack to the junction of the Fourth of July and Cerro Blanco Trails. From there, continue straight along Cerro Blanco Trail. The remaining 1.5-mile descent to FR 55 is a cakewalk. The trail is well established and navigable up to the last flicker of dusk. After a few switchbacks, it squeezes between rocky outcrops and looming cliffs as it drops down to a stream that's often flowing.

At the junction ahead, consider turning right for a detour to a grottolike bend in the canyon. The foliage on this 0.3-mile spur matches Fourth of July's, making it an attractive option for a romantic stroll on its own. (Starting from the Cerro Blanco Trailhead on FR 55, this easy hike is about 0.8 mile out and back.) Otherwise, bear left at the junction, and you'll soon arrive at FR 55. Turn left and follow this pleasant creekside road 1.4 miles downhill to the gate at the Fourth of July Campground.

NEARBY ACTIVITIES

With very few services on NM 337, the **Ponderosa Family Restaurant & Grill** stands out like an oasis. It has recently been rejuvenated and has the typical array of steaks, burgers, and New Mexican food. To find the restaurant, look for a log-cabin lodge on NM 337, about 7 miles north of Chilili or 12 miles south of Tijeras, or call 505-281-1181.

GPS TRAILHEAD COORDINATES N34° 47.400' W106° 22.767'

DIRECTIONS From I-40, take Exit 175 to Tijeras. Follow NM 337 south 29 miles to the T-junction with NM 55. Turn right, going west 3.2 miles on NM 55 to Tajique. Turn right on FR 55 (also marked as A013) and follow signs to the Fourth of July Campground, 7 miles up the dirt-and-gravel road. Turn right through the gate and park in the hiker parking area. Note that the gate is locked November–March. If arriving then, park at the gate and walk up toward the campground. The trailhead is at the end of the campground.

17 GOLDEN OPEN SPACE

The multicolored layers of rock here will remind you of a miniature Grand Canyon.

***BEST-KEPT SECRET* IS** the worst kind of cliché, but the City of Albuquerque hid this one in a neighboring county for more than 40 years. Established trails now allow you to walk the rim above San Pedro Creek and Arroyo Seco. Newer trails explore these deep, multicolored drainages.

DESCRIPTION

The City of Albuquerque acquired this 1,200-acre parcel in Sandoval County in 1964 under the federal Recreation and Public Purposes Act, which required the city to develop it for recreational purposes or return it to the Bureau of Land Management (BLM). Early plans for the property had it slated as a campground, one of several that would form a camping ring around the city. The idea never reached fruition. In retrospect, it's probably best it didn't.

Set aside for the preservation of nature, the land has since remained relatively undisturbed. Viewing it from La Madera Road, you might guess it extends for miles as monotonous grazing lands, but a short hike beyond the fence reveals a fascinating corrugated landscape.

The Golden Open Space is 6 miles west of its namesake ghost town and has been a work in progress for many years. What started out as the 2.25-mile Los

DISTANCE & CONFIGURATION: 7.2-mile loop hike with a long out-and-back spur; options to extend the spur or opt for a shorter 2.25-mile loop hike

DIFFICULTY: Moderate; the short loop hike is easy

SCENERY: Views of multiple mountain ranges; mesa-rim overlooks of the Arroyo Seco and San Pedro Creek; multicolored canyons

TRAIL TRAFFIC: Moderate

TRAIL SURFACE: Packed dirt, sand

HIKING TIME: 4 hours; 1 hour for short loop

DRIVING DISTANCE: 31 miles from the Big I

ELEVATION GAIN: 6,279' at trailhead; 6,388' at high point; 6,078' at low point

ACCESS: Daylight hours

WHEELCHAIR ACCESS: No

MAPS: Golden Open Space Map at cabq.gov/parksandrecreation/open-space; USGS *Hagan*

FACILITIES: None

CONTACT: Albuquerque Open Space, cabq.gov/parksandrecreation/open-space, 505-987-8831

LOCATION: Golden

COMMENTS: Leashed dogs are allowed on trails.

LAST-CHANCE FOOD/GAS: Convenience store–gas station at junction of NM 14 and NM 536, about 11 miles from the trailhead

Duendes loop trail to the overlook has now been expanded into a network of trails that explore all corners of this breathtaking landscape. Earlier editions of this book attributed trail construction to *los duendes.* Some people describe *los duendes* as industrious elves, others as evil dwarfs. In his 1910 paper "New-Mexican Spanish Folk-Lore," Aurelio Macedonio Espinosa identified *los duendes* as "individuals of small stature who frighten the lazy, the wicked and in particular the filthy." Their origins and motives remain a mystery. Regardless of who, some group or entities have been busy building trails here.

The hike begins in the parking area at the GOLDEN OPEN SPACE sign behind an equestrian access gate. Rules for the open space are posted nearby.

A groomed trail runs south up a gently sloping plain. After 0.6 mile of ordinary juniper grassland scenery, the trail arrives at an overlook on the cusp of Arroyo Seco. The main channel of the arroyo heads from the eastern side of Capulin Peak, about 5 miles southwest of the overlook. Once it crosses La Madera Road, numerous tributary washes emerge and converge, creating the vast multicolored drainage network before you. At the point due south of the overlook, it's more than 1 mile wide and nearly 200 feet deep, and it is divided into four or five major channels. At an elevation of 6,400 feet, this overlook is the highest point in the hike.

Continue the hike by following the trail as it curves east along the mesa rim. At 1.2 miles, the trail splits. The left fork is your option for an easy 2.25-mile loop back to the car. The right fork leads to a better hike. About 100 yards later, the trail splits again. Again, we'll take the right fork. The left fork is a 0.25-mile loop to another overlook. A small cave, which you are free to explore, is directly beneath the overlook. If you have trouble finding the cave, you can spot it from the trail down below in the arroyo.

The hike cuts back to the west as the trail ramps down into the arroyo. The earth will darken to rust red, and along the way you'll navigate through red, yellow,

Golden Open Space

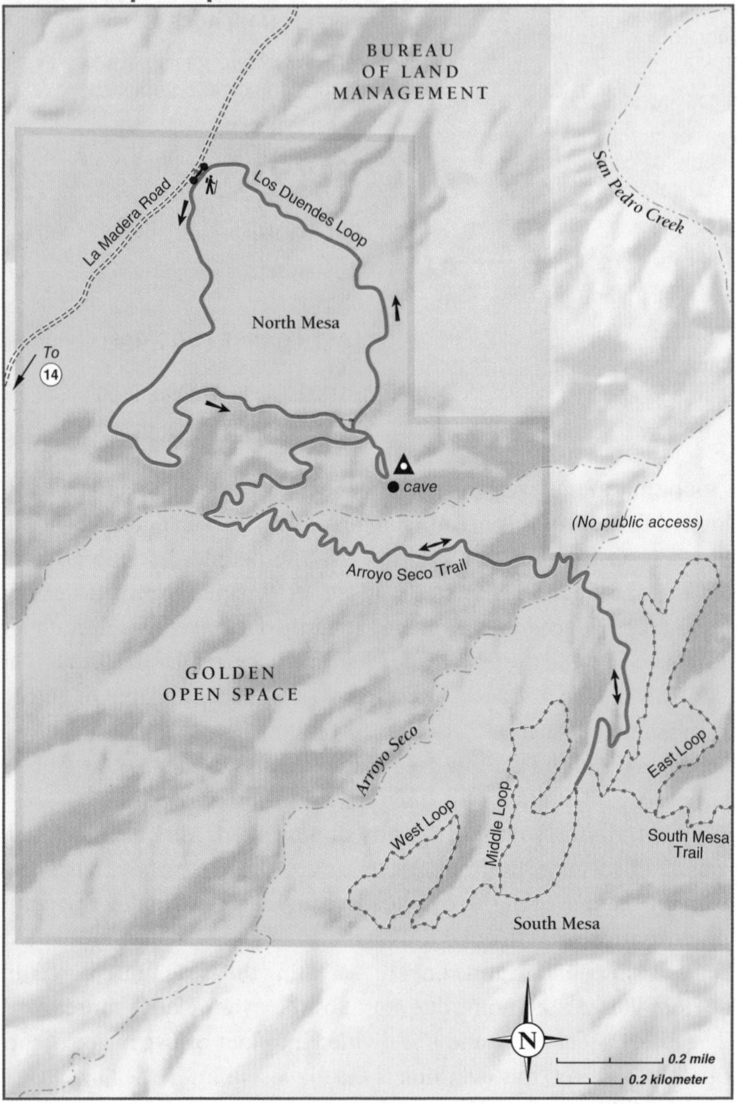

BUREAU
OF LAND
MANAGEMENT
La Madera Road
Los Duendes Loop
San Pedro Creek
North Mesa
To
14
cave
(No public access)
Arroyo Seco Trail
GOLDEN
OPEN SPACE
Arroyo Seco
East Loop
West Loop
Middle Loop
South Mesa
Trail
South Mesa
N
0.2 mile
0.2 kilometer

6,600 ft.
6,500 ft.
6,400 ft.
6,300 ft.
6,200 ft.
6,100 ft.
6,000 ft.
1 mi.
2 mi.
3 mi.
4 mi.
5 mi.
6 mi.
7 mi.

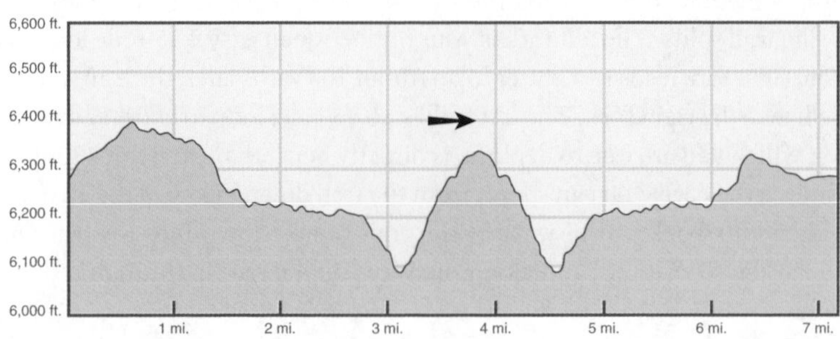

You'll pass many twisted landforms on this hike.

and gray sandstone twisted into every shape imaginable. When the trail reaches the bottom, it will cut back to the east and follow the arroyo from the other side. This is a chance to get another look at what you have been walking through. Every step of the hike inside the arroyo is stunning. In some ways it will remind you a little bit of the Grand Canyon.

Navigation should not be a problem on this hike, as there is trail the entire way. You are free to poke around and explore arroyos coming in from the sides. If you do have trouble spotting where the trail continues after crossing an arroyo bottom, just take a moment to walk in both directions until you find footprints, bicycle tire tracks, a cairn, or something else to tell you this is the trail.

The trail continues east through this colorful and distorted landscape until it meets another arroyo coming down from the south. The trail will turn south and follow that arroyo up to the rim. At this point, you have reached the other side of Arroyo Seco and have probably been hiking for 2 hours. You have walked around 3.6 miles.

You now have several choices. There are several trails on the far side of Arroyo Seco. They are there for you to explore and will lead you to fantastic views of the canyon. If you wander in the juniper savannah, you're likely to see flocks of pinyon jays and other birds. If you're really ambitious, you can continue east to San Pedro Creek and even go farther to explore BLM land east of the open space. But for this hike, we'll turn around and retrace our steps back to the other side.

This will give you another chance to walk through Arroyo Seco and another chance to spot the cave beneath the overlook. You might even want to pick out some places to explore on your next trip. When you reach the other side, turn right (north) on the trail you came in on. The trail will loop back to the parking lot. This leg is a little shorter than the outbound leg of the loop.

NEARBY ACTIVITIES

La Madera Road (also appearing on maps as Madera Road, Hagan Road, Indian Route 844, and County Highway 53) deteriorates quickly with a little rain or snow. But if conditions are good, reset your odometer at the Golden Open Space gate and continue north. The sites listed below are on private land but can be viewed from the road. Hiking or biking La Madera is also an option.

1.8 miles: A few rock walls are all that remain of a forgotten settlement on the right.

4.2 miles: The ruins of Hagan appear on the east bank of the Arroyo Tuerto. In the mid-1920s, the town boasted a grand hotel, a train station, and a mercantile store, but by 1950 Hagan was officially a ghost town.

5.1 miles: Petroglyphs can be found in the facing cliff almost within reach from the road. Look for the shapes of deer or antelope. One of the more curious works features a head with a pair of lollipop-shaped extensions. Is it an Indian with a feathered headband? An insectlike character stemming from Anasazi mythology? Evidence of a prehistoric visitation from antennaed aliens? Interpretation is open to debate.

7.5 miles: The little town of Coyote emerged in anticipation of the Hagan Spur of the Rio Grande Eastern Railroad. The train finally arrived in 1924—three years after citizens of Coyote had given up waiting for it. A few rock foundations remain on the right, along with pieces of off-white bricks stamped TONQUE.

8.8 miles: The ruins of Tonque Brick Factory are on the left, near the site of a precolonial pueblo of the same name. The road runs into a gate at San Felipe Reservation. It is no longer possible to drive to I-25, and you'll have to turn around.

GPS TRAILHEAD COORDINATES N35° 16.270' W106° 19.684'

DIRECTIONS From I-40 East, take Exit 175 toward Cedar Crest. From the I-40 overpass, go 6.9 miles north on NM 14. Turn left on La Madera Road and go 9.5 miles to the signed gate on the right. Note: The first 7.5 miles of La Madera Road are paved but narrow and twisty, and can be difficult in winter conditions. The remaining 2 miles are gravel and dirt but adequately maintained and fairly level. The parking lot for the open space will be on your right.

18 MARS COURT TRAILHEAD-DAVID CANYON

David Canyon's ponderosa parkland will remind you of Flagstaff.

TUCKED AWAY IN a far corner of the Manzanita Mountains, a well-marked network of singletrack and former logging roads winds across canyon meadows and forested ridges. Though the trails are easily accessible from a residential area, views from high points give the illusion of deep wilderness surroundings.

DESCRIPTION

Over the past few years the Sandia Ranger District has developed an extensive trail network in the Manzanita Mountains south of I-40. You can pick up a map of the trails (*Manzanita Mountains Trail System*) at the Sandia Ranger Station on NM 337 in Tijeras or you can download the map at fs.usda.goc/cibola.

Many of the Manzanita trails are open to motorized recreation and are not the best for a hike. David Canyon found at the Mars Court trailhead off of Raven Road on the right (west) side of NM 337 is far enough away from the other trails to offer a quiet and wonderful hike. It may be one of the best hikes close to Albuquerque. The ponderosa forest and magnificent views of the Manzano Mountains make you feel like you're in a remote wilderness, and in some places the ponderosa parkland will remind you of Flagstaff.

DISTANCE & CONFIGURATION: 4.8- to 6.8-mile loop options

DIFFICULTY: Moderate

SCENERY: Forested ridges, meadows, abundant birdlife, wildflowers

EXPOSURE: Half shaded

TRAIL TRAFFIC: Light

TRAIL SURFACE: Dirt roads, rocky trails

HIKING TIME: 3–4 hours

DRIVING DISTANCE: 25 miles from the Big I

ELEVATION GAIN: 7,596' at trailhead; 7,155' at low point

ACCESS: Year-round; no fees or permits required

WHEELCHAIR ACCESS: No

MAPS: USFS Manzanita Mountains Trail System; Sandia Ranger District; USGS *Escabosa*

FACILITIES: None

CONTACT: Cibola National Forest, fs.usda.gov/cibola, 505-281-3304

LOCATION: South of Tijeras

COMMENTS: Leashed dogs are allowed on trails.

LAST-CHANCE FOOD/GAS: Small grocery and cafe on NM 337, 0.8 mile south of Raven Road; gas station on NM 14 in Cedar Crest

On your way to David Canyon you'll pass both Tunnel Canyon and Otero Canyon Trails on the right side of NM 337. Both of them are very nice trails. They are, however, extremely popular with mountain bikers and are not the best place for a quiet hike. Sabino Canyon and Juan Tomas Open Spaces (Hike 20, page 115) on the left (east) side of NM 337 do, however, offer nice, quiet hikes. The next hiking options are almost 30 miles farther south.

The David Canyon hike begins at the Mars Court trailhead. If you check the map at the trailhead or a printed trail map, you'll see that there are over 15 miles of trails in and around David Canyon. The 1-mile-by-3-mile canyon area is bordered by the U.S. Air Force on the west, Isleta lands on the south, residential development on the east, and U.S. Forest Service on the north. Despite the confines, a hike here approximates the wilderness experience of any backcountry forest—minus the long drive up rugged access roads. There is a good chance that, except for a few stray mountain bikers, you'll have the forest to yourself.

With trails running on both sides of the canyon, in the bottom of the canyon, and going across the canyon, you can configure a hike for as long or as short as you want. Our 6.8-mile loop hike (with an option for a shorter 4.8-mile loop hike) is a good introduction to David Canyon. With the canyon being so close to Albuquerque, there is a good chance you'll want to come back again to hike it a different way.

The route begins on the south side of the parking area where both the Turkey Trot Trail (05162) and Wild Turkey Trail (05161) begin. Our hike bears to the left and follows the Turkey Trot Trail south. The trail descends at a very nice grade through a mixture of ponderosa, piñon, juniper, and alligator juniper. The smell of the ponderosa is wonderful. And if you come in the summer you'll see plenty of wildflowers. You are also likely to see hawks, ravens, and other types of birds. On many days you'll hear woodpeckers pounding away on the ponderosa. If you look closely at the ponderosa, you'll see thousands of small holes from their pounding.

Mars Court Trailhead–David Canyon

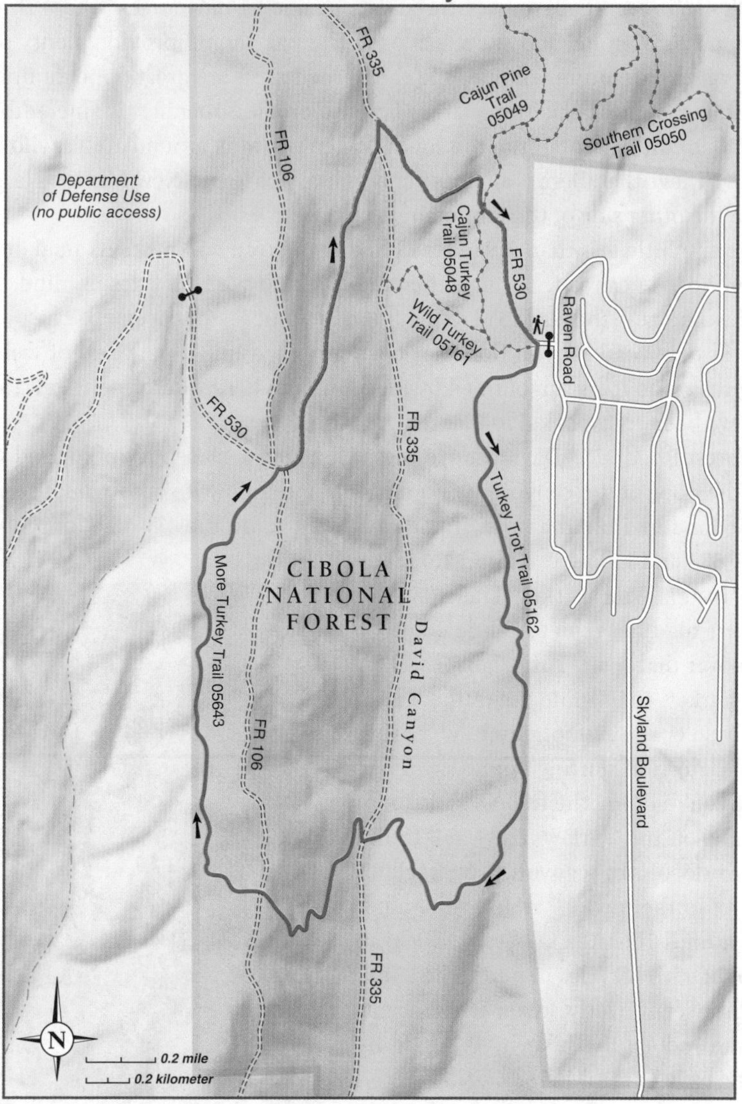

FR 335
Cajun Pine Trail 05049
Southern Crossing Trail 05050
FR 106
Department of Defense Use (no public access)
Cajun Turkey Trail 05048
FR 530
Wild Turkey Trail 05161
Raven Road
FR 530
FR 335
Turkey Trot Trail 05162
CIBOLA NATIONAL FOREST
More Turkey Trail 05643
David Canyon
FR 106
Skyland Boulevard
FR 335
N
0.2 mile
0.2 kilometer

8,000 ft.
7,800 ft.
7,600 ft.
7,400 ft.
7,200 ft.
7,000 ft.
6,800 ft.
1 mi.
2 mi.
3 mi.
4 mi.
5 mi.
6 mi.

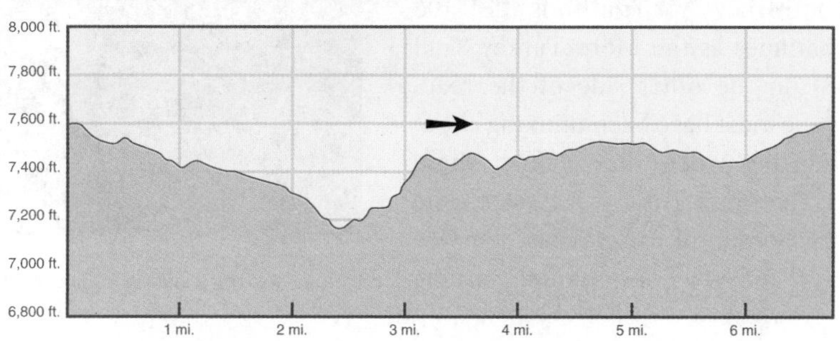

The trail eventually passes through a couple of burn areas where there is an abundance of Gambel and wavy-leaf oak. The oak should provide plenty of forage and coverage for future wildlife, and the burned areas are great opportunities to see how a forest comes back from a fire. They also provide openings for incredible views of the Manzano Mountains to the south. When you look around at this wild land, it's hard to believe that there is an important military base and New Mexico's largest city just on the other side of the mountains to the west.

After a little less than 2.5 miles of hiking the trail will make its final descent to the floor of the canyon. Because the trail was built with bicycles in mind, the 400-foot descent from the trailhead to the floor does not seem that steep. The ponderosa forest in the broad canyon floor has been groomed into a parkland of well-spaced ponderosa pine trees surrounded by meadows. It's here where you might think that you have been transported to Flagstaff, Arizona.

Forest Road 335 (David Canyon Road), which is closed to motorized vehicles, is on the floor of the canyon. If you turn left and follow it south, you'll reach Isleta Pueblo land in around a mile. If you only want to do the 4.8-mile loop, turn right on FR 335 and follow it around 1.6 miles north to the Wild Turkey Trail (05161). The dirt road has a nice, gentle 200-foot climb over that span. Turn right (east) on Wild Turkey. In 0.7 mile the trail, with its slightly steeper 200-foot climb, will bring you back to your starting point.

You're never far from a woodpecker in David Canyon.

If you're doing the full 6.8-mile loop, continue on the Turkey Trot Trail to the other side of the canyon. You'll climb 300 feet in the next 0.7 mile to the junction with FR 106. Again, because the trail was built with bicycles in mind, the climb does not seem overly steep. If you want, you can reduce the hike by 0.2 mile by turning right (north) here.

The Turkey Trot Trail ends at FR 106 and continues as the More Turkey Trail (05643) on the other side of the road. (Someone must have been thinking about Thanksgiving when they named these trails.) The More Turkey Trail skirts the western border of U.S. Forest Service property, and you'll see several warning signs about unexploded ordinance on Air Force land. You'll also notice that the forest has been thinned through controlled burns and actual cutting to reduce the risk of catastrophic fire. The thinning has groomed the forest into a beautiful parkland.

The More Turkey Trail ends after a little more than 1.5 miles at FR 530. You'll turn right (east) onto FR 530 to return to the Mars Court trailhead. FR 530 and most of the trails to the north allow motorcycles. But because this route is so far away from the main concentration of motorcycles, you are not likely to see any. If you wish, you can continue hiking north and choose another trail to return to the trailhead. There are many options to consider, but please consult a map to determine which one is best for you. If you make the turn onto FR 530, you'll have around 2.1 miles of hiking before reaching the trailhead. The grades across this end of the canyon are very gentle.

You'll know you're approaching the trailhead when you see a gate blocking motor vehicle access to FR 530. Your task now is to figure out your route for your next visit to this fabulous canyon.

NEARBY ACTIVITIES

Big Block Climbing Area presents an array of bouldering problems and sport climbing on limestone cliffs. The block itself is big enough for three routes rating around 5.7. The main wall has at least five established routes. Parking for Big Block is unmarked. Look for a trailhead between the guardrail and the road cut on the south side of NM 337 between mile markers 25 and 24. The trail to the area is short but steep.

• •

GPS TRAILHEAD COORDINATES N34° 59.050' W106° 20.989'

DIRECTIONS From I-40 East, take Exit 175 south to Tijeras. Go 8.8 miles south on NM 337. Turn right on Raven Road and follow it 1.6 miles. Turn right on Mars Court. Drive about 200 feet, through the open gateway, and park along the loop before the second gate. The trailhead is next to the first gate on the south side of the parking area.

19 RED CANYON

Fantastic outcrops like this make Red Canyon a favorite hike for many adventurers.

RED CANYON IS spectacular whether done as an out-and-back or as part of a longer loop. Most hikers come here for a 7.5-mile loop that incorporates Spruce Spring Trail. Our loop is slightly longer, but it explores a wider diversity of landscapes along paths less traveled, namely Box Spring Trail, Ox Canyon Trail, and a lonely stretch of Manzano Crest Trail. Either way, you'll witness old-growth conifers, mountain meadows, and the main attraction—the towering quartzite outcrops of Red Canyon.

DESCRIPTION

The best way to hike this route is open to debate. Photographers prefer to start with Red Canyon to take advantage of early daylight. Summer hikers start on Box Spring Trail to avoid the heat in Ox Canyon's exposed sections. The route described here opts for starting with Box Spring in a strategy that simply saves the best for last. If you don't have time for the loop, you can do a great out-and-back on Red Canyon. The lower canyon has fantastic geology and the top has great meadows with views. (It's a perfect place for lunch.)

Box Spring Trail (99) is an easy, well-shaded 1.4-mile path that climbs gently around the bulging ridge between Red Canyon and Ox Canyon. A sign for its trail-head stands on the south side of the road in the day-use area, near the restrooms and

DISTANCE & CONFIGURATION: 5.5-mile out-and-back or 8.6-mile loop

DIFFICULTY: Moderate–strenuous

SCENERY: Quartzite cliffs, dense woodland, subalpine meadows, views over the Estancia and Rio Grande Valleys

EXPOSURE: Mostly shaded

TRAIL TRAFFIC: Moderate

TRAIL SURFACE: Dirt, rock

HIKING TIME: 4 hours for out-and-back; 5–6 hours for loop

DRIVING DISTANCE: 62 miles from the Big I

ELEVATION GAIN: 7,921' at trailhead; 9,866' at high point for out-and-back; 9,942' for loop

ACCESS: FR 253 (access road) is subject to winter closures (call first); no fees or permits required for hiking; $7 campsite fee

WHEELCHAIR ACCESS: No

MAPS: Mountainair Ranger District–Manzano Division; Manzano Mountain Wilderness; USGS *Manzano Peak* and *Capilla Peak*

FACILITIES: Restrooms (no water), picnic tables, grills, and corrals at Red Canyon Campground

CONTACT: Cibola National Forest–Mountainair Ranger District, fs.usda.gov/cibola, 505-847-2990

LOCATION: Manzano

COMMENTS: Leashed dogs are allowed on trails.

LAST-CHANCE FOOD/GAS: Limited services along NM 337 and NM 55; convenience store–gas station in Tajique, 15 miles from the trailhead

picnic grounds. It starts by dropping south to cross an occasionally damp creek bed, then soon passes through an equestrian/pedestrian gate. From there it's a casual stroll on a narrow but obvious path that dips in and out of steep drainages.

You'll soon run into a few blackened pines that hint of a major forest fire not too long ago. Then suddenly, about a mile into the hike, you turn a corner and hit the burn zone—remnants of the Ojo Peak fire, a 19-day blaze that consumed nearly 7,000 acres in November 2007. Box Spring Trail ends here at its junction with **Ox Canyon Trail (190).**

Now more than 10 years after the Ojo Peak fire, there are still signs of the burn, but the forest is coming back. There are young, healthy ponderosa; thriving Gambel oak to provide forage for wildlife; and great open views. It's a good place to hike. A nearby signpost indicates that Trail 190 runs 0.5 mile southeast to FR 422 and 3.5 miles west to join the Crest Trail. Turn right here and start climbing west. The lower trail is as broad as a boulevard and as easy to follow. Trail workers installed numerous signs and laid down branches to keep you from straying onto discontinued routes, and mature pines emphasize the way with rectangular blazes scored many decades ago. New signs are scheduled to be installed.

Evidence of the fire soon fades as the singed landscape yields to lush woodland ripe with fern, moss, and mushrooms. The trail stays near the canyon floor, meandering near the intermittent stream that (sometimes) flows from the upper and lower Ox Springs. It switches back to traverse a rockslide and continues climbing to a point at 8,840 feet. By now you're in aspen territory, and just high enough to catch a glimpse of salt lakes in the Estancia Basin. They're sometimes hard to spot, but at the right time of day they seem to mirror the sky. The big one, Laguna del Perro, is about 12 miles long and 1 mile wide. Pueblo Indians harvested salt from these *salinas* to trade with Plains Indians. (See Nearby Activities.)

Red Canyon

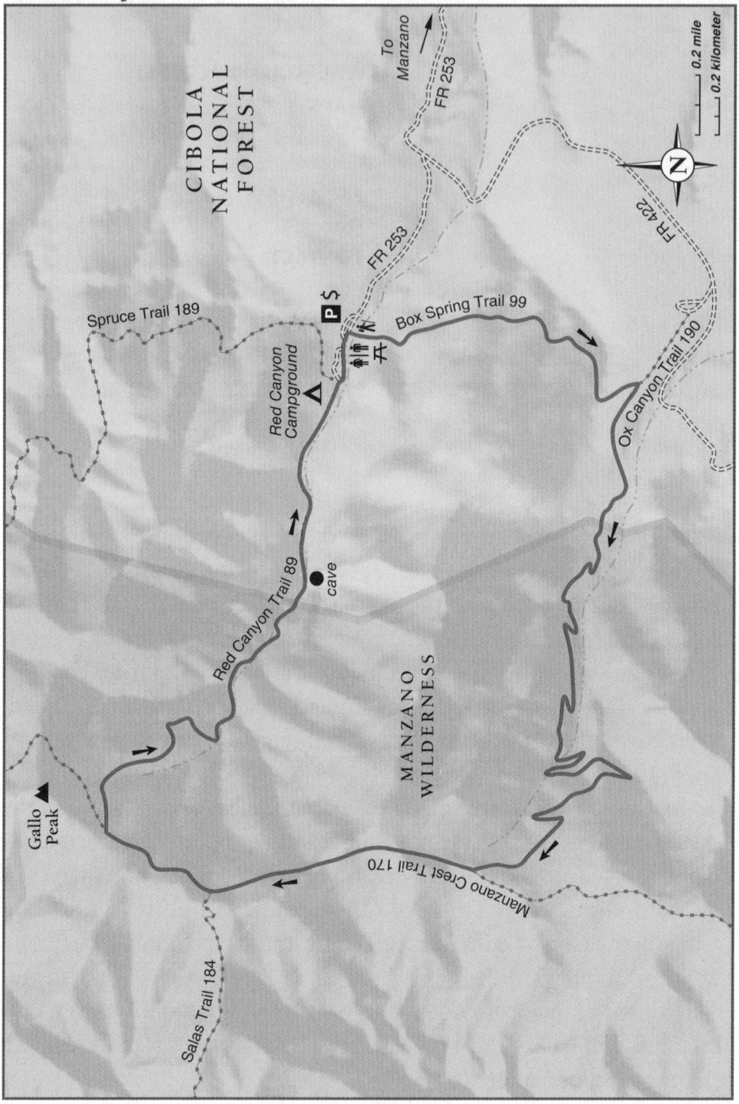

CIBOLA NATIONAL FOREST
MANZANO WILDERNESS
To Manzano
FR 253
FR 422
0.2 mile
0.2 kilometer
N
Spruce Trail 189
Red Canyon Campground
Box Spring Trail 99
Ox Canyon Trail 190
Red Canyon Trail 89
cave
Gallo Peak
Manzano Crest Trail 170
Salas Trail 184

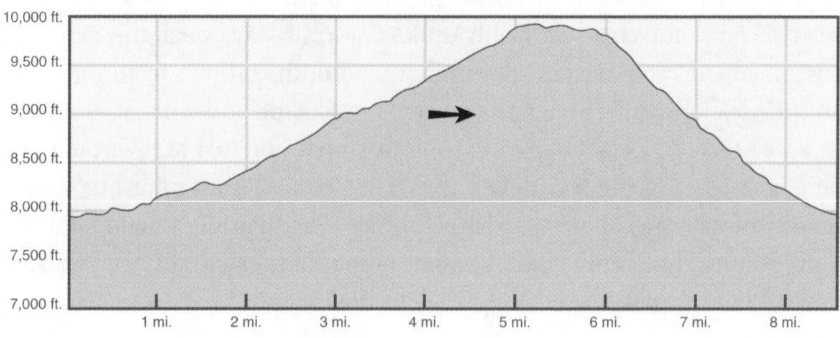

10,000 ft.
9,500 ft.
9,000 ft.
8,500 ft.
8,000 ft.
7,500 ft.
7,000 ft.
1 mi.
2 mi.
3 mi.
4 mi.
5 mi.
6 mi.
7 mi.
8 mi.

Fires cause pine cones to open and release their seeds, which is why pine trees are often the first to appear after a fire.

After a brief respite on relatively level terrain, the trail crosses to the south side of the stream and the switchbacks turn severe. Over the next 1.2 miles or so on this narrow and coiled trail, you'll travel a linear distance of only 0.18 mile, half of which is a gain in elevation. After the fifth switchback, the trail eases over a hump to arrive at a perfect spot on the crest to break for lunch.

The **Manzano Crest Trail (170)** is a lonely stretch of trail that starts out deceptively easy. Monumental cairns stand along the stretch heading south, and a cluster of signs gives distances in all directions. The segment for this hike is 1.5 miles north to Red Canyon Trail. You soon enter a steep meadow where the trail fades out. Maintain your direction and you should be able to spot diminutive cairns in the tall grass. The trail regains its definition farther uphill. The saddle just ahead is the high point of this hike. Gallinas Peak is visible about 45 miles southeast. Climb the rocks on your left for better views west over the Rio Grande Valley and down into Monte Largo Canyon (Hike 54, page 283).

Manzano Crest Trail then descends on the west side of the ridge. Rest assured it will soon return to the east side, where it enters dense woodland and fades out. Again, maintain your direction and you should soon spot the posted junction with Salas Trail (184). Continue on the Crest Trail into a meadow where it vanishes once again. You know the drill by now. The next posted junction is about 200 feet northeast.

Red Canyon Trail (89) is the steepest segment of this hike, but it's all downhill from here, and its entire 2.4 miles is easy to follow. A signpost here points the ways to trails running north, south, and east but says nothing of the one running west. (Take a quick jog in that direction to find its sign. TRIGO is the only word remaining on this bear-clawed sign. It refers to an old alignment of the discontinued Trigo Canyon Trail.)

Back at the junction, head east on Red Canyon Trail. It quickly drops into the shade of fir, spruce, aspen, and a smattering of massive ponderosa. The narrow path crosses a creek a few times. Crossings can get tricky with a good spring runoff, but that usually dies down to a trickle by summer. Stony walls rise to flank both sides of the stream. (Geologists, take note: In this area, where the Sais directly overlies the White Ridge Quartzite without the intervening Estadio Schist, the two quartzites look very much alike. It's also interesting to note that bedding, which was originally horizontal, is now subvertical due to folding and thrusting during the Precambrian.) At this point Red Canyon becomes fabulous and may become one of your favorite hikes. Just past a waterfall is an alcove with the shelter cave. From there, the canyon widens and the trail continues about 0.7 mile to the campground.

The Red Canyon Trailhead is marked with the standard map and info board. It's located at the top of the campground loop, so either way you go is less than 0.2 mile back to the day-use area.

NEARBY ACTIVITIES

Salinas Pueblo Missions National Monument: Like the plantations that would later come to plague the American South, these imposing missions fueled fierce discontent. Three far-flung units—Abó, Quarai, and Gran Quivira—now make up the national monument. Quarai is the nearest and is open daily, Memorial Day–Labor Day, 9 a.m.–6 p.m. The rest of the year you can visit 9 a.m.–5 p.m. Entry is free. To get there from Manzano, drive 5 miles southeast on NM 55. Turn right at Punta de Agua and go west 1 mile. For more information, call 505-847-2585 or visit nps.gov/sapu.

GPS TRAILHEAD COORDINATES N34° 37.314' W106° 24.688'

DIRECTIONS From I-40 East, take Exit 175 to Tijeras. Drive south on NM 337 and NM 55 about 41 miles, passing through the villages of Escobosa, Chilili, Tajique, Torreon, and Manzano. On the south side of Manzano, veer right at the fork onto NM 131, following the signs toward Red Canyon. Go 2.4 miles, then turn right before the entrance to Manzano State Park. NM 131 soon becomes Forest Road 253. About 2.5 miles past the Manzano State Park entrance, turn right and continue 0.4 mile toward Red Canyon Campground. Unless you plan to stay the night, park in the day-use area.

20 SABINO CANYON AND JUAN TOMAS OPEN SPACES

The Sandias from Juan Tomas Open Space

TWO EAST MOUNTAIN sites provide a range of hiking options over meadows, forested hills, and a historic site. Both trails are an island of calm in an area noted for motorized recreation.

DESCRIPTION

Over the past few years the Sandia Ranger District has developed an extensive trail network in the Manzanita Mountains south of I-40. You can pick up a map of the trails (*Manzanita Mountains Trail System*) at the Sandia Ranger Station on NM 337 in Tijeras or you can download the map at fs.usda.gov/cibola.

Many of the Manzanita trails are open to motorized recreation and are not the best for hiking. Sabino Canyon and Juan Tomas Open Spaces on the east side of NM 337 are two exceptions. There is also great hiking in David Canyon (Hike 18, page 105) on the west side of NM 337.

You'll pass both Tunnel Canyon and Otero Canyon Trails on the west side of NM 337 on your way to Sabino Canyon and Juan Tomas. Both are very nice trails, but they are extremely popular with mountain bikers and not the best place for a hike.

DISTANCE & CONFIGURATION: Sabino Canyon 2-mile loop hike; Juan Tomas Open Space 3.7-mile loop hike

DIFFICULTY: Easy–moderate

SCENERY: Woodland, meadows, nearby 20th-century ruins

EXPOSURE: Half shaded

TRAIL TRAFFIC: Moderate

TRAIL SURFACE: Packed dirt

HIKING TIME: 1 hour (Sabino Canyon); 2 hours (Juan Tomas Open Space)

DRIVING DISTANCE: 22 miles (Sabino); 26 miles (Juan Tomas) from the Big I

ELEVATION GAIN: Sabino Trailhead 7,100', with little change in elevation; Juan Tomas Trailhead 7,520', with a low point of 7,285' on trail

ACCESS: Year-round; Sabino Canyon is open sunrise–sunset

WHEELCHAIR ACCESS: No

MAPS: USFS Manzanita Mountains Trail System; USGS *Sedillo*

FACILITIES: Interpretive signage at Sabino

CONTACT: Bernalillo County Open Space, bernco.gov/openspace, 505-314-0400; Albuquerque Open Space, cabq.gov/parksand recreation/open-space, 505-987-8831

LOCATION: South of Tijeras

COMMENTS: Leashed dogs are allowed on trails.

LAST-CHANCE FOOD/GAS: All services at Exit 167 (Tramway Boulevard and Central Avenue); restaurants in Tijeras

Sabino Canyon offers a short stroll that takes you back a hundred years to the Reidmont Fur Farm, an enterprise that was, for better or worse, destined for failure. Stables and cages in ruins add a melancholic twist to the otherwise serene site.

For the definitive guide to this area, download *Sabino Canyon Open Space: An Interpretive Guide* from the Bernalillo County Open Space website (bernco.gov/openspace). For a quick recap, read on: About a mile south of Cedro Peak, Cibola National Forest surrounds an island of open space. From the early 17th century to the late 19th century, farmers cultivated the land for pinto beans and potatoes, but the site is best known for a short-lived attempt to capitalize on the fur craze of the flapper era. In the late 1920s, Austrian immigrant Alexander Riedling built the Riedmont Fur Farm, complete with hundreds of silver foxes, minks, and rabbits. But the fur market soon tanked with the onset of the Depression, and Riedling died on the farm a few years later.

In October 1999, Bernalillo County purchased the 117-acre parcel. The county thinned the trees and built 2 miles of trails with interpretive signs. The trails are open sunrise to sunset. Forest Road 252 splits the open space in two. Each side of the open space has a loop trail. Put together, they create a 2-mile figure eight hike. Parking is on the east side of the road.

If you don't have time for the full figure eight, the former fur farm is on the west loop. The east loop begins with a short stem across a shallow drainage. From there you can go either direction as the loop goes through both junipers and meadow. If you come in the summer, you may want to bring a flower guide as there are many varieties of flowers and other plants to identify. Look closely at the limestone along the way, as there is a very good chance of spotting seashells and other fossils. And

Sabino Canyon and Juan Tomas Open Spaces

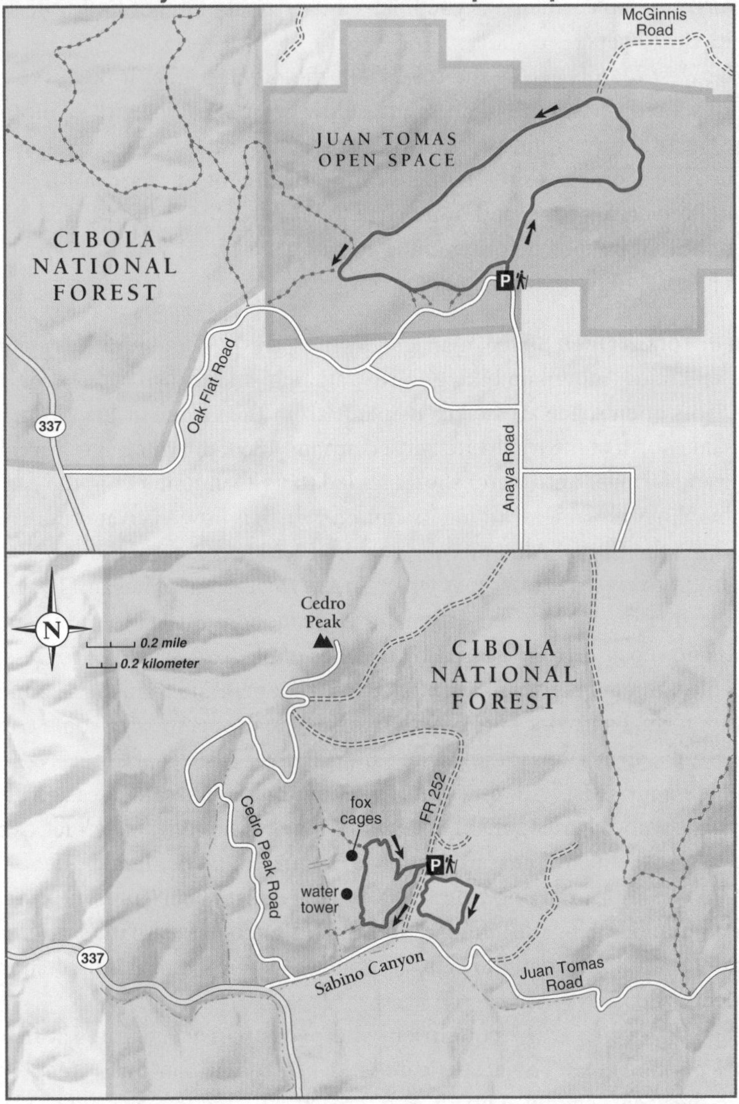

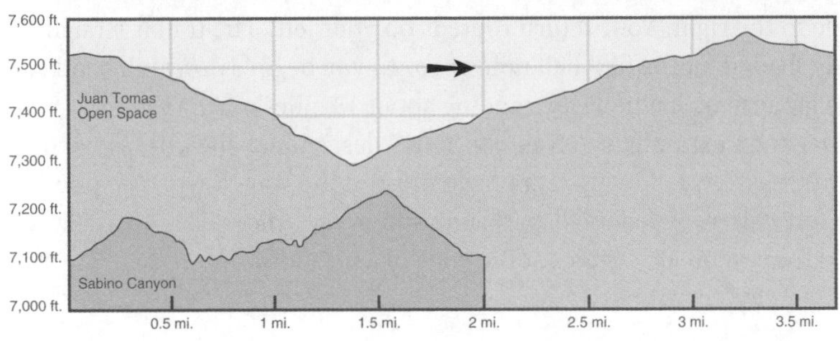

don't forget to look around, as you'll have many great views of Cedro Peak. It's the one with the towers.

The west loop is across the road from the parking area. It begins on a gravel road but soon diverts south to cross a meadow before heading into a piñon–juniper forest. The trail turns right (north) when it reaches the U.S. Forest Service boundary. The hike soon passes the remains of the Riedmont Fur Farm. You'll go by the old water tower, fox pens, and other structures. After the pens, the trail loops back through piñon–juniper before coming to the gravel road where the hike started. Turn left (east) to return to the parking lot.

Juan Tomas Open Space, managed by the City of Albuquerque, is an ideal spot for casual hiking, mountain biking, bird-watching, and (timed right) cross-country skiing. This open space area takes its name from the village of Juan Tomas, about 2 miles due north of the trailhead. Settled around 1860, the village grew modestly on logging and farming until water shortages led to its abandonment in the early 1960s. A few buildings remain, including its church, which is now a private residence.

In 1983 the City of Albuquerque acquired 1,290 acres from the U.S. Forest Service (USFS) to create Juan Tomas Open Space. Development began 14 years later to make the area suitable for recreational use, including projects to reduce forest-fire hazards and repair damage caused by decades of off-road driving. Progress thus far has been commendable, thanks in large part to cooperation from local communities.

An informal network of trails crisscrosses the property, with some connecting to USFS trails. Juan Tomas adjoins the Sandia Ranger District of Cibola National Forest, yet it stands apart with quietude. True, mountain bikes do occasionally careen through the woods here. Can't blame them—miles of smooth singletrack over gently rolling hills make Juan Tomas irresistible to beginner and moderate riders.

With elevations ranging from 7,300 to 7,760 feet, Juan Tomas features Rocky Mountain juniper, alligator juniper, and piñon, interspersed with scattered stands of ponderosa, Gambel oak thickets, and open meadows. Local inhabitants include mule deer, wild turkey, and elk.

The hike begins at the equestrian- and pedestrian-access gates at the edge of a gravel parking area. The access gate is identified with an OPEN SPACE sign. Go through the access and head north. You'll reach a T-junction very soon. You'll want to angle to the right. Your return route is on your left. The trail is straight, flat, and sparsely shaded for the first half mile or so. As you begin a downhill bend east, you'll catch a glimpse of Sandia Peak standing about 18 miles northwest.

Over the next mile, the trail continues descending and curves northwest into denser tree cover, following a drainage most of the way down. The ponderosa and piñon forest is well-groomed parkland and a very nice place to walk. The well-defined trail eventually arrives at the edge of a meadow.

From here the trail curves southwest for a modest climb up a 1.5-mile canyon. As it becomes steeper and rockier, look on your left for a broad trail (N35° 00.057' W106° 18.558'). (It still shows as a U.S. Forest Service road on some maps; but if you see signs for the Open Space–U.S. Forest Service boundary, you passed it about a quarter mile back.)

Head east on the broad trail about 0.3 mile until it splits into four trails. If you have time for a detour, the path on your left heads north into denser woods. To stick to this route, take the uphill singletrack going east. This 0.5-mile segment twists over a shaded hillside and arrives at a signed fork. Follow the arrow pointing right to return to the parking area.

NEARBY ACTIVITIES

Visit the **Tijeras Pueblo Archaeological Site** for self-guided tours of the 14th-century ruins. Excavations from 1948 to 1976 uncovered 200 rooms. The museum and interpretive trail are pleasant and informative. Entered into the National Register of Historic Places in 2005, the site is behind the Sandia Ranger Station in Tijeras. The ranger station is also worth a visit as it has an information desk, exhibits, maps, and plenty of brochures. Call 505-281-3304 or visit fs.usda.gov/cibola.

• •

GPS TRAILHEAD COORDINATES

Sabino Canyon N35° 02.393' W106° 20.635'
Juan Tomas Open Space N35° 00.030' W106° 17.851'

DIRECTIONS *Sabino:* From I-40 West, take Exit 175 to Tijeras. Go 5 miles south on NM 337. Turn left on Juan Tomas Road and go 0.7 mile east to FR 252. Turn left on FR 252 and drive 0.3 mile north to the open space. The parking area is on the right (east) side of the road.

Juan Tomas: From I-40 West, take Exit 175 to Tijeras. Go 8.7 miles south on NM 337. Turn left on Oak Flat Road and go 2.7 miles east. Park in the area on the left, across from the junction with Anaya Road.

21 SAN PEDRO MOUNTAINS MINING AREA

The San Pedro Mountains provide a beautiful background for this hike.

A WEB OF old roads makes up this route through the western hills of the San Pedro Mountains. Riddled with holes and scraped to the bone, this stout, rugged range bore the brunt of gold fever.

DESCRIPTION

This hike is not for everyone, and it is probably best to leave the kids at home, as there are many deep mining pits near the route. If you like to explore unusual places with some history, this hike is for you. The hike takes you through a corner of the San Pedro Mountains with many old mines and relics from when it was an active mining district.

Since it has only been a few years since the Bureau of Land Management (BLM) acquired access to this area, the BLM (along with the state and Santa Fe County) has not finished its work in removing hazards. This means that even though this tract is open to hiking and exploring, the BLM is not ready to promote the area for recreation. The county has already acquired adjacent land to add to the future recreation area. So if you hike here now, you'll have a chance to see the "before" picture.

As you explore this area, you'll also see that there are still many small-scale miners and mining clubs with active claims. There is a good chance that you'll see modern-day prospectors panning for and actually finding gold. With no streams in

DISTANCE & CONFIGURATION: 3.2-mile out-and-back with options to extend the hike

DIFFICULTY: Moderate; the climb to Cerro Columbo is strenuous

SCENERY: Piñon–juniper hills, historic mines, mountain vistas

EXPOSURE: Little shade

TRAIL TRAFFIC: Low

TRAIL SURFACE: Dirt, sand, rock

HIKING TIME: 2–3 hours

DRIVING DISTANCE: 32 miles from the Big I

ELEVATION GAIN: 6,905' at trailhead; 7,572' on summit of Cerro Columbo

ACCESS: Year-round; no fees or permits required

WHEELCHAIR ACCESS: No

MAPS: USGS *San Pedro* and *Golden*

FACILITIES: None

CONTACT: Bureau of Land Management–Taos Field Office, blm.gov/office/taos-field-office, 575-758-8851

LOCATION: Golden

COMMENTS: Open shafts along route pose serious hazards; watch your step and avoid hiking in the area after dark. The area has active mining claims; pay attention to no-trespassing signs. Leashed dogs are allowed on trails.

LAST-CHANCE FOOD/GAS: Convenience store–gas station at junction of NM 14 and NM 536, about 11 miles from the trailhead

the San Pedro Mountains, today's prospectors bring jugs of water and plastic tubs to separate the gold from the gravel.

As for the history of the area, the San Pedro (formerly Tuerto) Mountains stand near the south end of a mining belt that has endured at least 10,000 years of continuous human occupation. Evidence of early mining activity includes remnants of an ancient Native American copper-smelting industry found in the Cañon del Agua, near to the west of Cerro Columbo.

In 1839 the Mexican government awarded the San Pedro Land Grant to families in the area, hoping to deter Plains Indians from raiding the main settlements farther west. That same year, gold was discovered in the mountain streambeds. Mining settlements sprang up overnight and quickly developed into formal town sites with hotels, mercantile stores, and saloons. Within a decade, miners scalped the peaks of their natural surface terrain and essentially transformed the slopes into giant prairie dog colonies. Shortly after World War I, large-scale operations ceased, and town sites were razed.

In recent years most residents of the San Pedro community have consistently opposed attempts to revive mining operations, but they have no jurisdiction over 2,200 acres of BLM land in the San Pedro Mountains. Yet for decades this chunk of public land was available for recreation in theory only. A ring of private holdings kept it strictly off-limits.

The private stranglehold on public land did not escape the notice of the BLM–Taos office. Their plan for securing a public-access corridor was more than 20 years in the making, but on November 19, 2010, they succeeded in obtaining a 30-foot-wide ribbon of land totaling 2.96 acres—the piece that connects NM 344 with the mountain interior.

San Pedro Mountains Mining Area

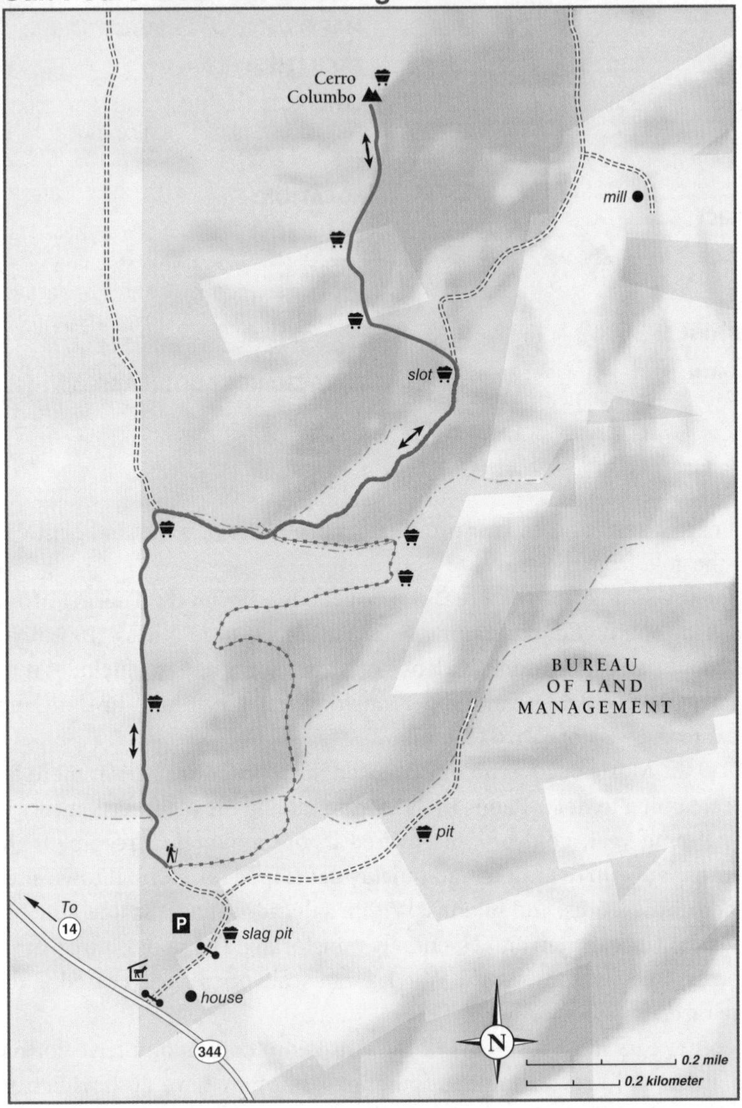

Cerro
Columbo
mill
slot
BUREAU
OF LAND
MANAGEMENT
pit
To
14
slag pit
house
344
N
0.2 mile
0.2 kilometer

7,800 ft.
7,600 ft.
7,400 ft.
7,200 ft.
7,000 ft.
6,800 ft.
6,600 ft.
0.25 mi.
0.5 mi.
0.75 mi.
1 mi.
1.25 mi.
1.5 mi.

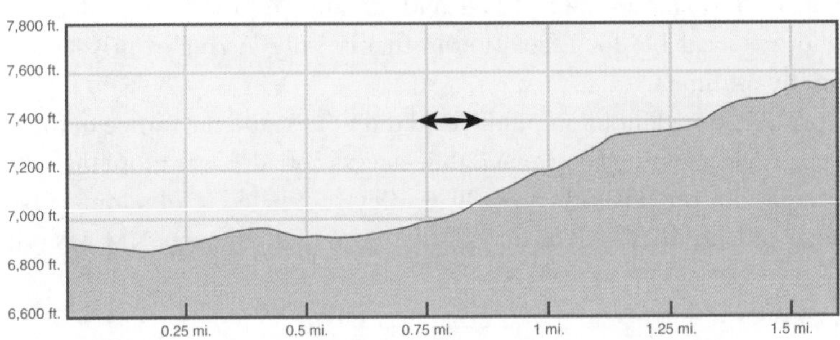

Keep an eye out for slot mines along the route.

As for hiking and exploring this area, when you reach the gate and dirt access road to the left of NM 344 (N35° 14.358' W106° 12.660'), there will be no warm greeting welcoming you to your public lands. Instead you'll see what appears to be an abandoned stable on the left and a house that could use some repairs on the right. Your first reaction will be that you are at the wrong place. But if you can see a second gate a short distance ahead on the access road and the number 1660 on a post, you're at the right place. If you don't want to hassle with unchaining the gates, you can park here and walk up the road. The parking area for the hike is around a quarter mile up the road.

As you head up to the parking area, keep an eye out to the right for a black wall of slag (residue waste from smelting copper) next to the road. Although the slag pile is on private land, you can still get a good look at it from the road. If you look closely, you'll see that much of the slag is in the shape of cones. The shape comes from the iron pots used to carry the cooling slag. This was very much a horse and wagon operation that managed to produce a very impressive pile.

You'll know that you are at the parking area because you will have gone up to a small ridge where several dirt roads come together. There will also be a large metal tank cut in half in front of you and a utility line running overhead. You can also see a beat-up cinder block building beyond and to the left of the tank. For orientation, the cinder block building is to the west.

The described hike follows old dirt roads and eventually ends at the top of Cerro Columbo. If you do not want to make the steep climb to the top, you are welcome to follow other old roads to explore the area. Just keep track of where you are and be careful not to fall into a hazard. Keep west to remain on BLM land.

The hike begins by following the dirt road on the left that goes to the south of the building. In a very short time you'll be at the western edge of BLM land. The road turns right and starts heading north. There are NO TRESPASSING signs on the fence. Continue following the road north as it goes over the flank of the hill to the east. There will be old mines and shacks to your right. There are also some deep pits not far from the road. So be careful about where you explore.

In a little more than 0.5 mile, you'll reach a road junction (N35° 14.911' W106° 12.650'). Turn right and head east. In less than 0.25 mile you'll reach another junction (N35° 14.881' W106° 12.494'). The road on the right continues up the arroyo. The hike follows the road to the left. It is a steep climb to the northeast. You'll see old mines, openings, trails, and roads all the way to the top. Stay right at a Y-junction near the top. As the road levels out, look down to your left for a slot. It leads to a horizontal shaft that extends through rock directly beneath your feet.

Cerro Columbo, the high point of the area, is off to the northwest. Turn left at the junction just ahead. Take a good look around and memorize the turn, because it's the easiest one to miss on the way back. Proceed about 0.25 mile northwest. Just before the road bends right and heads downhill, look for a campfire ring in the clearing on the left. Continue straight past it, going off-road to climb the hill. About 0.25 mile up, cairns mark the 7,572-foot summit of Cerro Columbo (N35° 15.373' W106° 12.341').

A stamp mill stands out among the abandoned structures in the valley to the immediate east. The view also includes San Pedro Mountain peaking at 8,242 feet, less than a mile southeast. Placer Mountain, the high point of the Ortiz, stands at 8,897 feet, 6 miles north-northeast. Sandia Crest at 10,678 feet is 14 miles west.

When you're ready to return, retrace your steps back to the car, and pick out places you might want to investigate on your next visit.

• •

GPS TRAILHEAD COORDINATES N35° 14.498' W106° 12.635'

DIRECTIONS From I-40 East, take Exit 175 toward Cedar Crest. From the I-40 overpass, go 16 miles north on NM 14 and turn right on NM 344. Drive 0.9 mile southeast and turn left at the double gate. Drive about 0.2 mile northeast on this dirt road. Park in a clearing near the five-way intersection. (See Description above for more information.)

22 TREE SPRING-CREST TRAIL

This steep hike rewards you with amazing views at the top.

THIS CLASSIC HIKE combines the 2-mile Tree Spring Trail with a 1.6-mile segment of the Crest Trail to reach the upper terminal of the Sandia Peak Tramway. Aspen shades the upper trail to the subalpine mountaintop, where views encompass 11,000 square miles. Many people are satisfied with the 2-mile hike to the top of the ridge for a fabulous view of Albuquerque and the Rio Grande Valley.

DESCRIPTION

In 1936 the U.S. Forest Service cleared the slopes and established a system of trails at Tree Spring to accommodate the fledgling Albuquerque Ski Club. These were the first runs in what would become La Madera Ski Area. By 1946 it expanded to the current location of Sandia Peak Ski Area and featured the nation's longest T-bar lift. A lift ticket cost $1. Diminutive by comparison, the original slopes at Tree Spring were soon considered a mere practice area.

You won't see a trace of ski runs at Tree Spring today, but the fee box standing at the trailhead is hard to miss. A large board displays the usual rules, safety info, and trail map. Nearby signs alternate between the singular and plural spelling of the trail, but there's no mistaking the way.

DISTANCE & CONFIGURATION: 4- or 7.2-mile out-and-back

DIFFICULTY: Moderate for the 4-mile out-and-back; moderate–strenuous for the 7.2-mile out-and-back

SCENERY: Marine fossils, aspen and fir, wildflowers, fantastic views

EXPOSURE: Mostly shaded

TRAIL TRAFFIC: Popular

TRAIL SURFACE: Dirt, rock

HIKING TIME: 2.5–5 hours

DRIVING DISTANCE: 27 miles from the Big I

ELEVATION GAIN: 8,469' at trailhead; 9,436' at the end of Tree Spring; 10,256' at tram

ACCESS: Year-round; day-use fee $3/car; free with Sandia Mountain Annual Pass or National Parks and Federal Recreation Lands Annual Pass; no permits required

WHEELCHAIR ACCESS: No; wheelchair-accessible restroom

MAPS: Sandia Ranger District; USGS *Sandia Crest*

FACILITIES: Restrooms (no water) at trailhead; visitor center, tramway terminus, restrooms, and emergency phone at Sandia Peak

CONTACT: Cibola National Forest–Sandia Ranger District, fs.usda.gov/cibola, 505-281-3304

LOCATION: Sandia Park

COMMENTS: Leashed dogs are allowed on trails.

LAST-CHANCE FOOD/GAS: Convenience store–gas station at the junction of NM 14 and NM 536

Tree Spring Trail (147) is the easiest and a very popular way to hike to the top of the ridge for incredible views of Albuquerque and the Rio Grande Valley. Because the elevation gain is relatively reasonable, this is a great hike for all ages.

The path begins as a paved sidewalk that leads straight to the pit toilets. The actual trail of hard-packed dirt starts just to the right of the facilities. Just ahead in 0.3 mile is the marker for Oso Corredor (265) going off to the left. This easy, though occasionally soggy, 2.7-mile side trail was named for the numerous black bear sightings in its inaugural season in 1989, a particularly dry summer in the Sandias.

If you look behind the pit toilets, you'll see a casual trail following an old roadway. That trail passes through open meadows full of wildflowers before joining the Oso Corredor Trail. Your challenge on that walk is to not see more than a dozen varieties of wildflowers.

Returning to our hike on Tree Spring Trail, the trail is well maintained and has nice grades the entire way. Credit the Adopt-a-Trail volunteers who cast aside large stones and terraced the grounds to facilitate your ascent. Just over a mile into the hike, the forest opens to meadows that thrive with wildflowers in warmer seasons. After 1.5 miles, the Sandias' limestone cap pokes through the soil. Look closely at the smooth gray rock for marine fossils. Gastropods (snails) about the size of a quarter are the easiest to spot. Trilobites and crinoids also riddle the rock from here to the peak.

The limestone is part of the 300-million-year-old Madera group. Beneath it is Precambrian granite that dates back some 1.4 billion years. It seems a few intermediary layers have gone missing. Landscapes often lose bits of their geologic records. Such absentmindedness is called an *unconformity.* The Sandias, however, blacked out for more than a billion years in what geologists worldwide refer to as "the Great Unconformity."

Tree Spring–Crest Trail

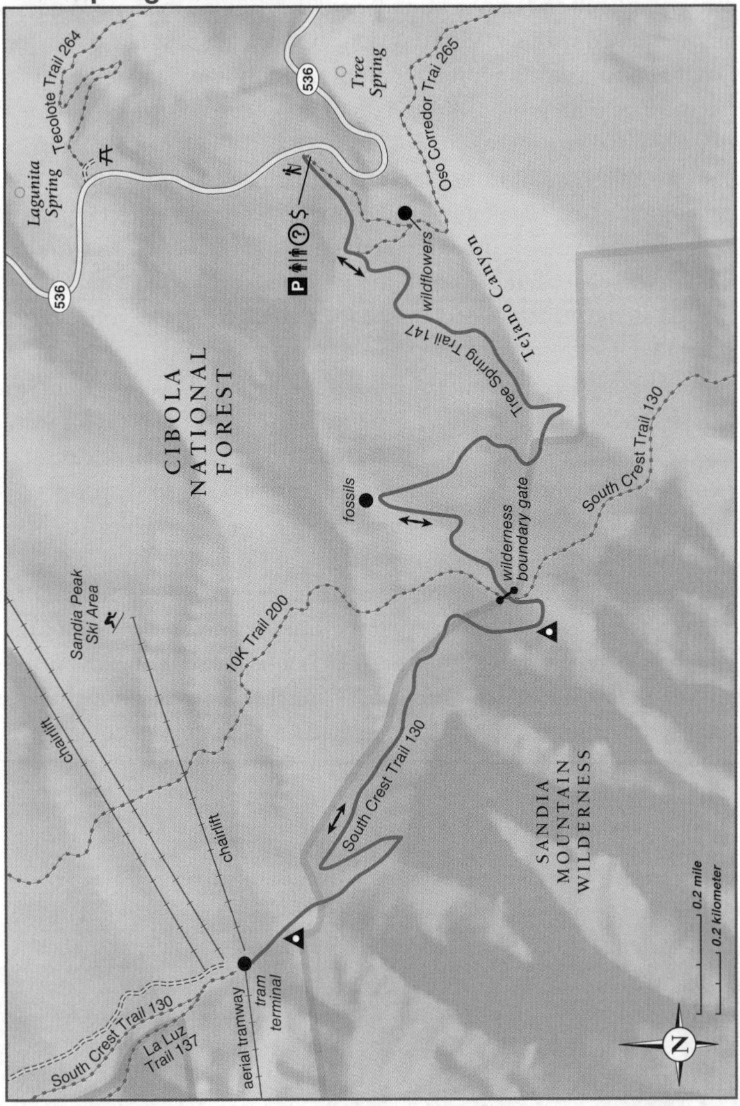

Lagunita Spring
Tecolote Trail 264
536
Tree Spring
Oso Corredor Trai 265
wildflowers
Tejano Canyon
Tree Spring Trail 147
CIBOLA NATIONAL FOREST
fossils
wilderness boundary gate
South Crest Trail 130
Sandia Peak Ski Area
10K Trail 200
chairlift
chairlift
South Crest Trail 130
SANDIA MOUNTAIN WILDERNESS
0.2 mile
0.2 kilometer
N
aerial tramway
tram terminal
South Crest Trail 130
La Luz Trail 137

11,000 ft.
10,500 ft.
10,000 ft.
9,500 ft.
9,000 ft.
8,500 ft.
8,000 ft.
0.5 mi.
1 mi.
1.5 mi.
2 mi.
2.5 mi.
3 mi.
3.5 mi.

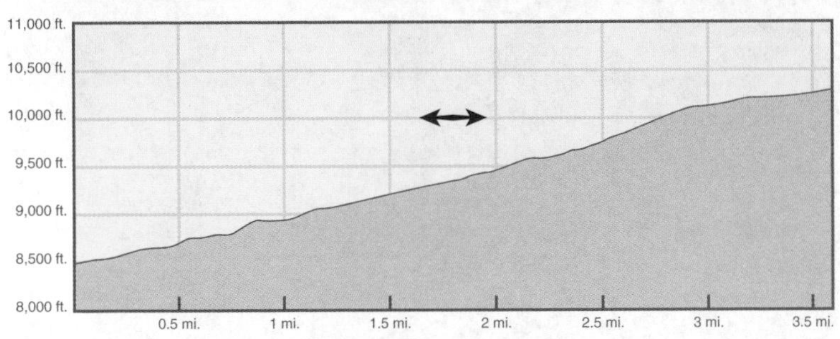

Tree Spring Trail ends at the boundary of the Sandia Mountain Wilderness. The boundary is marked with a wilderness sign and wooden post fence. The opening in the fence is almost a small minihub with three trails joining together at this point. To the immediate right is the 10K Trail (200). It proceeds north on a route that runs below the ridge and crosses the runs of the ski resort before reaching the Crest Highway about 5.5 miles uphill from the Tree Spring parking area. The 10K continues north to rejoin the Crest Trail near the Del Agua Overlook (Hike 15, page 91).

Going left takes you southbound on the Crest Trail (130). If you go south a little less than 2 miles, you'll catch up with the terminus of the Pino Trail (Hike 10, page 64). If you go all the way to the end of the trail, you'll reach Canyon Estates (Hike 2, page 26) in 13 miles.

The northbound Crest Trail proceeds straight ahead. At this point, the northbound Crest Trail is like a maze of little trails. Most of them go off to the left to overlooks of Albuquerque and the Rio Grande Valley on the other side of the ridge. Be careful near the edge; the drop-off is precarious. For most people hiking the Tree Spring Trail, this view is the main attraction and a good place to have a snack and then turn around.

If you're not turning around and want a longer walk, you can continue north on the **Crest Trail (130)** all the way to the tram terminal. Because of higher altitudes and steeper grades, this part of the hike is much harder than the first part. The nature of the trail is also much different, as you'll be passing through dense stands of mature fir, intermittent groves of aspen, and sporadic colonies of mushrooms and lichens. The green, shaggy growths resembling Spanish moss are an unrelated plant known as "old man's beard."

Look for marine fossils (gastropods) embedded in the limestone here.

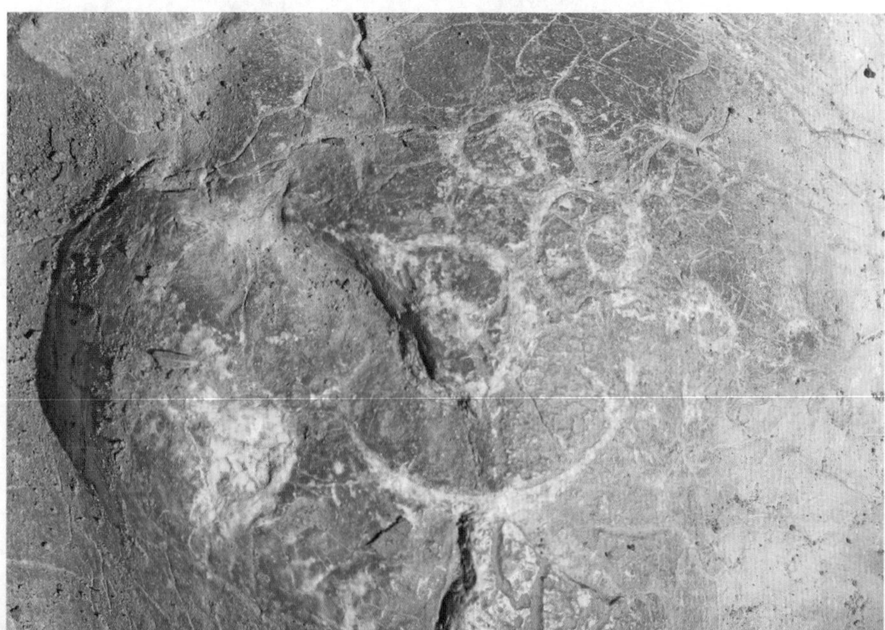

After a couple of long switchbacks, the trail runs near the ridgeline. Opportunities abound for short detours to secluded overlooks. If the wind dies down for a moment, you'll hear the hum of the tram's pulley system. Follow that sound and you'll soon emerge from the woods at the top of the ski trails. The red benches and blue poles of the chairlifts are impossible to miss, as is the steep view down the slopes.

The stairs up to the tramway terminal are by the second lift. Once on the wooden deck above, you've reached an altitude nearing 10,300 feet—squarely in subalpine spruce–fir forest archaically known as the Hudsonian Zone. To reach the highest point in the Sandias, you'd have to hike another 1.8 miles north on the Crest Trail. At 10,678 feet, Sandia Crest is the highest point in Bernalillo County.

Stations located on the deck identify peaks and landmarks in every direction. On an average day, the view overlooks 11,000 square miles—essentially everything within 60 miles of Albuquerque. In the past the deck featured a restaurant. At the time of this writing the restaurant building has been removed, but there are plans for a new restaurant to open in 2019.

Sandia Peak Tramway is featured in Hike 6 (page 45). Up until 2011 it was the world's longest aerial tramway. At 2.7 miles, it's still quite a ride. The tram operates year-round with occasional shut-down periods for maintenance. The upper tram terminal, the Four Seasons Visitor Center (open spring, summer, and fall), contains interpretive exhibits on natural history, including an explanation of how fossilized sea creatures ended up atop these mountains. For more information on the tram, call 505-856-7325 or visit sandiapeak.com.

BONUS HIKE

With parking sometimes difficult at the Tree Spring Trailhead, there is an alternative hike, **Tecolote Trail (264),** only 0.5 mile up Sandia Crest Scenic Byway. There is plenty of parking in a now defunct picnic area on the right side of the road just beyond mile marker 6. The 1.3-mile out-and-back trail begins behind the now shut-down pit toilet. The relatively flat trail features old mineshafts, great views, and a turnaround loop at the end. This is a good backup hike if you cannot park at Tree Spring.

• •

GPS TRAILHEAD COORDINATES N35° 11.618' W106° 24.273'

DIRECTIONS From I-40 East, take Exit 175 toward Cedar Crest. From the I-40 overpass, go north 5.9 miles on NM 14. Turn left on NM 536 (Sandia Crest Scenic Byway) and follow it 5.7 miles up to the Tree Spring parking area on the left.

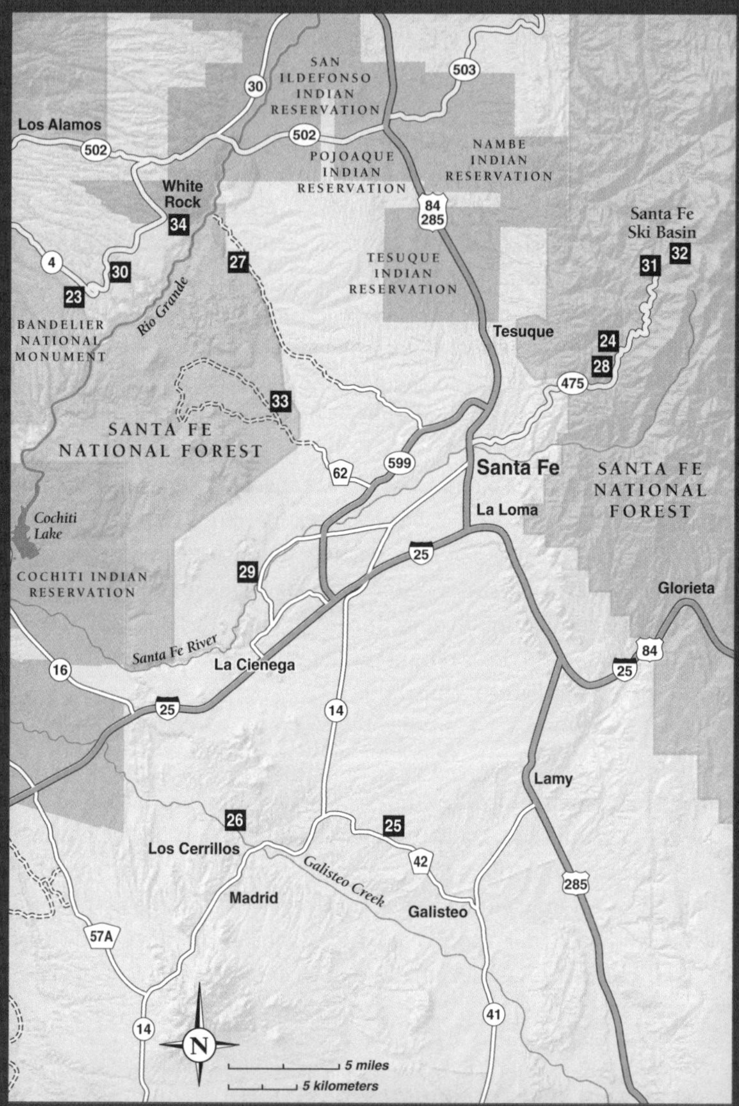

SAN ILDEFONSO INDIAN RESERVATION
Los Alamos
White Rock
POJOAQUE INDIAN RESERVATION
NAMBE INDIAN RESERVATION
TESUQUE INDIAN RESERVATION
Santa Fe Ski Basin
BANDELIER NATIONAL MONUMENT
Rio Grande
Tesuque
SANTA FE NATIONAL FOREST
Santa Fe
SANTA FE NATIONAL FOREST
La Loma
Cochiti Lake
COCHITI INDIAN RESERVATION
Glorieta
Santa Fe River
La Cienega
Lamy
Los Cerrillos
Madrid
Galisteo Creek
Galisteo
5 miles
5 kilometers

GREATER SANTA FE

23 Bandelier National Monument: Falls Trail 132
24 Borrego Trail 137
25 Cañada de la Cueva 141
26 Cerrillos Hills State Park 146
27 Diablo Canyon–Buckman 151
28 Hyde Memorial State Park 156
29 La Cieneguilla Petroglyph Site and Cañon 161
30 Lower Water Canyon–Lion Cave Trails 166
31 Nambe Lake 171
32 Puerto Nambe–Santa Fe Baldy 176
33 Twin Hills 180
34 White Rock Canyon: Red Dot/Blue Dot Trails 185

23 BANDELIER NATIONAL MONUMENT: Falls Trail

View toward the Rio Grande at the end of the Falls Trail

THE EXTENSIVE TRAIL SYSTEM in Bandelier National Monument allows for a wide range of hikes, from leisurely strolls among ancient cliff dwellings to weeklong treks into backcountry wilderness. The Falls Trail is geared for casual hikers and has many rewarding views.

DESCRIPTION

Bandelier is an obligatory day trip for many Santa Fe vacations. And for good reason: when you drive in from NM 4 at the top of Pajarito Plateau down to the Bandelier visitor center at the bottom of Frijoles Canyon, it's like you've dropped into Shangri-La. You almost have to pinch yourself to make sure you're not in a dream.

The pockmarked sheer canyon walls of volcanic tuff look like the bubbles and crevices inside an English muffin and are worth a drive across the country to see! The abundant ponderosa on the canyon floor fill the air with the scent of pine. The perennial stream running the length of the canyon makes it feel cooler on a warm day. The abundant Abert's squirrels with their big tufted ears and the mule deer with their short tails only add to what makes Bandelier special. And all of this is accented by the bright blue New Mexico sky, high above the canyon walls.

DISTANCE & CONFIGURATION: 3-mile out-and-back plus optional 3-mile extension

DIFFICULTY: Moderate

SCENERY: Waterfalls, canyon woodland, tent rocks, majestic cliffs, ruins

EXPOSURE: Some tree cover and canyon shade

TRAIL TRAFFIC: Heavy

TRAIL SURFACE: Packed dirt

HIKING TIME: 2–3 hours

DRIVING DISTANCE: 98 miles via San Ysidro or 104 miles via Santa Fe from the Big I

ELEVATION GAIN: 6,088' at trailhead; 5882' at Upper Falls

ACCESS: All trails open daily, sunrise–sunset, except December 25 and January 1. Day-use fees (subject to change): $25/vehicle or $15/person traveling on foot or bicycle. Annual Park Pass available. Federal Recreational Land Passes are accepted.

WHEELCHAIR ACCESS: No; limited access on the Main Loop

MAPS: Brochure map available at park entrance station; USGS *Frijoles*

FACILITIES: Visitor center, gift shop, snack bar (subject to seasonal closure), restrooms, campgrounds, interpretive exhibits and programs

CONTACT: National Park Service, nps.gov/band, 505-672-3861

LOCATION: White Rock

COMMENTS: No dogs allowed on trails. Shuttle bus from White Rock runs during the busy season, mid-May–mid-October.

LAST-CHANCE FOOD/GAS: All services in White Rock (11 miles northeast); convenience store in La Cueva (32 miles northwest); gas station in San Ysidro (58 miles southwest)

The combination of being a special place, abundant Ancestral Puebloan ruins, and great hiking trails makes Bandelier very popular. During the busy summer season (mid-May–mid-October) visitors arriving between 9 a.m. and 3 p.m. need to take the shuttle bus from the visitor center on NM 4 in White Rock to enter the canyon.

The ancestral Puebloan cliff dwellings and large ruins on the floor of the canyon are clearly the main attractions at Bandelier. By the mid-1200s people were coalescing into larger groups and began building small villages. The height of development was in the 1400s, and by the mid-1500s the people had moved on to the Rio Grande. The people of Cochiti Pueblo consider the people of Frijoles Canyon to be their ancestors.

As for hiking, the hike described in this book follows the Falls Trail downstream to the upper falls and then visits the main ruins in the heart of the canyon. It is a good introduction to Bandelier.

There are many more hiking options, and with 70 miles of trails to choose from, picking a route in this 33,750-acre monument can be tough. To thoroughly appreciate Bandelier, you need at least three days—your pass is good for a week. Keep in mind, however, that Bandelier trails are not to be taken lightly. They wind in and out of numerous canyons cut 500 feet deep into the southernmost Pajarito Plateau. Formed by the ash flow on the eastern flank of the Valles Caldera, this sloping plateau is not as flat as you might guess.

The good news is that the trails are easy to follow. Built by the Civilian Conservation Corps in the 1930s, they seem as sturdy today as the day they were constructed. More about that project, and everything else you could possibly want to

Bandelier National Monument: Falls Trail

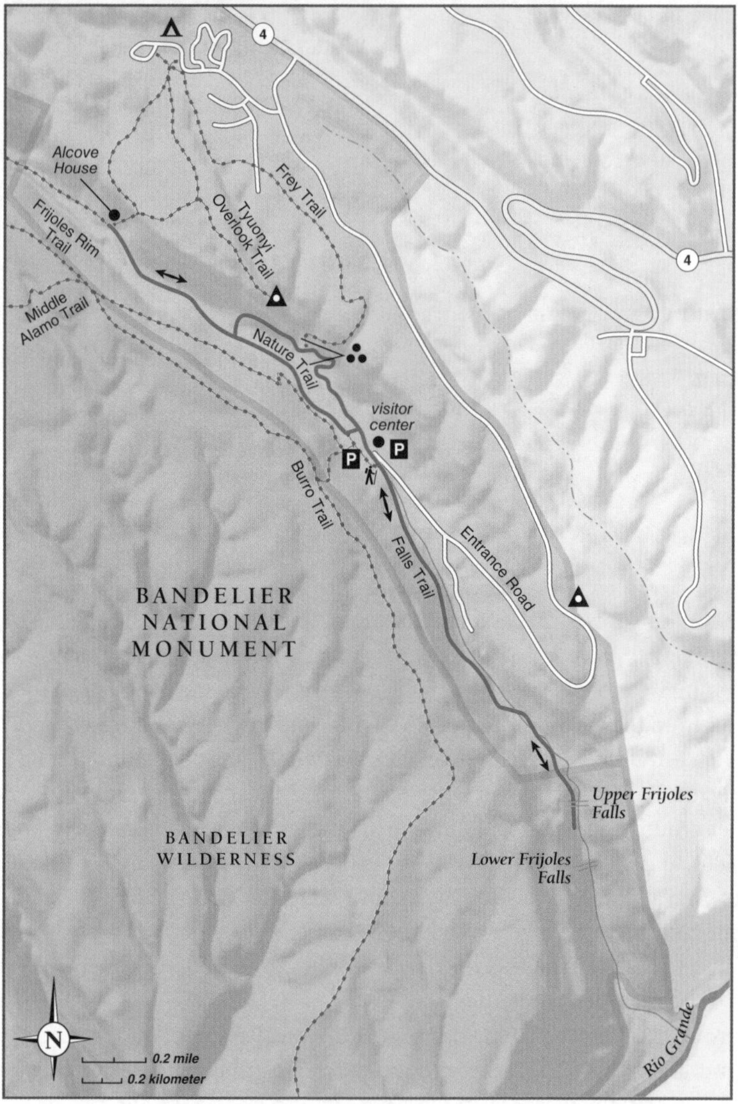

4
Alcove House
Frijoles Rim Trail
Tyuonyi Overlook Trail
Frey Trail
Middle Alamo Trail
Nature Trail
visitor center
P
Burro Trail
Falls Trail
Entrance Road
BANDELIER NATIONAL MONUMENT
BANDELIER WILDERNESS
Upper Frijoles Falls
Lower Frijoles Falls
Rio Grande
N
0.2 mile
0.2 kilometer

6,800 ft.
6,600 ft.
6,400 ft.
6,200 ft.
6,000 ft.
5,800 ft.
5,600 ft.
0.25 mi.
0.5 mi.
0.75 mi.
1 mi.
1.25 mi.
1.5 mi.

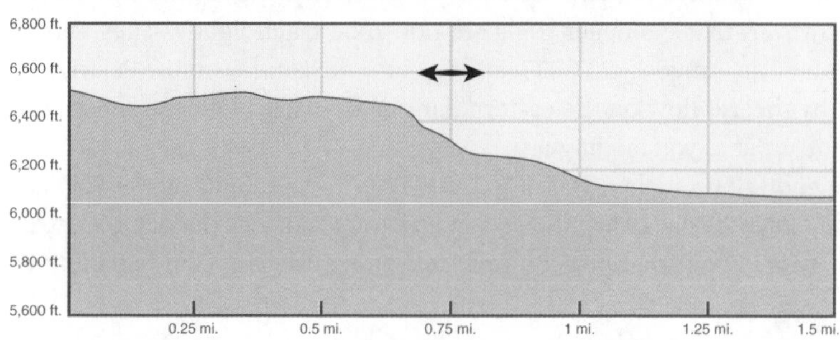

Visitors must climb four ladders to reach Alcove House.

know about the monument, can be learned in the visitor center. Spend some time with the exhibits and dioramas to prepare for any questions that might pop up on the trail. For this hike, be sure to pick up the 15-page booklet *A Guide to the Falls Trail.*

Keep in mind that weather in the park can be unpredictable. So please make sure that you are prepared for sudden changes. Snow and ice buildup add extra challenges in the winter, especially in canyons. Sun exposure and thunderstorms can get fierce in the summer. Park rangers are diligent about monitoring current conditions, so it's worth stopping by the visitor center before hitting the trail.

This hike begins at the south end of the backpacker's parking area, across the stream from the visitor center. The trail descends 400 vertical feet in 1.5 miles on its way to the very impressive Upper Frijoles Falls. Prior to the 2011 Las Conchas fire, the trail went all the way down to the Rio Grande. The severe floods that followed the fire washed out the trail below the Upper Falls. The shortened trail is still a great hike and provides time to extend the trip for exploring the ruins on the back side of the visitor center.

The hike to the falls begins as a very pleasant walk along the stream through the woods. You'll be passing both soft volcanic tuff and very hard basalt for the entire way. You'll even pass various forms of tent rocks. As the walk progresses, you may notice that the stream has cut deeper into the tuff and is now way below the trail. It is right around that time that you'll catch your first glance of the Rio Grande off in the distance and down below.

Although it may be difficult to tell, you are almost at the Upper Falls. The trail will end very soon at the Upper Falls overlook. The view is amazing. The falls plunge

80 feet at the point where the stream ran out of soft tuft to cut through and ran into a layer of hard basalt. The falls alone are wonderful, but there are also many different colors and layers from different volcanic events to add to the view. The pinkish rocks are volcanic tuff. The deep red layers were produced when one lava flow baked layers from previous flows. The dark, dense rock is basalt. And, if it is cold enough, you'll see various ice formations beneath the falls.

Because this is the end of the trail, you'll have to turn around. If you decide to call it a day, you'll have done a very nice 3-mile hike in Shangri-La. If you're not quite ready to leave, there's more on the other side of the visitor center.

The Main Loop starts from the back side of the visitor center and passes Big Kiva and Tyuonyi (a 400-room ruin). From here the trail becomes very interesting as it uses a combination of stairways and paths to follow the cliff line so you can examine the dwellings and pass through fantastic tuff formations. You can climb ladders to reach many of the rooms and cavities dug out of the tuff. From the cliff dwellings, you can return to the visitor center or extend your walk a little more than a mile by going to Alcove House. You'll have to climb 140 feet on a combination of four ladders and many steps to get to Alcove House. If you're worried about heights, you won't like the climb. Otherwise, it's pretty cool.

From here you can return to the visitor center or do some more exploring. Doing the Main Loop and Alcove House adds about 3 miles to your hike for a total of 6 miles.

• •

GPS TRAILHEAD COORDINATES N35° 46.714' W106° 16.200'

DIRECTIONS Bandelier is fewer than 40 linear miles from Albuquerque, but there are no reasonable shortcuts to its main entrance. From I-25 North, take Exit 276 to NM 599. Go north 13.5 miles to its end at US 84. Go north 14 miles to Pojoaque and turn left onto NM 502 (Los Alamos Highway). Go west 11.2 miles and bear left on NM 4 toward White Rock. (Note that the Tsankawi section, on the left 1.4 miles past the junction, features a 1.5-mile self-guided hike through an Ancestral Pueblo village.) Drive 12 miles on NM 4 to the main entrance.

Alternate route: From I-25 North, take Exit 242 at Bernalillo. Turn left on US 550 and go 23.5 miles to San Ysidro. Turn right on NM 4 and follow it 57 miles to the main entrance. Follow the road down to the visitor center. The Falls Trailhead is at the south end of the backpacker parking area.

24 BORREGO TRAIL

The Borrego Trail meanders through a mixed aspen-fir forest.

THIS WONDERFUL HIKE, on a well-maintained historic trail through a lush forest with running water, is suitable for all ages and seasons and is a great place to get away from the heat in the summer.

DESCRIPTION

Long before the idea of recreational hiking appeared on anyone's radar scope, local populations made use of the Sangre de Cristo Mountain's resources. Before the Spanish arrived, Native American populations depended upon the bounty derived from all ecologic zones ranging from the lowest river valley to the tallest mountain. Deer antlers and pine boughs are still incorporated into traditional dances and artistic representations to portray the mountains' bounty.

When Spanish settlers arrived and introduced sheep to the area, they used the mountain meadows as summer pastures. Even today, cattle grazing remains a traditional use of the mountain meadows. The Borrego Trail was a route that connected communities to the north and the mountain pastures to the Santa Fe market. *Borrego* means "lamb" in Spanish, and the trail is still there for you to hike. It runs almost due north from its trailhead for about 22 miles and crosses several creeks and drainages before reaching its terminus on the north side of Santa Fe National Forest. With some

DISTANCE & CONFIGURATION: 4-mile balloon

DIFFICULTY: Easy–moderate

SCENERY: Mountain views, mixed forest, Tesuque creek, wildflowers

EXPOSURE: Mostly shaded

TRAIL TRAFFIC: Popular

TRAIL SURFACE: Dirt, rock

HIKING TIME: 2–2.5 hours

DRIVING DISTANCE: 69 miles from the Big I

ELEVATION GAIN: 8,881' at trailhead; 8,241' at low point

ACCESS: Year-round; no fees or permits required

WHEELCHAIR ACCESS: No

MAPS: Santa Fe National Forest, East Half; USGS *Aspen Basin* and *McClure Reservoir*

FACILITIES: None

CONTACT: Santa Fe National Forest–Española Ranger District, fs.usda.gov/santafe, 505-753-7331

LOCATION: Santa Fe

COMMENTS: Leashed dogs are allowed on trails.

creative route finding and a couple of rural road walks, you could use this as a route to the traditional communities of Chimayo and Cordova on the "high road" to Taos.

Our hike is a very nice introduction to the Sangre De Cristo Mountains, and at about 4 miles it is considerably shorter than 22 miles. The trailhead is at the northern boundary of Hyde Memorial State Park. There is no sign on NM 475 for the trailhead. The only hint of a trailhead is a small paved parking area on the left side of the road. One indicator for knowing that you are at the right place is a small low sign saying LEAVING HYDE MEM. STATE PARK on the right side of the road. If you are not paying attention, you are likely to blow by the trailhead without knowing what you're missing.

The trailhead is at the far end of the parking area and has a sign with a trail map. The Borrego Trail (150) goes down a few dirt steps to descend into a thick fir and aspen forest. In about 0.5 mile, you'll reach a junction with Bear Wallow Trail (182). Bear Wallow is part of our route, and you can hike it now or wait to hike it on your return. The description in this book continues on Borrego and returns on Bear Wallow.

Up to now the Borrego Trail has been a wide track through the woods. Soon after the junction with Bear Wallow, there will be brush blocking access to the traditional wide route. To your right will be a well-defined and newer trail. The Borrego Trail has been rerouted here for resource protection. Don't worry; the new trail will rejoin the traditional route farther up.

The hike continues to be a very pleasant walk as it begins climbing to cross a ridge into a new drainage. There will be some switchbacks along the way and a few glimpses of the old route every now and then. Once you cross the ridge, the trail trends downhill to Tesuque Creek. You'll start seeing ponderosa pines joining the mix of trees as you get lower in elevation and reach the creek after 1.5 miles of hiking from the trailhead.

Just before you reach the creek, you'll see a smaller trail going off to the right that goes through a large log that has been cut to accommodate the trail. You are always welcome to walk in the creek, but it is much easier to take the trail on the right and follow it over a bridge. The bridge was built to make it easier for mountain bikers.

Borrego Trail

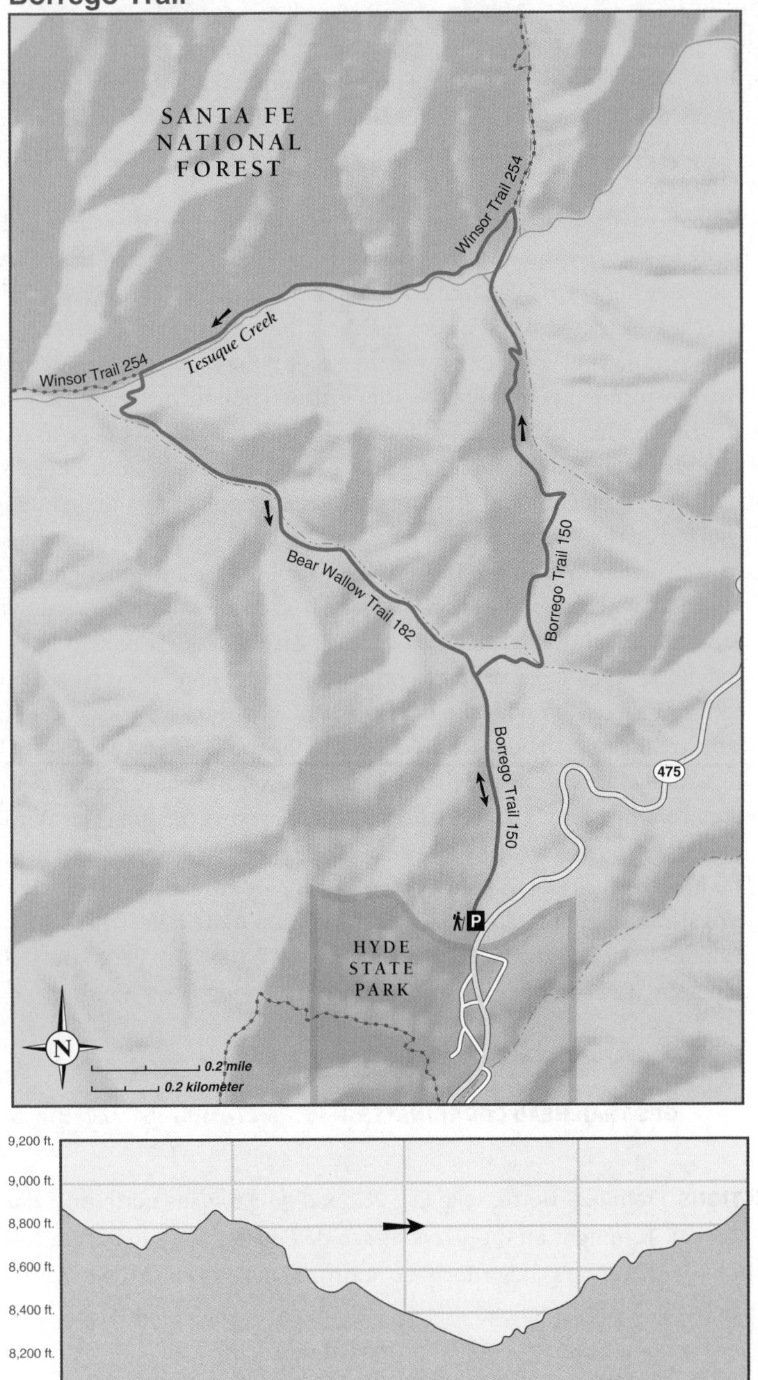

When you cross the bridge, keep going. You'll pass through a beautiful ponderosa meadow almost immediately. Very soon you'll be climbing to the bank of Tesuque Creek to join the Winsor Trail (254). Turn left (south) on the Winsor Trail to follow it downstream along Tesuque Creek. The Borrego Trail turns right (north) to share the route of the Winsor Trail until the two trails go their separate ways at Pacheco Canyon Road in around 2 miles.

Winsor is an important trail that begins north of Santa Fe in the village of Tesuque. It generally follows Tesuque Creek up to the Santa Fe Ski Basin and then climbs over a ridge to enter the Pecos Wilderness. From there it continues through the wilderness until it reaches the trailhead at Winsor Creek near the settlement of Cowles on the Pecos River. The Winsor Trail is the gateway to the Pecos Wilderness for Hikes 31 and 32.

With our planned hike following the Winsor Trail downstream, we'll be going through a predominantly ponderosa forest with the creek down below us to the left. Along the way there will be some openings of ponderosa parkland. There is a good chance that you'll meet mountain bikers, as this is a popular mountain biking route. After walking on the Winsor for about 0.8 mile you will have descended 300 feet and reached your junction with the Bear Wallow Trail (182). The junction has two log benches where you can grab a snack and take in the views of the creek down below and the mountains above. It's hard to beat the peacefulness of this setting.

From here, you'll cross the creek on a small bridge and follow the Bear Wallow Trail back to its junction with the Borrego Trail. You'll then backtrack on the Borrego to the trailhead. It's about 1.5 miles back to the trailhead and a gain of 650 feet in elevation. Along the way there will be fabulous views, and you'll get to see the forest transition from ponderosa back to the fir–aspen forest at the top. The Winsor Trail continues along the creek to Tesuque.

This hike has the right mixture of views, changing vegetation, climbs, and peacefulness to always keep it interesting. And if you want more miles, there are plenty of opportunities to extend the hike. Plus, the drive on NM 475 to get to the trailhead is not too shabby. The combination of all of them makes for a very nice day.

GPS TRAILHEAD COORDINATES N35° 44.770' W105° 50.059'

DIRECTIONS From I-25 North, take Exit 282 and go 3.6 miles north on Saint Francis Drive (US 84). Turn right on the *second* Paseo de Peralta. (It's a loop.) Go east 1 mile, then turn left on Bishop's Lodge Road. Go north 0.18 mile and turn right on Artists Road, which becomes Hyde Park Road (NM 475). Continue 8.5 miles. Parking is just north of the Hyde Memorial State Park border on the left side of the road.

25 CAÑADA DE LA CUEVA

If you still have energy after your hike, you can also explore the top of the canyon.

AN UNOFFICIAL yet intuitive route follows a dry wash across seldom-visited terrain in the hill country of the Galisteo Basin. Steep rock walls punctuate 20 twists and turns in this fascinating segment of the Cañada de la Cueva.

DESCRIPTION

The Galisteo Basin, as defined by the Galisteo Creek watershed, encompasses approximately 470,000 acres spanning northeast to the Sangre de Cristo Mountains, southwest to San Pedro Mountain, and reaching as far west as the Rio Grande near its confluence with the Santa Fe River.

This vast lowland is a sag in the earth's crust formed where rock layers are depressed and thickened. Runoff from surrounding mountains flows into the basin and carves numerous arroyos, creeks, and cañadas. Throughout New Mexico's fractured landscape, many places use the Spanish word *cañada* to describe a gulch or shallow ravine made by erosion or by volcanic activity.

A 3.3-mile segment of the Cañada de la Cueva snakes diagonally across 2,000 acres of Bureau of Land Management (BLM) land east of the Turquoise Trail and a bit south of Santa Fe. With its obscure trailhead, Cañada de la Cueva is almost like

DISTANCE & CONFIGURATION: 7.4-mile out-and-back

DIFFICULTY: Moderate

SCENERY: Sinuous arroyos, piñon–juniper hills, views of Sangre de Cristo and Jemez Mountains

EXPOSURE: Some canyon shade

TRAIL TRAFFIC: Low

TRAIL SURFACE: Sand

HIKING TIME: 3–4 hours

DRIVING DISTANCE: 55 miles

ELEVATION GAIN: 6,153' at trailhead; 5,850' at low point

ACCESS: Year-round; no fees or permits required

WHEELCHAIR ACCESS: No

MAPS: USGS *Picture Rock*

FACILITIES: None

CONTACT: BLM–Taos Field Office, blm.gov/office/taos-field-office, 575-758-8851

LOCATION: East of Cerrillos

COMMENTS: This route follows an intermittent stream that can be hazardous with heavy rainfall. Leashed dogs are allowed on trails.

LAST-CHANCE FOOD/GAS: Restaurants in Madrid, 10 miles from the trailhead; convenience store–gas station at junction of NM 14 and NM 536, 33 miles from the trailhead

a secret hike in the Galisteo Basin. If plans turn out as expected, the Cañada will become a link in a regional network of trails.

As of this writing, the Santa Fe County Commission has approved plans to develop a network of trails in the 2,400-acre Thornton Ranch. The ranch was acquired by the county many years ago for open space and is immediately to the east of the BLM land. The county has even made an agreement with the state to include a section of State Trust land in the upcoming outdoor recreation area. Adding to the possibilities are several hundred acres of adjacent land acquired by the BLM to protect archaeology sites from development. The bottom line is that over time there will be more trails for hikers to follow and land to explore in the Galisteo Basin.

Returning to our hike, stream corridors like Cañada de la Cueva support willow, tamarisk, and cottonwood trees. They also function as convenient avenues for animal life. Local species include frogs, salamanders, antelope, bear, chipmunk, coyote, deer, fox, prairie dog, and rabbit. If you walk through the Cañada after a rain, you'll see their tracks, and they will be everywhere.

These avenues are part of a larger migration corridor for wildlife, a kind of mass-transit system that animals use to commute between the surrounding rivers and ranges. Species that prefer aerial routes depend on the flora and fauna below for rest and refueling layovers. The bird checklist includes hawks, eagles, falcons, owls, hummingbirds, and a virtual choir of songbird species.

The popularity of this wildlife corridor owes largely to the relative scarcity of humans. Though it's poised to become Santa Fe's next major subdivision, great efforts are in place to protect what lives here now, as well as things left behind by those who lived here long ago.

Archaeological surveys conducted between 2002 and 2006 turned up more than 180 sites in the vicinity. Innocent strollers would be hard pressed to distinguish any

Cañada de la Cueva

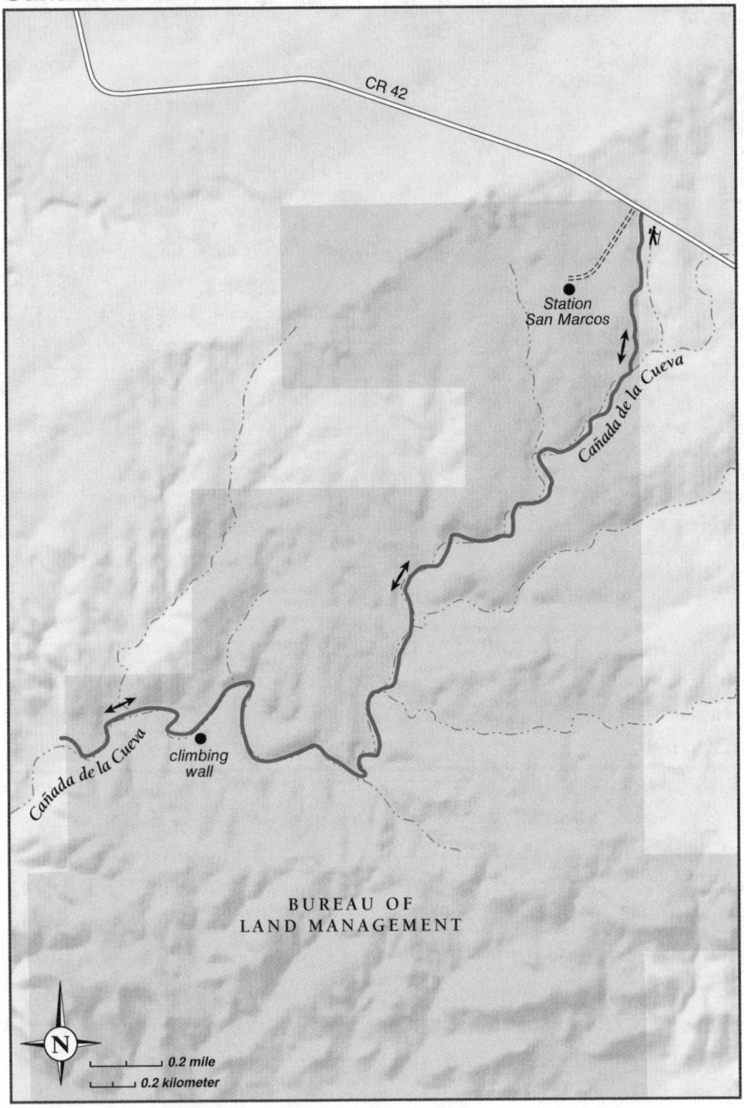

CR 42
Station San Marcos
Cañada de la Cueva
climbing wall
Cañada de la Cueva
BUREAU OF LAND MANAGEMENT
N
0.2 mile
0.2 kilometer

6,400 ft.
6,300 ft.
6,200 ft.
6,100 ft.
6,000 ft.
5,900 ft.
5,800 ft.
0.5 mi.
1 mi.
1.5 mi.
2 mi.
2.5 mi.
3 mi.
3.5 mi.

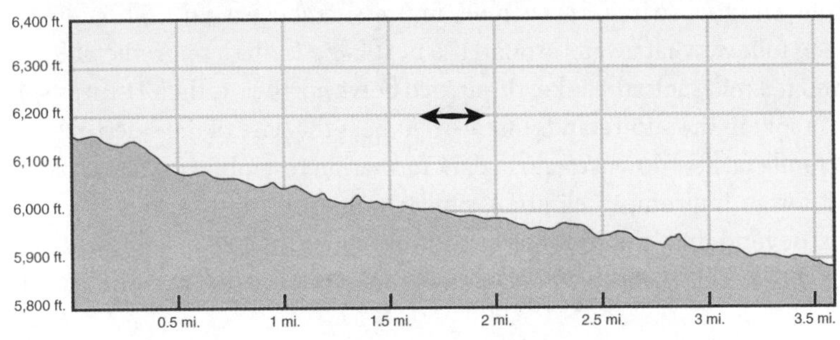

Even your four-legged friends will find plenty to check out on this hike.

one of these pueblo mounds from a hole in the ground. The route described below sticks to the streambed to avoid the inadvertent trampling of fragile ruins. If you must wander off course, please tread lightly. And remember: whatever you find there stays there.

The hike begins at the gate to Station San Marcos, a solid-waste and recycling facility. No, it's not an ideal way to kick off a backcountry trek, but rest assured the scenery soon improves. And don't worry about the fortified gate and reinforced chainlink fence. They're just there to secure the waste station. You need only step over a strand of barbed wire to access land filled with sensitive archaeological sites.

A BLM sign reading NO MOTOR VEHICLES marks the trailhead on the left side of the station gate. Start by heading due south on a faint doubletrack. You'll intersect the Cañada de la Cueva in less than half a mile. At this point the streambed is shallow and nearly 200 feet wide. Turn right and follow it downstream. Within minutes you'll pass bulging walls of rock as the arroyo narrows to 20 feet across. It soon widens again, and rock features grow more impressive at every turn. Though the route is simple to follow, what awaits around the next bend is often unpredictable.

About 3 miles into the hike, the arroyo bows northeast, then U-turns southwest. There, a solitary hoodoo stands on the right near the base of the steep, white bank. A quarter mile farther downstream, a dark formation resembling stacked blocks seems perfect for an impromptu climb. A similar wall crops up less than 0.5 mile downstream. Beyond that, the channel spreads out more than 200 feet across and fills up with chamisa. This is about where you run out of public land, according to the maps.

You may notice some fencing and gates along the banks of the arroyo indicating the end of public land (N35° 24.931' W106° 02.927'). And if you've come this far, it's time to turn back anyway. You've got nearly 4 miles to backtrack to the trailhead, and the slight upward grade on soft sand makes the return noticeably more difficult than the way down.

On the other hand, if you still have the energy, you'll find many opportunities to exit the arroyo for short scrambles to higher ground. Clifftops along the embankment are ideal for views over hilly terrain that extend to the Sangre de Cristo and Jemez mountain ranges. Additionally, several tributaries radiate from the main cañada. These tighter drainages also feature rock walls, some with caves that you might enjoy from a safe distance. (If nearby bear scat and mountain lion tracks don't deter you from entering caves, take into consideration that these rocky niches are also ideal for rattlesnakes.)

NEARBY ACTIVITIES

The Museum of New Mexico Foundation (MNMF) leads field trips to Galisteo Basin sites that are otherwise closed to the public. Check the MNMF Friends of Archaeology events calendar at museumfoundation.org, or call 505-982-6366. The Museum of Indian Arts and Culture also leads tours in the area. Check miaclab.org or call 505-476-1269. Be aware that these tours are often fully booked weeks in advance. For additional local information, visit galisteo.nmarchaeology.org and turquoisetrail.org.

GPS TRAILHEAD COORDINATES N35° 26.311' W106° 01.122'

DIRECTIONS From I-40 West, take Exit 175 (Tijeras) and go 36 miles north on NM 14. Turn right on CR 42 and go 3.8 miles east to the San Marcos Station. Park in the dirt pulloff by the gate.

26 CERRILLOS HILLS STATE PARK

You'll encounter many sealed mine shafts at Cerillos Hills State Park.

CERRILLOS HILLS STATE PARK is divided into two distinct areas. The northwest corner (**Exploratory Hike**) has an unmarked network of canyons, closed dirt roads, and horse trails that create several possibilities for extensive wandering between Waldo Canyon Road and Grand Central Mountain. The heart of the park (**Interpretive Trails**) has well-marked trails with enough interpretive signage for a dissertation on local history and geology.

DESCRIPTION

A visit to Cerrillos Hills State Park is an opportunity to walk through a thousand years of mining history. Mining began around A.D. 900, when Puebloans began working veins of blue-green stones. Believed to be an effective evil repellent, worked turquoise was strong currency in the Rio Grande Valley. Galena (lead sulfide) further boosted the mining economy when lead-glazed pottery suddenly became a hot commodity in the early 1300s. The tradition of mining continued with the Spanish and by Anglo prospectors. Most of the mines you see today date from the mining boom of 1879–1884. Large-scale mining ended when the boom collapsed. The New Mexico Abandoned Mine Land Program sealed the last of the hazardous shafts in the 1990s.

DISTANCE & CONFIGURATION: 4.5-mile balloon with spurs and 5-mile loop

DIFFICULTY: Moderate

SCENERY: Rolling hills, canyons, abandoned mines

EXPOSURE: Some canyon shade

TRAIL TRAFFIC: Moderate

TRAIL SURFACE: Sandy streambeds, dirt trails

HIKING TIME: 3 hours

DRIVING DISTANCE: 55 miles

ELEVATION GAIN: 5,678' at Exploratory trailhead; 5,689' at Interpretive trailhead; 6,300' maximum elevation

ACCESS: Daylight hours; $5/vehicle State Park Day Pass

WHEELCHAIR ACCESS: No

MAPS: State park trail map at pay station; USGS *Madrid*

FACILITIES: Restrooms (no water) at main parking area

CONTACT: nmparks.com, 505-474-0196; BLM–Taos Field Office, 575-758-8851

LOCATION: Cerrillos

COMMENTS: Leashed dogs are allowed on trails.

LAST-CHANCE FOOD/GAS: Convenience store–gas station at junction of NM 14 and NM 536, about 26 miles south and 7 miles north of Cerrillos; café and bar in Cerrillos

In 2000 the Santa Fe County Open Space Division acquired 1,100 acres of land in the Cerrillos Hills area that became Cerrillos Hills Historic Park in 2003 and a state park in 2009. The county is still acquiring land and has plans to expand the trail network.

In the meantime, two hike routes are described for the park. Both hikes require a daily $5 park pass, which can be at purchased at the main parking area.

Exploratory Hike: This hike is on the west side of the park. The road to the trailhead crosses 500 feet of private land before reaching the park boundary. At press time, the trailhead road is open to park visitors, but there is always the possibility that an owner could close the road.

The hike follows the road into the canyon. There are park signs and a cable gate at the mouth of the canyon. The scenery changes dramatically inside the steep-walled canyon, as it is shady and has fabulous rock formations. In around 0.75 mile you'll pass a series of low rock dams built to rehabilitate a small spring. At 1.5 miles into the hike there will be a road going off to the left (N35° 27.756' W106° 07.562'). To the right is a cable gate and a NO TRESPASSING sign.

Turn left (northwest) and follow the road out of the arroyo to an open landscape of interwoven dirt roads and horse trails. You'll soon pass the park boundary and enter Bureau of Land Management (public) land.

You'll pass more mine openings (now filled in or covered and safe to explore) than you can count. With so many holes you'll think you're in the middle of a prairie dog colony. Can you imagine what this area was like when all the mines were active?

As for the hike, continue uphill about 0.1 mile and go right at the Y-junction. About the same distance ahead, a horse trail starts on the left. You can cut the distance of this hike by turning now. Otherwise, continue another 0.1 mile. Three wooden posts propped up in rock piles are claim markers. The road from here fades

Cerrillos Hills State Park

BUREAU OF LAND MANAGEMENT
claim markers
CR 59
private property
Escalante Trail
Mirador
Mirador Trail
Cortez Mine Trail
Coyote Trail
Elkins Canyon Trail
Escalante Trail
Jane Calvin Sanchez Trail
CERRILLOS HILLS STATE PARK
Camino Turquesa
Waldo Canyon Road
private property
CR 59
Yerba Buena Road
N
0.2 mile
0.2 kilometer

6,600 ft.
6,400 ft.
6,200 ft.
6,000 ft.
5,800 ft.
5,600 ft.
5,400 ft.
interpretive trail
exploratory trail
1 mi.
2 mi.
3 mi.
4 mi.
5 mi.

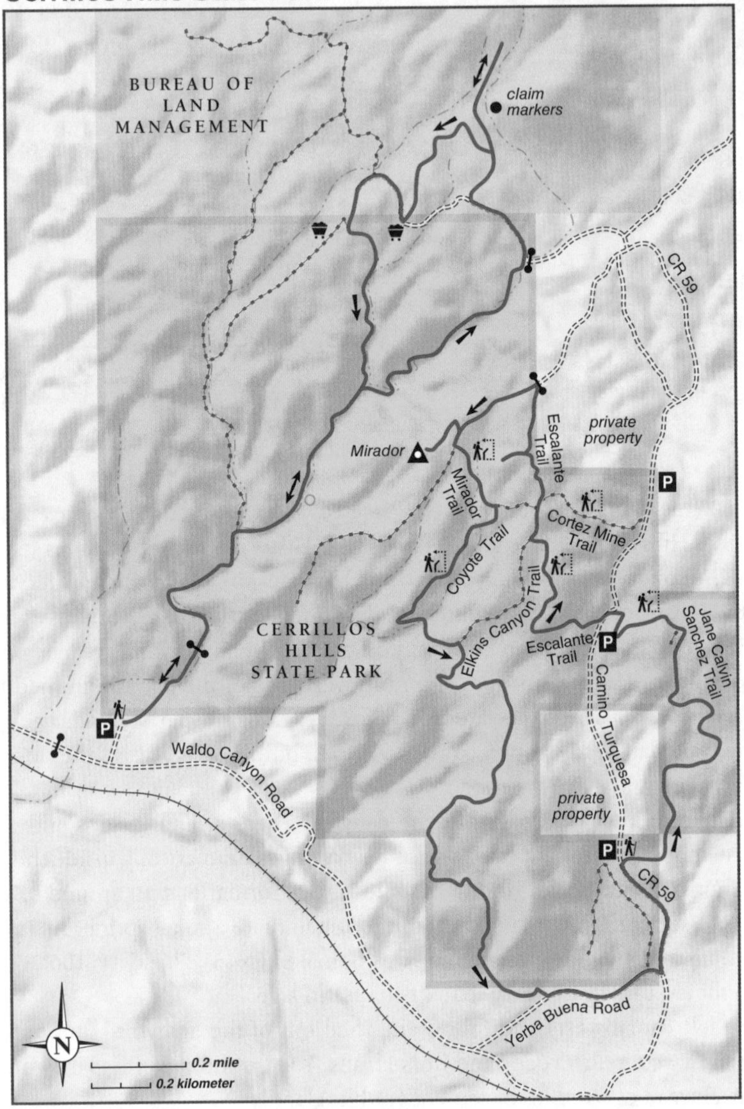

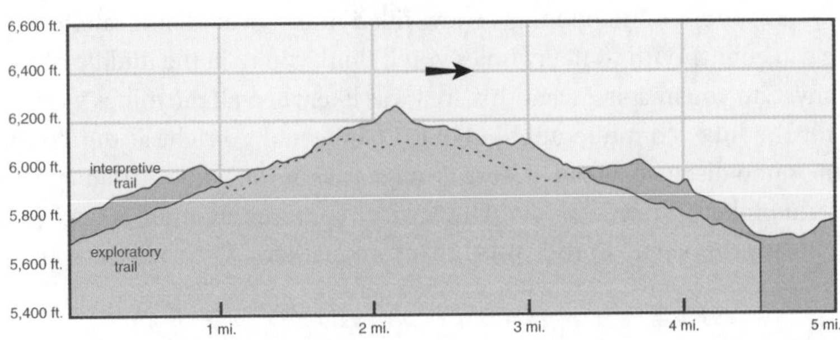

fast as it climbs the mountain. Less than 0.25 mile past the claim markers, down in the arroyo on the left, is a boarded mine that's losing its battle against the elements. Anywhere here is a good place to turn around to return to the horse trail that we passed earlier (N35° 27.941' W106° 07.626').

The tall hill that you've been walking toward is Grand Central Mountain. The county is in the process of buying private mining claims on the side of the hill so they can build a trail to the top.

When you reach the horse trail, turn right to cut back to the northwest. The trail winds around several old mines as it curves around to the south. In about 0.35 mile, the trail will reach an old road. Turn right again to cut back to the northwest. The route circles back to the south and passes more mines. Here the road becomes a trail. Go straight ahead on the trail. In around 300 feet, there will be another trail (N35° 27.806' W106° 07.945') going off to your left (east) and down into an arroyo.

From here the navigation is easy. Just follow the arroyo all the way back to the main canyon. Once in the main canyon, turn right and head 1 mile back to the trailhead to complete a very nice 4.5-mile hike.

Interpretive Trails: This hike begins at the main trailhead. To get there from Cerrillos, cross the railroad tracks and drive another 0.25 mile to the Y. Bear left onto County Road 59 (Camino Turquesa) and go 0.5 mile north, following the signs for Cerrillos Hills State Park.

The interpretive trails amount to a seminar in New Mexico culture and natural history. Only instead of a sleep-inducing lecture hall, the classroom is rolling terrain with scenic vistas, high-desert wildlife, and historic mines. A recommended 4.8-mile loop starts at the trailhead across the road from the main parking area. Begin on the steep, wide Jane Calvin Sanchez Trail. Within 1 mile, you'll pass three fenced mine shafts then descend to the springs on Camino Turquesa.

Turn left and head down the road about 60 yards to pick up Escalante Trail on the right. After a steep 0.5-mile climb past Cortez Mine Trail, look left for a 60-yard spur to Escalante View, the highest point on this route.

Return to the main trail and continue 0.1 mile north to a fence that crosses the road. Take a sharp left before the gate and follow signs to the Mirador. A sign there identifies the many mountain peaks and ranges in view.

From the Mirador, return to the main trail and turn right. Within the 0.5-mile descent ahead, four mines dot the trailside. Protective mesh allows you to gape into each one without the risk of falling in. When the trail starts uphill again, you have slightly more than a 0.5-mile climb before the sharp drop into Elkins Canyon.

At the canyon floor, turn right and follow the streambed trail as it squeezes through a rocky chute. When you emerge from the south end, take the first path on the left and follow a 300-yard easement to Yerba Buena Road (CR 59A). Turn left on this dirt road and go 0.25 mile to Camino Turquesa. Turn left again to go north past the cemetery and return to the parking area.

NEARBY ACTIVITIES

For more local lore and information on Cerrillos and the mines, visit the Casa Grande Trading Post and Mining Museum, at the west end of Waldo Street in Cerrillos. Call 505-438-3008 or visit casagrandetradingpost.com.

Madrid, New Mexico, is only a few minutes south on NM 14 from Cerillos. With bars, shops, and places to eat, it is always worth a stop. Madrid became a ghost town after its coal mines closed in the 1950s and was revived when artists and other creative people started moving in during the late 1960s.

• •

GPS TRAILHEAD COORDINATES N35° 26.958' W106° 08.443'

DIRECTIONS From I-40 East, take Exit 175 toward Cedar Crest. From the I-40 overpass, go 32 miles north on NM 14 and turn left onto Main Street toward Cerrillos. Once in the village, turn right at the first stop sign onto First Street. Cross the railroad tracks, take an immediate left onto CR 57 (Waldo Canyon Road), and go 1.3 miles northwest. (If you cross a cattle guard after the horseshoe curve, you've gone about 0.15 mile too far.) Turn right onto an unmarked dirt road, drive about 500 feet north to a state park boundary sign, and park by the gravel pit on the left.

Alternate route (50 miles): From I-25 North, take Exit 267 and turn right on CR 57. Drive 6.5 miles south-southeast, then look for the unmarked dirt road on the left about 0.15 mile past the cattle guard. Note that most of Waldo Canyon Road is unpaved and can get tricky in wet weather.

27 DIABLO CANYON-BUCKMAN

The sheer basalt faces of Diablo Canyon make it a popular spot for rock climbers and filmmakers.

TWO HIKES ARE featured at the northern end of the Caja del Rio Plateau. One is an awesome stroll through Diablo Canyon. The other is a longer hike into the always impressive White Rock Canyon. The combined hikes make for a wonderful day in a remote area west of Santa Fe.

DESCRIPTION

The Diablo Canyon–Buckman area hikes explore the Santa Fe side of White Rock Canyon near the long-gone lumber town of Buckman on the east side of the Rio Grande. Even though the area is less than 16 miles from the plaza in Santa Fe, most of it feels very remote. Reaching this area includes a 10.2-mile drive on Old Buckman Road as it skirts around the northern edge of the Caja del Rio Plateau.

Although it's unpaved, Old Buckman Road is significant. It is Santa Fe's easiest and quickest route to the Rio Grande. It follows the path of the Camino Real heading north out of Santa Fe and is the same route used by Juan de Oñate when he established the Spanish colony of New Mexico in 1598. The Denver and Rio Grande Western Railroad followed this corridor for its narrow gauge rail line from Santa Fe to Colorado. The railway was oftentimes referred to as the Chili Line, and you can still see parts of its former right-of-way along the road. The City of Santa Fe has 13

DISTANCE & CONFIGURATION: 2-mile out-and-back at Diablo Canyon; 6-mile out-and-back at Buckman

DIFFICULTY: Easy, Diablo Canyon; moderate, Buckman

SCENERY: Basalt canyon, high-desert chaparral, seasonal wildflowers, river gorge, volcanic mesas

EXPOSURE: Mostly sunny

TRAIL TRAFFIC: Moderate

TRAIL SURFACE: Dirt, sand, rock

HIKING TIME: 1 hour, Diablo Canyon; 3 hours, Buckman

DRIVING DISTANCE: 76 miles from the Big I

ELEVATION GAIN: 5,843' at Diablo trailhead, 5,678' at end of canyon; 5,440' at Buckman trailhead, 5,608' at high point

ACCESS: Year-round; no fees or permits required

WHEELCHAIR ACCESS: No

MAPS: Santa Fe National Forest–West Half; USGS *White Rock*

FACILITIES: Pit toilets

LOCATION: West of Santa Fe

COMMENTS: Leashed dogs are allowed on trails.

CONTACT: Santa Fe National Forest–Española District, fs.usda.gov/santafe, 505-753-7331; Bureau of Land Management–Taos Field Office, blm.gov/office/taos-field-office, 575-758-8851

LAST-CHANCE FOOD/GAS: Convenience store–gas station on Airport Road, 0.25 mile east of NM 599 (20 miles from trailhead)

water wells and a pipeline from the river in the corridor to fulfill much of its drinking water needs. Because of the pipeline, Old Buckman Road is open year-round. The road has a few soft, sandy spots, especially as you get closer to the river, but is generally well maintained and drivable. It can get bumpy if it hasn't been graded in a while.

You'll see **Diablo Canyon** in around 7.5 miles. You can't miss it. It's the massive split basalt formation just off to the left in front of you. You'll also see a Bureau of Land Management (BLM) sign for the Diablo Canyon Recreation Area. Turn left and follow the road to the parking area.

Diablo Canyon is a must-do attraction that you'll want to check out. It's an easy hike into and back from the canyon. If you hike the entire length of the canyon, you'll have a 2-mile out-and-back hike. The sheer basalt faces and other features make it a popular spot for rock climbers and moviemakers. The opening stagecoach ambush scene in the 2007 film *3:10 to Yuma* was filmed in the canyon.

The hike is quite simple. Just follow the path along the fenceline from the parking area into the broad gravel arroyo of Cañada Ancha. There is an information sign at the trailhead with a map and a picture of some of the climbing routes. Once in the arroyo, follow it into the canyon. You'll be amazed at the massiveness of the basalt walls on both sides of the canyon. There is a good chance that you'll see some water in a few places where the underground stream has reached the surface. It's not a lot of water, but it is some.

When you've had enough, just turn around and return to your car. If you want, you can follow the arroyo all the way to the river, but that would be anticlimactic, as the main attraction is clearly the canyon. You'll be driving down to the river for a hike along the Rio Grande when you get back to the car.

Diablo Canyon–Buckman

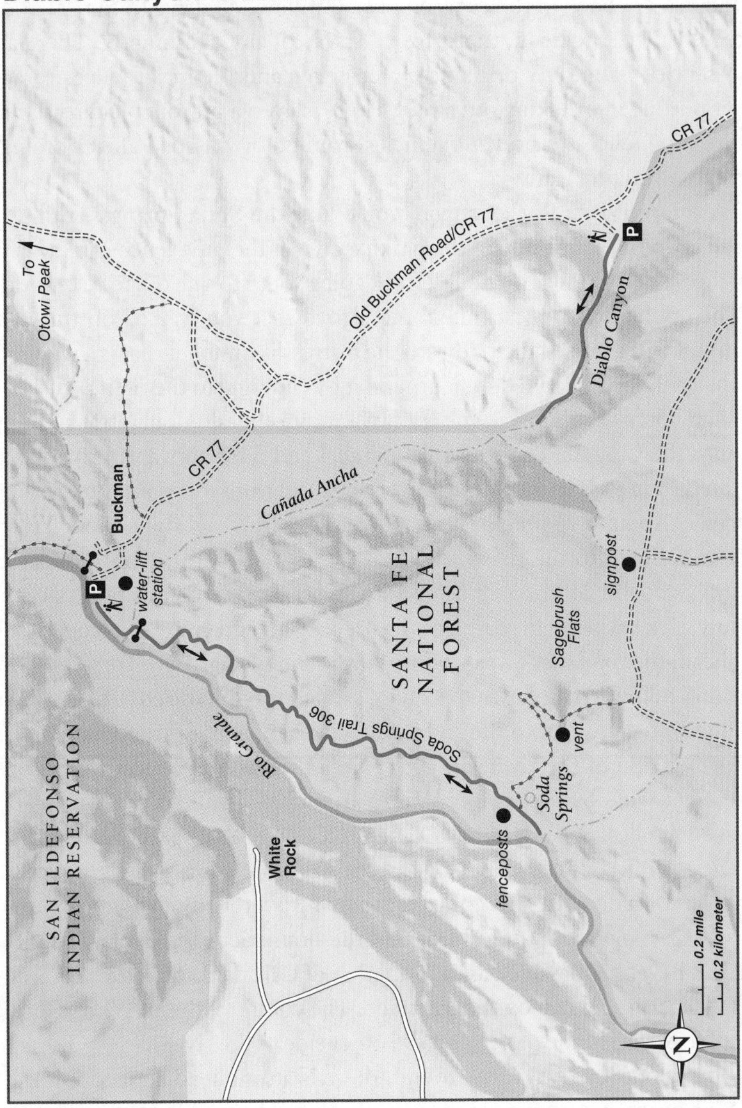

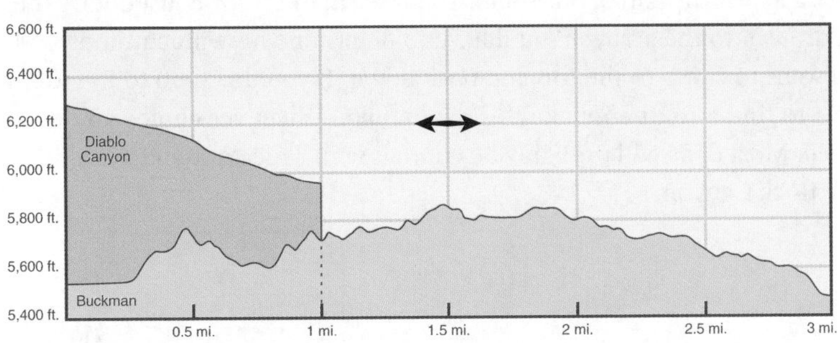

Once you're back in the car it's only a 3-mile or so drive to the river. Although the area is called Buckman, there are no traces of any community. There are buildings to service Santa Fe's drinking water needs and plenty of places to access the river for putting in or taking out a raft. There is even a pit toilet facility. Even better, there are pipe fences to prevent vehicles from going off-road and zooming around the arroyos or hiking trails.

To explore White Rock Canyon, you'll take the **Soda Springs Trail (306)**. The trailhead is on the south side of the parking area at the pipe fence gate near the river. The first part of the trail is on doubletrack going south to one of the waterworks buildings. The doubletrack crosses the same arroyo that you walked on through Diablo Canyon and will climb a hill up toward the fortresslike bunker that is a well. When you reach the well, the trail will detour around it by climbing to the right.

When you clear the well, the trail will rejoin the old doubletrack and continue south into the canyon. The trail runs parallel and a bit above the river over rolling hills. You'll soon pass under some power lines and from this point on the hike will be very scenic. About 0.25 mile past the power lines, the trail splits. Bear left (the right branch goes down to the river). About 0.1 mile past that, the trail forks again; this time turn right (the left branch drops into an arroyo). From this point on, the way is clear. Just stick to the main road, put the book away, and enjoy the scenery. About 2.3 miles ahead, the road dies out as it drops into a wooded arroyo. Turn right before the arroyo, and follow a path down to a quiet, shaded spot on the edge of the Rio Grande.

When you get down to the river, you'll be right across from Hike 34 (page 185) on the other side of the river. To get to the other side of a river that is only a few hundred feet wide by car would require around a 40-mile drive. At this point you have hiked 3 miles. For our hike we'll be returning the same we way came to look at the scenery from a different perspective. If you time your hike right, you might be sharing the solitude with migrating cranes flying overhead. If you miss crane season, you'll still have plenty of other birds and the dramatic features of White Rock Canyon. You'll have the massive basalt formation of Caja del Rio on the east side and the towering Pajarito Plateau on the west side. The communities of White Rock and Los Alamos are on top of the plateau on the other side of the river.

If you're not ready to turn around, there is a trail heading east toward the face of the Caja near the end of our route. You'll see markers for it just before the doubletrack drops into the arroyo. You'll have to determine how much time you have and if you want to climb to the top and back down. If you do climb to the top, you may be able to find a route to make this a loop hike. Whatever choice you make, it will be steep. Most of us will probably be content with a nice out-and-back hike through White Rock Canyon.

NEARBY ACTIVITIES

In the summer of 2018, the Santa Fe County Open Space Division, along with the BLM and U.S. Forest Service, opened a multipurpose trail near Old Buckman Road to retrace the Camino Real. The trail has several access points and connects Diablo Canyon with the plaza in Santa Fe. The trail incorporates parts of the old Chili Line right-of-way.

GPS TRAILHEAD COORDINATES N35° 50.139' W106° 09.719' (Buckman)

DIRECTIONS From I-25 North, take Exit 276 and go 9.8 miles northeast on Veterans Memorial Highway (NM 599). Exit at Camino La Tierra, turn left, and go 4.8 miles northwest. Turn right off pavement onto Old Buckman Road and continue 10 miles northwest to the water-lift station. (It resembles a small prison in a sinkhole. You'll know it when you see it.) Bear left and follow the road 0.25 mile to a wide sandy wash. Park on either side of the wash and continue following the road uphill on foot. The hike begins at the gate about 100 feet south of the wash.

You can extend your hike by following trails to the top of Caja del Rio.

28 HYDE MEMORIAL STATE PARK

The waterfall at Hyde Memorial State Park is well worth the 30-minute detour.

AN OLD FAVORITE at the southernmost tip of the Rockies is a short drive from the Santa Fe Plaza. The nostalgic campgrounds in Hyde Memorial State Park attract wildflower enthusiasts in the summer and aspen lovers in the fall, whereas winter crowds come for the sledding, snowshoeing, and cross-country skiing.

DESCRIPTION

On this loop, the segment on the west side of the road boasts the better views, but it's a steep mile up, followed by a steep mile down. For an easier hike, stick to the lower, shadier trails on the east side of the road. Start up the stepped trail near the northeast corner of the visitor center to follow the route counterclockwise. Pressed for time? Enjoy a 1.7-mile out-and-back to the waterfall.

To follow the route clockwise, as described here, start by locating the trailhead directly across Hyde Park Road. The trail starts out deceptively quaint, with a wooden fence by the roadside, a rock border, and a stone bridge over Little Tesuque Creek. On the far side of the bridge are an interpretive sign and a black mailbox that (sometimes) contains trail brochures.

Take a moment here to limber up, giving the calves and hamstrings an extra stretch. The first mile is like a good workout on a StairMaster, only far more scenic.

DISTANCE & CONFIGURATION: 3.3-mile loop

DIFFICULTY: Moderate–strenuous

SCENERY: Campgrounds, views of Santa Fe from 9,400 feet, evergreen, alder, aspen

EXPOSURE: Mostly shaded

TRAIL TRAFFIC: Popular

TRAIL SURFACE: Fine gravel, rock

HIKING TIME: 2.5 hours

DRIVING DISTANCE: 68 miles from the Big I

ELEVATION GAIN: 8,395' at trailhead; 9,408' at summit

ACCESS: Day-use activities: 6 a.m.–9 p.m.; gate hours: 8 a.m.–10 p.m.; $5/vehicle or New Mexico State Parks Annual Pass

WHEELCHAIR ACCESS: No; wheelchair access in picnic area and campgrounds

MAPS: Trail maps available at visitor center and trailhead; USGS *McClure Reservoir*

FACILITIES: Water, restrooms, campsites, RV hookups, picnic shelters, grills

CONTACT: nmparks.com, 505-983-7175

LOCATION: Santa Fe

COMMENTS: Leashed dogs are allowed on trails.

You ascend from a lush creekside forest to thinner stands of fir and pine as the trail climbs steadily from an elevation of 8,400 to just over 9,400 feet. It seems longer than a mile, and maybe it is if you count backsliding on loose gravel. Multiple switchbacks contribute to the illusion that the top is just around the bend. Park benches near the 0.25- and 0.75-mile marks provide brief respites from exertion.

Keep an eye out for garter snakes and horned lizards prowling through the pine needles. Black bear, mule deer, and porcupine also inhabit the area but are rarely sighted. A favorite among the summer wildflowers is scarlet gilia, or skyrocket. Oregon grape blooms in the spring and resembles holly with blueberry clusters when it ripens in the late summer. The plant is better known for its medicinal uses than for its snacking value. The berries are edible, though bitter, and children have been known to feel queasy after eating a few. You'd be better off foraging for wild strawberries.

You know you're near the top when the rocks begin to sparkle with mica. When the trail finally does level off, push on just another 0.25 mile. Past an area of storm-felled trees you will find two picnic tables and the best views in the park. Santa Fe sits near to the west, while the Jemez Mountains make up the bulk of the shadowy heaps in the distance.

When you're ready to continue, follow the arrow back down the mountain through another course of switchbacks. Some impatient hikers have trampled shortcuts straight down—refrain from following in their footsteps.

A signpost on an otherwise unmarked fork turns up about 2 miles into the hike. This is *not* the small loop seen on park maps. Instead, the left fork leads to the RV area. Unless you need the shortest route to the restrooms, avoid the detour.

The trail turns south and leads you to a fork with signs indicating that the left branch belongs to the Circle Trail and the right is the Girl Scout Trail. Both paths feature rock borders and labeled plants. They end up in the same place, though the Girl Scout Trail is slightly longer. The history of the Scouts in this area predates the founding of Hyde Park. Benjamin Hyde, affectionately known as Uncle Bennie,

Hyde Memorial State Park

475
Little Tesuque Creek
Girl Scout Trail
Piggyback Trail
SANTA FE NATIONAL FOREST
East Circle Trail
Waterfall Trail
West Circle Trail
Hyde Park Road
HYDE MEMORIAL STATE PARK
475
visitor center
lodge
N
0.2 mile
0.2 kilometer

9,600 ft.
9,400 ft.
9,200 ft.
9,000 ft.
8,800 ft.
8,600 ft.
8,400 ft.
0.5 mi.
1 mi.
1.5 mi.
2 mi.
2.5 mi.
3 mi.

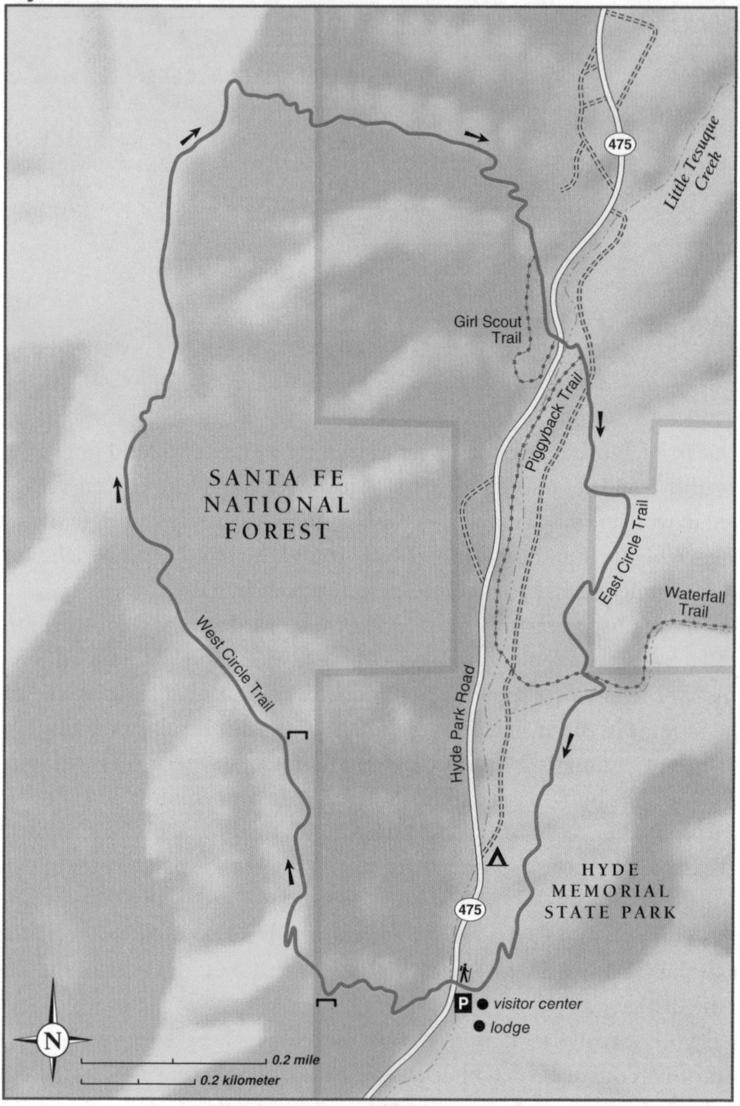

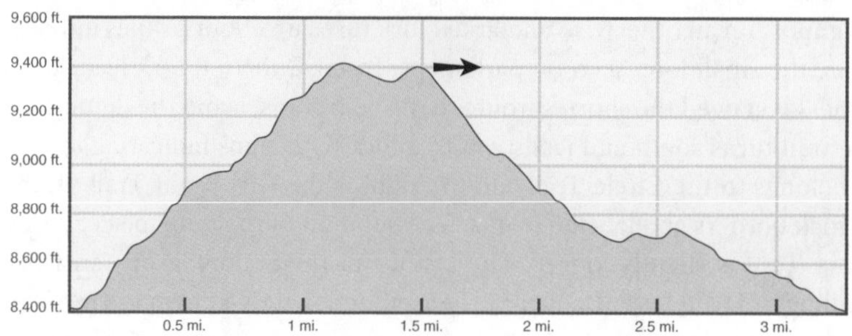

became Santa Fe's scoutmaster shortly after moving to town in 1927. His wife, Helen, bequeathed the land to the state in the year following his untimely death in 1933.

You soon return to Hyde Park Road, about 0.7 mile north of where you began. Cross back over the road. Park maps show a skating pond in this vicinity, but warm winters in recent years may see it soon replaced with an amphitheater. In any case, look for a nearby bridge, followed by a staircase in the embankment. At the top of the stairs are an Adirondack shelter and, beyond that, a dirt road. Straight across the road is a trail sign showing two hiker icons. If you don't find it, follow the dirt road south, passing campsites en route back to the lodge. The trail runs parallel to the road and offers a bit more seclusion, though you may still be able to spot campsites through the trees, hear campers' songs, and smell what's cooking on the grills. The area is mellower when the main camping loop closes for the winter (November 1–Easter).

About 0.25 mile into the upper trail, or 2.7 miles into the hike, you'll reach an unmarked fork. The branch continuing straight is the old Waterfall Trail. Veer right here to stay on the Circle Trail and go downhill toward the Group Shelter 2 area. A small black sign behind the group shelter indicates where Circle Trail resumes, and another sign shows where the new Waterfall Trail begins. This 0.25-mile spur is a cool side trip up a shady little canyon. Routed to follow a rocky stream, the riparian path seems a world away from the rest of the park. Though it flows only after heavy rains or snowmelt, it's well worth a 30-minute detour, even when it lacks a waterfall.

To continue on Circle Trail, return to the Waterfall trailhead and cross the wooden footbridge. At 0.25 mile or so past the bridge, a steep clearing begins to show through the trees. That's the sledding area. In the 1940s and 1950s, it was Santa Fe's first and only ski basin, complete with a towrope powered by a Cadillac engine. The structure at the base was built by the Civilian Conservation Corps in 1938 and allegedly used then as a cooking school. You'll recognize it now as Hyde Park Lodge. A couple of switchbacks take you back down to the parking area.

BONUS HIKE

Chamisa Trail (183) Trailhead is 2 miles west (heading toward Santa Fe) of the Circle Trail on the right (north) side of NM 475. It was near this trail that Tim McElvain, a retired geologist, found what he believed to be a shatter cone from meteor impact event in 2005. Even though all evidence of a crater eroded away millions of years ago, additional research has confirmed that there was an impact event in this area. The evidence is the distortions in the rock caused by the impact. You can check out the evidence for yourself by examining the rock faces along the Chamisa Trail. At the same time you can take in a nice easy to moderate 2.3-mile loop by going out on the lower Chamisa Trail and returning on the upper trail. If you wish to extend your hike, you can connect to the Winsor Trail (254) and hike for days. Doing both the Circle Trail and Chamisa Trail on the same trip makes for a great day of hiking.

NEARBY ACTIVITIES

Hyde Park is the gateway to endless opportunities for outdoor recreation. Start by driving north 8.4 miles on Hyde Park Road, also known as the Santa Fe National Forest Scenic Byway. (Hikes 24, 31, and 32 are along this road.) It ends at the Santa Fe Ski Area, near the southwest corner of the vast Pecos Wilderness. The Hyde Park Visitor Center has all the information you need for exploring this corner of Santa Fe National Forest.

• •

GPS TRAILHEAD COORDINATES N35° 43.834' W105° 50.221'

DIRECTIONS From I-25 North, take Exit 282 and go 3.6 miles north on Saint Francis Drive (US 84). Turn right on the *second* Paseo de Peralta. (It's a loop.) Go east 1 mile, then turn left on Bishop's Lodge Road. Go north 0.18 mile and turn right on Artists Road, which becomes Hyde Park Road (NM 475). Continue 7.4 miles and turn right at the Hyde Memorial State Park Visitor Center and Lodge. Park near the lodge and pay at the station next to the visitor center.

29 LA CIENEGUILLA PETROGLYPH SITE AND CAÑON

From the mesa top, you can look down on the petroglyphs or back toward Santa Fe.

TWO HIKES ARE featured in this timeless area southwest of Santa Fe. The first explores the spectacular La Cieneguilla Petroglyph Site, and the other includes a peaceful moment along the Santa Fe River and then climbs to the top of a 500-foot hill.

DESCRIPTION

The Santa Fe River valley southwest of Santa Fe was a route of the Camino Real and is home to many archaeological sites and early Spanish settlements. It is also home to two very nice and sometimes spectacular hikes on Bureau of Land Management (BLM) land. When you get off the interstate you'll be passing through a quiet corner of New Mexico with settlements that might remind you of Milagro, the fictional hamlet of John Nichols's *Beanfield* trilogy.

The hike at **La Cieneguilla Petroglyph Site** has over 4,000 fantastic petroglyphs concentrated in one small area. It is a must-do hike. There is a BLM parking lot and information kiosk on the west side of County Road 56 (Paseo Real) with a 0.5-mile approach trail to the escarpment with the petroglyphs.

There are primitive trails that let you work your way through the huge basalt rocks to give you a closer look at one petroglyph after another. Almost every rock

DISTANCE & CONFIGURATION: 2- and 3-mile out-and-back options at La Cieneguilla; 3.5-mile loop hike with spurs at Cañon

DIFFICULTY: Moderate; the climb to the top of Cerro Seguro is strenuous.

SCENERY: Amazing petroglyphs, river canyon, volcanic hills, broad mesas

EXPOSURE: Some canyon shade

TRAIL TRAFFIC: La Cieneguilla is very popular; Cañon is light.

TRAIL SURFACE: Dirt, rock

HIKING TIME: 1–2 hours at La Cieneguilla; 2.5 hours at Cañon

DRIVING DISTANCE: 54 miles from the Big I

ELEVATION GAIN: 6,153' at La Cieneguilla trailhead, 6,292' at high point; 6,114' at Cañon trailhead, 6,473' at high point

ACCESS: Year-round; no fees or permits required

MAPS: USGS *Tetilla Peak*

FACILITIES: None

CONTACT: BLM–Taos Field Office, blm.gov/office/taos-field-office, 575-758-8851

LOCATION: Southwest of Santa Fe

COMMENTS: Leashed dogs are allowed on trails.

LAST-CHANCE FOOD/GAS: Convenience store, food, gas at Exit 259, 17 miles from the trailhead

face is coated with petroglyphs. They are everywhere and have every figure and shape you can imagine. This is something you'll have to see to believe.

When you are done examining the petroglyphs, you can head back to your car or continue your hike by going to the top of the escarpment to look at the rock art from above and for incredible views of the area. The views alone are worth the extra hiking.

To reach the top of the escarpment, return to where the approach trail passes through the fenceline. Instead of returning to your car, stay on the west side of the fence and follow the trail as it arcs to the west at the base of the escarpment. The trail will enter a notch and work its way up to the north before doubling back south to reach the top. The top of the escarpment is flat and open.

From there, you can follow trails in almost every direction. For the best views and to see the petroglyphs from above, you'll want to turn left and head east to the edge of the escarpment.

The **Cañon** trip starts 3 miles south of Cieneguilla near the old settlement of Cañon. The hike drops down to the Santa Fe River, passes some old mines, and climbs to the top of Cerro Seguro. You'll find the Santa Fe River so peaceful that you might not want to leave it.

To reach the trailhead from Cieneguilla, turn right (south) from the parking lot and drive 1.5 miles south on CR 56 to CR 54A. Follow CR 54A southwest 1.5 miles. You will pass CR 54B along the way. (It goes off to the left and looks like the main route.) Stay on CR 54A. When the road turns to the right (northwest), stop and park on the left side of the road (N35° 34.626' W106° 07.884'). There is plenty of room for parking and an opening in the fence where the trail starts.

The area is primarily juniper grassland with unobstructed views and has a network of trails and dirt roads for you to follow. You'll see two trails at the fence opening. Our hike goes out on the right trail and has the option of returning on the left trail.

La Cieneguilla Petroglyph Site and Cañon

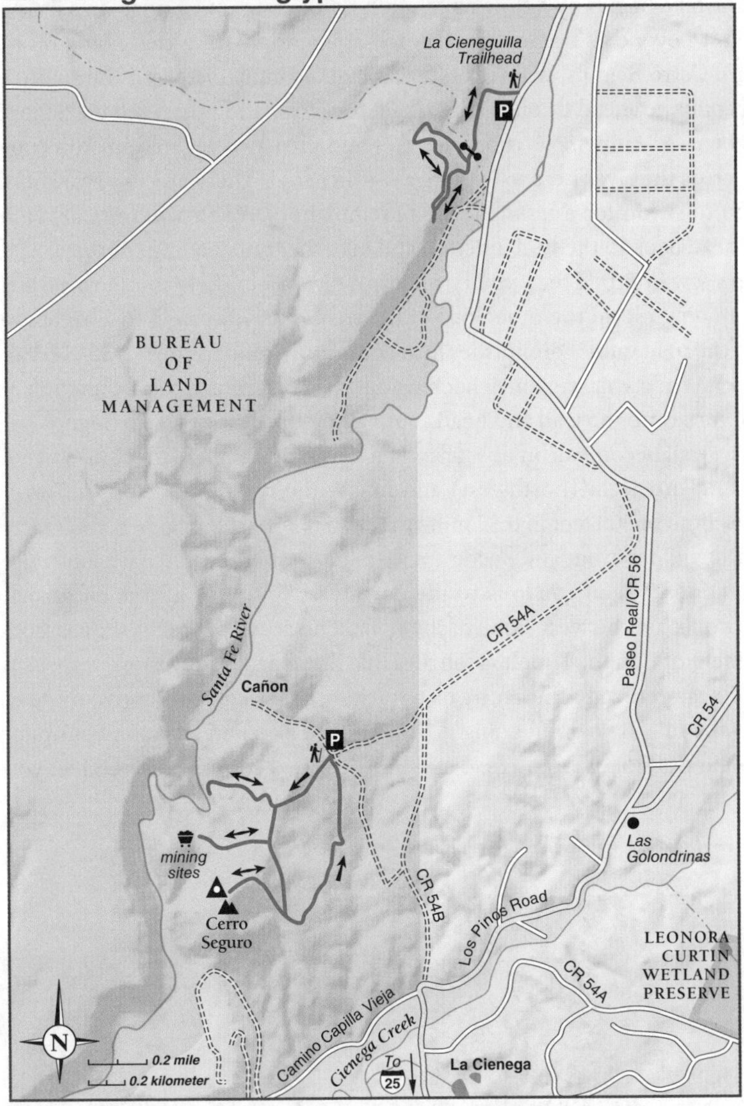

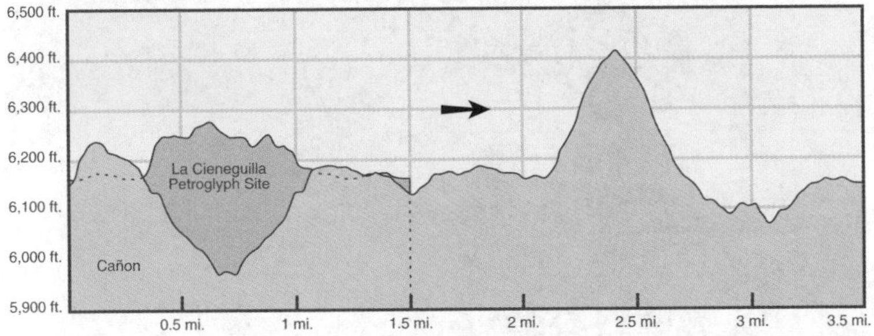

The hike begins by following the trail southwest up to a ridge. In a little over 0.25 mile, just beyond the ridge, you'll reach a junction with a trail going off to the left (south). Cerro Seguro, which you'll visit later, is immediately to the south. For now, you'll continue ahead through some great rock formations to reach the Santa Fe River.

The river canyon has running water and plenty of vegetation. You could, if you want, cross the river here to explore the other side. There are also two rock benches for you to sit on for a moment of contemplation. When you're ready to leave the river, head back to the trail junction and take the trail heading south.

In a few hundred feet, you'll run into a dirt road. There is a cairn at the junction and a mining pit on the other side of the road. For now, we'll turn right (west) and follow the road until it diminishes near some more mining sites (N35° 34.385' W106° 08.355'). When you are done checking out the area, return to the junction and make a right turn onto the trail and head south along the base of Cerro Seguro.

The trail becomes a bit obscure when it reaches an old road (N35° 34.166' W106° 08.044'). Turn right (northwest) and follow the road to the top of Cerro Seguro. With a climb of 300 feet in 0.35 mile, the road is very steep. When you reach the top, the road will peter out and become a path. From there, you'll have fantastic views in all directions. When you look to the northwest you'll see a large cross made out of white stones on the west slope of the river. The cross is directly across from the old settlement of Cañon. Timeless touches like these make New Mexico special.

You can return to the car by backtracking or take an alternative route when you get off the hill. Be careful going down. For the alternative route, continue past the outbound trail to a Y in the road and bear left. In a couple hundred feet you'll reach

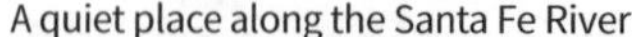
A quiet place along the Santa Fe River

another junction; turn left again to head north. In less than 0.5 mile the trail will bear to the right, and you'll come to another junction with a cairn (N35° 34.368' W106° 07.846'). Turn left and follow the trail back to your car now less than 0.5 mile away.

NEARBY ACTIVITIES

La Bajada Road was a featured hike in previous editions of this book. Because of access issues, the hike was removed from this edition. Although access from the south has been denied, you can still reach La Bajada from the north. It is 7.9 miles from La Cieneguilla parking lot. Turn left onto CR 56. In 0.1 mile, turn left again onto CR 56C. Follow 56C past the sign for the Santa Fe Ranch Recreation Area to the top of the Caja del Rio plateau. Once on top, stay on the road and drive another 7.2 miles to the end. The road is rough and subject to closures. But if you would like to see La Bajada Road, this is the way to do it.

El Rancho de las Golondrinas is a living-history museum in a 200-acre farming valley. Villagers in period clothing inhabit the original buildings, which date from the early 18th century. (Imagine a northern New Mexico version of Colonial Williamsburg, and you'll get the idea.) Hours vary by season; call 505-471-2261 or visit golondrinas.org for more information. The entrance is on Los Pinos Road, 1 mile northeast of Entrada La Cienega.

Leonora Curtin Wetland Preserve is a 35-acre preserve featuring a nature trail that winds through an open meadow to a natural ciénaga, or marsh. A second trail covers an arid upland area. Open weekends May–October (no dogs allowed). For information on hours and fees, call Santa Fe Botanical Gardens at 505-471-9103 or visit santafebotanicalgarden.org. To get there, head back to I-25 and turn left onto West Frontage Road immediately before the exit ramps. The entrance to the preserve is 1.4 miles ahead on the left.

• •

GPS TRAILHEAD COORDINATES N35° 36.519' W106° 07.196'

DIRECTIONS From I-25 North, take Exit 271. Turn left on NM 587 (Entrada La Cienega) and go north 1 mile. Turn right on CR 54 (Los Pino Road). Go 1 mile straight northeast on Los Pinos Road to where it bears north to become CR 56 (Paseo Real). Continue north another 2.8 miles. The La Cieneguilla parking lot is on the left.

30 LOWER WATER CANYON–LION CAVE TRAILS

Admire the Sangre de Cristo Mountains from Lower Water Canyon.

AN EASY MILE down a wooded canyon leads to two options. Turning right provides a scenic 2-mile loop hike back to the car. Continuing another 0.15 mile provides options to hike left or right on trails that climb gently to overlooks and rocky promontories on either rim of Water Canyon. Both options connect to other trails, which could lead to a full day of exploring this amazing landscape.

DESCRIPTION

Los Alamos County is New Mexico's smallest, with only 109 square miles, 42 of which are occupied by Los Alamos National Laboratory (LANL). Its trail network, however, is not to be taken lightly. Nearly 60 miles of official trails link canyons and mesas on the Pajarito Plateau, a rugged volcanic extension of the Jemez mountain range. Elevations on this tilted landscape range from 5,600 feet at the Rio Grande to 7,800 feet where the plateau meets the Valles Caldera.

The best-known attraction on the east side of the Pajarito Plateau is Bandelier National Monument, visited in Hike 23 (page 132). Canyons to the northeast of Bandelier, LANL land, share many of the monument's characteristics of fantastic scenery and pockmarked caves. They are as wonderful as Bandelier to explore.

Most of the canyons are open to hiking. As you drive on NM 4 from Bandelier toward White Rock, the land on the left side is actively used by the labs and is strictly

DISTANCE & CONFIGURATION: 2.2-mile loop; 5-mile loop plus spur; options for a much longer hike

DIFFICULTY: Moderate

SCENERY: Wooded canyon, sculpted rock, mesa-rim views

EXPOSURE: Half shaded

TRAIL TRAFFIC: Moderate

TRAIL SURFACE: Dirt, rock

HIKING TIME: 1.5 hours (loop); 2–3 hours (loop plus spur)

DRIVING DISTANCE: 99 miles via San Ysidro or 97 miles via White Rock from the Big I

ELEVATION GAIN: 6,425' at trailhead; 6,211' at low point; 6,484' at high point

ACCESS: Daylight hours

WHEELCHAIR ACCESS: No

MAPS: USGS *White Rock*

FACILITIES: None

CONTACT: U.S. Department of Energy/LANL, lanl.gov/trails, 505-667-3792

LOCATION: White Rock

COMMENTS: Leashed dogs are allowed on trails. Trails are Los Alamos National Laboratory property.

LAST-CHANCE FOOD/GAS: All services in White Rock (4 miles northeast); convenience store in La Cueva (33 miles northwest); gas station in San Ysidro (60 miles southwest)

off-limits. But most of the land on the right side is open to hiking and has a network of well-marked and well-maintained trails. If you are driving from White Rock the orientation will be reversed.

Access to the trails is from a series of gates along the right side of NM 4. The gates are not identified by any signage along the road. The only way to recognize them is to notice a doubletrack or pulloff on the side of NM 4. Parking is very limited at the gates, so you'll probably have to park along the road. There are photomaps of the trail network and a list of restrictions posted at the gate trailheads. Generally, hiking, snowshoeing, mountain biking, horseback riding, and dogs are permitted. Motorized vehicles, firearms, smoking, campfires, overnight camping, and geocaching are not permitted. Gates are subject to closure depending on the needs of LANL. Continued access to the trails is contingent upon users adhering to the restrictions and treating the land with respect.

The trailhead for our hike is at gate 5. The gate is difficult to spot if you're coming from White Rock. So it might be easier to drive to mile marker 60 and then come back (see Directions). Once you spot the gate, it is easiest to park on the side of road. Gate 5 is a few yards down a steep, rutted doubletrack on the east side of NM 4. It is the trailhead for both the Lower Water Canyon Trail and Lion Cave Trail. Our hike goes out on Lower Water Canyon and returns on Lion Cave.

There is no sign at the gate identifying it as gate 5. The only identifier is on the aerial photomap on the information sign just inside the gate. The gate is really not hard to find and well worth your effort.

Lower Water Canyon follows an old dirt road that hooks right and runs southeast alongside a shallow streambed. The north side of the canyon, a wall of pocked tuff, soon becomes visible through the pine. You'll get a closer look at Swiss cheese

Lower Water Canyon–Lion Cave Trails

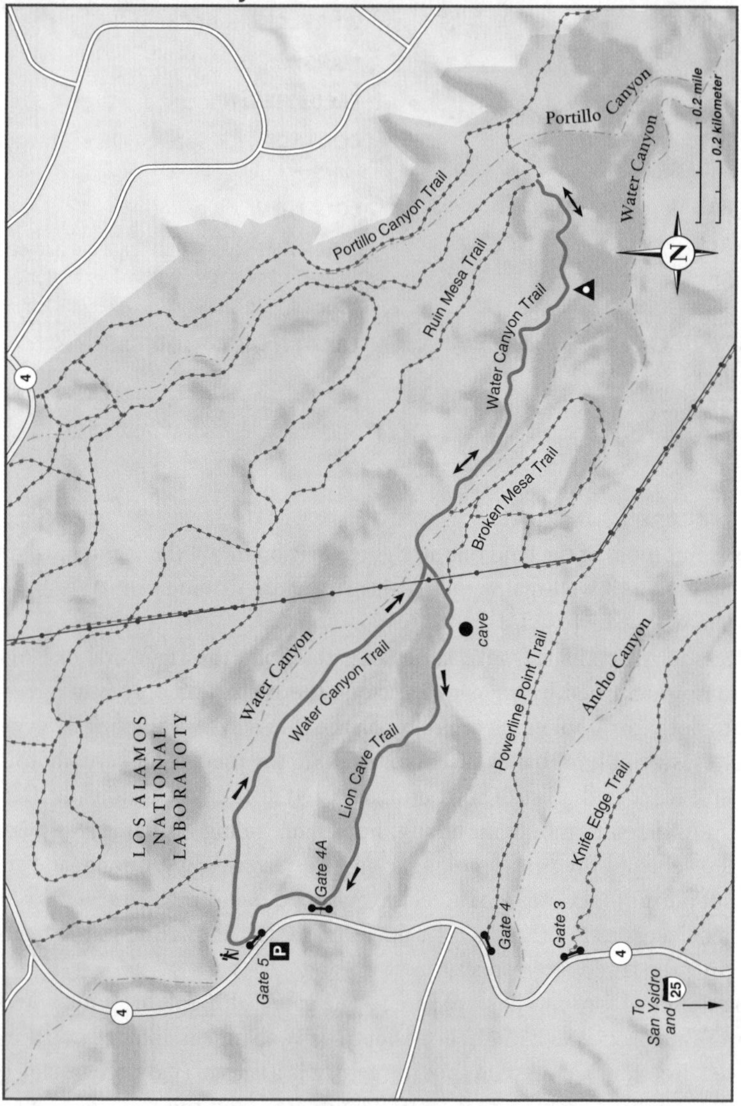

Portillo Canyon
Water Canyon
0.2 mile
0.2 kilometer
N
Portillo Canyon Trail
Ruin Mesa Trail
Water Canyon Trail
Broken Mesa Trail
cave
Water Canyon
Water Canyon Trail
Lion Cave Trail
Powerline Point Trail
Ancho Canyon
Knife Edge Trail
LOS ALAMOS
NATIONAL
LABORATOTY
Gate 4A
Gate 5
P
Gate 4
Gate 3
4
To
San Ysidro
and
25

6,600 ft.
6,500 ft.
6,400 ft.
6,300 ft.
6,200 ft.
6,100 ft.
6,000 ft.
1 mi.
2 mi.
3 mi.
4 mi.
5 mi.

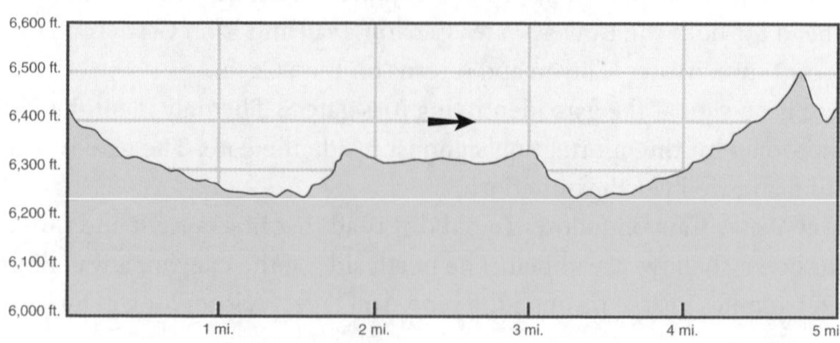

The Rio Grande flows below this overlook.

cliffs later. For now take a moment to smell the ponderosa, which have an aroma reminiscent of vanilla and butterscotch. In around 1 mile, you'll reach the junction with Lion Cave Trail. If you only have time for a short 2-mile loop hike, you can turn here and follow Lion Cave back to the gate. If you continue another 0.15 mile you'll reach the junction with Broken Mesa Trail and have the choice of going on Broken Mesa or staying on Lower Water Canyon.

Broken Mesa Trail goes off to the right and climbs through interesting landforms and passes many pockmarked caves. It connects with Powerline Point Trail in a little over 1.1 miles. If you turn left and go southeast another mile or so, you will have fabulous views of the Rio Grande 1,000 feet below. Going to the end of Powerline Point Trail is a 6-mile-plus out-and-back hike. You can turn right on Powerline Point Trail and reach NM 4 at gate 4 in less than 1 mile. It is a 0.5-mile road walk back to gate 5.

For an all-day adventure you could extend your hike by picking up the Ancho Springs Trail toward the end of Powerline Point Trail and taking it down to the river. From there you can hike along the river or climb back up. If you are interested in a hike going down to the river see Hike 34 (page 185).

Lower Water Canyon Trail veers left and climbs away from the rocky streambed. The trail is easy to follow and the most logical route for this hike. From the junction it climbs steadily to a bench, where it begins to level out. The streambed meanwhile has trenched into a gorge 400 feet below you. There are plenty of places for outstanding views of the gorge and the pockmarked caves around you. Some of the views can be vertigo inducing, and in others you can see the Rio Grande.

From the bench, the trail works its way northeast along the canyon to skirt around and then go over a small ridge to Portrillo Canyon. Right after the crossing there is a junction with Ruin Mesa Trail. The next junction is Portrillo Canyon Loop Trail. The most interesting feature is how foot traffic has worn a trench into the soft volcanic tuff. It makes you wonder how long this trail has been used.

From here you can hike all the way to the edge of White Rock or find other trails to explore. Since you're close to 2.5 miles into the hike, turn around and walk back 1-plus miles to the junction with Lion Cave Trail.

Lion Cave Trail runs through a side canyon of Water Canyon. Because this canyon is smaller, Lion Cave runs very close to the pockmarked caves on the canyon wall. This is a good opportunity to explore the Bandelier tuff formations. The tuff was created from the slurry of ash and gases that flowed from the caldera eruption. Gas bubbles were trapped inside the solidifying tuff, which later eroded to form irregular patterns of arches, niches, and windows. Pueblo people modified some of these pockets into *cavates,* or carved rooms. You may find some in your exploring.

The trail reaches gate 4A, below NM 4, in a little more than 0.8 mile. From here the trail turns right (north) to climb over the small ridge separating the two canyons to reach our starting point at gate 5 in less than 0.4 mile.

With its fantastic scenery and so many hiking options and places to explore, this hike is well worth the drive from Albuquerque. If it were closer, it could easily be an everyday go-to hiking area.

• •

GPS TRAILHEAD COORDINATES N35° 48.218' W106° 14.758'

DIRECTIONS Via San Ysidro: From I-25 North, take Exit 242 toward Bernalillo. Turn left on US 550 and go 23.5 miles to San Ysidro. Turn right onto NM 4 and follow it 60.3 miles. After passing mile marker 60, look for an unpaved pulloff on the right. (If you reach the bottom of the hill, you've just missed it.)

Via White Rock: From I-25 North, take Exit 276 and turn left onto NM 599. Go 13.5 miles north to merge onto US 84. Continue 14 miles north to the Los Alamos exit. Turn left and go 11.6 miles west on NM 502. Merge onto NM 4 toward White Rock and follow it 7.9 miles south. After mile marker 61, just past the bottom of the hill, look for a gravel pulloff on the left. It's harder to spot coming from this direction.

31 NAMBE LAKE

Nambe Lake is one of the most scenic spots in this entire book.

IF YOU CAN handle a strenuous workout, this high-country hike to an alpine lake should be on your must-do list. It's that amazing!

DESCRIPTION

If you're looking for a high-country hiking adventure, you don't have to drive to Colorado to find one. They're right here within our 60-mile radius of Albuquerque in the Pecos Wilderness just outside of Santa Fe. Nambe Lake is the closest alpine lake to Albuquerque and Santa Fe and is a great high-country adventure.

The hike is tough, but it is gorgeous the entire way. You'll find alpine meadows, lakes, glacial features, and fantastic views on this hike. And when you reach the goal, the view of the alpine lake surrounded by mountain peaks poking above timberline will take your breath away.

The hike begins with a gorgeous drive on NM 475 from Santa Fe into the Sangre de Cristo Mountains. The Sangre de Cristo Range is an extension of the Rocky Mountains and has New Mexico's tallest peaks. If you want to see fall colors, this is the drive and hike to take. You'll be immersed in yellow-gold aspen leaves.

The best time for this hike is in the fall. There is year-round access, but there could be too much snow in the winter and spring. Summer is also a good time for

DISTANCE & CONFIGURATION: 7-mile out-and-back

DIFFICULTY: Strenuous

SCENERY: Alpine lake, glacial features, amazing views, aspens

EXPOSURE: Mostly shaded

TRAIL TRAFFIC: Popular

TRAIL SURFACE: Dirt, rock

HIKING TIME: 5 hours

DRIVING DISTANCE: 75 miles from the Big I

ELEVATION GAIN: 10,274' at trailhead; 11,427' at Nambe Lake

ACCESS: Year-round; snow in the winter; no fees or permits required

WHEELCHAIR ACCESS: No

MAPS: Santa Fe National Forest–East Half; USGS *Aspen Basin*

FACILITIES: Pit toilet at trailhead

CONTACT: Santa Fe National Forest–Española Ranger District, fs.usda.gov/santafe, 505-753-7331

LOCATION: Santa Fe

COMMENTS: Leashed dogs are allowed on trails.

this hike, as the mountain temperatures are much cooler than down below. But if we're having a good monsoon season, there can be thunderstorms almost every afternoon. If you do hike in the summer, it's best to start early and be off the mountain before the storms roll in.

NM 475 ends at the Santa Fe Ski Basin parking area. The trailhead is off to the left near the restroom facilities. The **Winsor Trail (254)** is just across the stream. We'll be taking it uphill into the Pecos Wilderness.

The Winsor Trail is a very popular hiking, biking, and equestrian trail that starts 13 miles downhill from our entry point in the village of Tesuque. A ride downhill is a favorite for mountain bikers. If your timing is right, you might see cowboys on horseback moving cattle to or from pastures high in the mountains. Grazing continues to be a traditional use of the mountains.

The hike begins by following the small stream through the woods. When you see a meadow off to the right, the trail will turn left and leave the stream. After a few switchbacks you'll reach a log fence that marks the Pecos Wilderness boundary. At this point you've hiked 0.75 mile and climbed 550 feet. This is the end of the trail for mountain bikers, as wheeled vehicles are not allowed in wilderness areas.

The next 1.4 miles of the trail generally trend downhill for an elevation drop of around 350 feet. The trail slabs along the side of the mountain through aspens and fir with the upslope to your right. Doing this walk in late September and early October when the leaves are changing is one the most wonderful experiences you can have.

The Lower Nambe Trail (403) goes off to your left and heads downhill in about 0.3 mile after entering the wilderness. Stay with the main trail as it works its way around the mountain. There are breaks in the woods for nice views of Santa Fe Baldy as you proceed. At 12,622 feet it is the highest point in Santa Fe County. After passing through a rocky stretch, you'll be able to see Nambe Creek down below.

So far you've had a very nice hike of a little more than 2 miles on a well-defined trail through beautiful country. The hike is now going to get really interesting. When

Nambe Lake

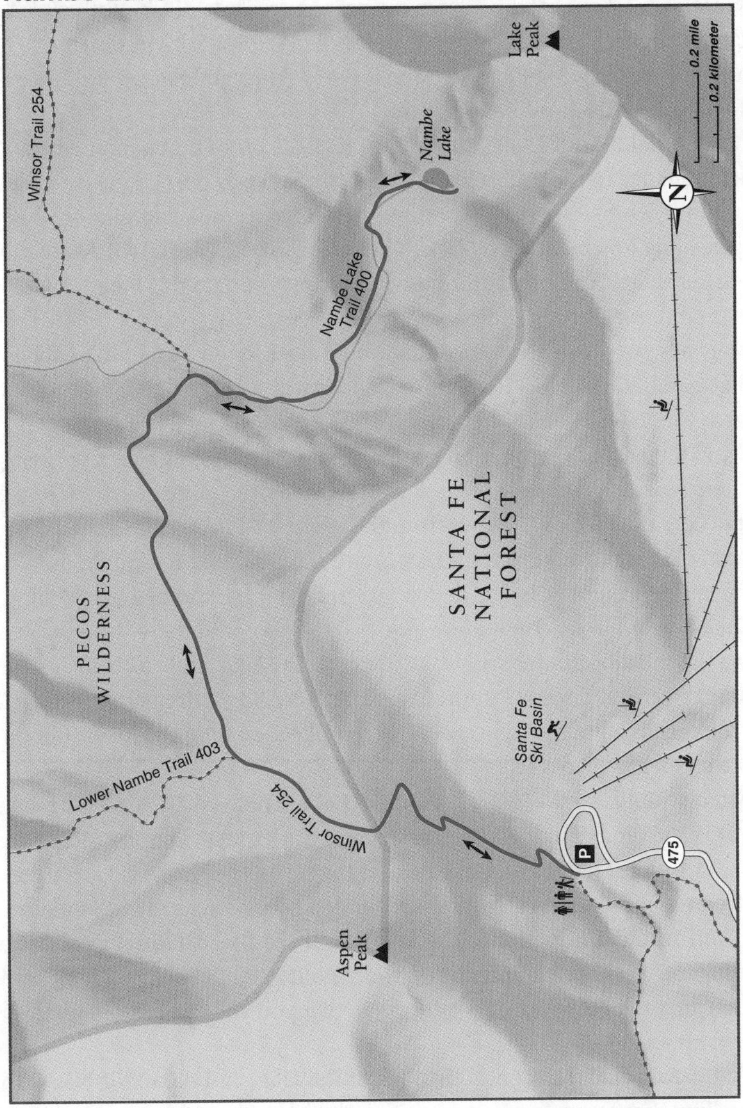

Winsor Trail 254
Lake Peak
0.2 mile
0.2 kilometer
N
Nambe Lake
Nambe Lake Trail 400
SANTA FE NATIONAL FOREST
PECOS WILDERNESS
Santa Fe Ski Basin
Lower Nambe Trail 403
Winsor Trail 254
P
475
Aspen Peak

11,400 ft.
11,200 ft.
11,000 ft.
10,800 ft.
10,600 ft.
10,400 ft.
10,200 ft.
0.5 mi.
1 mi.
1.5 mi.
2 mi.
2.5 mi.
3 mi.
3.5 mi.

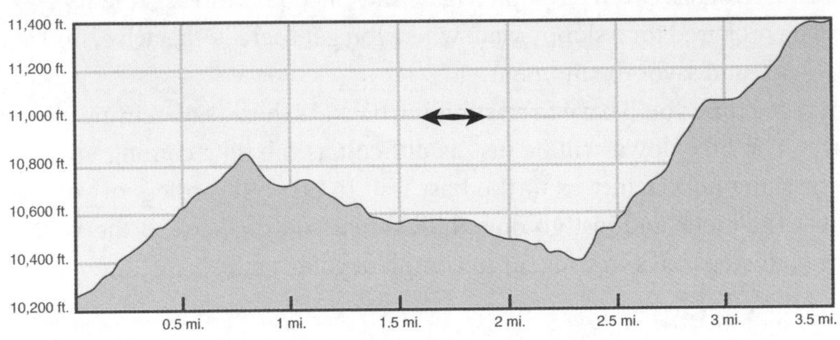

the Winsor Trail starts heading down toward the creek, look for another trail continuing straight ahead. If you look around, you should see a sign saying NAMBE LAKE. If you miss the trail or if the sign is gone, don't worry. You can hike toward the creek until you do pick up a trail heading upstream.

Nambe Lake Trail (400), the trail to the lake, is an unmaintained trail because any maintenance to the trail is likely to be washed away every time the creek floods. Again, don't worry. There is a braided network of trails and almost always other hikers heading upstream to the lake. The setting of the lake is worth any difficulty it takes to get there. And no matter how many times you do this hike, you are likely to do it a bit differently each time.

Your best bet is to recognize that you have a steep 1-mile hike ahead of you. You'll be gaining 1,000 feet in that mile, and it will seem like an elevator shaft. If you stay near the creek, you'll be going in the right direction. Because of the braided trails, you'll be asked by other hikers more than once if they're going the right way. And there is a good chance you'll ask another hiker the same question. Just go uphill and stay near the creek as it flows from the lake.

Along the way you'll pass meadows and scree slopes. You might even see cattle grazing in the meadows. In a little over 0.6 mile on the Nambe Lake Trail, you'll see a flat meadow off to the right and wonder if the lake is in there. It's not. Feel free to explore the meadow, but if you want to get to the lake angle to your left and find a trail near the creek. Several hundred feet later you'll see a dramatic cirque full of gray scree rock again off to the right. Feel free to poke around in the rocks, but remember that the creek has veered left.

After around a mile on the Nambe Lake Trail, you'll reach the lake (N35° 48.046' W105° 46.603'). It will be better than you expect. The lake sits at the base of a glacial cirque at 11,400 feet. Lake Peak at the top of the cirque is 12,400 feet. As you look around, you'll see that you're surrounded by massive gray mountains on three sides. And when you look into the lake you'll see the shallow, crystal-clear water mirroring the trees and mountains that surround it. And when you look behind you, you'll see that the only way out is the creek that you've been following. In short, the setting is amazing!

There are small trails on both sides of the lake, and plenty of places to sit and take it all in. You can even circumnavigate the lake, but it does get marshy at the far end, so be prepared for a sloppy walk when you get there. Otherwise, find a place to have a snack and savor the moment.

At some time you'll have to start hiking back, as there is no tenting allowed near the lake. The hike down will be just as difficult as the hike coming up. And it will have the same uncertainty as to the best trail to take. Regardless of your decision, stay near the creek and just go downhill. When you get back to the Winsor Trail, retrace your steps back to your car to complete your 7-mile hike.

Check out Santa Fe Baldy from the Winsor Trail.

Although this hike is not the easiest, it is a fantastic mountain hike. And if your health and stamina allow, it is one that you are likely to enjoy. It's hard to believe that we have such a diversity of hikes within our 60-mile radius of Albuquerque.

• •

GPS TRAILHEAD COORDINATES N35° 47.698' W105° 48.262'

DIRECTIONS From I-25 North, take Exit 282 and go 3.6 miles north on Saint Francis Drive (US 84). Turn right on the *second* Paseo de Peralta. (It's a loop.) Go east 1 mile, then turn left on Bishop's Lodge Road. Go north 0.18 mile and turn right on Artists Road, which becomes Hyde Park Road (NM 475). Continue 14.6 miles to the end of the road. Park in the lower lot of the Ski Basin. The trailhead is on the left near to restrooms and creek.

32 PUERTO NAMBE–SANTA FE BALDY

Looking into the heart of the Pecos Wilderness, with the Truchas Peaks in the distance (center left)

WITH GORGEOUS MOUNTAIN views, forests, meadows, streams, and gray jays, the hike to Puerto Nambe is a walk through a high-country paradise. This is a moderate hike suitable for almost everyone. If you have more energy, optional extensions can turn this into an epic adventure.

DESCRIPTION

At 10,950 feet, Puerto Nambe is a beautiful high-country meadow in the heart of the Pecos Wilderness. Since it's about 4.2 miles from the Winsor Trailhead at the Santa Fe Ski Basin, it is a fantastic destination for a day hike. On your way to Puerto Nambe you'll walk through magnificent aspen and fir forests, cross several streams, and grab wonderful views of the mountains around you. This hike is a true gem. As an added bonus you'll have more than a few gray jays asking you to share your lunch with them.

Because Puerto Nambe is a trail crossroad, there are plenty of options to extend your hike beyond the 8-mile-plus round-trip to this point. If you continue east on the Winsor Trail (254) for a little less than 2 miles you'll reach Spirit Lake for a 12-mile out-and-back hike. If you follow the Skyline Trail (251) north for 1.5 mile you will have climbed to 11,600 feet and will be standing on a ridge with views that go on forever. The entire Pecos Wilderness will be in front of you and will look like a bowl full of aspens, fir, and adventure.

DISTANCE & CONFIGURATION: 8.4-mile out-and-back, with longer options up to a 14-mile out-and-back

DIFFICULTY: Moderate with a strenuous extension

SCENERY: High-country mountains, aspen, fir, spruce, meadows, streams, gray jays

EXPOSURE: Mostly shaded

TRAIL TRAFFIC: Popular

TRAIL SURFACE: Dirt, rock

HIKING TIME: 5–10 hours depending upon the options you choose

DRIVING DISTANCE: 75 miles from the Big I

ELEVATION GAIN: 10,274' at trailhead; 10,950' at Puerto Nambe; 11,600' at Pecos Wilderness overlook; 12,622' at Santa Fe Baldy

ACCESS: Year-round; snow in winter; no fees or permits required

WHEELCHAIR ACCESS: No

MAPS: Santa Fe National Forest–East Half; USGS *Aspen Basin*

FACILITIES: Pit toilet at trailhead

CONTACT: Santa Fe National Forest–Española Ranger District, fs.usda.gov/santafe, 505-753-7331

LOCATION: Santa Fe

COMMENTS: Leashed dogs are allowed on trails.

Off in the distance a bit to the left are the Truchas Peaks. And looming to your immediate left is a trail to the top of Santa Fe Baldy. At 12,622 feet, it is the highest point in Santa Fe County and the highest point in our entire 60-mile radius of Albuquerque.

A hike to the top of Santa Fe Baldy will add another mile of hiking each way and another 1,000 feet of climbing. If you choose to do that, you'll have a very strenuous 14-mile day hike. It will probably take about 8–10 hours to complete, so you'll want to get a very early start. If you're up to it, it is a fantastic and gratifying hike.

If you're not up for a 14-mile day hike, you might consider a backpack trip to the area. With abundant water and lush meadows, you can't pick a better spot to pitch a tent. If you're already spending the night at Puerto Nambe, a hike to the top of Santa Fe Baldy would only be a 5-mile out-and-back side trip. And you'll still have plenty of time to check out other trails and places.

The trail to Puerto Nambe is open year-round. With its high elevation, there will be snow in the winter. During the summer you should be prepared for afternoon thunderstorms. Your best bet during summer is to start early enough to avoid any storms and to make sure that you're not on an exposed ridge if a storm should come. Fall is a wonderful time to visit, but with shorter days you'll want to be aware of how much daylight is left, so you give yourself plenty of time to get back before dark. If you choose to backpack in the fall, be aware that it can be very cold at night.

The actual hike to Puerto Nambe is quite simple and straightforward. You'll begin with a fabulous drive up NM 475 to its end at the Santa Fe Ski Basin and park in the lot close to the Winsor Trailhead. The trailhead is just beyond the pit toilet facilities on the other side of the small stream.

The hike follows **Winsor Trail (254)** upstream as it makes several switchbacks to climb to the ridge that marks the Pecos Wilderness boundary. It's 0.75 mile and 550 feet of climbing to the ridge. This is the hardest part of the hike. From here the trail will be rocky in places, but the grades will be much gentler. The Winsor Trail

Puerto Nambe–Santa Fe Baldy

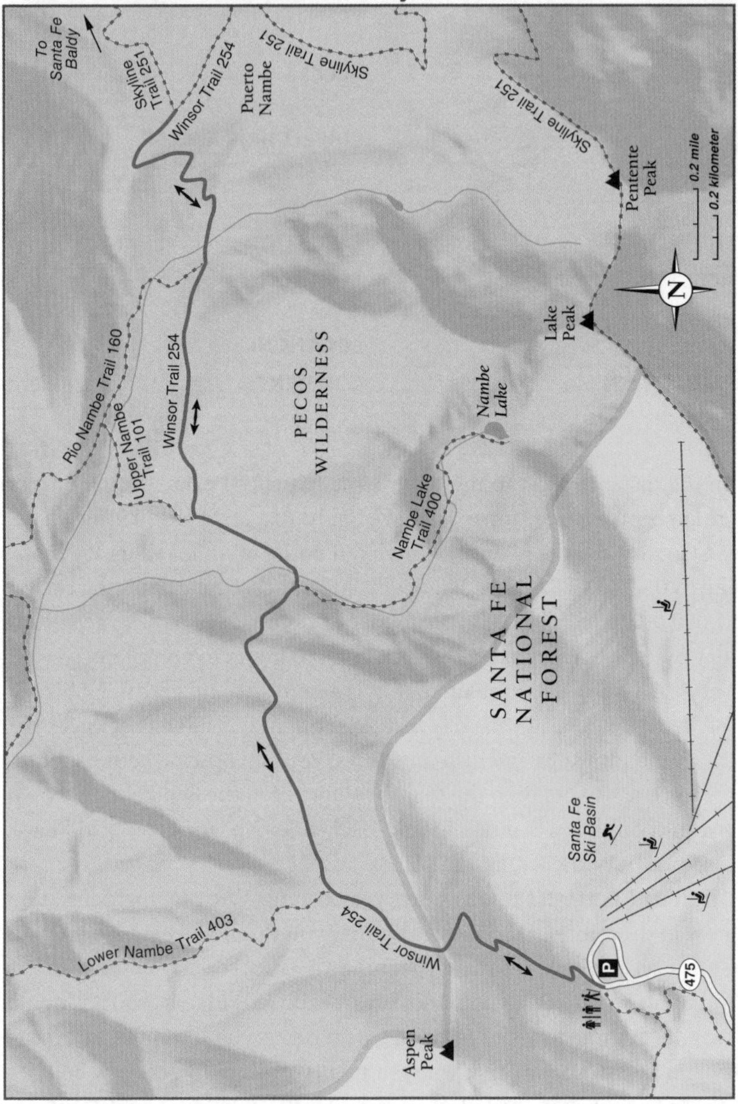

To Santa Fe Baldy
Skyline Trail 251
Winsor Trail 254
Puerto Nambe
Skyline Trail 251
Skyline Trail 251
Pentente Peak
0.2 mile
0.2 kilometer
N
Lake Peak
Nambe Lake
PECOS WILDERNESS
Rio Nambe Trail 160
Upper Nambe Trail 101
Winsor Trail 254
Nambe Lake Trail 400
SANTA FE NATIONAL FOREST
Santa Fe Ski Basin
Lower Nambe Trail 403
Winsor Trail 254
P
475
Aspen Peak

11,200 ft.
11,000 ft.
10,800 ft.
10,600 ft.
10,400 ft.
10,200 ft.
10,000 ft.
0.5 mi.
1 mi.
1.5 mi.
2 mi.
2.5 mi.
3 mi.
3.5 mi.
4 mi.

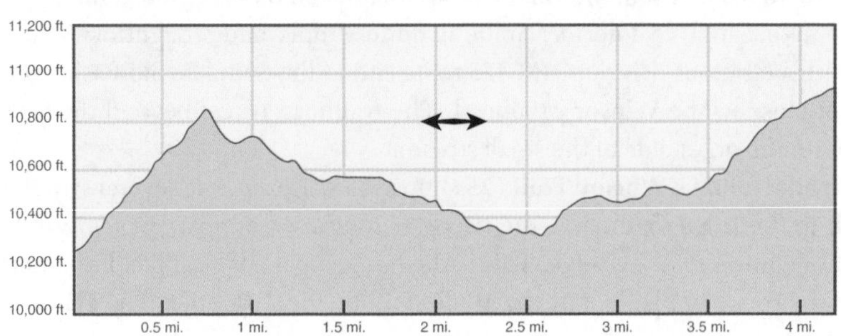

will now trend downhill to lose 350 feet over the next 1.5 miles to a small bridge crossing Nambe Creek. The hike is in an aspen–fir forest the entire way, but there are enough openings to provide excellent views of Santa Fe Baldy and other mountains. Along the way you'll pass Lower Nambe Trail (403) and the trail to Nambe Lake (Hike 31, page 171).

From the bridge it is 2 miles of hiking and 550 feet of climbing to Puerto Nambe. When you leave the bridge, most of the hike will be through thick stands of aspens. If you time your trip right you could be bathing in a sea of yellow-gold aspen leaves shimmering in the sky. A few days later you could be walking through a shower of falling aspen leaves. And a few days after that, you could be passing naked aspens waiting for next spring. No matter how you time it, it will be good.

Over the remaining 2 miles to Puerto Nambe you'll cross at least two streams and pass two trails splitting off from Winsor. Our hike follows Winsor all the way to Puerto Nambe. If it has been a good water year there could be additional stream crossings. And with the forest openings, you'll have many fantastic views of Santa Fe Baldy. As you gain elevation the aspens will decline and be replaced by a fir–spruce forest. In around 1.3 miles, right after crossing the second strong stream, the trail will climb 300 feet in a series of switchbacks over the next 0.5 mile, and then make a sharp turn to the right to enter a meadow. Depending on the year, this particular area can get marshy.

You are now entering Puerto Nambe. It's a large meadow dotted with fir trees surrounded by mountains. You are likely to see some cattle during the summer, as grazing has been and still is a traditional use of the mountains by local people. Keep walking until you reach the junction of the Winsor and Skyline Trails. The junction is marked with a sign. Anywhere in here is a good place to stop for a snack and to decide on your next step.

While eating, you may be joined by several gray jays (also called Canada jays) looking for handouts. They aren't easily intimidated and are likely to hang out on a nearby branch waiting for you to turn around so they can swoop down for a quick snack.

And as you look around, you'll probably decide that this is one of your favorite places on Earth. From here you can extend your walk or return the way you came in. Your choice, no matter what it is, will be a good one in this high-country paradise.

GPS TRAILHEAD COORDINATES N35° 47.698' W105° 48.262'

DIRECTIONS From I-25 North, take Exit 282 and go 3.6 miles north on Saint Francis Drive (US 84). Turn right on the *second* Paseo de Peralta. (It's a loop.) Go east 1 mile, then turn left on Bishop's Lodge Road. Go north 0.18 mile and turn right on Artists Road, which becomes Hyde Park Road (NM 475). Continue 14.6 miles to the end of the road. Park in the lower lot of the Ski Basin. The trailhead is on the left near to restrooms and creek.

33 TWIN HILLS

Admire the vast expanse of undeveloped land as you look toward Santa Fe and the Sangre de Cristos.

KEY ADVICE FOR hiking on the plateau: head for the hills. Lightly forested volcanic formations provide a haven for unique geological sculptures and a flurry of wildlife. The volcanic features, including a bottomless vent, make this hike worth doing.

DESCRIPTION

This hike on the Caja del Rio is for those who like to explore and make discoveries. With much of this hike off-trail, there is a very good chance that you'll do it differently each time you go out.

The Caja del Rio ("Box of the River") is a dissected volcanic plateau that stands between Santa Fe and the Rio Grande. Stretching about 20 miles north from La Bajada to Buckman (Hike 27, page 151), it's mostly grassy plains with several clusters of moderate hills, few of which rise more than 500 feet. The plateau makes up the bulk of the exposed part of the Cerros del Rio volcanic field, which consists of about a dozen volcanoes and more than 70 vents of cinder cones, plugs, and tuff rings. Volcanic activity here peaked between 2.3 and 2.5 million years ago, leaving the basalts and lavas that dominate the landscape today.

DISTANCE & CONFIGURATION: 6.9-mile figure eight (shorter if you park farther in)

DIFFICULTY: Easy–strenuous depending on where you are

SCENERY: Volcanic formations, hilly terrain, mountain vistas

EXPOSURE: Little shade

TRAIL TRAFFIC: Low

TRAIL SURFACE: Packed dirt, loose rock

HIKING TIME: 4 hours (more if you do a lot of exploring)

DRIVING DISTANCE: 63 miles from the Big I

ELEVATION GAIN: 6,490' at trailhead; 7,300' at high point

ACCESS: Year-round, though subject to road closures; no fees or permits required

WHEELCHAIR ACCESS: No

MAPS: Santa Fe National Forest–West Half; USGS *Agua Fria* and *Montoso Peak*

FACILITIES: None

CONTACT: Santa Fe National Forest–Española Ranger District, fs.usda.gov/santafe, 505-753-7331

LOCATION: West of Santa Fe

COMMENTS: Rough roads provide the only access to hills on the plateau. This is a good place for a bike-and-hike. Leashed dogs allowed on trails.

LAST-CHANCE FOOD/GAS: Convenience store–gas station on Airport Road, 0.25 mile east of NM 599 (10 miles from trailhead)

Aside from stock ponds, you won't likely find much water on the plateau. Average rainfall amounts to less than an inch per month. Intermittent stream channels and ephemeral swales tend to stay dry outside of monsoon season.

The Caja del Rio Allotment of the Española Ranger District covers nearly 67,000 acres with well over 100 rugged roads and mapped trails. The area is popular with jeep tourists, target shooters, equestrians, and mountain bikers. What tends to deter most hikers are the relatively featureless plains that stretch (and yawn) between questionable roads and scenic hills. As a result, few hikers know what they're missing. These hills are packed with fascinating geologic features, abundant wildlife, and a smattering of remnants from ancient pueblos. You could wander for days out here and you'd still miss half of it. This hike just scratches the surface. The point is merely to get you into nearby hills quickly and effortlessly, without damaging your vehicle, and to acquaint you with endless possibilities for exploration upon the Caja del Rio Plateau.

The hike begins wherever you decide that your car has taken enough abuse. Under ideal conditions, the road holds up fine until you get past the second cattle guard, less than a mile up Forest Service Road 24. A few bumpy patches follow over the next half mile or so, but most cars with normal clearance can crawl over it to reach the T-junction. The road heading west from here is less forgiving. You can attempt to drive it to shave a few miles off the hike. For those eager to get their boots on the ground, it's probably best to get out here and start walking.

For orientation, when you turn off of FR 24 you are facing west. The fenceline to your left is south. The dirt road whether you drive or walk is heading west. The prominent pair of stark, volcanic plugs (sometimes mistaken for Twin Hills, which stand less than a mile farther northwest) are to the west. The hike is headed to the plugs.

Twin Hills

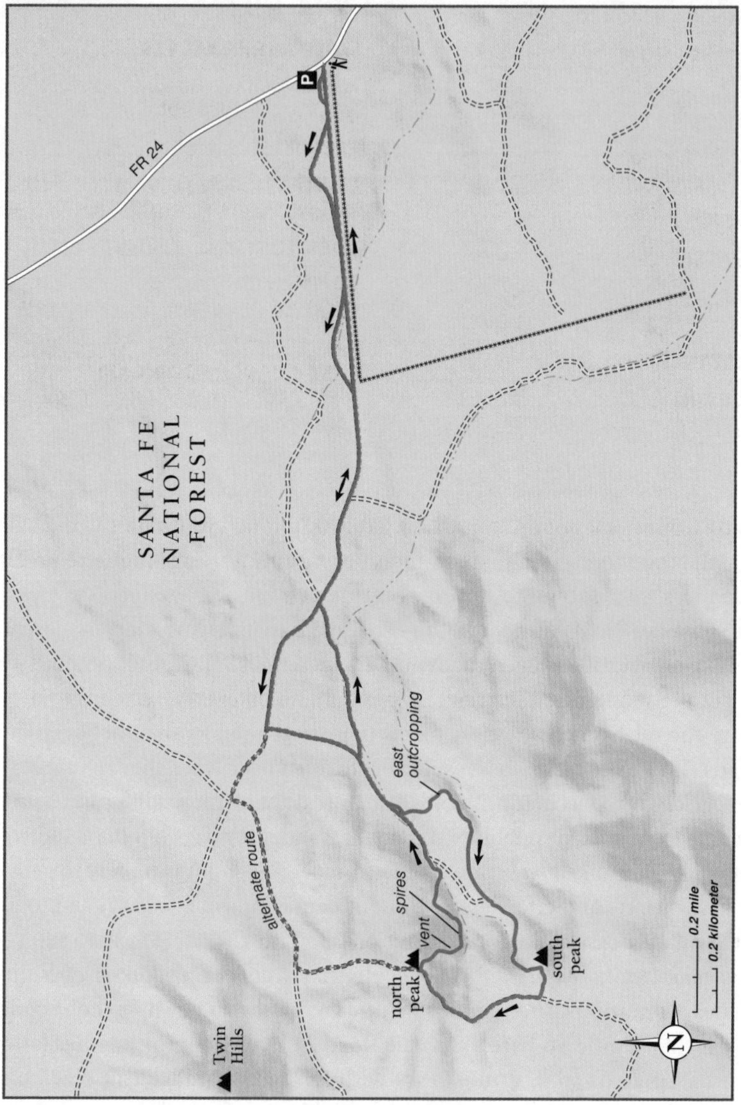

FR 24
SANTA FE NATIONAL FOREST
east outcropping
alternate route
spires
vent
north peak
south peak
Twin Hills
0.2 mile
0.2 kilometer
N

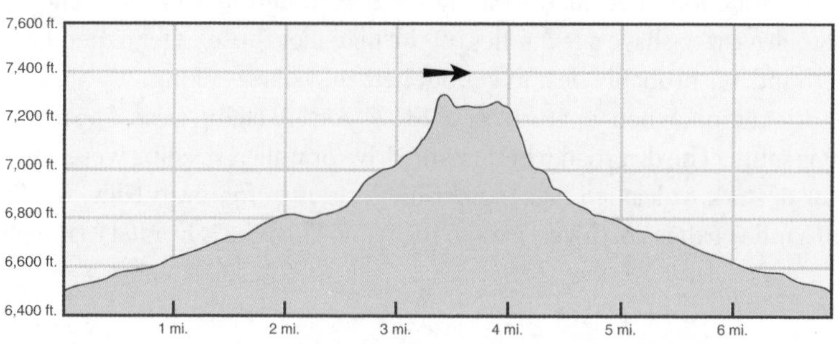
7,600 ft.
7,400 ft.
7,200 ft.
7,000 ft.
6,800 ft.
6,600 ft.
6,400 ft.
1 mi.
2 mi.
3 mi.
4 mi.
5 mi.
6 mi.

There is much to discover on this hike, but the main event is an eerie volcanic vent (N35° 41.951' W106° 09.300') that seems to have no bottom. It's almost spooky to look into it. The vent is at the north peak.

The hike description visits the south vent first and then goes to the north vent. A description of a faster route to the vent will follow.

For the first mile, braided doubletracks follow a fenceline and aim directly at the plug on the north peak. Stay on the road another mile as it bends north. After it dips south, and just before turning north again, look for a lesser road veering south (N35° 42.307' W106° 08.233').

At this junction, you're 2 miles into the hike, and so far the immediate scenery has been a dusty display of overgrazed grasslands with a colorful potpourri of spent shotgun shells. It gets much better.

Turn left on the side road heading south. It soon curves right to pass between the points of two low ridges. Both ridges ramp up to peak at a pair of conjoined volcanic hills, roughly forming one continuous horseshoe-shaped ridgeline. The idea of the hike from here is simple: follow the ridge on your left up to the south plug, cross over to visit the one to the north, then follow the other ridge back down to the road. (That's the basic idea, anyway, but be prepared for curiosities along the way that may cause you to deviate from this simple course.)

Start by looking for a rocky outcrop on the near end of the ridge on your left. It's not as prominent as either peak, but easy enough to spot from the road. Leave the road for a quick climb to that point. Views from here include an unobstructed panorama of the Sangre de Cristo range rising on the far side of Santa Fe.

Climb southwest, toward the south peak. As the ridge bends west, a hogback (volcanic dike) begins to emerge on your right. Hiking on the upper side of a 0.3-mile-long wall is easier, due to thinner vegetation, though you'll better appreciate its immensity from below. If you stick to the high road, a good spot for a quick look below comes at a gap in the middle. A road once passed through here, but only a trace of it remains. Also keep an eye out for interesting rock formations on the far side of the drainage.

The hogback leads you to a short but steep ascent to the south plug. A red-dirt road parallels the ridge between the peaks. You can follow it to the north peak or stay on the ridge for better views. The ridge area would have been a perfect place for prehistoric hunters to observe game animals grazing on the flats to the west. From the north peak, a short jeep road (more of a footpath now) splits off to visit the volcanic vent. Be very careful, as it's steep and deep. Make sure your dogs and kids are under control.

About 300 feet south of the vent are spires that you probably spotted from the hogback. They rise near the steep, lushly vegetated head of the main drainage. You may spot a few more curiosities in this area. Feel free to wander off course to explore whatever catches your attention. You can return to the ridge above to finish the intended route, or just follow the drainage downstream for a shortcut to the road that brought you in.

If you only have time to visit the vent, follow the road west as mentioned in the description. Continue past the road where the description has you turning south and go to the next road (N35° 42.521' W106° 08.827'). Turn left (south) and follow that road to the top of the north plug. The road up to the plug is very steep, as it climbs almost 300 feet in a 0.4-mile stretch. Once on top, the path to the vent is on the south side of the plug.

• •

GPS TRAILHEAD COORDINATES N35° 42.300' W106° 06.583'

DIRECTIONS From I-25 North, take Exit 276 and turn left on NM 599. Go north 6 miles to Exit 6. Navigate the roundabouts on each side of the highway to get on the West Frontage Road heading south. Go southwest 1.4 miles and turn right on Caja del Rio Road. Go north 2.9 miles and turn left on CR 62. After 1.2 miles, CR 62 crosses the first cattle guard and becomes FR 24. Continue northwest another 1.6 miles, crossing two more cattle guards along the way. Turn left (west) and park in a clearing at the T-junction. Drive slowly as the T-junction is easy to miss and the braided road has more than one openings joining FR 24.

34 WHITE ROCK CANYON: Red Dot/Blue Dot Trails

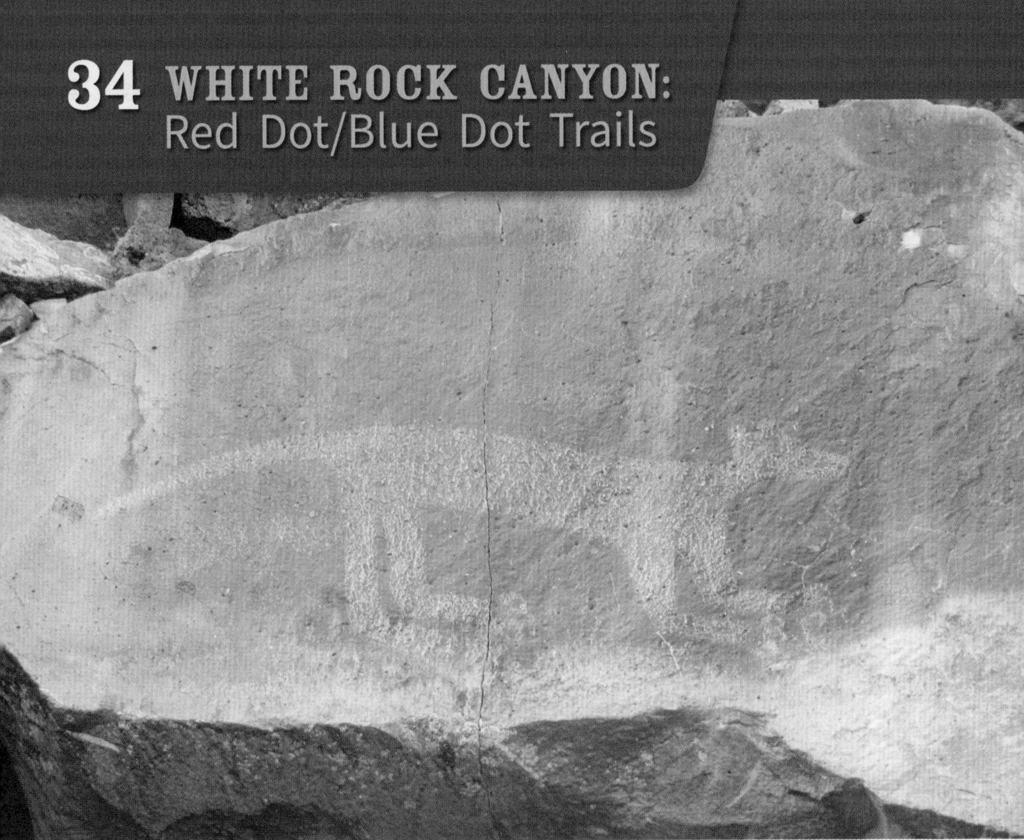

This mountain lion petroglyph is almost 5 feet wide.

THE HIKE DROPS into White Rock Canyon from Overlook Park in the community of White Rock. With fantastic views, an oasis with waterfalls and lagoons, and fabulous rock art, this tough walk is one of the best in New Mexico.

DESCRIPTION

The Los Alamos bedroom community of White Rock, at 57 miles by air from Albuquerque, is just inside the 60-mile-radius criterion for selecting hikes. With the rugged Jemez Mountains and Caja del Rio between the two, it's almost a 100-mile drive to get there. Separating the Jemez and the Caja is the rugged 1,000-foot-deep White Rock Canyon. The canyon was formed by the Rio Grande, which runs on the bottom.

The west side of the canyon is the gem of Los Alamos County Open Space properties. In addition to great outdoor recreation potential, it is also home to endangered plant and wildlife species. And according to the county, it is the only canyon listed on the National Register of Historical Places.

The community of White Rock sits on the rim of the canyon and offers one of the most fantastic hikes in New Mexico. Its Red Dot/Blue Dot network of trails takes you from the rim to the river and then follows the river to another trail back to the rim. Along the way you'll have lagoons, small waterfalls, fabulous rock art, and incredible

DISTANCE & CONFIGURATION: 6.5-mile loop

DIFFICULTY: Strenuous

SCENERY: Breathtaking views of White Rock Canyon, distant mountains, river, lagoons, falls, rock art

EXPOSURE: Mostly exposed, some shade along the river

TRAIL TRAFFIC: Popular

TRAIL SURFACE: Dirt, rock

HIKING TIME: 4–5 hours

DRIVING DISTANCE: 95 miles from the Big I

ELEVATION GAIN: 6,270' at trailhead; 5,416' at canyon bottom

ACCESS: Year-round; no fees or permits required

WHEELCHAIR ACCESS: No

MAPS: USGS *White Rock;* trail maps at White Rock visitor center (see Nearby Activities)

FACILITIES: Restrooms and water at Overlook Park

CONTACT: Los Alamos County Open Space, losalamosnm.us, 505-663-1776

LOCATION: White Rock

COMMENTS: Leashed dogs are allowed on trails. The canyon and basalt boulders can get hot in the summer.

LAST-CHANCE FOOD/GAS: All services in White Rock

views. There are even places to pitch a tent near the river if you want to camp out. And when you're back on the rim, there's another trail to take you back to your jump-off point to complete a challenging and fulfilling 6.5-mile loop hike.

If you are up for a tough hike, this one is for you. You won't regret the long drive to get there. Because the canyon is hot in the summer, this is a good fall, winter, or spring hike. If you time it right, you might even be joined by migrating cranes flying overhead.

The hike begins at White Rock's Overlook Park. Parking for the trailhead is near the dog park, and you'll find signs describing the trails near the parking area.

Begin by taking the Blue Dot Trail down to the river. It was built in the 1930s for livestock access. Follow it through an old fence into the canyon. Keep an eye out for painted blue dots showing the way. (The trails are named for their painted dots.) The rim has great views of the Sangre de Cristo Mountains far to the east, the Caja del Rio closer in, and the Rio Grande down below. Hike 27 (page 151) is just on the other side of the river.

The steep, well-defined trail switches back and forth several times as it descends through the basalt to a bench. After crossing the bench, the trail continues its steep but slightly easier descent toward the river. In about 0.75 mile you'll leave the basalt and enter a wooded section with a small running stream and soon reach the junction with the River Trail. The junction is well marked with signs. The Blue Dot Trail continues down to the riverbank. If you find yourself at the river's edge, you've gone too far. When you reach the junction you will have descended over 800 feet.

Turn right and follow the River Trail south. For the next 0.4 mile or so the trail crosses several small streams as it winds through a juniper forest. In less than 0.5 mile there will be unobstructed views of the river. In another 0.5 mile or so, you'll come to a sign that says RED DOT TRAIL 1 MILE on one side and BLUE DOT TRAIL 1 MILE on the other side. After about 2 miles of walking along the river you'll reach a strong stream and almost be at the junction with Red Dot.

White Rock Canyon: Red Dot/Blue Dot Trails

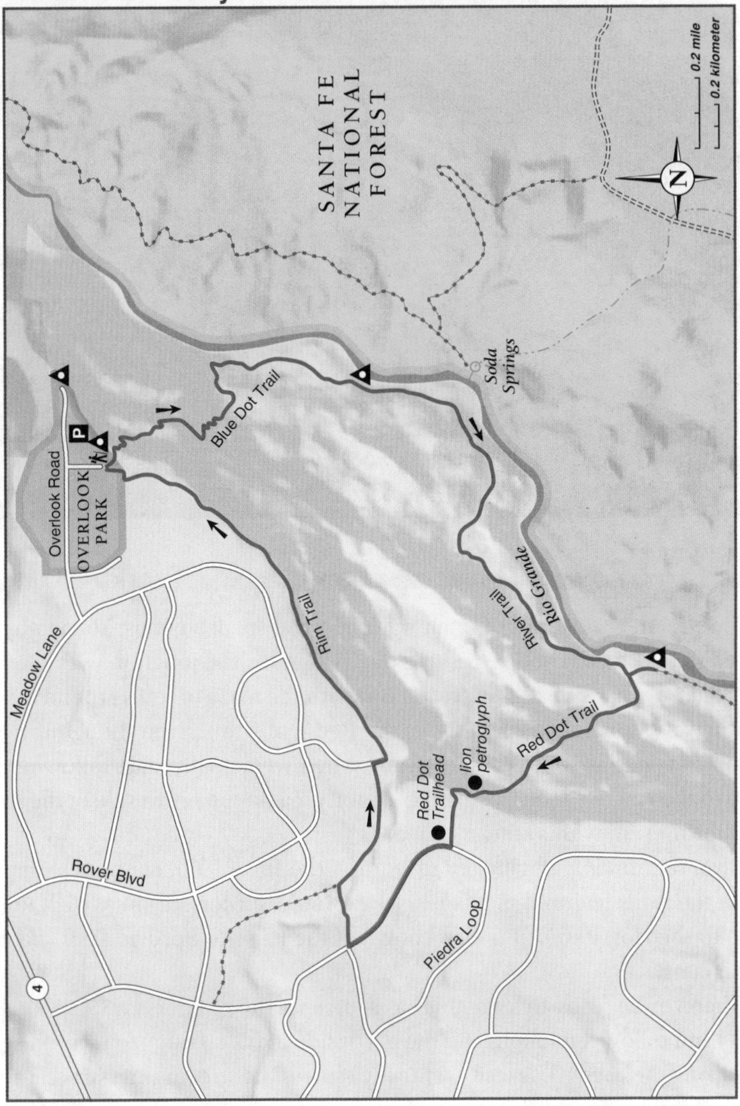

SANTA FE NATIONAL FOREST
0.2 mile
0.2 kilometer
N
Soda Springs
Blue Dot Trail
Overlook Road
OVERLOOK PARK
P
Rim Trail
River Trail
Rio Grande
Red Dot Trail
lion petroglyph
Red Dot Trailhead
Meadow Lane
Rover Blvd
Piedra Loop
4

6,600 ft.
6,400 ft.
6,200 ft.
6,000 ft.
5,800 ft.
5,600 ft.
5,400 ft.
1 mi.
2 mi.
3 mi.
4 mi.
5 mi.
6 mi.

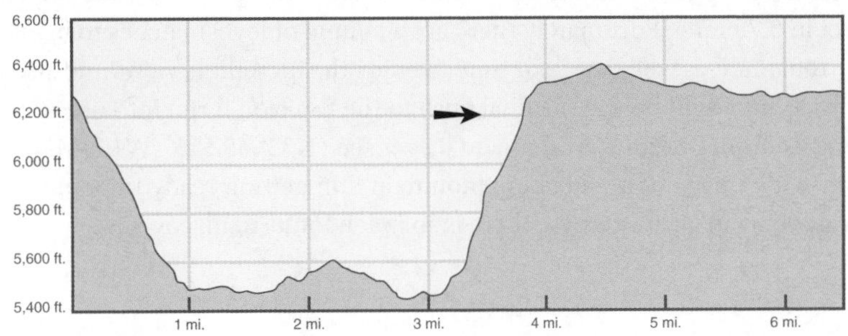

Lagoons along the riverside create a little paradise.

The stream has a series of small waterfalls and small lagoons. You might even be tempted to take a cool and refreshing dip. A sign for the junction with the Red Dot Trail is on the other side of the stream. But with the maze of trails around the lagoons it's not always apparent which one is the Red Dot Trail. Even though the Red Dot junction trail sign is south of the stream, when we actually start following the Red Dot up to the rim, we'll be leaving the lagoon area on the north side of the stream. In the meantime, enjoy this fantastic area.

If you're thinking of a longer adventure, the River Trail continues south to link up with the trails featured in Hike 30 (page 166). But for our hike, we'll follow Red Dot up to the rim. Red Dot is also known as the Pajarito Springs Trail and has been used for centuries.

When you're ready to leave this oasis, pick up the red dots (N35° 48.122' W106° 11.733') and follow them uphill on the north side of the stream. You'll soon see petroglyphs along the route. The trail eventually crosses the stream and starts climbing.

This may be one of the steepest climbs that you'll ever do. You'll be climbing 800 feet in 0.75 mile. Fortunately there are a couple of level benches to break up the climb. You might as well take your time to enjoy the incredible views and also to look at the rock art. Right before the final push to the top, you'll run into one of the most amazing examples of rock art that you'll ever see (N35° 48.510' W106° 12.067'). It's a 5-foot-wide image of a crouching mountain lion getting ready to pounce. We are fortunate to be in an area where there is so much for us to discover.

And with one final push, you'll be back on top. Once on top, turn right to follow the trail for another 0.15 mile west to the Red Dot Trailhead. It's on a residential street (Piedra Loop) and about 2.4 miles from the starting point.

Because of a deep gulch between here and the starting point, it's necessary to do a short road walk to get around the gulch. For that, turn right and walk on Piedra Loop northwest. When you reach the first road coming in from your left (La Senda), look to your right for a marker for a trail going off into the juniper woods. (It's right behind the road barrier.) Turn right and follow the trail east as it passes some houses to get around the head of the gulch and to the Rim Trail (N35° 48.752' W106° 11.948'). It's actually quite cool to pass a residential area to reach our goal, as little trails like this can help make our communities more walkable.

Once on the Rim Trail, head in a northeast direction back to Overlook Park. There will be houses to the left and the rim to the right. Between the two is a braided network of paths. Every trail has wonderful views toward the rim. Eventually you'll see light towers for the athletic fields at Overlook Park to guide you back to your starting point to conclude a fabulous adventure.

NEARBY ACTIVITIES

While in White Rock, you might want to stop by the visitor center at 115 NM 4. It's just west of where you turned for Rover. It is open daily and has exhibits, hiking maps, information on area attractions, water, restrooms, picnic tables, RV hookups, and parking, and it is also where you pick up the free shuttle to Bandelier. For more information, call 505-672-3183 or visit visitlosalamos.org.

• •

GPS TRAILHEAD COORDINATES N35° 49.441' W106° 11.070'

DIRECTIONS Via Santa Fe: From I-25 North, take Exit 276 and turn left onto NM 599. Go 13.5 miles north to merge onto US 84. Continue 14 miles north to the Los Alamos exit. Turn left and go 11.6 miles west on NM 502. Merge onto NM 4 toward White Rock and follow it 3.7 miles to Rover Boulevard in the center of White Rock. There are signs pointing the way to Overlook Park. Turn left onto Rover. In 0.2 mile, turn left onto Meadow Lane. In 0.8 mile, turn left onto Overlook Road. Pass by the ballfields, and in 0.4 mile, turn right onto the road leading to the trailhead parking area near the dog park area.

Via San Ysidro: From I-25 North, take Exit 242 toward Bernalillo. Turn left on US 550 and go 23.5 miles to San Ysidro. Turn right onto NM 4 and follow it 63.1 miles to Rover Boulevard in the center of White Rock. (See Via Santa Fe for details on reaching the trailhead.)

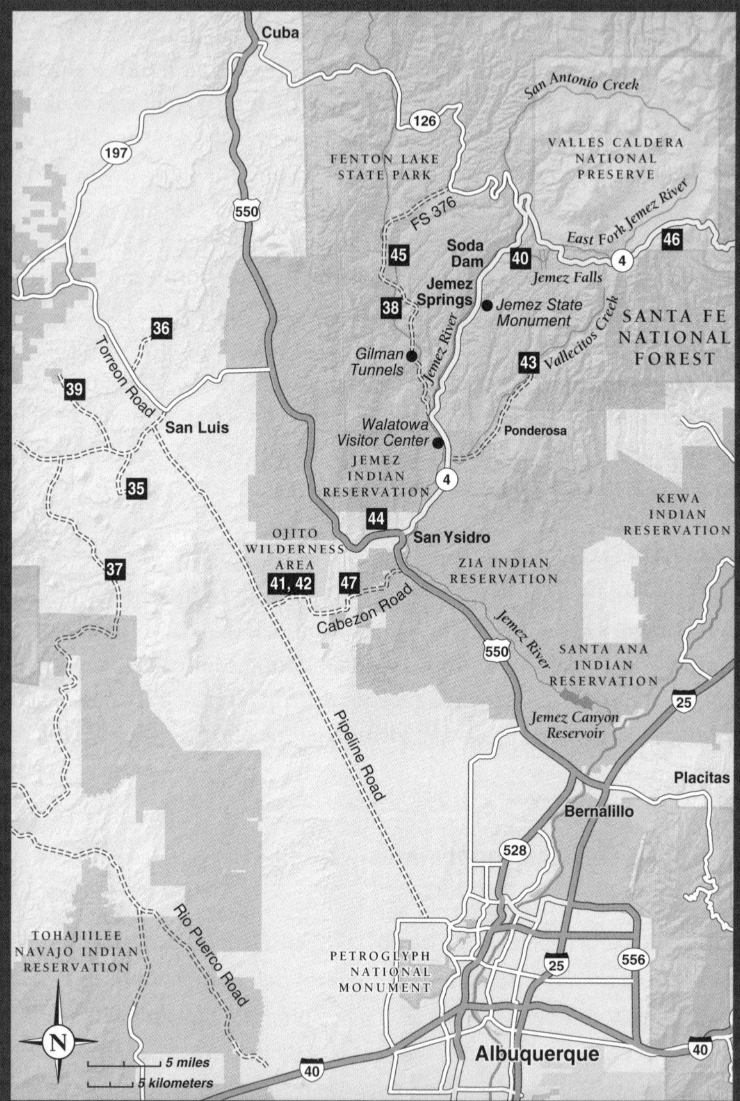
Cuba
San Antonio Creek
126
197
FENTON LAKE
STATE PARK
VALLES CALDERA
NATIONAL
PRESERVE
550
FS 376
East Fork Jemez River
Soda
Dam
40
4
46
45
Jemez
Springs
Jemez Falls
38
Jemez State
Monument
36
SANTA FE
NATIONAL
FOREST
Gilman
Tunnels
Jemez River
Vallecitos Creek
43
Torreon Road
39
San Luis
Walatowa
Visitor Center
Ponderosa
JEMEZ
INDIAN
RESERVATION
35
44
KEWA
INDIAN
RESERVATION
San Ysidro
OJITO
WILDERNESS
AREA
ZIA INDIAN
RESERVATION
37
41, 42
47
Cabezon Road
Jemez River
550
SANTA ANA
INDIAN
RESERVATION
25
Pipeline Road
Jemez Canyon
Reservoir
Placitas
Bernalillo
528
Rio Puerco Road
TOHAJIILEE
NAVAJO INDIAN
RESERVATION
PETROGLYPH
NATIONAL
MONUMENT
25
556
N
5 miles
5 kilometers
Albuquerque
40
40

NORTHWEST OF ALBUQUERQUE

35 Cabezon Peak 192

36 Continental Divide Trail (CDT): Deadman Peaks 196

37 Guadalupe Outlier 200

38 Holiday Mesa 204

39 La Leña WSA: Empedrado Ridge-CDT 209

40 McCauley Hot Springs 213

41 Ojito Wilderness: Hoodoo Trail 218

42 Ojito Wilderness: Seismosaurus Trail 222

43 Paliza Canyon Goblin Colony 227

44 San Ysidro Trials Area 232

45 Stable Mesa 237

46 Valles Caldera National Preserve 242

47 White Ridge Bike Trails Area 247

35 CABEZON PEAK

Looking west from Cabezon, you'll take in magnificent formations as far as you can see.

THIS LOOP ON the shoulders of a giant volcanic plug offers amazing vistas at every turn. This entire area could easily qualify as a national park if more people knew about it. A nontechnical but nonetheless harrowing spur presents the option of climbing to the top of its towering neck.

DESCRIPTION

The pedestal of Cabezon stands well over 1,000 feet high. Jutting up another 800 feet is a ribbed column of basalt that once filled the throat of a great volcano. The cinder cone has long since eroded to expose this monolithic core.

The Navajo name for it is *tse najin,* or "black rock." Their legends tell of the Twin Warrior Gods who decapitated a giant. The blood from the fatal wound spilled to the south and congealed into the lava flow at El Malpais (Hike 51, page 269), and its head became what the Spaniards would later call *Cabezón,* which translates as "big head."

Spanish settlement here in the upper Rio Puerco Valley began shortly after the reconquest, but the early ranchos were soon under continual attack from Navajo neighbors to the west. Relations with eastern neighbors were strained in 1815 when the Spanish government awarded tracts of Zia, Jemez, and Santa Ana pueblo lands to Cabeza de Baca. The resulting dispute over this grant, known as the Ojo del Espiritu Santo, lasted well over a century.

DISTANCE & CONFIGURATION: 2.5-mile balloon, plus optional summit spur

DIFFICULTY: Strenuous approach, moderate–strenuous loop, insane spur

SCENERY: National park–quality views over mixed grassland steppe and volcanic fields

EXPOSURE: Mostly sunny

TRAIL TRAFFIC: Low–moderate

TRAIL SURFACE: Dirt, rock

HIKING TIME: 2.5 hours, another 2–3 hours for the summit spur

DRIVING DISTANCE: 74 miles from the Big I

ELEVATION GAIN: 6,476' at trailhead; 7,273' high point of balloon; 7,785' at summit

ACCESS: Year-round; no fees or permits required

WHEELCHAIR ACCESS: No

MAPS: USGS *Cabezon Peak*

FACILITIES: None

CONTACT: BLM–Rio Puerco Field Office, blm.gov/office/rio-puerco-field-office, 505-761-8700

LOCATION: San Luis

COMMENTS: The last 7 miles of roads, especially the approach road, and the trail can turn treacherous in wet conditions. A brochure on the Cabezon Peak Wilderness Study Area can be acquired from the Bureau of Land Management (BLM) office in Albuquerque, or you can download it from blm.gov/visit/cabezon-wsa. Dogs cannot do the summit; they can do the trails.

LAST-CHANCE FOOD/GAS: Convenience store–gas station in San Ysidro, about 35 miles from the trailhead

Cabezon Peak straddles the western boundary, with its summit just inside the Ojo del Espiritu Santo Grant, though land on both sides is currently administered by the BLM. The property was badly eroded and overgrazed when the US government purchased it in 1934. Over the past 70 years, resource-management programs have brought modest improvements to the upper Rio Puerco Valley. The once-fertile farmlands have yet to return, but the terrain does support an impressive array of wildlife. Common creatures include three toad species, beavers, badgers, bobcats, and porcupines. Golden eagles, great horned owls, and a variety of hawks often nest by the peak.

Cabezon is often described in some variation of New Mexico's little Devils Tower. But check the stats: Devils Tower rises 1,267 feet from the Belle Fourche River to peak at 5,112 feet, whereas Cabezon rises 2,020 feet from the Rio Puerco to peak at 7,785 feet. So why the diminutive comparison? Maybe because Devils Tower, America's first national monument, is a solitary landmark that dwarfs everything else in its empty corner of Wyoming. By contrast, Cabezon stands in the company of about 50 other plugs in the shadow of Mount Taylor (Hike 55, page 288), the volcano peaking at 11,301 feet about 35 miles to the southwest. Or maybe because the vertical rock on Devils Tower exceeds Cabezon's by just enough to pose a significantly more challenging climb.

Cabezon's primary summit route is not considered a technical climb, but that doesn't make it easy or particularly safe. A hardhat is well advised (a bike helmet should suffice in a pinch). If the prospect of scrambling through talus and clawing your way up a chimney sounds daunting, don't let it keep you away from Cabezon. You can enjoy a hike here without a trip to the summit.

The hike begins on the eastern side of the parking area, where an aging signboard marks the trailhead. Start up the steep trail toward the volcanic neck. After a steady climb for nearly half a mile, the trail splits. Take your pick—both branches soon cross

Cabezon Peak

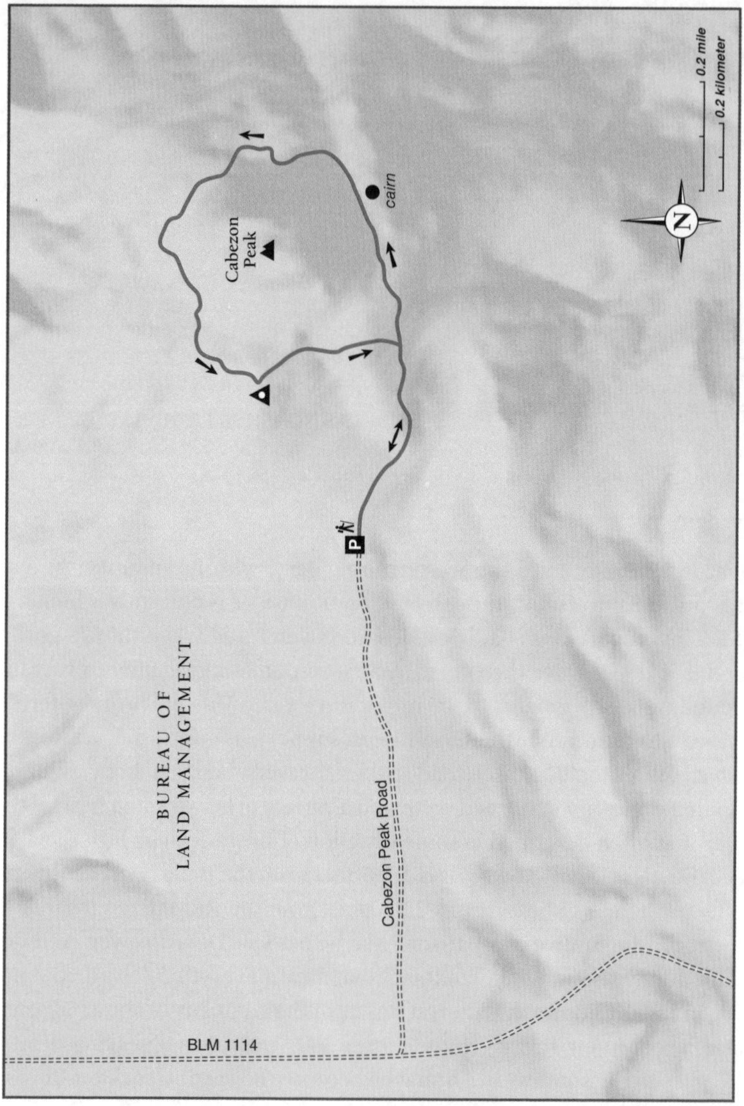

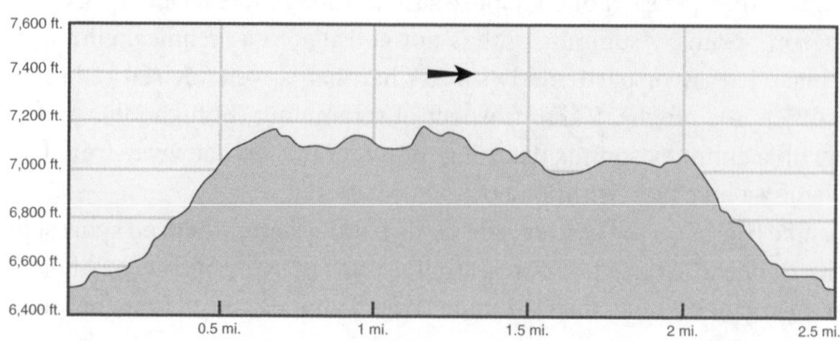

an old barbwire fence that marks the western boundary of the Ojo del Espiritu Santo Grant. If the trail fades on you, do a couple of zigzag patterns to pick it up again.

The branches merge shortly thereafter. Continue around to the south side of the neck. Less than 0.25 mile past the fence, look for the marker for the summit route (N35° 35.833' W107° 05.607'). Stones arranged into a 10-foot arrow point the way. There's no clear trail through the scree, so aim for the chimney. There you'll find rock ledges adequate for handholds and footholds to pull your way to the rim. Another short scramble through loose rock on the domed peak and you're at the top. Something to remember before attempting any ascent: descents are invariably more challenging.

After several minutes of contemplating the vertical route, you might wonder if circumnavigating the peak would be more fun than scaling it. Those prone to the slightest fits of acrophobia or who are hiking with dogs will certainly enjoy the loop more than the climb. Hearty hikers bent on doing both should do the ascent first, while their legs are still strong. Continuing with the hike, follow the path around to the southeast shoulder. There you'll find what appears to be an easier summit route. It isn't. From here the loop path fades as it drops into a boulder field. Few cairns mark the way, but the strategy from this point is obvious: keep the boulder fields on your left and the edge of the shoulder on your right.

Some boulder-hopping and a short climb are necessary to round the corner to the north side. Drop back down one level to get around the boulder field there. Just be patient to find the best route. You'll also find the shadow side of Cabezon a bit eerie, with lichen on the tower and relentless boulders at the base. Soon you'll cross a downed fence and continue around to the west side. An outcrop pointing due west provides fantastic views of other plugs like Cerro Cuate ("twins hill"), 4 miles west-northwest, and beautiful formations as far as you can see. And just in case you forgot where you parked, look down to your left.

The final quarter of the loop is across a steep slope. Avoid drifting too far downhill, or you'll face more difficulty in crossing the ridge ahead. Once over that last hump, you'll intersect the trail that brought you up here. Turn right and follow it back down to the parking area.

• •

GPS TRAILHEAD COORDINATES N35° 35.806' W107° 06.301'

DIRECTIONS From I-25 North, take Exit 242 at Bernalillo. Turn left on US 550 and go northwest 23 miles toward San Ysidro. Stay left on US 550 and continue another 18 miles toward Cuba. Turn left on County Road 279 to San Luis. The paved portion ends after 8.5 miles. Continue 3.8 miles straight on the dirt road. Veer left at the Y onto BLM 1114 and go south 2.9 miles. Turn left at the sign for Cabezon Peak and go east 0.9 mile on a rough road to the parking area at the end of the road.

36 CONTINENTAL DIVIDE TRAIL (CDT): Deadman Peaks

Interesting rock formations abound on this hike.

HIKE A WONDERFUL portion of the Continental Divide National Scenic Trail (CDT) close to Albuquerque with fantastic views of Cabezon and other volcanic plugs of the Mount Taylor volcanic field. The loop described here uses equal parts dirt road and the CDT to circumnavigate a cluster of red hills known as Deadman Peaks.

DESCRIPTION

Upon arrival at the base of Deadman Peaks, the first thing everyone wants to do is check out the hoodoos. They're an odd sight, standing out there on the caliche like a colony of giant mushrooms sprouting from snowy-white earth. Next they want to know where the CDT is. Fact is, they're standing right on it.

The Continental Divide National Scenic Trail, more often referred to as the CDT, is a 3,100-mile-long distance hiking trail that runs on, or within 50 miles of, the Continental Divide from Mexico to Canada; 770 miles of the trail are in New Mexico. The CDT along with the Appalachian Trail (AT) and the Pacific Crest Trail (PCT) make up the triple crown of long-distance hiking trails in this country.

Hiking the entire CDT across New Mexico is a serious endeavor. A short day hike like this is a great way to get a taste of the CDT experience without the effort required for a longer hike. Hikes 39 and 55 (pages 209 and 288, respectively) also touch on portions of the CDT within our 60-mile radius from Albuquerque.

DISTANCE & CONFIGURATION: 2.8-mile loop or 4.9-mile loop

DIFFICULTY: Easy

SCENERY: Mesa vistas, rock formations, burned-out coal deposits, skittish cows

EXPOSURE: Minimal shade

TRAIL TRAFFIC: Low

TRAIL SURFACE: Rocky trail, dirt road

HIKING TIME: 1.5 or 2.5 hours

DRIVING DISTANCE: 73 miles from the Big I

ELEVATION GAIN: 6,550' at trailhead; 6,932' at high point

ACCESS: Year-round, no fees or permits required

WHEELCHAIR ACCESS: No

MAPS: USGS *San Luis* and *Headcut Reservoir*

FACILITIES: None

CONTACT: BLM–Rio Puerco Field Office, blm.gov/office/rio-puerco-field-office, 505-761-8700

LOCATION: San Luis

COMMENTS: Driving the dirt road can get tricky in wet conditions. Leashed dogs are allowed on trails.

LAST-CHANCE FOOD/GAS: Convenience store–gas station in San Ysidro, about 35 miles from the trailhead

The challenge of a long hike on the CDT in New Mexico is the scarcity of naturally occurring water. A long hike on the CDT revolves around where to find water, treating the water, and how much to carry to get to the next water source. The Continental Divide Coalition at continentaldividetrail.org can provide information on the trail and, more important, provide information on how to successfully hike the CDT.

This hike follows a stretch of the CDT that was built in the late 1990s and early 2000s. Building the trail through the upper Rio Puerco Valley was sponsored primarily by volunteers from the New Mexico Mountain Club. The hike begins where BLM 1102 makes a left turn and heads north. There is plenty of room for several cars to park, and the hoodoos will be right in front of you.

Start hiking from the hoodoos. Just turn your back to them and walk straight north along the road. You should spot the cairns within a minute. Each is a pyramid stacked about knee high. Keep them in sight, and you'll never lose the trail.

About 0.2 mile from the hoodoos, the trail deviates east from the road and climbs the side of a ridge pointing south from the pedestal of Deadman Peaks. About 0.25 mile farther up is the first of six switchbacks leading to the biggest of Deadman's three peaks.

At first glance, the peaks appear as ordinary volcanoes capped with the usual rust-red cinders. A closer look reveals a shade of reddish-orange that's not quite as common in these otherwise dun mesa lands, though many roads around Torreon are the same fiery shade. This surfacing material is sometimes referred to as red dog or clinker. Pick up a few scatters along the path, and you'll see it isn't lava. This red rock forms when heat from coal-seam fires causes low-grade metamorphic changes in the mudstones sandwiched between the coals.

The trail levels out for the next 0.6 mile as it follows the rim. On your left, the main peak rises another 200 feet. On your immediate right, the drop from the rim is 100 feet or so. The views south to Cabezon and beyond are stunning!

Continental Divide Trail: Deadman Peaks

Continental Divide Trail

Continental Divide Trail

Deadman Peaks

Cerros Colorados

BUREAU OF LAND MANAGEMENT

To CR 279

BLM 1102

P

Continental Divide Trail

N

0.2 mile

0.2 kilometer

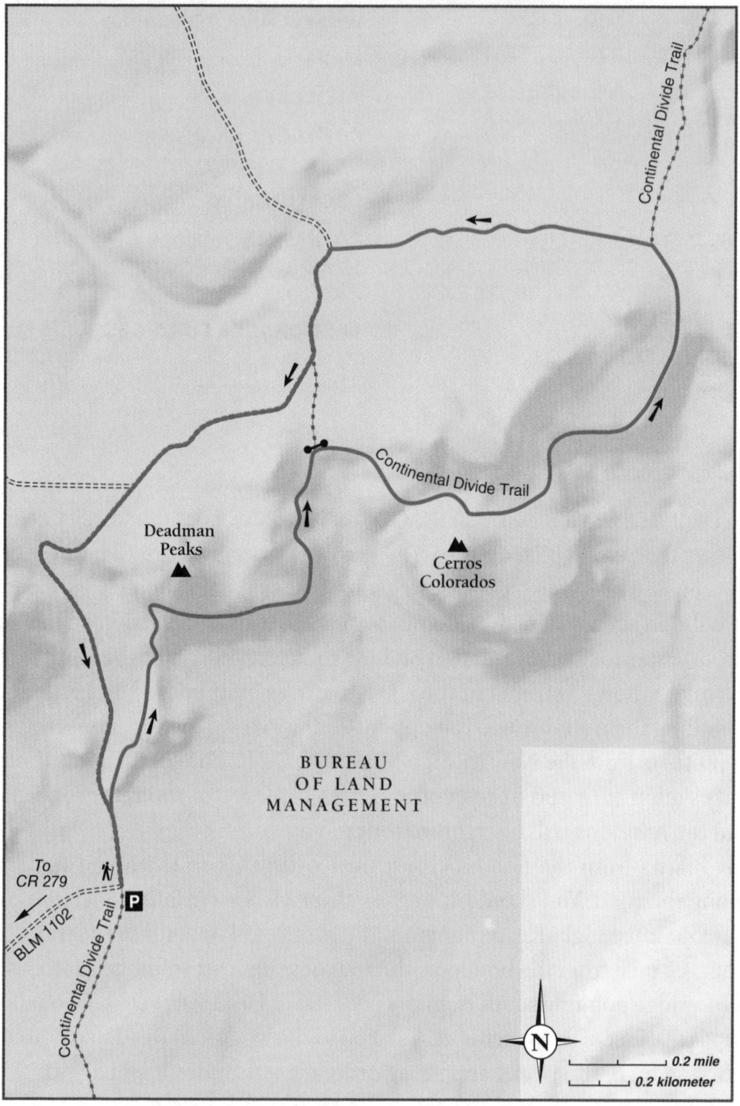

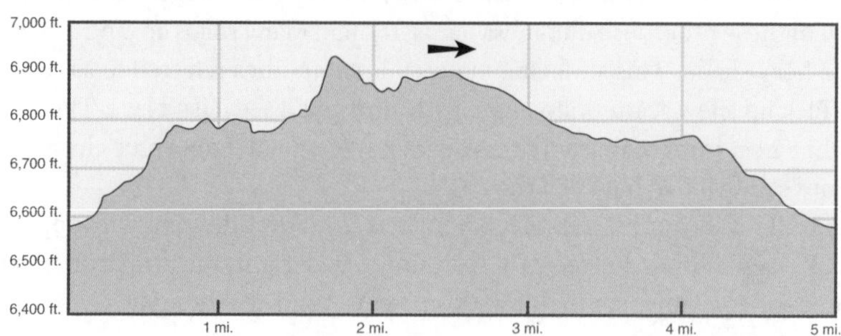

One mile into the hike, the trail turns north along the rim of a canyon that separates Deadman Peaks from the somewhat bulkier Cerros Colorados. Once the trail reaches the back end of the canyon, it turns right and joins a former doubletrack. The old road comes in from the north through an opening in the fence (N35° 45.357' W107° 04.046') and heads east into the Cerros Colorados. There are several cairns in the area and brush blocking the old road. If you're pressed for time, it's best to leave the trail at this point for a 2.8-mile loop. The next opportunity to leave the CDT is in 1.2 miles farther north for a 4.9-mile loop.

If you continue on the CDT and turn the corner into the Cerros Colorados, you could easily lose half an hour gawking at rock formations in a 0.25-mile twist of waterways. Then there's always something else to lure you around the next bend. When you leave the rim you'll pass through a pedestrian gate and start running into white-painted posts to mark the trail. Very soon after the gate, you'll reach a doubletrack (N35° 45.718' W107° 03.303'). This is where this hike leaves the CDT by turning left (west) and starts heading back to your car. You can continue on the CDT, if you want, but before you know it, you'll be 6 miles from your car.

If you opt for the quick 2.8-mile loop, go through the fence opening and walk about 200 yards to the dirt road (BLM 1102). Turn left (west) and follow the road about 1.4 miles back to the junction where you parked.

If you choose the full 4.9 hike, continue west on the doubletrack. In less than 0.75 mile the doubletrack will join BLM 1102. Turn left again (south) and follow the road a bit less than 1.5 miles back to your car.

Once back at the hoodoos, you might be tempted to see what lies along the CDT to the southwest. You'll soon run into the same problem: one hyperscenic turn after another lures you farther along the trail, dropping to cross the Arroyo de Los Cerros Colorados and then quickly climbing past the 6,650-foot peak of San Luis. Next you're crossing pavement on Torreon Road and heading out on a high bench on Mesa San Luis. Before you know it, you're standing on the edge of a wind-sculpted sandstone ridge, once again with 6 miles of CDT between you and your car.

• •

GPS TRAILHEAD COORDINATES N35° 44.609' W107° 04.463'

DIRECTIONS From I-25 North, take Exit 242 at Bernalillo. Turn left on US 550 and go northwest 23 miles toward San Ysidro. Stay left on US 550 and continue another 18 miles toward Cuba. Turn left on County Road 279 to San Luis. The paved portion ends after 8.5 miles. Turn right here onto Torreon Road (also paved) and go north 3.7 miles. At the top of the hill, turn right onto BLM 1102. (Look for a stop sign and a yellow cattle guard.) You can park here to pick up the CDT, or follow the main dirt road northeast 3.4 miles to the next CDT intersection (our trailhead) on the south side of Deadman Peaks. Park on the side of the road in front of the mushroom-shaped hoodoos.

37 GUADALUPE OUTLIER

The 21-mile drive to Guadalupe Outlier rivals California Highway 1 for beauty.

AT THE CHACOAN outlier of Guadalupe Ruin, you can explore the ruin, wander along the roads, and take in scenery worthy of a national park. This is an opportunity for an adventure within our 60-mile radius of Albuquerque.

DESCRIPTION

Chaco Canyon, and its collection of amazing ruins of prehistoric great houses and kivas, is a UNESCO World Heritage site and beyond our 60-mile radius from Albuquerque. If you have never been there, it is well worth visiting. At its height around 1,000 years ago, the Chacoan influence extended beyond the limits of the canyon and into our 60-mile radius from Albuquerque.

That influence included a network of outlying great houses and roads to connect them to the center of Chaco Canyon. Guadalupe Ruin is the eastern-most Chacoan outlier. It is located on top of a small steep-walled mesa overlooking the Rio Puerco.

No one knows for sure why it was built. Some speculate that it was built to control the flow of turquoise coming out of the Cerillos Hills (Hike 26, page 146) near Santa Fe. Regardless of the reason, Guadalupe has a commanding view of what would have been the eastern edge of Chacoan influence.

DISTANCE & CONFIGURATION: 0.5-mile out-and-back, with options to wander for miles

DIFFICULTY: Easy with a strenuous climb to the ruin

SCENERY: Ancient ruin, national park–quality views, volcanic plugs, mesas, solitude

EXPOSURE: Mostly sunny

TRAIL TRAFFIC: Low

TRAIL SURFACE: Dirt, rock

HIKING TIME: 1–2 hours

DRIVING DISTANCE: 87 miles from the Big I

ELEVATION GAIN: 5,887' at trailhead; 6,042' at ruin

ACCESS: Year-round; no fees or permits required

WHEELCHAIR ACCESS: No

MAPS: USGS *Guadalupe*

FACILITIES: None

CONTACT: BLM–Rio Puerco Field Office, blm.gov/office/rio-puerco-field-office, 505-761-8700

LOCATION: San Luis

COMMENTS: Driving on the dirt road can get tricky in wet conditions. Leashed dogs are allowed on trails.

LAST-CHANCE FOOD/GAS: Convenience store–gas station in San Ysidro, about 37 miles from the trailhead

There are two reasons for including Guadalupe Ruin as one of the 60 hikes. One is for the opportunity to explore a very remote and astoundingly attractive location. The other is for the drive. The drive to Guadalupe is virtually unknown and deserves to be on the list of the greatest drives of the nation. It challenges the drive to Big Sur on California Highway 1 for scenery.

Although Sandoval County has improved the road to Guadalupe in the last few years, don't even consider driving on it if it is wet. It is easy to get stuck or to slide out of control when the road is wet. Portions of the road can be washed out if there has been a heavy rain, so please turn around if you run into an obstacle. And plan your trip accordingly to not drive at night. But if the road is dry and you have plenty of daylight, you'll have an amazing adventure that you'll long remember.

You'll reach Guadalupe Ruin from the same approach as Cabezon and our other hikes in the Upper Rio Puerco basin. When you leave the pavement, you'll have countless volcanic plugs of the Mount Taylor volcanic field and even more mesas in front of you. The scenery is worthy of national park designation. You might wish you had a scorecard to keep track of the scenic vistas. There are so many!

As the road curves west, you'll pass the approach road to Cabezon (Hike 35, page 192). The road will eventually turn south (see Directions) and cross a wide arroyo (Arroyo Chico). Soon after the arroyo, you'll reach a junction. It looks like the main road continues ahead. You want to turn left, to keep going south. At this point, you're 8 miles from your destination. And now the scenery is going to get even better.

You'll be totally immersed in volcanic plugs and mesas as you go up and over hills and cross arroyos on your journey south. To your left you'll soon see the two volcanic plugs (Cerro Santa Clara and Cerro Guadalupe) that were featured on the commemorative postage stamp issued to celebrate the centennial of New Mexico's statehood. Cerro Guadalupe is the plug that looks like it has horns on its southern flank.

Guadalupe Outlier

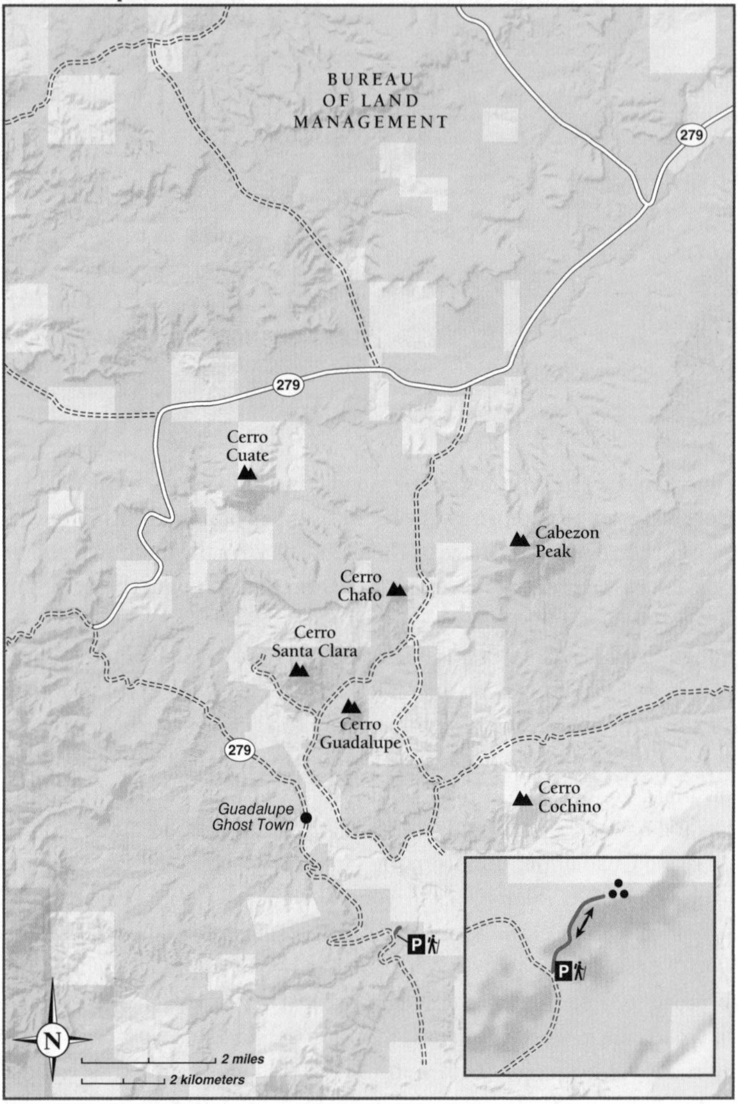

BUREAU
OF LAND
MANAGEMENT
279
279
279
Cerro Cuate
Cabezon Peak
Cerro Chafo
Cerro Santa Clara
Cerro Guadalupe
Cerro Cochino
Guadalupe Ghost Town
P
N
2 miles
2 kilometers

6,300 ft.
6,200 ft.
6,100 ft.
6,000 ft.
5,900 ft.
5,800 ft.
5,700 ft.
0.1 mi.
0.2 mi.
0.25 mi.

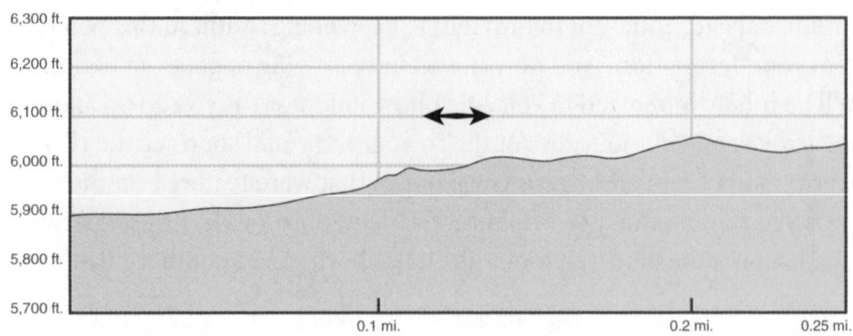

The sandstone scenery on the right side is also fantastic. There are mesas, pillars, walls, and other contorted formations. Eventually you'll reach the melting-adobe ghost town of Guadalupe. The two-story building was once a hotel. Guadalupe is on private land and is an active ranch, so you'll have to enjoy it from the car. Once you clear the ghost town you'll be on Bureau of Land Management land for the rest of the way.

You'll reach Guadalupe Ruin after driving 29.5 miles from US 550. The mesa with the ruin is on your left. The easiest place to park is south of the mesa on the left side of the road. From here the hike is quite simple: walk back to the mesa. The trail starts at the interpretive sign.

The trail is short but very steep. When you get to the top, take your time to notice the details of the ruin. The extremely fine stone work is unmistakably of Chacoan origin. And feel free to climb into the excavated kivas. When you're done checking out the ruin, check out the views. They, too, are worthy of a national park. The Rio Puerco is immediately to the east, and Cabezon is to the north.

When you're done with the ruin, it's a good time to walk around and explore the area. If you walk south, you'll probably see piles of stone that were once housing units associated with the mesa-top ruin. If you walk to the north, you might notice a black basalt dike near the bottom of the mesa. And you're welcome to keep walking north and do some exploring there. As long as you stay near the road you'll be on public land and won't get lost. Since very few people venture this way, you can have a nice quiet walk along the road and a chance to get a closer look at the land. Who knows what you'll discover.

And when you're done exploring, return the way you came in. The views will be just as great the second time around. And with it being later in the day, the different angle of the sun may reveal something you missed before. I'm sure you'll agree after taking this drive that there is no place anywhere else quite like it and that this is one of the great drives of the nation.

• •

GPS TRAILHEAD COORDINATES N35° 30.941' W107° 07.658'

DIRECTIONS From I-25 North, take Exit 242 at Bernalillo. Turn left on US 550 and go northwest 23 miles toward San Ysidro. Stay left on US 550 and continue another 18 miles toward Cuba. Turn left on County Road 279 to San Luis. The paved portion ends after 8.5 miles. Reset your odometer now. Continue straight on the dirt road. The road will arc to the west and turn south in 8.7 miles from the pavement to cross a wide arroyo. At 13 miles from the pavement, the road will reach a junction. The main road appears to go straight. Turn left (south) to remain on CR 279 and to reach your destination, 21 miles from the pavement. Park south of the mesa on the left side of the road.

38 HOLIDAY MESA

From the top of Holiday Mesa, look south to the Sandia Mountains.

IT'S HARD TO beat the combination of a scenic drive up one side of Rio Guadalupe and a wonderful hike on the other side to the top of Holiday Mesa. The hike has fantastic views and an optional extension to the ruins of an ancient pueblo. If you're OK with fording the Rio Guadalupe and a tough climb, you'll like this hike.

DESCRIPTION

Holiday Mesa is a massive sheer-wall formation in the Jemez Mountains that was once an ancestral homeland of Jemez Pueblo. More than 500 years later the mesa is still visited and held sacred by the people of Jemez. Later in the first half of the 20th century, the mesa top was heavily logged and was named after a lumberman. (See Hike 45, page 237, for more history of this area.)

The hike follows old logging roads to the top of the mesa for views that stretch all the way back to Albuquerque; a chance to see how the U.S. Forest Service is grooming the forest to prevent catastrophic fires; and if you're willing to walk a little farther, a chance to see an ancestral home of Jemez Pueblo.

As you drive up NM 4 from Jemez Pueblo you'll pass beautiful red rock formations on your right and the Walatowa Visitor Center to your left. As you continue,

DISTANCE & CONFIGURATION: 4.6-mile or 8.5-mile out-and-back

DIFFICULTY: Strenuous in parts; easy in others

SCENERY: Magnificent mountain and canyon views, ponderosa parkland, streams

EXPOSURE: Mostly shaded

TRAIL TRAFFIC: Low

TRAIL SURFACE: Dirt, rock, volcanic ash

HIKING TIME: 3–5 hours

DRIVING DISTANCE: 59 miles from the Big I

ELEVATION GAIN: 6,627' at trailhead; 7,528' on top of the mesa

ACCESS: May–mid-December; Forest Road 376 is closed in the winter; no fees or permits required

WHEELCHAIR ACCESS: No

MAPS: Santa Fe National Forest–West Half; USGS *San Miguel Mountain*

FACILITIES: None

CONTACT: Santa Fe National Forest–Jemez Ranger District, fs.usda.gov/santafe, 575-829-3535

LOCATION: Cañon

COMMENTS: Hike requires fording Rio Guadalupe; bring a pair of flip-flops for the ford. Leashed dogs are allowed on trails.

LAST-CHANCE FOOD/GAS: Convenience store, gas station, and visitor center on NM 4, about 11 miles south of the trailhead

you'll pass the small community of Cañon and eventually reach the junction of NM 4 and NM 485. The two mesas in front of you are Guadalupe Mesa (the shorter one in front) and Virgin Mesa. Holiday Mesa is farther north and west.

The mesas were once part of the Cañon de San Diego Land Grant. Over time, control of the grant fell into the hands of lumbering interests. When logging ceased in the middle of the last century, the land was transferred to Santa Fe National Forest.

To reach the trailhead, turn left and go north on NM 485. You'll soon enter Guadalupe Canyon with its red sandstone walls and go through the Gilman Tunnels. NM 485 becomes FR 376 when it crosses into U.S. Forest Service land just before the tunnels.

The trailhead is 2.7 miles after the tunnels. It is a wide area on the right side of the road with room to park several cars and a gate blocking access to a very rutted dirt road leading down to the Rio Guadalupe. Our destination is the top of the sheer-wall mesa on the other side of the river.

The hike begins by following the rutted road down to and across the river. You can either wade or hop rocks to cross the river. Fortunately, the river is neither deep nor wide. But don't cross it if it is flooded or a raging torrent. It helps to have a pair of flip-flops to wear while wading.

Once on the other side continue up the road. The old roadway along the river edge is not the way to go. The first few hundred feet of the road are steep. But you'll be turning right (southeast) very soon (N35° 46.231' W106° 47.184'). If you kept going straight, you'd join Hike 45 (page 237) in about 3 miles.

The route is wooded the entire way and gains 900 feet in the next 2.3 miles to reach the top. The road traces the face of the mesa by winding in and out of side notches on its upward trek. The route tends to make a steep climb, then finds a bench for a level stretch, and then resumes climbing. The intermittent benches give

Holiday Mesa

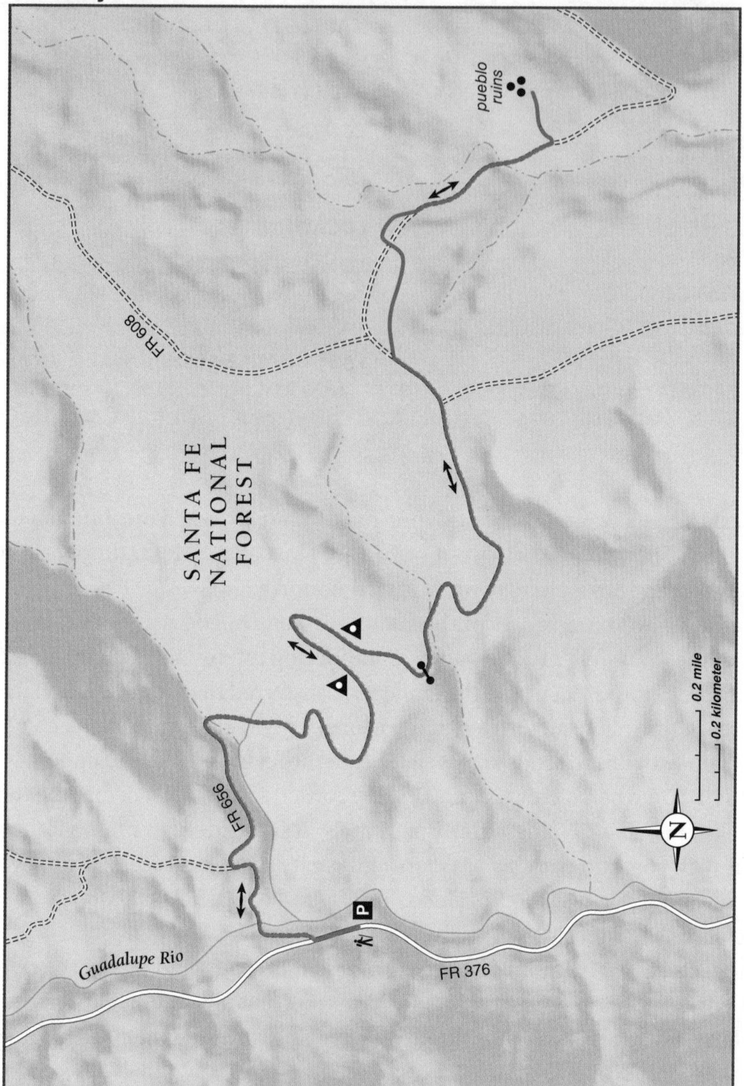

pueblo ruins
FR 608
SANTA FE NATIONAL FOREST
FR 656
Guadalupe Rio
FR 376
P
0.2 mile
0.2 kilometer
N

7,700 ft.
7,500 ft.
7,300 ft.
7,100 ft.
6,900 ft.
6,700 ft.
6,500 ft.
1 mi.
2 mi.
3 mi.
4 mi.

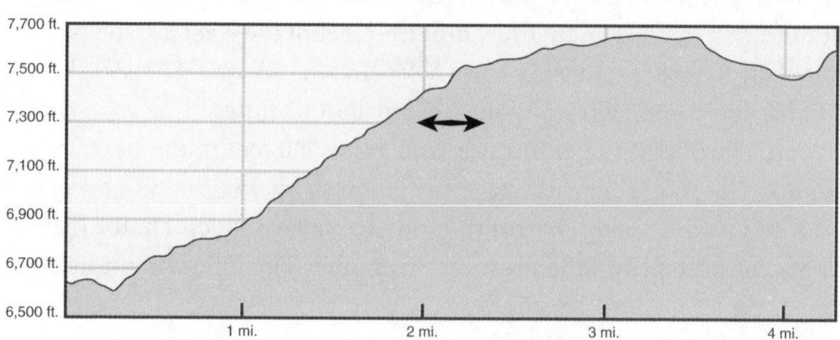

Cross this creek to reach the top of the mesa.

you a chance to catch your breath and make the climb much easier. Because of erosion the road can get very rocky, so pay attention to your footing. No matter what, you'll have fantastic views for the entire route to compensate for any difficulties.

Relatively early in the climb, if it has been a good water year, you'll run into a small stream and a couple of flowing springs in one of the notches. Farther up the road there will be a fenceline. Keep heading uphill. Soon after the fenceline the road will make a sharp turn to the right. There will also be a lesser road going to the left. Turn right and continue uphill.

When you reach the top, you will literally be on top of the world. The sheer drops are vertigo inducing, so don't get too close to the ledge. And you'll have stunning views everywhere. You'll see mountains, mesas, Rio Guadalupe canyon down below, and a sea of trees.

There is also a drop gate at the top. The gate is there to prevent vehicles on top of the mesa from going down the route you came up. From here, you have a decision to make. After taking in the views, you can turn around for a 4.6-mile out-and-back hike or continue on. Since the mesa is generally flat, the hiking is easy from this point on.

If you continue, you'll be walking through a ponderosa forest. The composition of the road is a soft volcanic ash that is much easier on the feet than the rocks on the washed-out road. The U.S. Forest Service is actively thinning the trees to reduce the likelihood of catastrophic fire.

The forest is an open and peaceful parkland. As an added bonus the trees cut down by the U.S. Forest Service are being processed by a Jemez Pueblo enterprise into various wood products. The enterprise is a continuation of the traditional connection between the mountains and the Jemez people.

If you wish to visit an ancestral pueblo, it's 2 miles from the gate. To get there, just stay on the road. Even if you don't go all the way to the ruin, the walk through the woods in itself is wonderful. In about 1 mile the road will join FR 608. Turn right and follow FR 608 as it goes east and then arcs to the south. In 0.8 mile, very soon after the road climbs out of a drainage, there will be a hill on your left. The ancestral pueblo is at the top about 600 feet away.

The buildings collapsed long ago into a series of long mounds that seem to go in all directions. It is extremely impressive. And the setting is spectacular. You can even see the Sandia Mountains in the far distance. The view alone is worth the hike. Enjoy the view, but remember to leave everything as you found it. This, like all archaeological sites, is still sacred and protected by law.

When you've finished taking it all in, it will be time to retrace your steps and return to your car. Be careful as you go over the rocks on the road going downhill. And don't forget that you still have to cross the river before wrapping up your 8.5-mile hike. And you'll still have the fantastic drive home through Guadalupe Canyon. You might even want to stop to take a picture in the afternoon light.

NEARBY ACTIVITIES

Walatowa Visitor Center is about 11 miles south of the trailhead on the west side of NM 4 (between mile markers 8 and 7), just north of the gas station. The visitor center has exhibits on the history of Jemez Pueblo, a gift shop, and U.S. Forest Service information. It is generally open daily from 8 a.m. to 5 p.m. and well worth a stop. For more information, call 575-834-9235 or visit jemezpueblo.com.

• •

GPS TRAILHEAD COORDINATES N35° 45.951' W106° 47.324'

DIRECTIONS From I-25 North, take Exit 242. Turn left on US 550 and go 23.5 miles to San Ysidro. Turn right on NM 4 (beware of speed traps) and go 9.5 miles to Cañon. Turn left on NM 485 and go north 5.7 miles. The road becomes FR 376, a narrow but well-maintained gravel road. Continue 2.7 miles beyond the tunnels to a parking area on the right side of the road. The hike begins at the gate ahead.

39 LA LEÑA WSA: Empedrado Ridge–CDT

Hoodoos and other great landforms await on this hike.

HOODOOS AND VIEWS dominate this off-trail hike in a remote wilderness study area northwest of Cabezon. The views are worthy of a national park, and the hike is a good one to take with fellow adventurers.

DESCRIPTION

In 1975 Congress directed the Bureau of Land Management (BLM) to identify roadless areas of 5,000 acres or more under their jurisdiction with wilderness characteristics to develop a list of possible candidates for wilderness protection. Because designating an official wilderness area takes an act of Congress, many of the candidates have been classified by the BLM as wilderness study areas (WSAs). The BLM manages WSAs as if they were official wilderness areas by discouraging off-road vehicle activity and development. WSAs are open to most outdoor recreation, such as hiking and hunting. The Ojito (Hikes 41 and 42) was a WSA before it became a wilderness in 2005.

The Upper Rio Puerco area has five WSAs (Cabezon, Ignacio Chavez, Chamisa, Empedrado, and La Leña). Except for the trails near Cabezon and the Continental Divide Trail (CDT), there are no developed hiking trails in the Upper Puerco WSAs. To remedy this situation Michael Woodruff and the WOW WE Meetup Hiking Group have developed a nice 5.5- to 6-mile easy-to-follow off-trail loop route in

DISTANCE & CONFIGURATION: 5.5- to 6-mile loop

DIFFICULTY: Moderate with a few tricky descents

SCENERY: Hoodoos, amazing rock formations

EXPOSURE: Mostly sunny

TRAIL TRAFFIC: Low

TRAIL SURFACE: Dirt, rock

HIKING TIME: 3 hours

DRIVING DISTANCE: 76 miles from the Big I

ELEVATION GAIN: 6,515' at trailhead; 6,295' at low point; 6,687' at high point

ACCESS: Year-round; no fees or permits required

WHEELCHAIR ACCESS: No

MAPS: USGS *Arroyo Empedrado*

FACILITIES: None

CONTACT: BLM–Rio Puerco Field Office, blm.gov/office/rio-puerco-field-office, 505-761-8700

LOCATION: San Luis

COMMENTS: Be cautious driving on the dirt road in wet conditions. Leashed dogs allowed on trails.

LAST-CHANCE FOOD/GAS: Convenience store–gas station in San Ysidro, about 37 miles from the trailhead

the upper basin of Empedrado Arroyo in the La Leña WSA. The La Leña WSA is 10,208 acres of badlands northwest of Cabezon. Because this area is very remote and off-trail, you might want to go with a partner or a group.

One of the attractions of this hike is the drive through national park–quality scenery to get there. The dirt roads can be impossible to drive when wet, so save this hike for dry weather. You'll have fantastic views that go on forever, hoodoos to explore, interesting rocks to examine, and to wrap up you'll follow a portion of the CDT.

When you get to your parking area on the right side of BLM 1102, you can, if you want, walk a few hundred feet to the end of the doubletrack for a very nice view. Otherwise, the hike starts on the other side of the road. The La Leña WSA is also on the other side of the road.

The hike begins as a walk through sagebrush–grassland with some junipers thrown in for variety. The entire hike is off-trail, so feel free to make your own adaptations. If you do make your own route, always keep in mind where you are in relation to your car. The route is reasonably intuitive, but having a GPS to navigate to critical decision points is helpful.

The first goal is to hike south a little less than 0.7 mile to the mesa edge (N35° 40.448' W107° 10.947') with its absolutely fabulous views. The views will be fantastic for the rest of the hike. Depending on the angle you took from your car, you could reach the edge a little bit earlier or later. It really doesn't matter, as you'll be following the edge to your right to our next decision point (N35° 40.660' W107° 11.200') in a little more than a mile. If you only hiked to here and returned to your car, you would still have a wonderful walk.

When you reach the decision point you should see an old fenceline in front of you. But the most important landmark will be a patch of brilliant white sandstone off to your left at the bottom of the mesa. The next step is to find a good way down to the white sandstone. It's really not that hard, but it can get tricky depending on the route you select. This is the trickiest part of the hike.

La Leña WSA: Empedrado Ridge–CDT

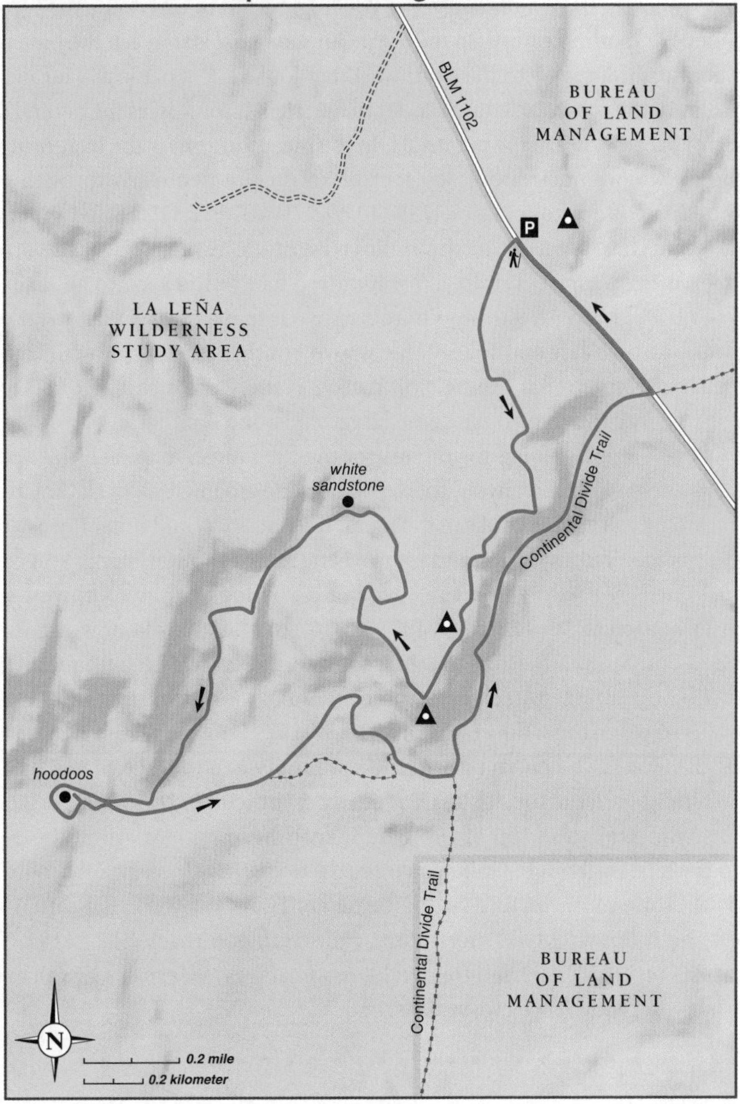

BLM 1102
BUREAU
OF LAND
MANAGEMENT
LA LEÑA
WILDERNESS
STUDY AREA
white
sandstone
Continental Divide Trail
hoodoos
Continental Divide Trail
BUREAU
OF LAND
MANAGEMENT
N
0.2 mile
0.2 kilometer

6,800 ft.
6,700 ft.
6,600 ft.
6,500 ft.
6,400 ft.
6,300 ft.
6,200 ft.
1 mi.
2 mi.
3 mi.
4 mi.
5 mi.

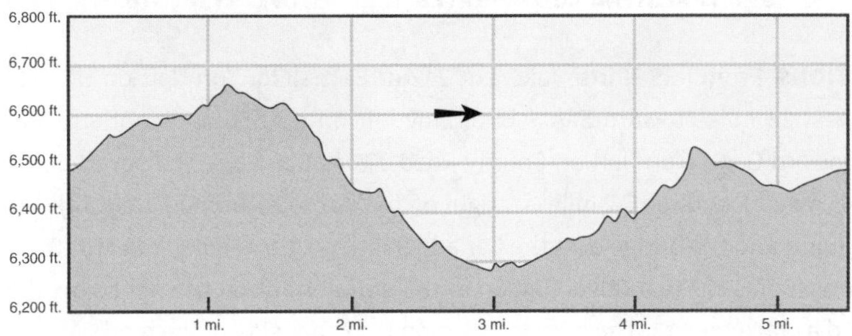

Once you're in the white sandstone, you might want to take some time to examine the hoodoos and other features in the area. Our next goal is to reach the base of a small uplift about 0.2 mile away to the southwest that looks like a peninsula jutting into the lower valley of the arroyo. It's much easier to find than it sounds, as the natural direction of the arroyo leads toward the peninsula. In the meantime enjoy the beautiful scenery.

The walk continues about 500 feet or so on the peninsula through beautiful sandstone formations to a place (N35° 40.492' W107° 11.419') where it is possible to work your way down off to the right (west) to a lower level of the arroyo valley. Once off the peninsula, walk a few hundred feet to the west to an arroyo (N35° 40.486' W107° 11.505'). At this point the arroyo is in exposed sandstone. From here you'll want to turn left and follow the arroyo south as it goes downhill through a small canyon. This stretch can be a bit tricky, as there are a couple of places where you have to climb down through some large sandstone boulders.

It will be smooth sailing for the rest of the hike once you reach the floor of the canyon. At the end of the canyon, there will be wide-open views in all directions. Feel free to examine the vertical walls of the mesa, the hoodoos, and other formations. This hike is as much about exploring and improvising as it is about walking. You could start working your way back to your car now, but if you look to the southwest you'll see another formation (N35° 40.185' W107° 11.816') on the valley floor worth exploring.

When you are ready to head back, look to the east. The tall mesa where you started will be a little left of center. There will be a shorter mesa a little to the right. Your goal is to reach the saddle (N35° 40.228' W107° 11.097') between the two mesas. In short, head east. When you get to the uplift between the two mesas, find a good place to scramble to the top. This is not nearly as difficult as the other two scrambles.

Once you reach the top of the saddle keep heading east. You'll be below the mesa to the left. In about 0.3 mile you'll see a fence. If you look closely you'll also see a trail with stone cairns on this side of the fence. That's the CDT. For this hike, you'll turn left and follow the CDT north for 1 mile until you reach BLM 1102. Turn left (northwest) on BLM 1102 and follow the road back to the car. It's less than 0.5 mile away from where the CDT crosses the road.

• •

GPS TRAILHEAD COORDINATES N35° 41.147' W107° 10.831'

DIRECTIONS From I-25 North, take Exit 242 at Bernalillo. Turn left on US 550 and go northwest 23 miles toward San Ysidro. Stay left on US 550 and continue another 18 miles toward Cuba. Turn left on County Road 279 to San Luis. The paved portion ends after 8.5 miles. Continue 5.2 miles straight on the dirt road. Immediately after crossing a cattle guard and the bridge over the Cañada Santiago, turn right on BLM 1102. Drive 4.6 miles north on 1102 to a ridge. Pull on to the doubletrack on the right side of the road and find a place to park. The hike will start on the other side of the road.

40 McCAULEY HOT SPRINGS

Take a break and soak your tired feet at McCauley Hot Springs.

IT'S HARD TO beat a hike to a hot spring. It's even better when the hike is through woods with fabulous views of the Jemez Mountains. McCauley is the best hot spring hike in our 60-mile radius of Albuquerque.

DESCRIPTION

The volcanism that created the Jemez Mountains and Valles Caldera still has an active magma chamber deep below the surface. As a result the Jemez Mountains have several thermal springs for us to enjoy, the most prominent being the bath house in the town of Jemez Springs.

There are also several primitive hot springs in the area. Some are on national forest land and open to visitation. Soda Dam is just north of Jemez Springs on NM 4. Spence Hot Springs north of the Battleship Rock picnic area is a short walk from NM 4. Because of its proximity to the road, it is heavily visited and can be crowded. San Antonio Hot Springs farther north is reached by Forest Road 376. The 5-mile drive on FR 376 to San Antonio is extremely rugged and is even worse on a mountain bike. But it is a wonderful place for a soak.

The best spring for a hike is McCauley Hot Springs. The water is not as warm as the Jemez Springs bath house and the setting is not as spectacular as San Antonio

DISTANCE & CONFIGURATION: 3.4-mile out-and-back from Battleship Rock; 3.2-mile out-and-back from Jemez Falls

DIFFICULTY: Moderate

SCENERY: Mountain views, streams, falls, ponderosa, rock formations, hot spring

EXPOSURE: Mostly shaded

TRAIL TRAFFIC: Popular

TRAIL SURFACE: Dirt, rock, volcanic ash

HIKING TIME: 2 hours, more if you decide to soak

DRIVING DISTANCE: 62 miles from the Big I

ELEVATION GAIN: 6,764' at Battleship Rock trailhead; 7,972' at Jemez Falls trailhead; 7,493' at McCauley Hot Springs

ACCESS: Year-round for Battleship Rock, May–mid-December for Jemez Falls; $5 parking fee at Battleship Rock; no permits required

WHEELCHAIR ACCESS: No

MAPS: Santa Fe National Forest–West Half; USGS *Jemez Springs* and *Redondo Peak*

FACILITIES: None

CONTACT: Santa Fe National Forest–Jemez Ranger District, fs.usda.gov/santafe, 575-829-3535

LOCATION: Jemez Springs

COMMENTS: Road to Jemez Falls is closed in winter. Leashed dogs are allowed on trails.

LAST-CHANCE FOOD/GAS: Convenience store, gas station, and visitor center on NM 4, about 16 miles south of the trailhead

Hot Springs. But for a nice walk in the woods and a great destination, McCauley Hot Springs is hard to beat. Because it requires a walk, you have a better chance of having a quiet experience when you reach the spring.

There are several ways to hike to McCauley Hot Springs. You can hike in from the west by starting at Battleship Rock picnic ground, or you can hike in from the east by starting at the Jemez Falls Campground. You also have the option of hiking from Battleship Rock to Jemez Falls and back. Or, if you have two cars, you can hike the entire length in one direction.

Battleship Rock picnic area is about 4.3 miles north of the National Forest Ranger Station at the north end of Jemez Springs. The trail begins in the picnic area on the right side (east) of NM 4.

The picnic area has an upper and lower parking lot; both have a $5 fee. (It's half price if you have a national pass.) To reach the trailhead, go through the parking lot and picnic area to a small bridge over San Antonio Creek. (San Antonio Creek and East Fork join at the picnic ground to form the Jemez River.) The East Fork Trail (137) starts on the other side of the pavilion. It is around 1.7 miles (for a round-trip of 3.4 miles) with around 700 feet of elevation gain to McCauley Hot Springs. The

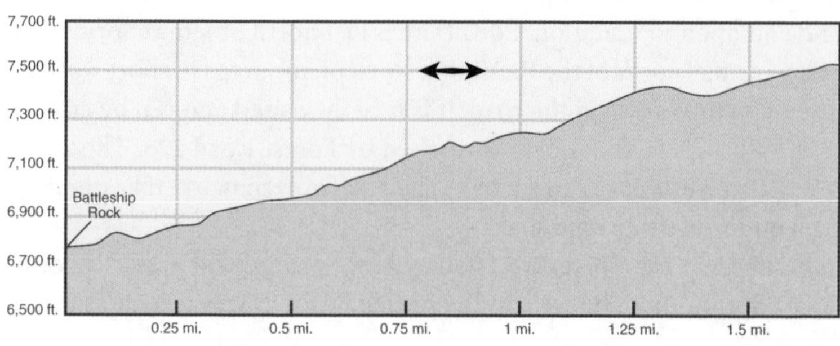

McCauley Hot Springs

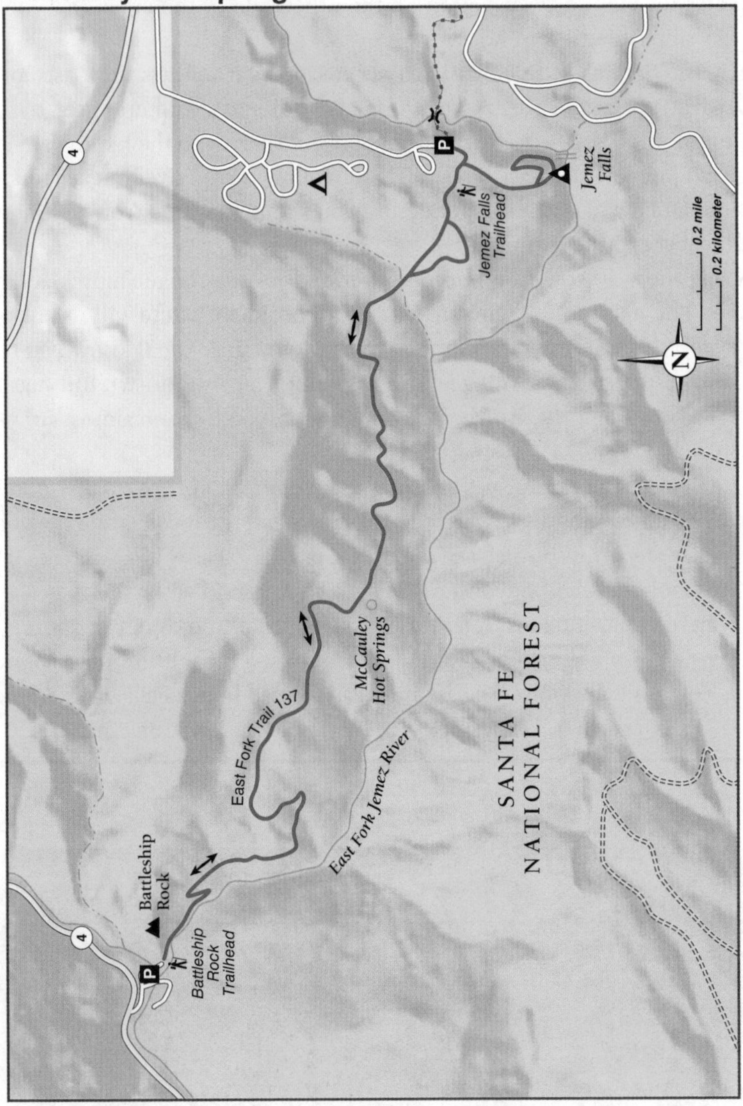

4
P
Jemez Falls Trailhead
Jemez Falls
0.2 mile
0.2 kilometer
N
McCauley Hot Springs
East Fork Trail 137
East Fork Jemez River
SANTA FE
NATIONAL FOREST
Battleship Rock
Battleship Rock Trailhead
4
P

8,200 ft.
8,000 ft.
7,800 ft.
7,600 ft.
7,400 ft.
7,200 ft.
7,000 ft.
Jemez Falls
0.25 mi.
0.5 mi.
0.75 mi.
1 mi.
1.25 mi.
1.5 mi.

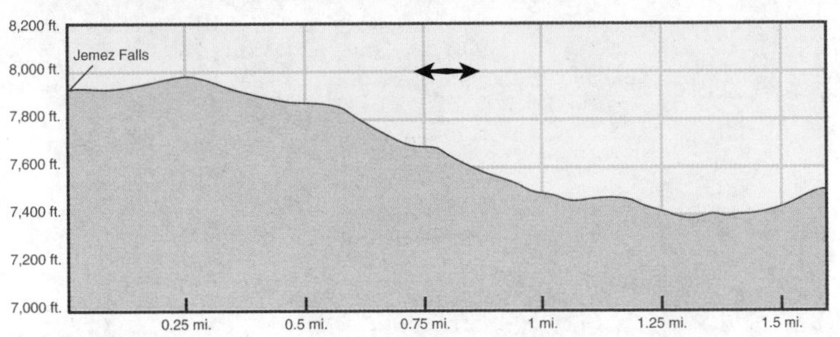

huge volcanic-rock rock formation on the other side of the creek that looks like a prow of a ship is Battleship Rock.

The trail begins in thick riparian vegetation as it follows the East Fork of the Jemez River upstream. Keep with the main trail and avoid any user trail leading down to the stream. The trail will eventually cut sharply to the left to gain elevation and enter a ponderosa forest. The trail is still following the river but at a much higher elevation. Once you reach the ponderosa you should have no trouble following the trail all the way to the spring.

Along the way you'll be hopping over and passing huge shiny black obsidian boulders. The Jemez Mountains are famous for obsidian. There will also be openings in the forest for fantastic views of the Jemez Mountains. You'll know you're getting close to the spring when you see a sign saying NO CAMPING WITHIN 400 FEET OF MCCAULEY WARM SPRING. And before you know it, you'll see an almost circular pond about 40 feet across.

The pond is the product of a rock-and-log dam. There are smaller pools downstream. The water ranges between the upper 80s and the low 90s and is a good place to soak your feet. You can also see the warm, crystal-clear water bubbling out of the sand and a population of tiny fish that like to play around with your toes.

If you're continuing on to Jemez Falls, go around the top of the pond to get to the other side. From there, look for the trail following the outflow of the pond downstream. The trail will soon turn east and head toward Jemez Falls. If you're not going to Jemez Falls, return to Battleship Rock the same way you came in.

A detour to Jemez Falls is well worth the extra mileage.

For the Jemez Falls option, you'll need to drive to Jemez Falls Campground and park in the free day-use parking area. Because of winter road closures, the Jemez Falls option is available May–mid-December. To reach Jemez Falls, take NM 4 past the junction with NM 126 at La Cueva to the entrance to Jemez Falls. (It is 12.8 miles from the ranger station.) Follow the campground road 1.3 miles to the day-use parking area.

The trailhead for the East Fork Trail (137) is on the right (west) side of the parking area. You'll start the walk by descending on a nice crusher fine ramp. When you reach the bottom, don't switch back to the left. That trail leads to Jemez Falls. However, if you have time, the falls are well worth exploring.

For the hike to McCauley, you'll want to cross the drainage at the bottom of the ramp to the sign for Trail 137 pointing the way to McCauley Springs. From here, it is 1.6 miles (3.2 miles round-trip) and a descent of 400 feet to the spring. With a detour to the falls your hike will probably end up being more than 4 miles.

Rather than climbing as you did from Battleship Rock, you'll descend from Jemez Falls to the spring. The walk is through a quiet ponderosa forest with fabulous views of the Jemez Mountains, including some tent rock–like formations. You'll also be stepping on small pieces of pumice.

And when you run into the sign about where to camp, you'll know that you're almost to the spring. And again you'll have a wonderful spring in front of you, only this time from the other side. And again, you'll have the option of returning or continuing. The return except for a detour to the falls will be the same as your outbound route.

BONUS HIKE

East Fork Trail (137) does not end at Jemez Falls. It continues east for about 5 miles to Las Conchas trailhead. Las Conchas is a great place for a little side trip. It has rock walls for climbing, running water, and a nice, easy 1.6-mile trail (3.2 miles round-trip) through a beautiful lush canyon full of knee-high grass and wildflowers. It is truly a wonderful place less than 5 miles from the Jemez Falls road at mile marker 36 on NM 4.

NEARBY ACTIVITIES

If you go through Jemez Springs on your way back, it is a great place to stop for a meal or a soak. You can call the Jemez Spring Bath House to reserve a tub at 575-829-3303.

• •

GPS TRAILHEAD COORDINATES N35° 49.706' W106° 38.667'

DIRECTIONS From I-25 North, take Exit 242. Turn left on US 550 and go 23.5 miles to San Ysidro. Turn right on NM 4 (beware of speed traps) and go 22.2 miles to Battleship Rock Picnic Grounds. There is parking on NM 4. The trail starts in the picnic ground on the other side of the bridge.

41 OJITO WILDERNESS: Hoodoo Trail

A collection of colorful sandstone hoodoos creates a hoodoo garden.

FABULOUS VIEWS AND amazing hoodoos are waiting for you in the Ojito Wilderness. This hike at the west end of the Ojito is perfect for all ages and the entire family.

DESCRIPTION

The Hoodoo Trail is one of two developed trails in the Ojito Wilderness. The other is Seismosaurus (Hike 42, page 222). Hoodoo is a wonderful walk through amazing scenery and is suitable for all ages and the entire family. The hike is easy and offers fantastic views, a hoodoo garden, and ponderosas where they shouldn't be. If you go beyond where the trail ends you can find old homesteads, unusual rocks, and many other surprises.

To reach the Ojito Wilderness and the trailhead turn left from US 550 2 miles short of San Ysidro at Cabezon Road (see Directions). There is a sign on the right side of US 550 pointing the way to the Ojito Wilderness. The road has been greatly improved over the years, but it is still a nightmare to drive when wet.

As you approach public land, you'll see angled sandstone formations on the right side of the road. They are part of the Tierra Amarilla Anticline, and the location of Hike 47 (page 247). The next portion of the drive may be a bit of a surprise, as it is a very popular place for target shooting. Don't worry; the Hoodoo Trail is well beyond the sound of gunfire.

DISTANCE & CONFIGURATION: 4-mile out-and-back with plenty of options for off-trail exploring

DIFFICULTY: Easy

SCENERY: Hoodoos, open vistas, mesas, mountains, painted desert, great geology, ponderosas

EXPOSURE: Minimal shade

TRAIL TRAFFIC: Low

TRAIL SURFACE: Sand, dirt

HIKING TIME: 2–3 hours

DRIVING DISTANCE: 49 miles from the Big I

ELEVATION GAIN: 5,786' at trailhead; 5,957' at high point

ACCESS: Year-round; no fees or permits required

WHEELCHAIR ACCESS: No

MAPS: USGS *Sky Village NE*

FACILITIES: None

CONTACT: BLM–Rio Puerco Field Office, blm.gov/office/rio-puerco-field-office, 505-761-8700

LOCATION: San Ysidro–Ojito area

COMMENTS: Driving on the dirt road can get tricky in wet conditions. Leashed dogs are allowed on trails.

LAST-CHANCE FOOD/GAS: Convenience store–gas station in San Ysidro (see Directions)

After 9 miles of very scenic driving from US 550, there will be a sign on the right side of the road identifying the Ojito Wilderness. Parking for the trailhead is 2 miles ahead. Before you reach the Hoodoo Trail you will pass the parking area for the Seismosaurus Trail. Parking for the Hoodoo Trail is on the left (south) side of the road.

The sign at the parking area says that the Hoodoo Trail is a 2-mile out-and-back. The trail is actually 2 miles in each direction. And, if you wish, the hike can easily be extended. The trail begins on the other side of the road.

The easiest way to reach the trail is to turn right and walk along the road for a few hundred feet until see you see an obvious trail with a vertical marker (N35° 29.718' W106° 55.272') on the north side of the road. You can also take the path immediately across from the parking lot, but it will soon become difficult to follow. When that happens, work yourself to the right (east) until you find the main trail.

The trail angles to the left through juniper grassland toward the base of the multicolored shale and sandstone Bernalillito Mesa to your left. The trail will climb to a bench at the base of the mesa and will stay on the bench to, more or less, follow the contour of the mesa. Much of the trail is a sandy footpath and almost seems like a beach. The vegetation here is a combination of juniper, scrub oak shrubs, and piñon. Soon after climbing onto the bench, you'll start seeing sandstone hoodoos. These hoodoos are extremely interesting, as they have very thin layers of different colored sandstone: white, yellow, pink, burnt red, and others.

The hoodoos are incredible, and at one point there will be so many of them that it will seem like a hoodoo garden (N35° 30.273' W106° 55.671'). And if you look around, you'll see that there are ponderosa pine trees at the edge of the hoodoo garden. Finding ponderosa pines below 6,000 feet (and the entire hike is below 6,000 feet) is very unusual. Outside of drainages with their cooler air, ponderosa pine trees in the Sandias generally start at around 7,000 feet. Perhaps the ponderosa in the Ojito are remnants from when the climate was moister and cooler.

Ojito Wilderness: Hoodoo Trail

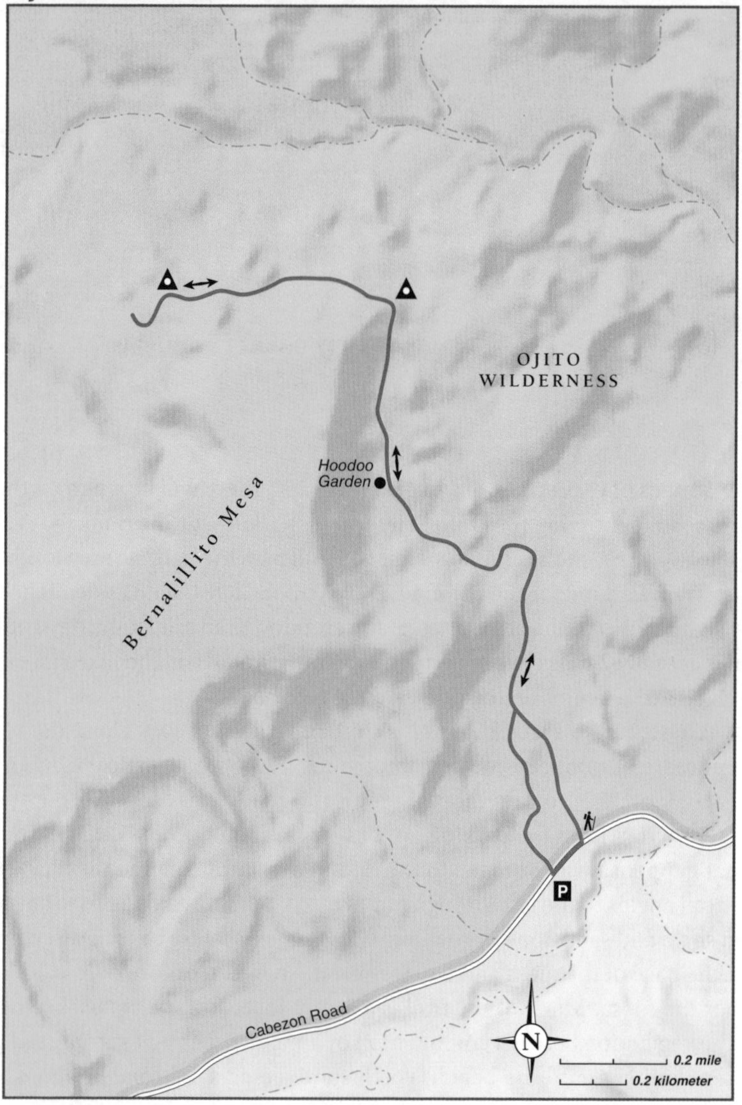

OJITO WILDERNESS

Hoodoo Garden

Bernalillito Mesa

Cabezon Road

N

0.2 mile

0.2 kilometer

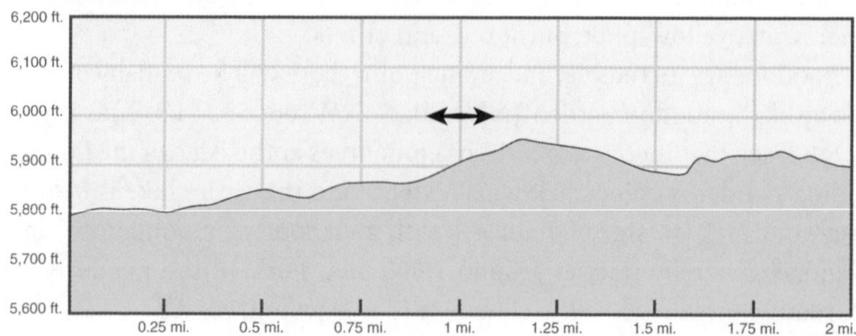

Although it may not be immediately obvious, the trail continues beyond the hoodoo garden. Just keep hiking in the direction that you have been hiking, and you should be able to pick up the trail cairns again beyond the ponderosa. As you continue along, you'll see fantastic places to camp out and will also spot several campfire rings. Can you imagine how many stars you would see and how many coyotes you would hear yipping away if you spent the night here.

With the trail following the base of the mesa it will eventually curve with the mesa to the west. When you reach the turn, there will be amazing views off to your right of the desert below. You'll see multiple colors and the mesmerizing patterns of eroded and deep-cut arroyos. You'll also pass several peninsulas jutting off to the side from the mesa bench. All of them have views and are worth exploring.

After about 2 miles of walking the cairns and the footpath seem to peter out near the bottom of a small arroyo (N35° 30.541' W106° 56.186'). From here, you can retrace your steps back to the trailhead. Or if you're comfortable with your navigation skills (and it certainly helps to have a GPS), you can work your way down to the bottom of the mesa bench and return to the trailhead by a different route.

If you stay near the bottom of the mesa, you'll always have the mesa in sight to help with navigation. If the mesa is to your right, you'll more or less be going in the right direction. If you do venture out, you might find an old homestead or two, an outcrop or two of unusual rocks, old roads, or something else. If you do find a cultural resource, leave it as it is, as it's protected by law. And always remember, it was two hikers who were out wandering who found New Mexico's largest dinosaur very close to here.

NEARBY ACTIVITIES

On your way back from the Ojito, you might want to make a quick stop in Bernalillo to check out **Coronado State Monument.** It features the ruins of the Tiwa Pueblo of Kuaua. The expedition of Spanish conquistador Francisco Vásquez de Coronado encountered the pueblo in 1540. Access the visitor center via Kuaua Road, on the north side of US 550, on the west bank of the Rio Grande in Bernalillo. Call 505-867-5351 or visit nmhistoricsites.org for more information regarding hours and fees.

• •

GPS TRAILHEAD COORDINATES N35° 29.645' W106° 55.330'

DIRECTIONS From I-25 North, take Exit 242 at Bernalillo. Turn left on US 550 and go northwest 21.2 miles. (San Ysidro is about 2 miles too far.) Turn left on Cabezon Road. (Look for the brown sign for Ojito Wilderness and White Ridge Bike Trails on the right, followed by a green street sign for Cabezon Road on the left.) Go left at the first fork ahead. After 11 miles on Cabezon Road, turn left into a parking area on the south side of the road. The trailhead is at the pedestrian gate on the other side of the road.

42 OJITO WILDERNESS: Seismosaurus Trail

This petroglyph led to the discovery of a dinosaur!

VISIT WHERE THE largest dinosaur in New Mexico was found. Along the way you'll have fantastic vistas and stumble upon great rock art and interesting geological curiosities. You might even spot a place to wander off and start exploring.

DESCRIPTION

Since the original Wilderness Act passed in 1964, the National Wilderness Preservation System has grown to include 765 areas nationwide. The first was New Mexico's own Gila Primitive Area, as it was then called. Another 22 followed in about as many years. With nearly 1% of New Mexico's public lands designated as wilderness, the state would let it rest at that for the next 18 years. The hiatus finally ended with the Ojito Wilderness Act of 2005, which permanently protects more than 11,000 acres of beautifully rugged land next to the Zia Reservation. Since the Ojito act, Sabinoso and Columbine Hondo have been added to the list of New Mexico wilderness areas.

The Ojito Wilderness, with its mixture of amazing landforms, painted deserts, unusual rocks, old homesteads, and other surprises, makes it a fabulous desert playground for us to explore. Even better, it is only 1 hour from Albuquerque. But the protection might not have happened without the efforts of two determined hikers.

In 1979 the Bureau of Land Management (BLM) and other groups, who were studying parcels of public land to consider for wilderness protection, had more or

DISTANCE & CONFIGURATION: 2.25-mile out-and-back with options for off-trail exploring

DIFFICULTY: Easy

SCENERY: Open vistas, mesas, mountains, painted desert, rock art, great geology

EXPOSURE: Minimal shade

TRAIL TRAFFIC: Low

TRAIL SURFACE: Sand, dirt

HIKING TIME: 1–2 hours; longer if you explore

DRIVING DISTANCE: 48 miles from the Big I

ELEVATION GAIN: 5,889' at trailhead, with no significant change

ACCESS: Year-round; no fees or permits required

WHEELCHAIR ACCESS: No

MAPS: USGS *Sky Village NE*

FACILITIES: None

CONTACT: BLM–Rio Puerco Field Office, blm.gov/office/rio-puerco-field-office, 505-761-8700

LOCATION: San Ysidro–Ojito area

COMMENTS: Driving on the dirt road can get tricky in wet conditions. Leashed dogs are allowed on trails.

LAST-CHANCE FOOD/GAS: Convenience store–gas station in San Ysidro (see Directions)

less discarded the Ojito area as a candidate. The two hikers disagreed, and they set out to provide evidence that the Ojito was worth protecting.

While on their way to photograph some petroglyphs that they knew were in the area, they stumbled on what "looked like a huge chicken neck laying half in and half out of the sandstone." The "chicken neck" and other bones turned out to be a 110-foot-long dinosaur that the excavators named "Seismosaurus."

Seismosaurus has since been classified as a *Diplodocus*. Regardless of its classification, it is the largest dinosaur ever found in New Mexico and is now on display at the New Mexico Museum of Natural History in Albuquerque. Even better, the Ojito was returned to the list of candidates for wilderness protection.

The hike to Seismosaurus is an easy 2.25-mile out-and-back hike. To reach the trailhead, leave US 550 a couple of miles short of San Ysidro, and turn left (west) onto unpaved Cabezon Road. The road has had several improvements over the years but it can get rough in spots if it has been a while since the last grading. And don't even consider it if it is wet. But most of the time the road should be fine. The drive is stunning!

As you approach public land you'll see incredible land formations to the right. Those angled rocks are part of the Tierra Amarilla Anticline and are the location of the White Ridge Bike Trails (Hike 47, page 247). The next portion of public land is popular with target shooters. Don't worry; our hike is beyond them. After several turns, there will be a sign for the Ojito Wilderness. The trailhead is less than a mile away. There is a small parking lot on the left (south) side of the road.

The hike begins on the other sign of the road at the pedestrian access. The trail follows an old two-track through juniper grassland. There are fantastic views of sandstone mesas in all directions, and off to the left you'll see Cabezon Peak (Hike 35, page 192) poking over a mesa. As you continue walking, you'll see multicolored deserts to your right. The path will soon turn to the left, and you'll see ropey-looking sandstone formations that you might mistake for petrified logs. As you continue, the

Ojito Wilderness: Seismosaurus Trail
unusual rock formations
petroglyphs
OJITO WILDERNESS
Cabezon Road
P
N
bomb target
0.2 mile
0.2 kilometer

6,200 ft.
6,100 ft.
6,000 ft.
5,900 ft.
5,800 ft.
5,700 ft.
5,600 ft.
0.25 mi.
0.5 mi.
0.75 mi.
1 mi.

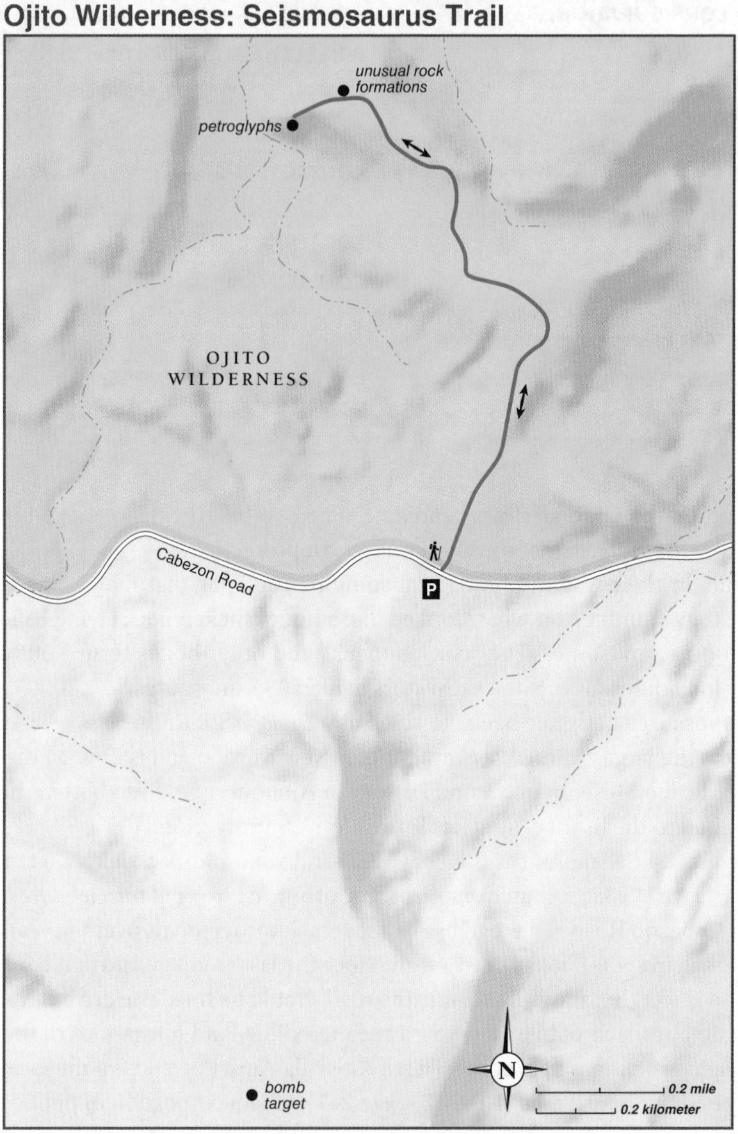

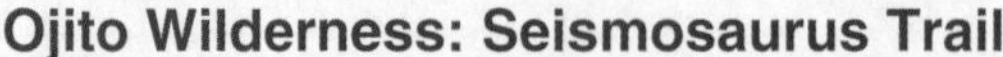

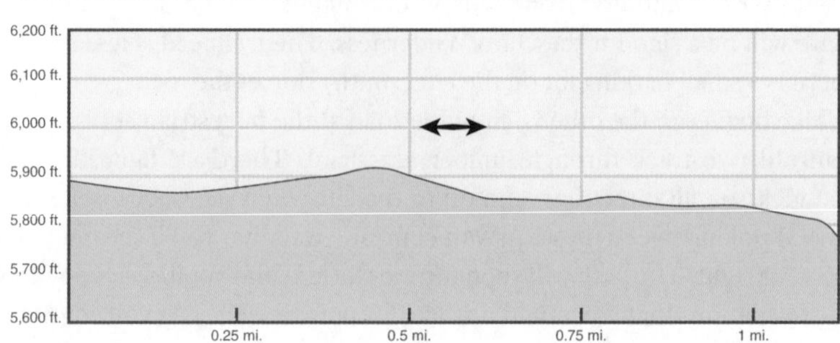

A mesa top that once functioned as a bomb target now serves as an overlook with incredible vistas.

path becomes so sandy that you'll think you're walking on a beach. The path angles to the left again, and you'll start running into the petroglyphs (N35° 30.355' W106° 54.632') that led to the discovery of Seismosaurus down below.

When you reach the end of the mesa, you'll see eroded valleys and other mesas. If you're comfortable with your backcountry skills, you might want to go off-trail and start exploring. Who knows what you'll find. Otherwise, you can turn around and enjoy the walk back. Either option is wonderful.

BONUS HIKE

As part of the Ojito Wilderness Act of 2005, the BLM agreed to sell the sections of public land adjacent to the wilderness to Zia Pueblo. Zia in turn agreed to allow public access to their newly acquired lands for day-use only. The parking lot for the Seismosaurus Trail is on Zia day-use land.

The tall sandstone mesa directly south of the parking lot is also on Zia day-use land. In World War II the Army Air Force had a bomb target on top of the mesa for training bomber crews. Although the target is difficult to see on the ground, you can still barely see it on Google Earth. You can see plenty of bomb fragments on top of the mesa.

If you're an adventurous explorer and up for a steep scramble, there is a notch in the mesa where you can climb to the top. You could head out from the Seismosaurus parking lot to reach the notch, but that involves a difficult walk through broken ground.

An easier way to the top is to drive back about 1.75 miles to a turnoff on the right (south) side of the road (N35° 28.955' W106° 53.408'). Find a good place to park, and follow the dirt road south 0.3 mile to the fenceline. Turn right (west) and follow the fenceline to the top of the mesa. The notch is to the right of where the fenceline reaches the mesa top. The land to the south of the fence is Zia Pueblo land and off-limits. There are plenty of cow paths north of the fence that you can follow for a little more than 0.5 mile to the base of the mesa. Some of the land on the north side of the fence is State Trust Land, so you might want to check with the State Land Office (nmstatelands.org) for their latest policies on recreational access.

When you get to the base of the mesa you'll have a bit of a scramble to get to the mesa top. If you look to the right of where the fenceline reaches the top you should see the notch (N35° 28.776' W106° 54.349'). There is a small section of fence in the notch to control cattle. Just climb around it.

Once on top it will be smooth sailing. It's very flat and sandy with a mixture of shrubs, juniper, cactus, and grasses. The target is now about 0.5 mile away (N35° 29.056' W106° 54.712'). You'll probably need a GPS to find the center. But the increase in bomb fragments will help you find it. Please do not gather fragments as they are a cultural resource and protected by law.

The views from the top of the mesa are fabulous. You'll see all of the land formations, colors, and views that make the Ojito such a fantastic playground. But please be careful when you get near the edge. There are huge cracks in the ground near the edge where the sandstone is starting to break away. When you're ready to return, retrace your steps back to the notch and work your way down to the base of the mesa. You might find it harder going down than it was going up.

The hike to the mesa top is doable, but it does require that you be careful and be comfortable with off-trail exploring.

• •

GPS TRAILHEAD COORDINATES N35° 29.734' W106° 54.400'

DIRECTIONS From I-25 North, take Exit 242 at Bernalillo. Turn left on US 550 and go northwest 21.2 miles. (San Ysidro is about 2 miles too far.) Turn left on Cabezon Road. (Look for the brown sign for Ojito Wilderness and White Ridge Bike Trails on the right, followed by a green street sign for Cabezon Road on the left.) Go left at the first fork ahead. After 10 miles on Cabezon Road, turn left into a parking area on the south side of the road. The trailhead is at the pedestrian gate on the other side of the road.

43 PALIZA CANYON GOBLIN COLONY

Each goblin here seems to have its own character.

NEAR THE PALIZA FAMILY CAMPGROUND, this hike starts on a primitive road alongside a wooded creek, follows it into a ponderosa-shaded canyon to visit an assembly of standing rocks known as hoodoos and goblins, then continues up to a ridgeline viewpoint for a look out over the canyon.

DESCRIPTION

Welcome to the famous Jemez (pronounced HAY-mess), a mountainous land so vast it would take several books to describe half of it. Here are a few recommendations to get you started: In *Jemez Spring,* the Aztlán literary guru Rudolfo Anaya concocts a plot to blow up Los Alamos National Laboratories for the final installment in the Sonny Baca mysteries. For considerably slimmer and more practical reads, try *Guide to the Jemez Mountain Trail* by Judith Ann Isaacs and the classic *Exploring the Jemez Country* by Roland A. Pettitt.

This hike visits a spot that Pettitt described as "the wildest half-acre in the Jemez." His comments were brief and his directions vague, which helps explain why so few people know about it today. He also underestimated the extent of the bizarre features found here: they occupy an area of at least 30 acres. However, he did an admirable job in describing the landscape: "There are gargoyles, Cleopatra's

DISTANCE & CONFIGURATION: 3.6-mile loop or 5.25-mile out-and-back (add 1.6 miles if Forest Road 10 is gated)

DIFFICULTY: Easy to moderate, but exploring the goblin area can be strenuous

SCENERY: Towering ponderosa, riparian habitat, sculpted rock

EXPOSURE: Mostly shaded

TRAIL TRAFFIC: Moderate

TRAIL SURFACE: Dirt roads

HIKING TIME: 2–3 hours

DRIVING DISTANCE: 56 miles from the Big I

ELEVATION GAIN: 6,814' at trailhead; 7,546' at endpoint

ACCESS: Year-round; FR 10 is subject to winter closures from December to April or May, contact Jemez Ranger District for current conditions; no fees or permits required

WHEELCHAIR ACCESS: No; wheelchair access at campground

MAPS: Santa Fe National Forest–West Half; USGS *Ponderosa* and *Bear Springs Peak*

FACILITIES: Camping, picnic tables at Paliza Family Campground

CONTACT: Santa Fe National Forest–Jemez Ranger District, fs.usda.gov/santafe, 575-829-3535

LOCATION: Ponderosa

COMMENTS: Leashed dogs are allowed on trails. Though not required for this hike, entry to Paliza Family Campground is $8/vehicle.

LAST-CHANCE FOOD/GAS: Convenience store, gas station, and visitor center on NM 4, about 2 miles north of the turnoff for Ponderosa

needles, backs of Triceratops and Stegosaurus dinosaurs, tents, haystacks, exploded solidified bubbles, roller coaster rides."

Indeed, these volcanic-rock formations also evoke Swiss cheese, Japanese cemeteries, and Easter Island. Add totem poles and hooded clowns to the inventory, and you begin to get the idea. And as if the rocks weren't naturally odd enough, mysterious images have been carved into some of them. Ancient petroglyphs depict antennaed humanoids and at least one creature resembling an armadillo.

The hike: To see the spectacle for yourself, walk north on the rutted red road. You'll soon cross beneath power lines, which follow much of this route. Early in the hike you might catch a glimpse of a tent rock in the distance. It hints at the shape of things to come.

For now the trail crosses a patchwork of vegetation types, moving quickly from grassland to piñon and juniper to ponderosa. There's also a lush riparian habitat along Vallecito Creek and a smattering of Gambel oak for good measure. It's a fair sampling of Jemez Mountain flora, minus the aspens found at higher elevations.

In just less than a mile, the road splits, with the right branch going through an open gateway. Do not go through the gate. Instead, follow the road to the left. A few sandy washes cross the road within the next 0.5 mile. Stay on the road until you spot a cluster of unusual formations a short ways upstream. (You'll know it when you see it.) This is your cue to turn left (N35° 43.449' W106° 37.206') to the northwest and begin exploring the goblin colony.

They're not as big as the tent rocks at Kasha-Katuwe (Hike 5, page 41) on the east side of the Jemez, nor are they as uniform. Each figure seems to have its own character. In *Dry Rivers and Standing Rocks: A Word Finder for the American West,* Scott

Paliza Canyon Goblin Colony

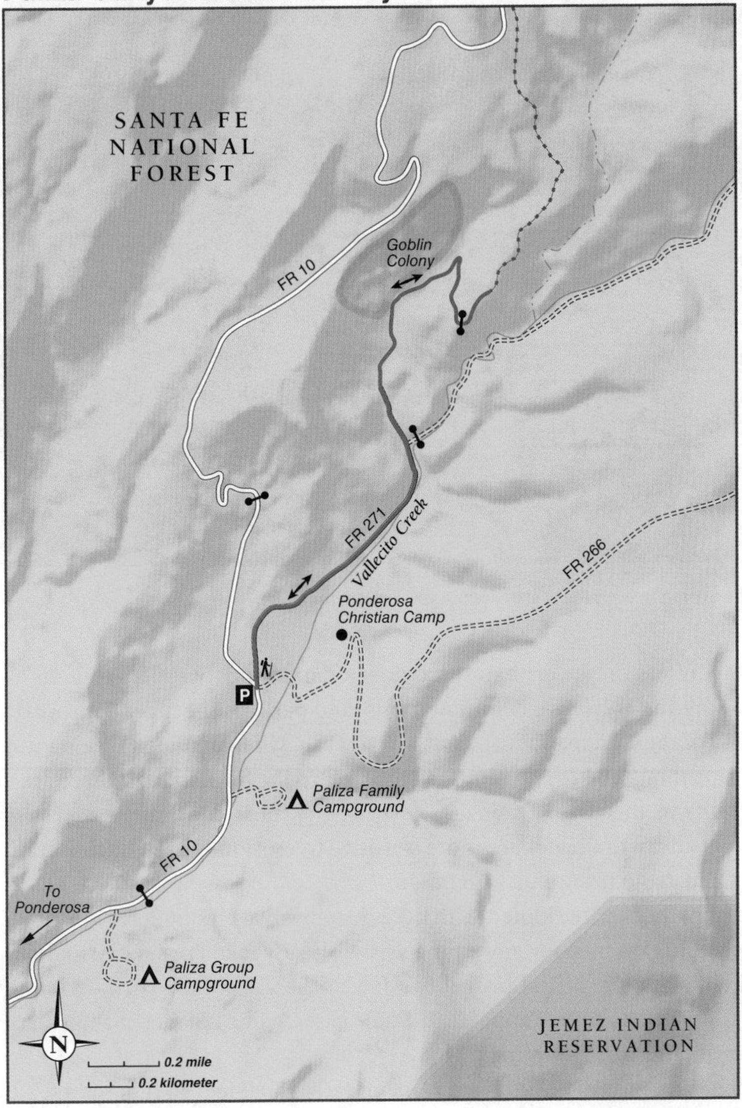

SANTA FE NATIONAL FOREST
Goblin Colony
FR 10
FR 271
Vallecito Creek
Ponderosa Christian Camp
FR 266
Paliza Family Campground
FR 10
To Ponderosa
Paliza Group Campground
JEMEZ INDIAN RESERVATION
N
0.2 mile
0.2 kilometer

7,400 ft.
7,300 ft.
7,200 ft.
7,100 ft.
7,000 ft.
6,900 ft.
6,800 ft.
0.5 mi.
1 mi.
1.5 mi.
2 mi.
2.5 mi.

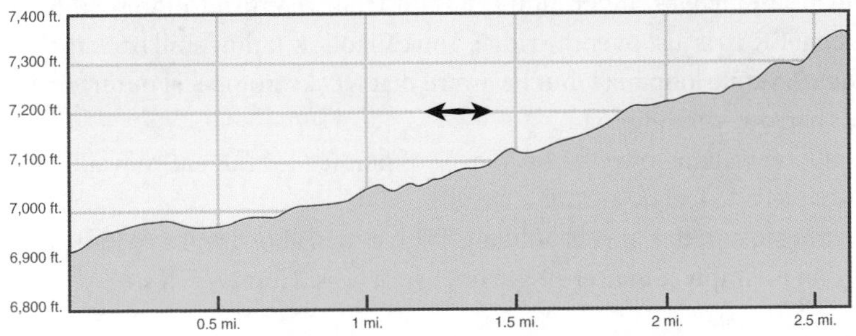

You'll be treated to amazing scenery when you explore the Goblin Colony.

Thybony offers no fewer than three dozen names for rocks like this. In New Mexico, *hoodoo* and *goblin* are common terms, and perhaps the most appropriate for the majority of rocks here, but use your imagination when naming these figures.

Some things to keep in mind as you explore the formations: There are no developed trails in this area. Drainages provide the most convenient access corridors. Areas outside of drainages are more sensitive to erosion caused by foot traffic. Tread lightly, and avoid trampling vegetation.

Though rocks are riddled with holes ostensibly well suited for footholds, refrain from climbing on them. Many animals have already taken residence in them, including birds, chipmunks, and probably a few snakes. Also, the rock—compacted ash, really—is not as solid as it appears. In some cases, a fine balancing act is all that keeps slender goblins from toppling over.

The canyon wall is very steep, rising nearly 300 feet in less than 0.2 mile. Use caution around ledges. If you find it too difficult to return to the road below, keep ascending. FR 10 is just over the ridge. You can follow it downhill back to the parking area for a 3.6-mile loop hike, but be aware that trucks from local pumice mines often use this narrow, winding road.

You'll be walking over, or by, pieces of pumice for the entire walk. Feel free to pick up a piece to feel how little it weighs.

Getting lost in this area is unlikely. With a road above and a road below, finding either one is simply a matter of gravity awareness. However, it's easy to lose track of fellow hikers, particularly the little ones. Consider establishing a nearby meeting point in case you get separated.

Finally, don't let the rocks steal all the attention. The scaly bark of alligator juniper contributes to the variety of textures, while seasonal wildflowers add to the color palette. Petroglyphs are few and far between. It takes a good eye to spot them.

When you're ready to move on, return to the road below and turn left. That is, if you haven't exhausted yourself racing up and down the arroyos. (The Goblin Colony is certainly the main event of this hike, but the extension that follows is well worth doing on this or on a future hike.) Stick to the main road as it winds uphill. At the second hairpin turn is another open gateway. Take a moment here to enjoy the view of canyons below to the east and west.

The road levels out somewhat from here for a short but pleasant walk along the ridge. Feel free to turn back anywhere along this stretch. The route ends about 0.4 mile from the gateway, where it splits around a pueblo mound. You might not recognize the mound as anything of significance; today it is only a pile of basalt rocks, but it is under the protection of the Antiquities Act of 1906. The roads ahead continue to split and proliferate into a network of unauthorized roads and informal tracks. Even with the most detailed maps, it can get a bit confusing and probably requires a GPS unit to navigate.

Stroll back the way you came, watching for details you may have missed on the way up. Birdlife is abundant. Raven and red-tailed hawk frequently patrol the canyon. With an audacious call and a crest to match, Steller's jay enlivens picnic areas and campsites. The brilliant hues of the western tanager strike a sharp contrast against the dark conifer. Burrowing owls often stake out roads and trails shortly after dark. If you happen to be out that late, revisit the goblin colony. It's a different world by moonlight.

• •

GPS TRAILHEAD COORDINATES N35° 42.512' W106° 37.628'

DIRECTIONS From I-25 North, take Exit 242. Turn left on US 550 and go 23.5 miles to San Ysidro. Turn right on NM 4 (beware of speed traps) and go 6.3 miles to the signs for Ponderosa. Turn right on FR 290 and go 6.9 miles, where it becomes FR 10, a maintained gravel road. Continue straight another 2.5 miles. About 0.5 mile past the paved entrance to Paliza Family Campground, a maintained gravel road (FR 266) starts on the right. Pull over to the left and park in the clearing ahead. The hike begins directly across the road on FR 271 heading north. During seasonal closures on FR 10, park at the gate and walk the remaining 0.8 mile to FR 271.

44 SAN YSIDRO TRIALS AREA

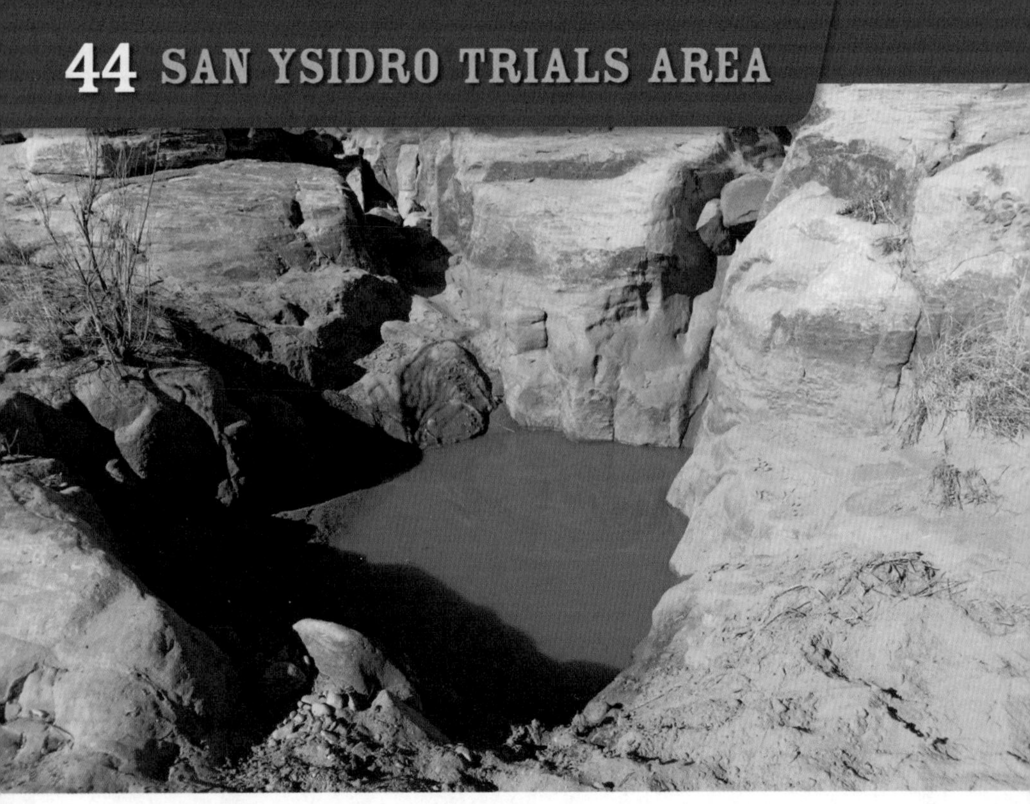

Discover plenty of slot canyons and water holes on this hike.

A UNIQUE SLOT CANYON area at the southern tip of the Sierra Nacimiento offers a comprehensive lesson in geology—or, for the layperson, just a lot of strange rocks to gawk at.

DESCRIPTION

The Sierra Nacimiento ("birth mountains," in reference to the birth of Christ) is a 50-mile range from San Ysidro to Gallina and is by far the elder of the two Rocky Mountain ranges that stretch down into the Jemez Pueblo. And since it also has the longer reach, the Sierra Nacimiento has been proclaimed "the southernmost tip of the Rockies." However, they share this distinction with the Sangre de Cristo Mountains, located about 60 miles due east.

Being on the flank of the San Juan Basin, the Sierra Nacimiento is in frontline position to intercept eastbound storms. Average annual precipitation at higher elevations is nearly 3 feet (compared to Albuquerque's 8 inches). The resulting runoff carves small but intricate canyons through the foothills, notably in the San Ysidro Trials Area.

The trials area is closed to off-road motorized vehicles, except during special-use events permitted to the New Mexico Trials Association (NMTA). They were among the first to recognize that the area's unique geologic features—namely "grippy rocks"—would enhance their motorcycle competitions and their practice events.

DISTANCE & CONFIGURATION: 3-mile loop, more if you explore; 5.4-mile balloon without gate key

DIFFICULTY: Easy–moderate

SCENERY: Sinuous canyons, hard-rock desert, sandstone-and-gypsum mesas

EXPOSURE: Some canyon shade

TRAIL TRAFFIC: Low

TRAIL SURFACE: Dirt, sand, rock

HIKING TIME: 2–3 hours (3–4 hours without gate key)

DRIVING DISTANCE: 43 miles from the Big I

ELEVATION GAIN: 5,633' at trailhead; 5,519' at low point; 5,733' at high point; 5,479' at US 550 parking area

ACCESS: Year-round, but see Comments about gate key; no fees or permits required

WHEELCHAIR ACCESS: No

MAPS: USGS *San Ysidro*

FACILITIES: Trailhead parking, marked trails

CONTACT: BLM–Rio Puerco Field Office, blm.gov/office/rio-puerco-field-office, 505-761-8700

LOCATION: San Ysidro

COMMENTS: Pick up a gate key from the Bureau of Land Management office at 100 Sun Ave. NE, Pan American Building, Suite 330 in Albuquerque. If you don't have a key, you can start the hike from the parking area on US 550. Leashed dogs are allowed on trails.

LAST-CHANCE FOOD/GAS: Convenience store–gas station in San Ysidro

The NMTA hosts four events here each year and sometimes will practice here when there are not events. Surprisingly, the dirt bikes haven't shredded the landscape. In terms of Leave No Trace ethics, cows seem to be the worst offenders. To catch or avoid motorcycle competitions, check the events schedule posted on the NMTA website (nmtrials.org), keeping in mind that competitors may show up for practice runs up to five days before an event.

The bottom line is that you'll probably have the whole place to yourself. With that, the hiking possibilities are almost unlimited. Just look around the parking area and you'll spot six or seven trailheads, each marked with a dirt bike icon. These markers appear on trails throughout the area. All signs are identical and hence useless for distinguishing one route from another.

For those in a hurry, the trailheads on the east side of the parking lot are the quickest way to access marvelous canyons. You'll also encounter a few protected pueblo sites along the short stroll to this rocky playground. Other nearby slots and sandstone pavements worth exploring begin just 0.2 mile northwest of the parking area and extend north to the Jemez fenceline.

The route described here is a simple combination of prominent paths and waterways in the heart of the trials area. For a quick orientation: the hike traverses a hilly valley bound by Red Mesa to the west, Mesa Cuchilla to the east, and White Mesa on the far side of US 550 to the south. To narrow it down further, it's confined to a triangular space defined by two major drainages that merge before crossing US 550.

Start the hike by walking straight past the left side of the signboard. Hop across a small wash. The wash deepens as you continue east and slightly to the north. You can walk in it or, during wetter seasons, take the track running parallel on the north

San Ysidro Trials Area

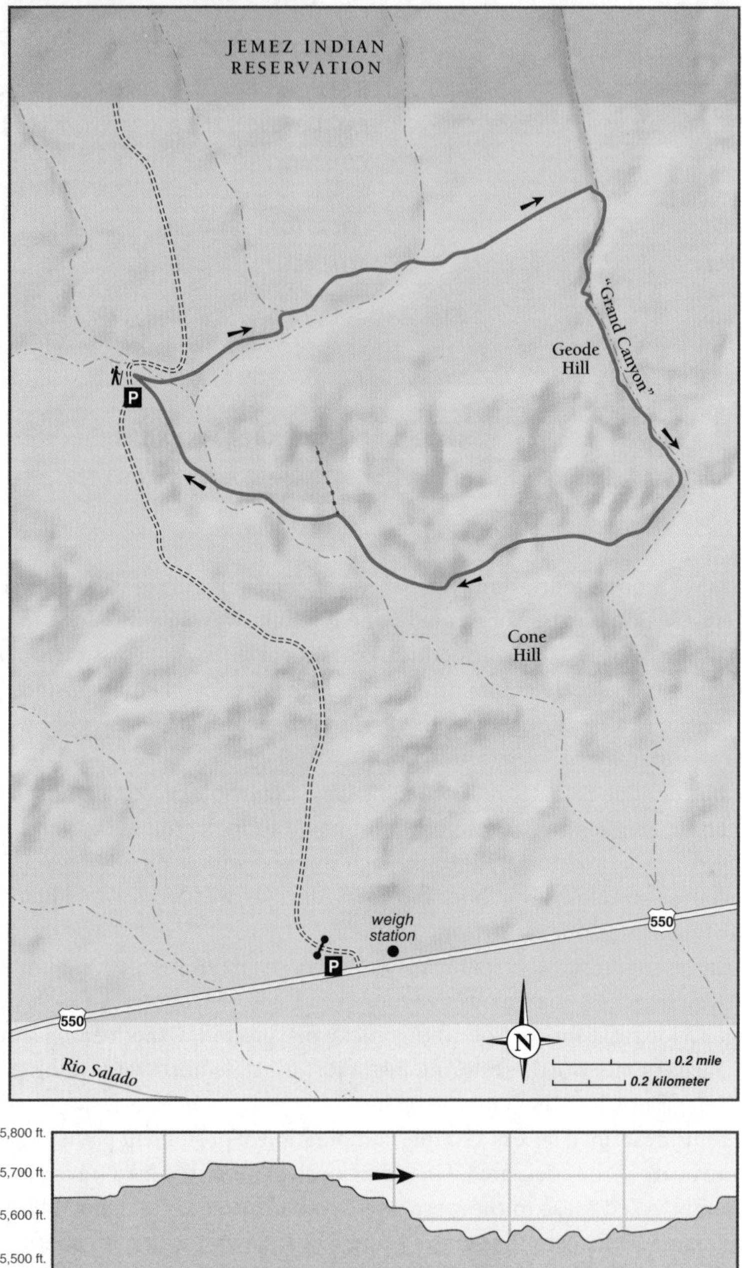

Features such as this make the San Ysidro Trials Area an intriguing place to explore.

bank. The wash gets very narrow after about 0.75 mile, so you'll probably opt for the high road anyway.

Maintain a fairly straight path and you'll intersect a canyon just under a mile from the parking area. You can't miss it—some bikers have dubbed it the Grand Canyon. That's an enormous exaggeration. It's not more than 50 feet across at its widest point, and it narrows to a classic slot in places.

A cairn near to the right marks an easy entry point, though there are several to choose from. You can also look upstream for easier ways in. Be advised, however, that the Jemez Reservation lies less than 300 yards to the north. Please respect its boundaries. Also, do not enter the canyon if the forecast calls for rain. Pay special attention to the northern skies. Storms up to 10 miles away could send torrents of water and debris through this channel, and emergency exits are few over the next 0.5 mile.

That said, walk down to the canyon floor, and turn right to head downstream. The wide sandy wash narrows into sinuous chutes with polished sandstone walls. Each turn reveals marvelous details. Scoured spillways and basins hint at the furious rapids and whirlpools that follow stormy weather.

You may encounter a few ponds en route. If they're too big to cross, you'll need to backtrack for an exit from the canyon. You can reenter the canyon downstream, but the hard-rock route along the rim is just as interesting, and smaller waterways on either side of the main canyon are worth exploring as well. If you poke around on the hill on the west bank there is a good chance of finding geodes and gypsum crystals. Or if you're confident in your sense of direction, wander off to the east—where there are more slot canyons, sandstone hoodoos, cliff shelters, and ancient petroglyphs—then return to this canyon to finish the hike.

Once the canyon squeezes past the hill, it shallows out to a stream that trickles through dense stands of willow and tamarisk. Do not follow the stream into this wooded area. Instead, pick up the motorbike trail that curves southwest as it wraps around the base of the hill. It will lead you away from the stream and into an open meadow. Follow the track through a low pass at the far corner of the meadow.

Once you cross the ridge, you'll see two cone-shaped hills on your left, about 100 yards south. Stay on track as the path continues west and slightly to the south through a stand of tamarisk in a small wash. From there, the motorbike trail bends around the base of a ridge on your right and then aims northwest, roughly parallel to a major arroyo about 500 feet to your left. You can't see it from here, but a tree line marks the spot.

At the next fork, stay left. As the trail bends closer toward the arroyo, cross over to walk along its streambed. From here, less than 0.5 mile remains in the hike, but the wavy bedrock makes an impressive finale. As the top end of the drainage curves to your right, exit left and walk uphill about 100 yards to the parking lot.

With its proximity to Albuquerque and so much to discover, this is a great place to visit again and again.

NEARBY ACTIVITIES

Perea Nature Trail is a 1-mile loop through restored wetland on the bank of the Rio Salado. Benches, boardwalks, and wildlife blinds enhance enjoyment of this shaded nook. The interpretive signs offer a good primer on the plants and wildlife in the area. The Perea Trailhead is at the end of a paved pulloff near the northwest corner of the Rio Salado bridge on US 550, about 0.8 mile south of the NM 4 junction.

• •

GPS TRAILHEAD COORDINATES N35° 34.097' W106° 48.778'

DIRECTIONS From I-25 North, take Exit 242 at Bernalillo. Turn left on US 550 and go 25 miles to a weigh station on the right (1.5 miles past the town of San Ysidro). The paved turnoff for the San Ysidro Trials Area is at the far end of the weigh station. Drive up to the locked gate on the left side of the parking area. (If you don't have the key, park here and walk through the pedestrian gate.) Follow the rugged dirt road 1.2 miles to the parking area, and park near the signboard.

45 STABLE MESA

A peaceful ponderosa parkland sits on top of Stable Mesa.

THE MOST SCENIC drive in the Jemez leads to the western base of Schoolhouse Mesa. The hike takes you to the western rim of its southern neighbor, Stable Mesa. From there you can explore windows and shelter caves in a mile-long pumice ridgeline. An optional extension ventures out to the ruins of an ancient pueblo and a historic logging camp.

DESCRIPTION

Pueblo Indians developed at least 40 settlements in the Jemez Province before the Spaniards arrived in 1541. They established many of the larger pueblos upon mesas, some as high as 8,000 feet. Evidence of later settlements in this area includes the town sites, camps, and cabins associated with the railroad logging period of 1922–1941. The road you drove up to Porter Landing is the most prominent legacy of this period. It traces the railroad grade of the Santa Fe Northwestern through the Gilman Tunnels and up the cascading Rio Guadalupe. With a population of 300, Porter was the center of operations from 1925 to 1937. Unusually high floods in 1941 washed out tracks and trestles. With the war increasing demands for steel, the rail wreckage was quickly salvaged and sold. The last remnant standing in Porter today, a stone hearth in a clearing

DISTANCE & CONFIGURATION: 6.6-mile out-and-back, with longer options

DIFFICULTY: Moderate, with a few short, strenuous sections

SCENERY: Ponderosa forest, volcanic formations, views of the Sierra Nacimiento

EXPOSURE: Mostly shaded

TRAIL TRAFFIC: Light

TRAIL SURFACE: Dirt roads, loose rock

HIKING TIME: 3–4 hours

DRIVING DISTANCE: 62 miles from the Big I

ELEVATION GAIN: 7,211' at trailhead; 7,800' on mesa top

ACCESS: May–mid-December; Forest Road 376 is closed in the winter; no fees or permits required

WHEELCHAIR ACCESS: No

MAPS: Santa Fe National Forest–West Half; USGS *San Miguel Mountain*

FACILITIES: None

CONTACT: Santa Fe National Forest–Jemez Ranger District, fs.usda.gov/santafe, 575-829-3535

LOCATION: Cañon

COMMENTS: Leashed dogs are allowed on trails.

LAST-CHANCE FOOD/GAS: Visitor center, convenience store, and gas station on NM 4, about 14 miles from the trailhead

by the river, is the fireplace from the superintendent's lodge. Other relics remain scattered upon the surrounding mesas and throughout the canyons.

Before setting out on the hike, look above the pines across the river and note a forested peak less than 1 mile southeast. That's the western corner of Stable Mesa. The destination of this hike lies on the rim that seems to dip back behind the treetops.

The hike begins with a short walk up FR 376. Immediately after crossing the bridge, turn right on a footpath through a stand of trees and walk south along the river. (It's just as easy to walk up to the gate 100 yards ahead, and follow the road down to the river.) The path soon intersects a well-defined dirt road that's closed to motor vehicles. About 200 feet ahead on the left is the fireplace from the superintendent's lodge; hidden behind scrub and trees, it's easier to spot coming from the opposite direction.

The road follows the east bank of the river. About 0.4 mile into the hike, Stable Canyon opens up on the left. Stable Spring sometimes keeps the lower canyon fairly damp, and the path is often cluttered with downed trees. Still, it's worth exploring. Marine fossils appear in the limestone cliffs less than 0.5 mile up on the left.

For now, continue south along the main trail to a fork about 200 yards or so past the mouth of Stable Canyon. Bear left and follow the rocky jeep road uphill. (A lesser road stays close to the river.) The terrain soon levels out. About 0.5 mile past the fork, shortly after dipping through an arroyo, the road forks again (N35° 48.317' W106° 46.862'). Head uphill to the left. The views to the west are astounding as you ascend to the next level.

If you see a sign that says Leaving Porter, you've missed the fork and have gone too far. If you continue on this road you'll eventually reach Hike 38 (page 204) in about 3 miles. So for this hike, turn around and go back to the fork.

Another fork is about 1 mile ahead. A fallen tree blocks a faint road going straight. You'll follow the road as it bends left, but first you might want to take a short rest here.

Stable Mesa

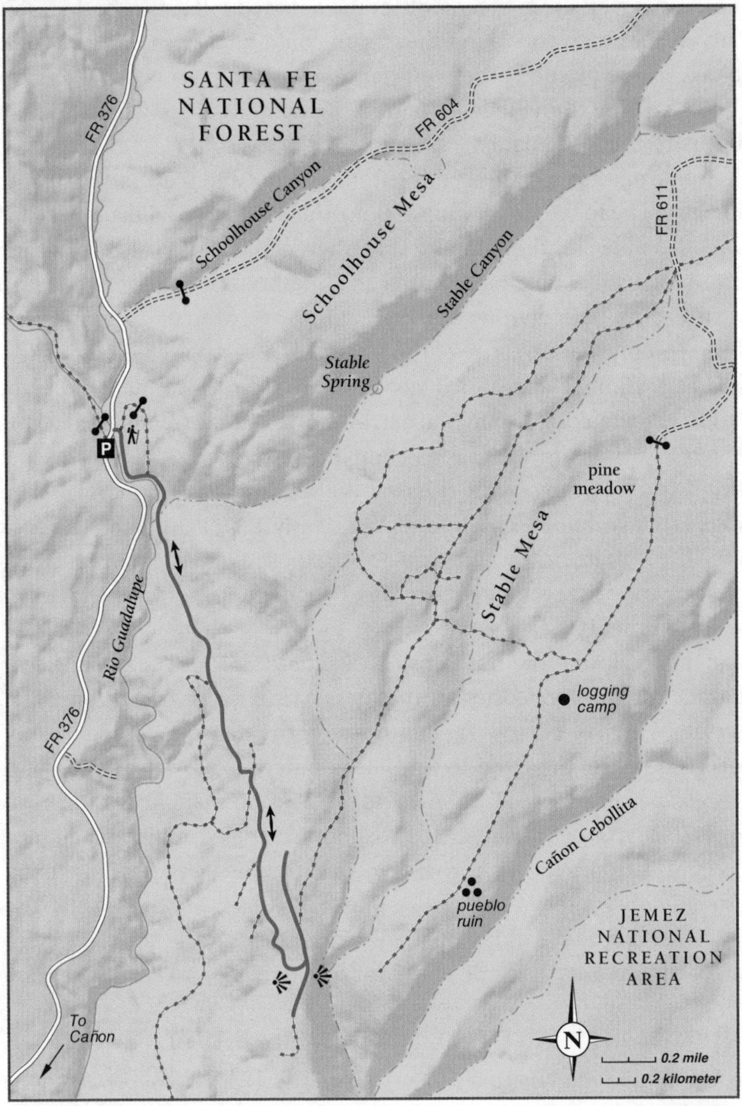

SANTA FE NATIONAL FOREST
FR 376
FR 604
FR 611
Schoolhouse Canyon
Schoolhouse Mesa
Stable Canyon
Stable Spring
P
pine meadow
Stable Mesa
Rio Guadalupe
logging camp
Cañon Cebollita
pueblo ruin
JEMEZ NATIONAL RECREATION AREA
To Cañon
N
0.2 mile
0.2 kilometer

8,200 ft.
8,000 ft.
7,800 ft.
7,600 ft.
7,400 ft.
7,200 ft.
7,000 ft.
0.5 mi.
1 mi.
1.5 mi.
2 mi.
2.5 mi.
3 mi.

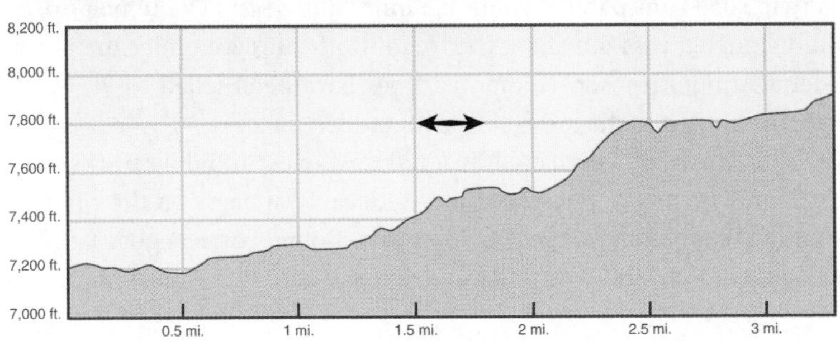

A campfire ring sits in the middle of the faint road. If you're in the habit of leaving trails cleaner than you found them, you could fill a trash bag or two here. Feel free to take all the plastic bottles you can carry, but don't touch any tins, bottles, or other refuse dating to the logging period. If you're not sure whether it's trash or a cultural artifact, leave it alone.

Continue on the road as it bends left, then right, and then up the steepest ascent on this route. The rocks are very loose along this stretch, so hiking poles can be helpful. About 0.3 mile past the campfire ring, the steep, rocky road ends at the junction with a pronounced doubletrack. Turn right and head over a flat outcrop about 100 yards to the south. Take another break to enjoy the views to the west and get oriented.

Sitting on the western edge of the Jemez Plateau, you're now 2.5 miles into the hike and have climbed almost 600 feet from the river. How much more you hike is up to you. But in looking around the narrow north–south-trending range to the west is the Sierra Nacimiento, the Laurel companion to the Hardy-shaped Jemez. More specifically, you're sitting on the rim near the southwestern corner of Stable Mesa. A low ridge extends about 0.2 mile south and nearly 1.5 miles north. The backbone of this ridge is volcanic rock, which appears in exposed outcrops all along the western flank. As you can see in the steep outcrop to your left, it's adorned with pocks, holes, grooves, and other intricate details.

Start by exploring the outcrops to the south. If you haven't noticed already, you're on a fingerlike extension of the mesa, with views over a gorge a few yards to the east. When you reach the end of the formations, turn around and head to the north side of the junction to find more outcrops off the left side of the road. The designs become more elaborate, with arches and shelter caves that evoke playful shapes, like grottoes and oversized fishbowl castles. Graffiti etched into the soft rock dates back from a few years to several decades and perhaps many centuries. You could spend hours among these fascinating formations, and then head back the way you came—or consider racking up a few extra miles on the alternate routes. If you choose to explore, keep track of where you are in relation to the return route.

THE RUINS AND THE LOOP

The road from the rim junction is relatively flat and easy to follow. As the map indicates, a twin road runs parallel about 0.5 mile to the east. The remains of a logging camp and a pueblo ruin are along that road. Both sites are under the protection of the Federal Antiquities Act. Numerous trees have been felled to prevent vehicles from approaching from the north, but with modest success.

The twin roads are connected by a few east–west-trending tracks that are difficult to spot. The first one to stand out noticeably appears on the right, 1.5 miles northeast of the junction on the rim. Two dirt-mound barriers obstruct this former road, which winds 0.7 mile over hills and across drainages to meet the parallel road.

The logging camp is about 0.3 mile south of this T-junction. The remains of log cabins are easy to spot on both sides of the road. The pueblo ruin—little more than a mound, really—is another mile south. Hence, a hike from the rim to the pueblo runs about 3.5 miles, one-way. If you intend to shorten your return route by heading east from either the camp or the ruin, be warned that this shortcut can involve considerable bushwhacking, and that the drainages between the two roads become increasingly difficult to cross as they trench south toward the gorge.

• •

GPS TRAILHEAD COORDINATES N35° 49.181' W106° 47.252'

DIRECTIONS From I-25 North, take Exit 242. Turn left on US 550 and go 23.5 miles to San Ysidro. Turn right on NM 4 (beware of speed traps) and go 9.5 miles to Cañon. Turn left on NM 485 and go north 5.7 miles. The road becomes FR 376, a narrow but well-maintained gravel road. Continue north another 7 miles to Porter Landing. A sign on a gate here reads ROAD CLOSED. Park alongside the barrier rail on the left, immediately before the bridge.

The entire hike features views like this.

46 VALLES CALDERA NATIONAL PRESERVE

This volcanic caldera contains surprisingly lush grass valleys as seen from the Valle Grande Trail.

THE TRAIL TAKES you up to a midlevel ridge for a glimpse of the landscapes hidden in Valles Caldera. Peaking over 9,100 feet, it's one of the cooler summer hikes. In winter, its modest gain in elevation is ideal for beginner and intermediate snowshoeing. This trail is outside of the caldera core and is always available for a wonderful hike with fabulous views of the caldera. It is suitable for the entire family.

DESCRIPTION

Valles Caldera along with Tent Rocks (Hike 5, page 41) is worth a trip across the country to see. The caldera is beautiful and is what's left of a huge volcano that ejected 150 cubic miles of rock and sent ash as far as Iowa 1.2 million years ago. The volcano hasn't stirred in the past 60,000 years, and nobody knows when or if it will erupt again.

The giant crater once belonged to the legendary Cabeza de Baca family. In 1860 the US Congress recognized a land debt to the heirs of Don Luis María Cabeza de Baca and offered them the vacant parcel of their choice. Topping their top-five countdown was a 95,000-acre tract in the northern Jemez. The property, which encompasses most of the caldera, is still known locally as Baca Location No. 1, the Baca Ranch, or simply the Baca.

DISTANCE & CONFIGURATION: 2.9-mile loop (Coyote Call); 2-mile out-and-back (Valle Grande)

DIFFICULTY: Easy

SCENERY: Aspen, fir, and ponderosa; views across the caldera, possible sightings of bald eagles and elk

EXPOSURE: Mostly shaded

TRAIL TRAFFIC: Popular

TRAIL SURFACE: Grass and dirt, or snow

HIKING TIME: 1–2 hours

DRIVING DISTANCE: 80 miles from the Big I

ELEVATION GAIN: 8,730' at trailhead; 9,193' at high point on the loop hike

ACCESS: Year-round; no permit or fee required for described hikes; permit required for Valles Caldera core

WHEELCHAIR ACCESS: No

MAPS: USGS *Bland*

FACILITIES: None

CONTACT: nps.gov/vall, 575-829-4100

LOCATION: North of Jemez Springs

COMMENTS: Leashed dogs allowed on described trails but not allowed in Valles Caldera core

LAST-CHANCE FOOD/GAS: Gas station at Jemez Pueblo visitor center on NM 4, about 33 miles before the trailhead; restaurants in Jemez Springs, about 23 miles before the trailhead

Ensuing years of livestock grazing, sulfur mining, and extensive logging took a toll on the land. In 1963 a third-generation oilman, James "Pat" Dunigan, bought the ravaged property for $2.5 million. A native Texan with a master's degree from New York University, Dunigan is perhaps most fondly remembered for his environmentally balanced ranching and caring stewardship of the Baca. When his sons sold it to the federal government for a cool $101 million in 2000, it was in relatively sparkling condition.

This purchase, made through the Valles Caldera National Preservation Act, would expand New Mexico's already supersized menu of recreational opportunities. But did we really need access to another 40 miles of trout streams, 66,000 acres of conifer forest, 25,000 acres of grassland, Sandoval County's highest peak, and the state's largest herd of elk? Absolutely. The bigger question is how long can we keep it all unsullied?

The task of keeping the land pristine was initially assigned to the Valles Caldera Trust. The trust was given a charter to protect the land and to operate it as a quasi-public enterprise that would be financially self-sufficient within 15 years. When it became apparent that this was not going to happen, the land was transferred to the National Park Service (NPS) in 2015 as a national preserve.

NPS management of the preserve is still very much a work in progress, and it is best to check the preserve's website (nps.gov/vall) for the latest information. At the time of this writing the preserve has a small interpretive center and offers 35 hiking permits daily on a first-come, first-serve basis. Where you can go is restricted, and very few of those places allow dogs. There are, however, two trailheads with fantastic hikes (Coyote Call and Valle Grande) outside of the central core of the preserve that are always open, do not require a permit, and allow dogs.

Valles Caldera National Preserve

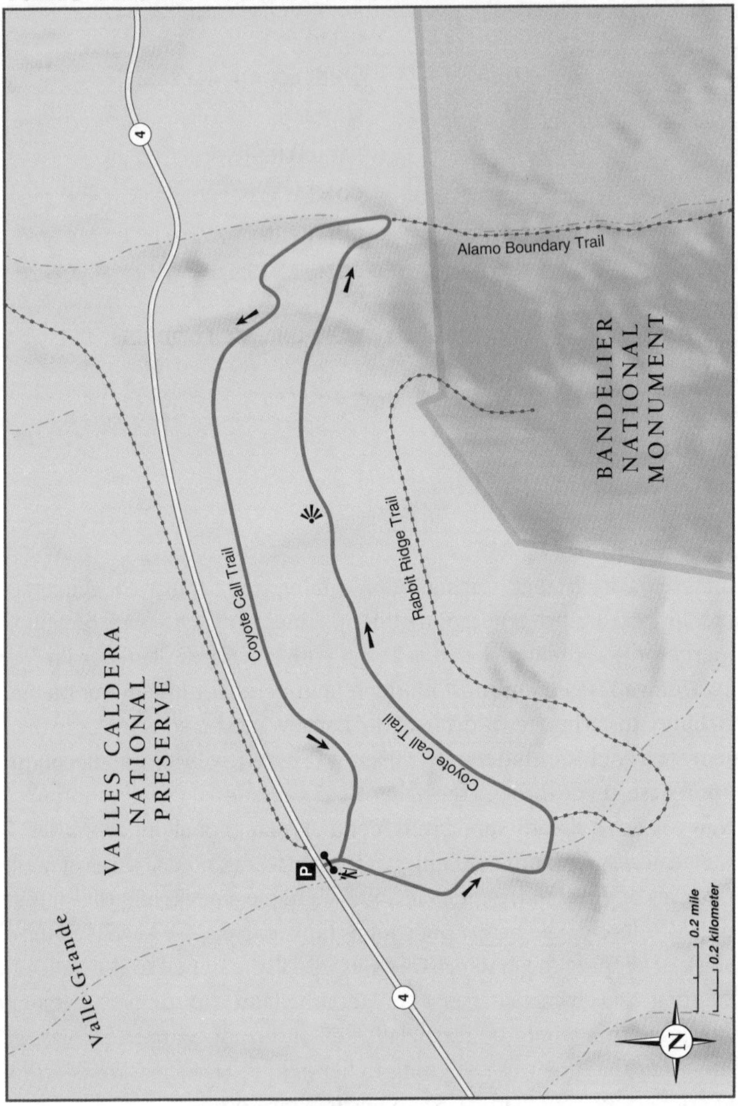

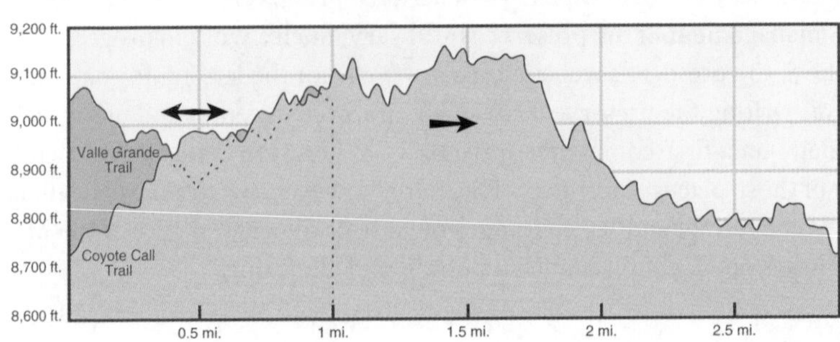

Young aspen flourish in a former burn zone on the Coyote Call Trail.

Coyote Call Trail on the south side of NM 4 takes you up to a midlevel ridge overlooking the caldera. The trail begins at the pedestrian gate with a metal box containing a register on the south side of NM 4. The trail is well marked and even has markers nailed to trees for cross-country skiing and snowshoeing.

Start by heading south across the meadow, bearing slightly to the right along an old logging road that climbs up about a half mile to the eastern side of the domed hill ahead. Midway up the ridge behind the hill, the road turns left.

About 100 yards after rounding the corner, you'll arrive at the junction with Rabbit Ridge Trail on the right. Rabbit Ridge is also open to hiking without a permit and allows dogs. It climbs 600 feet in about 1.25 miles from the trail junction to a higher overlook. It's a nice option for extending this hike, or something that you can save for a future date. The Valles Caldera is certainly worth more than one visit.

To stay on Coyote Call Trail, continue straight past the junction. The trail conforms to the curvature of the ridge, bowing out and back for the next mile. There are several places along the way for taking a break and enjoying the magnificent view of the caldera.

Many visitors mistake the Valle Grande for the Valles Caldera. To clarify, the Valle Grande is the largest of four valleys in the Valles Caldera. The actual caldera, a collapsed volcano, measures 12–15 miles in diameter. The Valle Grande, about 3 miles wide from north to south, is what drivers see from NM 4. In other words, the Valle Grande is merely the crescent, whereas the Valles Caldera is the full moon.

From the overlook, the view stretches clear across to the north rim, but the other valleys remain hidden behind the hills and domes that flank the far side of the

Valle Grande. The one on the left is Redondo Peak, Sandoval County's highest point, at 11,254 feet. The dome on the right is Cerro del Medio. The stream snaking across the meadow in front of it is the East Fork of the Jemez River.

In addition to fantastic views of the caldera, there is much else to see on the hike. If you look toward the ground, you might spot pieces of obsidian. Collecting rocks is strictly prohibited in the national preserve, so please leave everything in place. If you would like to learn more, there is a wonderful display of obsidian in the interpretive center. You also might notice the large number of young aspen trees along the route. Recent fires have opened gaps in the ponderosa pines to make it possible for aspens to thrive.

Continue on Coyote Call Trail another 0.5 mile or so to the junction with another old road merging from the right. Take a sharp left here, and head downhill. After another 0.5 mile, NM 4 comes into view. At that point the trail bends to the west and runs roughly parallel to the highway for the remainder of the loop.

Valle Grande Trail takes you down to the valley floor for an up-close look of the caldera. The trail begins just west of the preserve's boundary with Bandelier National Monument. To find the trailhead, look for an unmarked pulloff on the south side of NM 4, between mile markers 42 and 43. A tiny wooden sign on the north side marks the trailhead. Cross the road, and follow the fence for about 200 feet west to the registration box, then zigzag downhill through a lush forest of fir and aspen. The well-worn mile-long trail takes you to the edge of the meadow in the Valle Grande. It's a short hike, but tack on at least 20 minutes to take in the view.

• •

GPS TRAILHEAD COORDINATES N35° 50.887' W106° 27.916'

DIRECTIONS From I-25 North, take Exit 242 at Bernalillo. Turn left on US 550 and go 23.5 miles to San Ysidro. Turn right and go 41 miles on NM 4. On the left side of the road, near mile marker 41, is a pulloff big enough for four or five cars. Park there, or if it's full, another pulloff is about half a mile ahead. Coyote Call Trail begins at the signed gate across the road from the first pulloff.

47 WHITE RIDGE BIKE TRAILS AREA

Take in the fantastic Tierra Amarilla Anticline. That's Cabezon peeking over the top in the far distance.

FIFTEEN MILES OF hiking and biking trails explore a land packed with geological curiosities. The views are so spectacular that you'll have to pinch yourself to make sure that they are real. Though this hike hits most of the major features, it covers just a fraction of all possible routes on this endlessly fascinating terrain.

DESCRIPTION

The White Ridge trails have the distinction of being on the Tierra Amarilla (or San Ysidro) Anticline. It is one of New Mexico's most interesting landforms and attracts geology students from around the country. To visualize an anticline, think of pushing a rug against a wall; the upward folds are the same as an anticline. The area is spectacular.

You'll start seeing the anticline as you approach White Ridge from US 550. They are the angular sandstone formations to your right. Go to the second parking lot (right side) 0.5 mile ahead after crossing into public lands.

Maps are available inside the register box and refer to a series of several numbered trail junctions. At the time of this writing many of the junction signs have become difficult to read. The hike follows the numbers as follows: Outbound: 1–3, 21, 22, 12, 11, 10. Return: 10–17, 23, 1. The connecting segment between 17 and 23 is a well-defined dirt road that does not appear on the maps.

DISTANCE & CONFIGURATION: 5.5-mile loop and spur with options to lengthen or shorten the hike

DIFFICULTY: Moderate with a tricky descent

SCENERY: Gypsum ridges, painted desert, classic anticline

EXPOSURE: Minimal shade

TRAIL TRAFFIC: Moderate

TRAIL SURFACE: Sand, dirt, loose rock, gypsum

HIKING TIME: 3–4 hours depending on how much exploring you do

DRIVING DISTANCE: 42 miles from the Big I

ELEVATION GAIN: 5,850' at trailhead; 6,042' at high point; 5,652' at low point

ACCESS: Year-round; no fees or permits required

WHEELCHAIR ACCESS: No

MAPS: Trail maps available at trailhead; USGS *Sky Village NE* and *San Ysidro*

FACILITIES: Picnic tables and detailed maps at trailhead

CONTACT: BLM–Rio Puerco Field Office, blm.gov/office/rio-puerco-field-office, 505-761-8700

LOCATION: San Ysidro–Ojito area

COMMENTS: For an authoritative briefing on the complex geological features at White Ridge, visit geoinfo.nmt.edu/tour/landmarks/san_ysidro. Leashed dogs are allowed on trails.

LAST-CHANCE FOOD/GAS: Convenience store–gas station in San Ysidro (see Directions)

With the junctions not necessarily discernable, just head uphill on the wide trail leading from the parking area. You'll be walking on white gypsum and passing old gypsum diggings. In 0.3 mile the scenery changes abruptly. You'll be on the cusp of a scooped valley that looks like a leviathan took a bite out of the Earth's crust.

From here keep the rim to your left and head toward a white mound with a dark stumplike cylinder on its peak. The mound is the area high point and the cylinder is a USGS benchmark. There, you'll find the best views on the trail system; be careful, as the drop on the other side is 200 feet or more. Many casual hikers are content in making this their destination for a 1.6-mile out-and-back hike, but we're just getting started.

Take a moment to scope out the terrain ahead. The next leg of the hike is the narrow gypsum ridge reaching out on the left. It points toward an elongated dome informally known as Travertine Ridge, which stretches along the floor of the valley. Now note the yellowish sandstone ridge at the far end of the valley. It extends south for the entire length of the east rim—that's your return route.

To continue the hike, follow the white ridge down into the valley. The short section of trail coming off the ridge is very steep and can be tricky, so take your time with it and be very careful. The red valley floor can get sloppy after rain or snow, but you'll soon climb out of it as you ascend Travertine Ridge.

Once on the ridge, the trail follows an old road that skirts around the right side of a series of domed hills. The domes are the result of dissolved minerals precipitating from warm mineral springs. With many of the springs at the south end no longer active, their tops have collapsed into cavernous sinkholes. If you would like to check one out, there is an informal side trail (N35° 30.990' W106° 50.619') to a sinkhole.

The springs become more active as you go north, and you'll pass one bubbling up on the left that is about the diameter of a rain barrel. Enjoy this unusual little ecosystem from a distance, because the surrounding mud is deeper than you think.

White Ridge Bike Trails Area

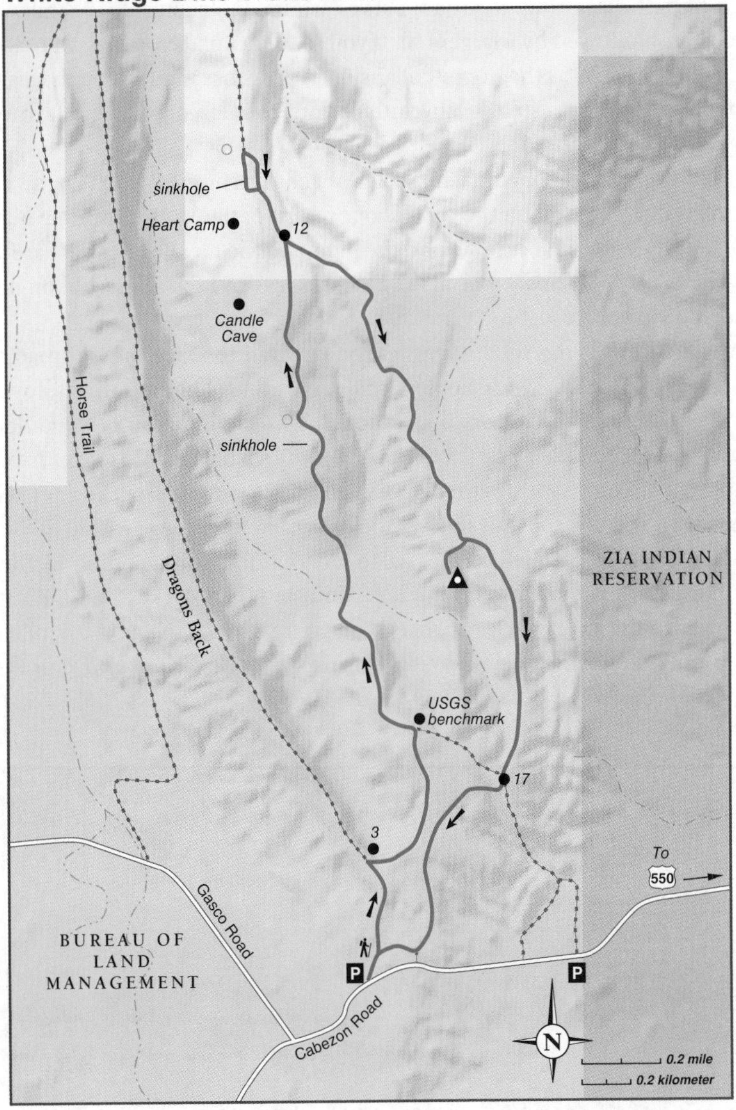

sinkhole
Heart Camp
12
Candle Cave
Horse Trail
sinkhole
Dragons Back
ZIA INDIAN RESERVATION
USGS benchmark
17
3
To
550
Gasco Road
BUREAU OF LAND MANAGEMENT
P
P
Cabezon Road
N
0.2 mile
0.2 kilometer

6,200 ft.
6,100 ft.
6,000 ft.
5,900 ft.
5,800 ft.
5,700 ft.
5,600 ft.
1 mi.
2 mi.
3 mi.
4 mi.
5 mi.

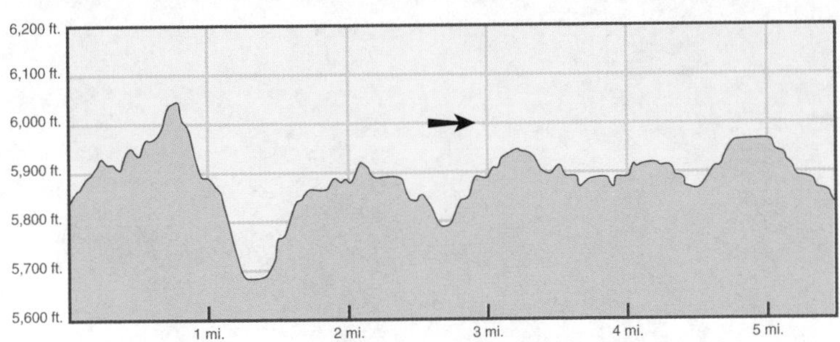

Once past the spring, the route curves around the right side of a hill with conjoined peaks, followed by a larger hill. If you're so inclined, you may want to explore the area to the west, as the dome-collapsing process has made deep fissures on that side of the ridge. The resulting labyrinth of slots, tunnels, cracks, and textures could take all day to explore.

Continuing on the main route, you'll reach Junction 12 when a trail comes in from the right. The trail on the right is our return path. Another sizable hump rises on the left. Junction 11 is just beyond the hump. In the meantime, there are wonderful views in all directions. You can even see US 550 and the white ribbon of the Rio Salado in the distance.

At Junction 11, the route turns left onto a trail to leave the old road to circle around an active spring with rippled mineral residue. The trail drops down below the spring to rejoin the old road at Junction 10. The junction is the official turnaround point for this hike. However, you are more than welcome to continue exploring, as there are more springs to the north and fissures to the south.

As for the return route, it follows the old road along the east side of the mound back to Junction 12. Bear left on the trail to Junction 13. From Junction 13, the smaller path on the right is more scenic and less confusing than the road on the left. It also runs closer to the rim, which you'll keep on your right for the next 0.8 mile to Junction 16. You're welcome to check out the many spurs to overlooks on your way back.

The incredible colors never end on this hike.

Just under 0.7 mile past Junction 16, the trail splits in at least four directions in a kind of roundabout at Junction 17. From here you have three options for returning to the parking lot. One is to return to the anticline overlook, about 0.25 mile to the northwest via Junction 20, and then backtrack to the parking lot from there. Another is to head southeast for a steep descent through banded terrain. This 0.55-mile segment leads to the first parking lot on Cabezon Road; turn right and follow the road about 0.5 mile from there back to the west parking lot.

The shortest way is to follow a dirt road not indicated on the maps. From Junction 17, make a soft right to follow the old doubletrack heading west. It will soon bend southwest. In 0.3 mile the old road splits into two routes. Turn right to rejoin our outbound route just below the first overlook.

BONUS HIKE

The **Horse Trail** is an easy hike along an old doubletrack on the west flank of the anticline and is part of the White Ridge trail network. The geology is fabulous, and if you search around enough, you'll find plenty of surprises. You can make the hike as long or as short as you want. And if you're really ambitious, you can circle the west flank of the anticline and examine the active springs north of where the main hike ended. To reach the trail, drive west 0.2 mile from the parking lot to the road on your right (Gasco Road). Drive north 0.5 mile to the first doubletrack going off to the right. Turn north. Almost immediately, there will be another doubletrack going to the right. Turn right again. Although the other route looks more substantial, turning here is the better option. Follow the road 0.2 mile to a drop gate. The Horse Trail starts at the drop gate and heads north.

• •

GPS TRAILHEAD COORDINATES N35° 29.898' W106° 50.477'

DIRECTIONS From I-25 North, take Exit 242 at Bernalillo. Turn left on US 550 and go northwest 21.2 miles. (San Ysidro is about 2 miles too far.) Turn left on Cabezon Road. (Look for the brown sign for Ojito Wilderness and White Ridge Bike Trails on the right, followed by a green street sign for Cabezon Road on the left.) Go left at the first fork ahead. After 4.4 miles on Cabezon Road, turn right, into a fenced parking lot for the White Ridge Bike Trails Area. The trailhead is at the opening in the northeastern corner of the parking lot.

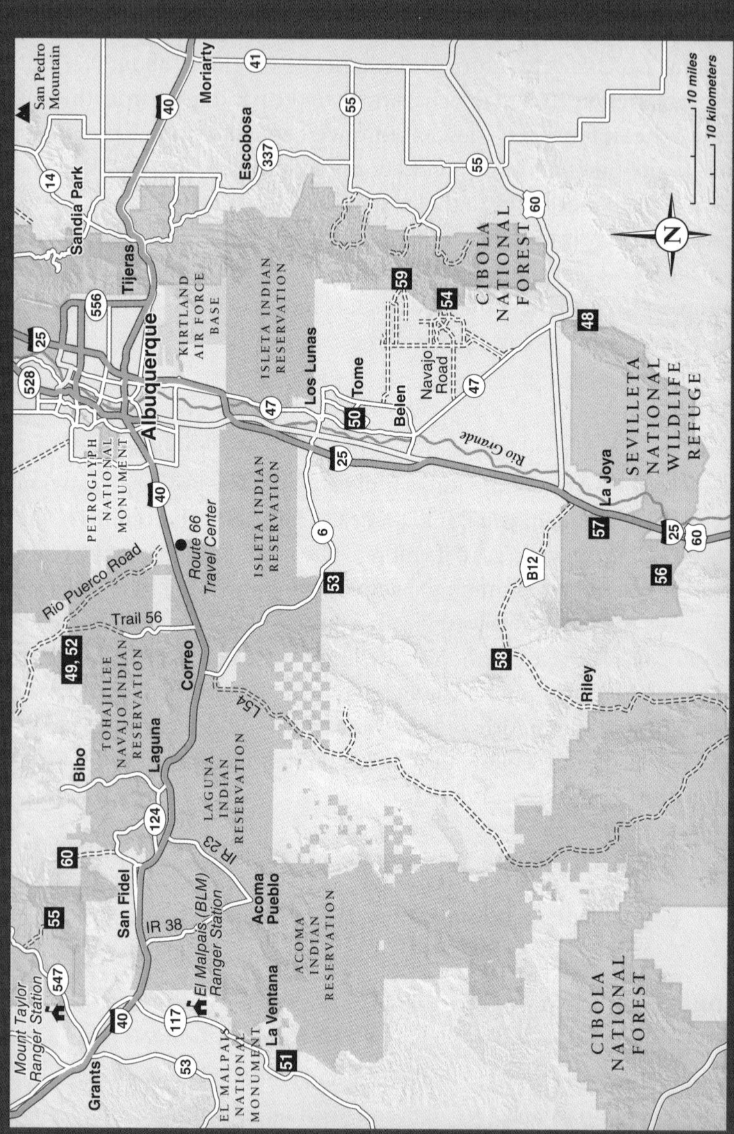
San Pedro Mountain
Moriarty
41
40
55
Escobosa
337
14
Sandia Park
55
60
Tijeras
556
Albuquerque
25
528
KIRTLAND AIR FORCE BASE
ISLETA INDIAN RESERVATION
CIBOLA NATIONAL FOREST
59
54
48
Los Lunas
Tome
50
Belen
Navajo Road
47
PETROGLYPH NATIONAL MONUMENT
Rio Grande
SEVILLETA NATIONAL WILDLIFE REFUGE
La Joya
57
56
B12
Route 66 Travel Center
6
53
Rio Puerco Road
Trail 56
49, 52
Correo
58
Riley
L54
TOHAJIILEE NAVAJO INDIAN RESERVATION
Bibo
Laguna
124
LAGUNA INDIAN RESERVATION
IR 23
60
San Fidel
55
IR 38
El Malpais (BLM) Ranger Station
Acoma Pueblo
ACOMA INDIAN RESERVATION
Mount Taylor Ranger Station
547
117
La Ventana
51
53
Grants
EL MALPAIS NATIONAL MONUMENT
10 miles
10 kilometers
N

SOUTH AND WEST OF ALBUQUERQUE

48 Abó Pass Area 254
49 Cañada del Ojo 259
50 El Cerro Tomé 264
51 El Malpais National Monument: Sandstone Bluffs 269
52 Herrera Mesa 274
53 Hidden Mountain 278
54 Monte Largo Canyon 283
55 Mount Taylor: Gooseberry Spring 288
56 San Lorenzo Canyon 293
57 Sevilleta National Wildlife Refuge 298
58 Sierra Ladrones 303
59 Trigo Canyon 307
60 Water Canyon Wildlife Area 312

48 ABÓ PASS AREA

Don't miss the amazing scenery of Manzano Peak from Abó Pass.

THERE ARE NO TRAILS on this tract of Bureau of Land Management (BLM) land south of Abó Pass. But there are plenty of arroyos and roads to make this an easy-to-follow route through open fields and red rock formations. Along the way you'll find fantastic views of the Manzano Mountains, antiquities, and remarkable fossils. This is a fun little hike in the southeast corner of our 60-mile radius of Albuquerque.

DESCRIPTION

This hike takes advantage of a small tract of BLM land overlooking historic Abó Pass. With Sevilleta National Wildlife Refuge to the west and private land to the north and east, this tract is an isolated oasis open to hiking and exploring in the southeast corner of our 60-mile radius of Albuquerque.

Abó Pass at the far south end of the Manzano Mountains is a natural corridor between the Great Plains to the Rio Grande Valley. It was used as a trading and raiding route by Native Americans long before the Spanish arrived. Abó Pueblo (see Nearby Activities) was located on the eastern approach of the pass.

More recently, the then Santa Fe Railway built the "Belen Cutoff" in 1908 through the pass to get around the steep grades of its route over Raton Pass on the Colorado–New Mexico border. The Belen Cutoff is now the BNSF Southern Transcon route,

DISTANCE & CONFIGURATION: 4.1-mile out-and-back with small balloon at the end; nearby bonus hike of 1–2 miles

DIFFICULTY: Easy–moderate

SCENERY: Piñon–juniper hills, panoramic mountain views, marine fossils

EXPOSURE: Some canyon and forest shade

TRAIL TRAFFIC: Low

TRAIL SURFACE: Sandy washes, gravel, grass, rocks

HIKING TIME: 2 hours (3 hours with the bonus hike)

DRIVING DISTANCE: 74 miles from the Big I

ELEVATION GAIN: 6,208' at trailhead; 5,994' at low point

ACCESS: Year-round; no fees or permits required

WHEELCHAIR ACCESS: No

MAPS: USGS *Becker*

FACILITIES: None

CONTACT: BLM–Socorro Field Office, blm.gov/office/socorro-field-office, 575-835-0412

LOCATION: Southeast of Belen

COMMENTS: Leashed dogs are allowed on trails.

LAST-CHANCE FOOD/GAS: All services in Belen, about 40 miles from the trailhead

and with around 90 freight trains a day, it is one the nation's busiest rail corridors. In 2011 the BNSF eliminated a serious bottleneck in its system by double-tracking the route through the pass. US 60 also goes through the pass. With I-40 to the north absorbing most of the east–west vehicle traffic, US 60 is a nice, quiet drive.

The hike begins by going east from the parking location and following the arroyo downstream. The arroyo is a nice path through juniper grassland. In a few hundred feet you'll run into a wire fence crossing the arroyo. It's BLM land on both sides of the fence, so feel free to go under or over the fence to continue your hike. In a few hundred more feet the arroyo will merge with another arroyo. Pay attention to this junction (N34° 22.639' W106° 31.202'), as you'll be returning this way.

At this point you'll have a tall wooded mesa on your right and beautiful views of the Manzano Mountains on your left. In a little more than 0.6 mile into the hike, the arroyo will reach a dirt road. Turn to the right and follow the road east. By this time you'll be away from the mesa and in more open country. In another 0.4 mile or so, you'll reach another road (N34° 22.931' W106° 30.442'); turn right and follow it south.

In around 0.2 mile the road will veer left, and there will be a smaller road continuing ahead to an overlook (N34° 22.806' W106° 30.400'). As you look to the south you'll see a flat-top knob surrounded by red rock. Between you and the knob is a grass-filled swale with a small drainage running down the middle. You'll often see bluebirds flying around in the swale. Our goal is to cross the swale and to explore the area around the base of the knob. From here the hike is cross-country, and you can take any route you want. With this being open country, you don't have to worry about losing sight of your landmarks or other people in your party.

When you reach the area of the knob, you'll be in the middle of a red rock formation. As you look to the northeast, you have a clear view of Abó Pass off in the distance. This would have been a perfect lookout location for observing the pass from a distance. As you continue walking around the area of the knob you may see

Abó Pass Area

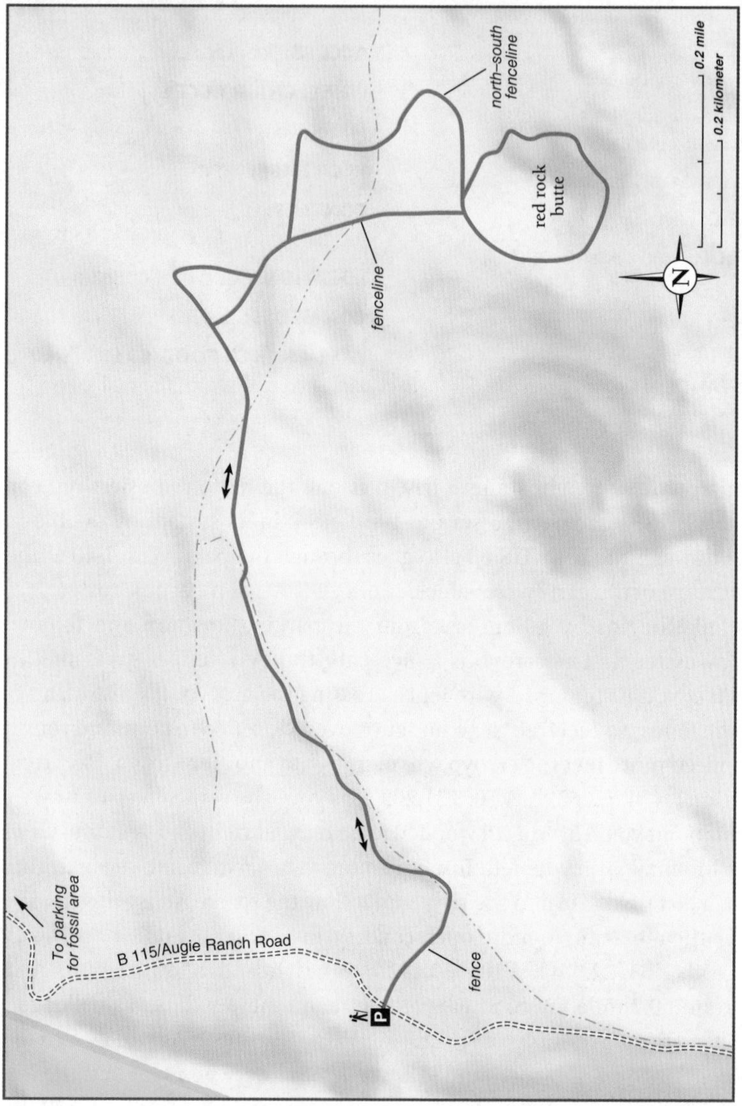

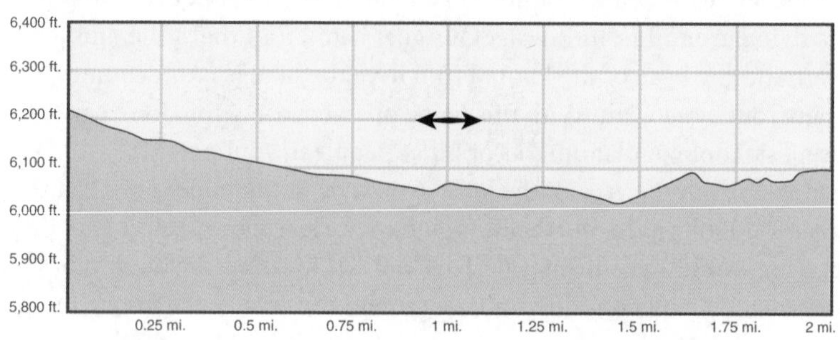

The red rock butte

some stacked rock walls. There's not much to indicate what they may have been, but they would have made a good hiding place in case raiders were causing havoc near the pass. Because the stacked rocks are clearly antiquities, leave them as you found them so the next person coming through can enjoy them. As antiquities, the stacked rocks are protected by law.

To the east of the knob, you'll see a north–south-running wire fence. BLM land extends another 0.25 mile beyond the fence. So feel free to walk around and explore as much as you want within the confines of BLM land. When it's time to return to the car, you may want to wrap up your exploration by circumnavigating the knob. From there, it's a matter of retracing your steps back to your car.

There are certainly more spectacular hikes in this book, but this is still a fun little hike. The scenery is splendid and the opportunity to do some off-trail exploring is always a plus. And you'll always find something unexpected when you explore and wander.

BONUS HIKE

Our hike and exploration of the knob was more or less confined to a layer of red rock. Had we been a little higher in elevation, we would have been on a layer of gray Madera Formation limestone. In the area near Abó Pass, the limestone is loaded with marine fossils. What makes these fossils special is that they are red from dissolved iron replacing their original material. If you would like to see red brachiopods and other red fossils, you can do so on your way home.

When you get back to your car and start driving, you'll have to drive over a limestone ridge before reaching the highway. The top of the ridge is around 1.2 miles from your parking spot. Once on top of the ridge, you'll see a small road going off to the east. Turn right and find a good place to park (N34° 23.622' W106° 30.929'). You are now on the limestone layer. From here, just walk in a northeast direction and stay near the edge of the ridge. You'll see the road you were on below you. Just wander around the limestone layer until you start finding the red fossils.

You may have to walk a little bit and be patient. And it might help to soften your eyes to see them. But if you keep at it, you'll find more than you can imagine. Just retrace your steps back to car and head on out when you're ready to leave.

NEARBY ACTIVITIES

Abó Ruins–Salinas Pueblo Missions National Monument: The unique buttressed walls of the Franciscan mission church of San Gregorio de Abó still dominate the Tompiro Pueblo of Abó. To visit this remarkable site, return to US 60, turn right, and drive 8 miles east. Turn left on NM 513 and go 0.5 mile north. Open daily, 9 a.m.–6 p.m., Memorial Day–Labor Day, and 9 a.m.–5 p.m. the rest of the year. 505-847-2585, nps.gov/sapu.

• •

GPS TRAILHEAD COORDINATES N34° 22.709' W106° 31.341'

DIRECTIONS From I-25 South, take Exit 175 at Bernardo and go 20.3 miles east on US 60. (Note: NM 47 from Belen to US 60 is 10 miles shorter but adds at least as many minutes.) After Abó Pass, as US 60 starts east again, look for an asphalt turnoff about 100 yards past the end of the guardrail on the right. Take a sharp right there and go through the gate, being sure to latch it behind you. The road shows up on some maps as B115, but a nearby sign indicates you're now on County Road 115/Augie Ranch Road. Veer left at the Y immediately ahead and drive 2 miles south on the main dirt road. Watch for an intersecting wash that's about as wide as the road itself. Turn right and park on the sandy streambed.

49 CAÑADA DEL OJO

This hoodoo is only a preview of what you'll find on this hike.

A COLLECTION OF hoodoos like you've never seen before and other fantastic surprises are waiting to be discovered in this little-known tract of Bureau of Land Management (BLM) land north of Tohajiilee. This 4.5-mile backcountry hike is easy to follow and a good introduction to an incredibly interesting area.

DESCRIPTION

Once you cross the Rio Puerco, as you drive west from Albuquerque on I-40, most of the land on both sides of the highway is tribal land and off-limits to hiking. There is, however, a tract of public BLM land north of Tohajiilee that is open to hiking. This tract has some of the most amazing landscapes near Albuquerque. Even better, this land is rarely visited and is almost a secret.

When you get off the interstate and start driving to the trailhead, the landscape along the road gives very little indication of what's waiting for you. It's only by getting out of the car and walking around that you'll discover what this area has to offer. It is only then that you can stumble into an amazing hoodoo village, pass by twisted sandstone formations, discover old homesteads, spot a stake from an old uranium claim, and maybe even find fossils, geodes, or other interesting items along the way.

DISTANCE & CONFIGURATION: 4.5-mile figure eight

DIFFICULTY: Moderate

SCENERY: Hoodoos, homestead ruins, grassland, views

EXPOSURE: Little shade

TRAIL TRAFFIC: Low

TRAIL SURFACE: Cross-country, high-desert grassland, sand, rock, cow paths

HIKING TIME: 2–3 hours

DRIVING DISTANCE: 44 miles from the Big I

ELEVATION GAIN: 5,924' at trailhead; 5,822' at low point; 6,000' at high point

ACCESS: Year-round; no fees or permits required

WHEELCHAIR ACCESS: No

MAPS: USGS *Herrera*

FACILITIES: None

CONTACT: BLM–Rio Puerco Field Office, blm.gov/office/rio-puerco-field-office, 505-761-8700

LOCATION: North of Tohajiilee

COMMENTS: Driving on the dirt road can get tricky in wet conditions. Leashed dogs are allowed on trails.

LAST-CHANCE FOOD/GAS: Convenience store–gas station on TR 56, about 11.5 miles from the trailhead

If you happen to find any archaeological or cultural artifacts on your walk, feel free to look at them, enjoy them, and then leave them where you found them. They are part of our heritage and are protected by law. Leaving them will allow the next person coming along to have the experience that you had.

When you reach the trailhead, pull off on the east side of the road, and park north of the fenceline. This will place you clearly on BLM land. The open landscape is easy to navigate and ideal for exploring. This hike will give you a good introduction to a place that you can come back to again and again.

For orientation, the road that you have been driving generally runs north and south with a bit of an angle to the northwest. The looming mesa on the west of the road is Herrera Mesa (Hike 52, page 274). Immediately northwest of you is a section of State Trust Land. (Check with nmstatelands.org for current regulations.) There is some private land a little bit to the south and east of here. (If you follow the route described in this book, you'll be on BLM land for the entire hike.) If wish to explore farther north, you'll soon discover that the road quickly deteriorates. So where you are right now is the best place to start your exploration of a true Albuquerque gem.

To begin the hike, start walking north along the west face of the nearby uplift. You can walk along the road, but that will have you crossing a small corner of state land. In less than 0.5 mile, you'll cross a shallow arroyo coming in from the west. Keep walking toward the sandstone mesa north of the arroyo to an old homestead (N35° 12.636' W107° 06.891').

Finding something like this is an opportunity to imagine. What was this? When was it built? Was it for sheep, cattle, or something else? When was it abandoned? And what was it like to live here?

After checking out the homestead, turn right and follow the base of the mesa to the northeast. In about 0.3 mile, when you near the end of the mesa, you'll reach another old homestead (N35° 12.793' W107° 06.718') tucked into a little rincon.

Cañada del Ojo

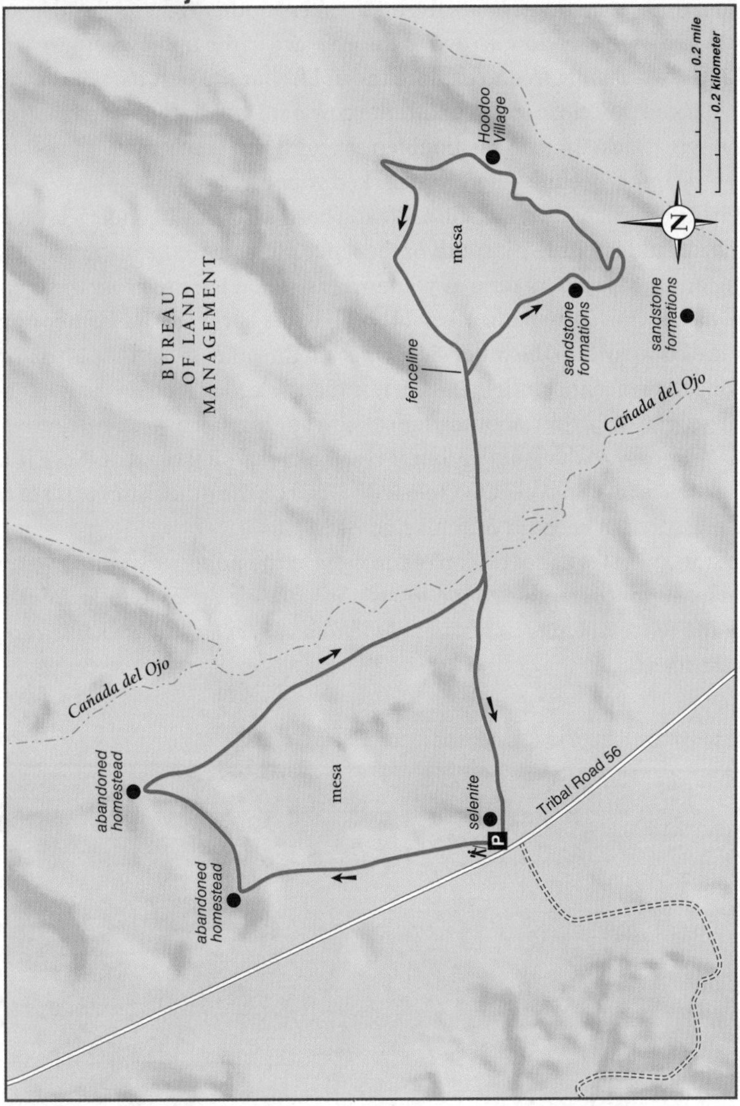

0.2 mile
0.2 kilometer
N
Hoodoo Village
mesa
BUREAU OF LAND MANAGEMENT
sandstone formations
sandstone formations
fenceline
Cañada del Ojo
Cañada del Ojo
abandoned homestead
abandoned homestead
mesa
selenite
P
Tribal Road 56

6,200 ft.
6,100 ft.
6,000 ft.
5,900 ft.
5,800 ft.
5,700 ft.
5,600 ft.
1 mi.
2 mi.
3 mi.
4 mi.

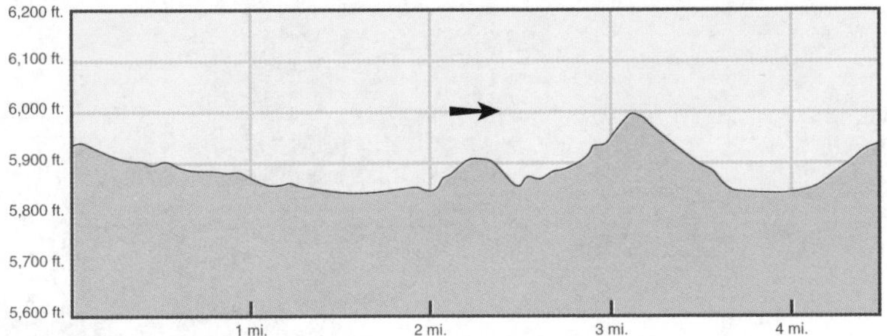

From the second homestead, the hike makes another right turn and heads southeast back across the shallow arroyo to the east face of the uplift where we started our walk. You are certainly free to explore the uplift, but the best part of this hike is yet to come. If you stay close to the uplift, the cow path will become the faint remains of an old doubletrack. Stay on the doubletrack until you reach an east–west fenceline. This is the same fenceline where you parked your car.

When you reach the fence, turn left and head east. The boundary between BLM and private land is a little bit south of the fence. Staying to the north will assure you of being on BLM land. As soon as you turn east you'll have to cross the main arroyo of Cañada del Ojo. (The namesake of this hike, the spring *ojo,* is farther north.) Just follow the cow paths to the other side. Once on the other side of the arroyo continue east along the fenceline until it ends in less than a third of a mile.

There you will find another fenceline running northwest to southeast. The fence is very easy to duck under, but if you look left you'll see that there is an opening in the fence just a few feet to the north. Once on the other side (east) of the fence you'll be assured of keeping your hike on BLM land.

Your next goal is to get on top of the mesa at the point where the two fencelines meet. The 30-foot scramble to the top is not hard. It's easier to follow the cow path leaving the fence opening at a slight angle to a very nice and walkable ramp to the top of the mesa.

The hoodoo village has amazing sandstone formations to explore.

Once you've reached the mesa top just follow the fenceline southeast for about 0.25 mile until you reach a red sandstone wall. You are now closing in on the main event of this hike. Even better, the fenceline is now well within the boundaries of BLM land and you are free to explore on both sides of the fence.

For this hike, pass under the fence to circle around to other side of the red sandstone formation in front of you. This spectacular formation is only the tip of the iceberg of what you'll be encountering. BLM land extends west to the sandstone formation downhill (southwest) from you, and you certainly are free to wander in that direction.

When you are ready to continue the hike, duck under the fence south of the red sandstone wall, and start heading up the drainage. You'll soon run into a fantastic hoodoo village. Feel free to wander around and explore these incredible sandstone formations.

When you are finished exploring, keep following the drainage uphill. It provides an easy path to the top of the canyon to check out the hoodoo village from above. From here, you can follow the canyon rim back to the fenceline and retrace your steps back to the east–west fence. Another choice, and the one shown on the map, is to drift off to the right until you reach the north edge of the mesa. From there you can follow the mesa edge back to the east–west fenceline.

The hike ends by following the fenceline west for less than 1 mile back to your car. Just before you reach your car, as you go over a small ridge, you might notice that the ground has several pieces or chunks of flat gypsum crystals. When the crystals are in flat sheets, they are usually called selenite. If they're more of a cluster, they are oftentimes called "desert rose" or acicular gypsum crystals. If you want to conduct a scientific experiment, you can put a flame under the crystal and watch it turn opaque white as it loses moisture.

With this introduction to Cañada del Ojo under your belt, you may want to vary your route the next time to see what else you can discover.

• •

GPS TRAILHEAD COORDINATES N35° 12.253' W107° 06.818'

DIRECTIONS From I-40 West, take Exit 131 and go north toward Tohajiilee on Tribal Road 56/Cañoncito School Road. At 7.8 miles, TR 56 jogs right and becomes a dirt road heading north. In 3.3 miles there will be a Y. Bear right to continue north on TR 56. In 3.4 miles there will be a cattle guard marking the northern boundary of Tohajiilee. Continue 1.2 miles to the next fenceline and park just beyond the wire fence. (This is the same parking place as for Herrera Mesa.)

50 EL CERRO TOMÉ

The *calvario* on top of Tomé Hill

THE TERMINUS OF New Mexico's most famous pilgrimage, Tomé Hill is also a font of inspiration for great art and literature, both secular and sacred. With views of the Manzano Mountains and over the Rio Grande, the hill has a natural beauty that makes it a great place for a short hike almost any time of year.

DESCRIPTION

In the mid-17th century, Tomé Domínguez, age 90, settled in the Sandia jurisdiction with his wife, Eleña Ramírez de Mendoza. Soon after both passed away, one of their three sons, Tomé Domínguez de Mendoza, moved to Fonclara, a site at the base of this volcanic hill south of Albuquerque. In 1659 he received permission to settle the land, along with the right to "recruit" unpaid laborers from nearby Isleta Pueblo to build a hacienda. The homestead was finished by 1661 but came under attack during the Pueblo Revolt in 1680. Mendoza fled back to Spain and never saw his hacienda again.

In 1739 the Tomé Grant was awarded to the local *genízaros,* a marginalized class of Hispanicized Indians and mixed-blood settlers. Ostracized by both Spanish and Pueblo societies, many genízaros developed their own customs, including religious practices based largely on native beliefs and Franciscan mysticism. Their unique traditions evolved into the Penitente Brotherhood, noted for acts of mortification, flagellation, and the Good Friday crucifixion of a Penitente brother.

DISTANCE & CONFIGURATION: 1.7-mile loop

DIFFICULTY: Moderate with a strenuous climb

SCENERY: Religious iconography perched atop a solitary volcanic mass, petroglyphs, views of the Manzano Mountains and Sierra Lucero

EXPOSURE: No shade

TRAIL TRAFFIC: Moderate; packed on Good Friday

TRAIL SURFACE: Dirt, rock

HIKING TIME: 1 hour

DRIVING DISTANCE: 31 miles from the Big I

ELEVATION GAIN: 4,892' at trailhead; 5,223' at summit

ACCESS: Sunrise–sunset; no fees or permits required

WHEELCHAIR ACCESS: No; sculpture garden is wheelchair accessible

MAPS: USGS *Los Lunas*

FACILITIES: Interpretive signage

CONTACT: Town of Tomé Land Grant, 505-565-0015

LOCATION: Los Lunas

COMMENTS: On Good Friday join thousands of pilgrims on a climb to the top of Tomé Hill. Dogs are not allowed on trails.

LAST-CHANCE FOOD/GAS: All services in Los Lunas

The annual passion play at Tomé Hill today is said to be the same as the one described by Fray Francisco Domínguez in 1776, with one possible exception. According to a disclaimer posted in Tomé Park, "No actual crucifixion is carried out."

Credit for organizing the installation of the *calvario* on Tomé Hill in 1947 goes to Edwin Antonio Berry, a World War II veteran and the son of a 19th-century Penitente leader. Berry also recorded the oral history and songs of his culture for posterity and remained the steward of Tomé Hill until his death in 2000. A stirring tribute to Tomé's most celebrated citizen can be found in Gregory Candela's locally published poetry collection, *Surfing New Mexico* (Crones Unlimited, 2001).

The route you walk here is known as Berry's Path. You hardly need a guidebook for this one. Abundant interpretive texts at Tomé Hill Park spell out just about everything you could want to know about this legendary hill. But to omit this hike would be a mortal sin, for nothing else encapsulates the essence of New Mexico quite like El Cerro Tomé. The cultural significance of the hill has earned it a listing on the National Register of Historic Places.

Park literature depicts the hill as a station at the crossroads of many cultures, but with an interesting slant. For instance, 1846 is recalled as "the year of the U.S. invasion and occupation of New Mexico." By contrast, the Spanish conquistadors are described as mere "explorers." If you don't have time to read all the signs—and unfortunately a few have vanished in recent years—get the equally comprehensive brochure; God willing, you'll find one in the black mailbox.

In 1968 a large portion, including the hill, of the Tomé Land Grant was sold to an out-of-state land-development corporation. The controversial sale created considerable discord within the community. Fortunately, after several years of negotiations, the hill was returned to the Town of Tomé Land Grant in November 2013.

If you have the chance to come here on Good Friday, you will have the opportunity to participate in a true New Mexico cultural experience. Thousands of people

El Cerro Tomé

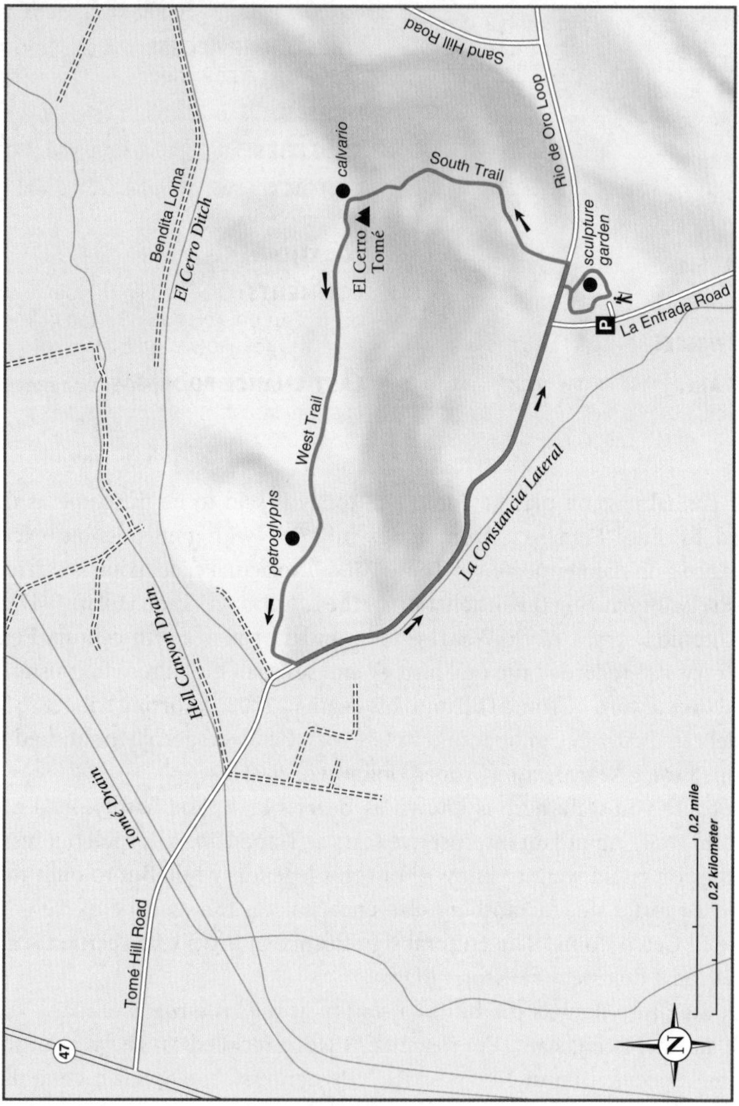

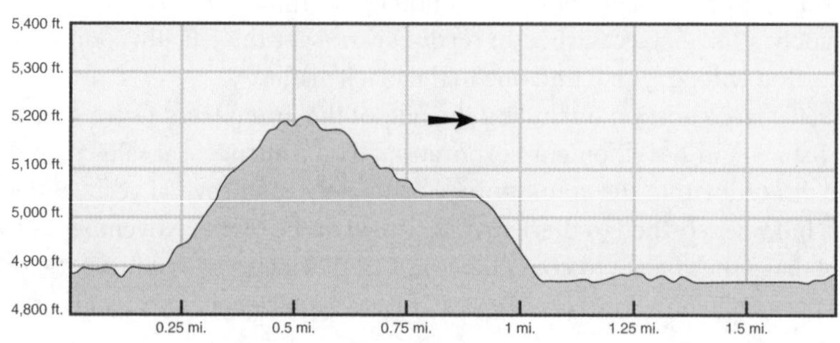

La Puerta del Sol on the south side of Tomé Hill

end their Good Friday pilgrimage at the top of the hill. Many of them start their walk from as far back as Albuquerque.

As you drive south on NM 47, the number of pilgrims along the road will be like a growing river. What started as a trickle near Albuquerque becomes a small stream of pilgrims by Isleta. By Los Lunas that stream has grown to a large creek or small river. And when you are within a mile or two of the hill it's a raging torrent. Pilgrims are everywhere. It's something you have to experience to understand.

Begin the hike by walking around *La Puerta del Sol,* the impressive sculptural centerpiece of Tomé Hill Park. The steel-and-rust artwork of the artist Armando Alvarez is a complex vision of the diverse groups who have traveled El Camino Real in the past 400 years. The $100,000 piece features a 25-foot-high gateway and the life-size likenesses of several historical archetypes. The work is often described as a celebration of cultural diversity; however, bold details evoke darker episodes of cultural conflicts.

Follow the sidewalk around a cable fence and up the road. A crosswalk ahead leads to the start of the steep South Trail. According to a sign back in the park, "The distance to the summit is over a quarter of a mile with an altitude gain of 1,200 feet." Don't worry—it's not quite that severe. The gain is a mere 400 feet. But with only two switchbacks, the rocky path takes some effort. The reward at the top is eternal salvation, along with a lovely view of the valley between the Manzano Mountains and Mesa Gallina.

Though highly discouraged now, leaving a mark on the hill is a custom that dates back 2,000 years or more. As the signs below suggest, petroglyphs appear on every flat slab of basalt on the hill. However, they're not easy to see from the trails, and the literature is a bit murky on how to find them. As a result, visitors often scour the hill in search of pecked rocks. With a good eye and better patience, you can spot a few petroglyphs from designated (though unmarked) spurs off South Trail near the top of the hill.

The calvario at the summit consists of three wood-and-metal crosses, each 16 feet high. A tin shrine sits at the base of the central cross, along with countless votive candles, rosaries, photographs, and handwritten prayers. It is at once a place of profound grief, joy, and hope. In addition to the permanent installation, temporary folk memorials and devotional artworks often crop up at various stations around the hilltop. There's always something new and fascinating on Tomé Hill.

Continue past the calvario on West Trail, also called Via Cruces ("Crosses Way"). The trail descends from the crosses and then flattens out. When the trail starts to descend again you may want to look at the rock faces to the right. They are loaded with petroglyphs. When you reach the base of the hill, turn left and follow the road 0.6 mile back to the parking lot at Tomé Park. Or for the scenic route, turn right, and follow the road about 3 miles clockwise around the hill.

For an enlightening and entertaining perspective on contemporary life in Tomé, read Ana Castillo's widely acclaimed novel *So Far from God.*

NEARBY ACTIVITIES

Tomé Plaza features the Immaculate Conception Church and Museum. You will definitely want to get out of the car and walk around the various nooks and crannies of the churchyard. A two-story courthouse once stood on the southwest corner of this historic plaza, but all that remains is the old Tomé jail. The walls are 4 feet thick and built of black igneous rock. To get to Tomé Plaza from Tomé Hill Park, return to NM 47 via Tomé Hill Road, turn left, and drive south 1.3 miles. Turn right on Church Loop and go about 0.1 mile to the small community park on the plaza.

• •

GPS TRAILHEAD COORDINATES N34° 45.078' W106° 42.322'

DIRECTIONS From I-25 South, take Exit 203 at Los Lunas and turn left (east) on NM 6 (Historic Route 66). Go 3.5 miles and bear right on Lujan Road. After 0.25 mile on Lujan Road, turn right (south) on NM 47. Go 3.4 miles to Tomé Hill Road. Turn left toward the hill and follow the signs to Tomé Hill Park, 1 mile ahead. Turn right on La Entrada Road, then left into the parking lot.

51 EL MALPAIS NATIONAL MONUMENT: Sandstone Bluffs

You'll pass by three beautiful arches on this hike.

MOST VISITORS AT Sandstone Bluffs seem content with the 30-mile view from the overlook. True, the sea of lava and distant mountain peaks are lovely, but the most impressive sights are along an informal path directly below.

DESCRIPTION

El Malpais (mall-pie-EES) refers to both the national monument and the national conservation area, administered by the National Park Service and the Bureau of Land Management, respectively. Between the two, El Malpais comprises 377,000 acres of public badlands.

Generally speaking, the terms *malpais* and *badlands* are used to describe any land that's inhospitable to humans. In New Mexico, there's usually a lava flow involved that makes them extra bad. Indeed, the lava flow of El Malpais National Monument is a most brutal terrain. And like most dangerous things in nature, its allure is irresistible.

The land wasn't always so bad. The shale and sandstone bluffs of the Colorado Plateau tectonic block quietly formed at the bottom of oceans and lakes for 500 million years. Sedimentary layers are obvious today in white-, tan-, and rust-colored bands running the length of the escarpment like bathtub rings.

DISTANCE & CONFIGURATION: 5.5-mile loop, or 4- to 6-mile out-and-back

DIFFICULTY: Moderate

SCENERY: Overlooks, lava fields, natural arches

EXPOSURE: Morning shade on lower trail

TRAIL TRAFFIC: Popular at overlook; low elsewhere

TRAIL SURFACE: Sand, rock

HIKING TIME: 3–4 hours

DRIVING DISTANCE: 81 miles from the Big I

ELEVATION GAIN: 6,993' at trailhead; 6,627' at low point below the bluffs

ACCESS: Year-round, sunrise–sunset; no fees or permits required

WHEELCHAIR ACCESS: No; part of the overlook is wheelchair accessible

MAPS: USGS *Los Pilares*

FACILITIES: Restroom at trailhead; no water

CONTACT: nps.gov/elma, 505-876-2783

LOCATION: Southeast of Grants

COMMENTS: Leashed dogs are allowed on trails. The El Malpais (Bureau of Land Management) Visitor Center, en route to the trailhead, has several very nice exhibits on the area and is a worthwhile stop if it is open.

LAST-CHANCE FOOD/GAS: Convenience store–gas station at Exit 89

Seventy million years ago, the plateau started rising above its neighbors. A north–south rift slowly opened the Rio Grande Valley between 30 and 10 million years ago. But the heaviest volcanic action started in the last 5 million years, with magma swelling into the deep fault in the crust that created Mount Taylor and the Valles Caldera 1–3 million years ago. It still smolders today from Raton to Springerville, Arizona; through the Jemez; and of course, El Malpais: the freshest volcanic field in the southwestern United States. Small cones erupted here at least five separate times between 120,000 and 1000 BC, until the valley filled with a river of lava 40 miles long and 5 miles wide. Stories of the nearby Acoma Pueblo suggest the latest outburst might even have been as recent as A.D. 1200.

With no formal trails but plenty of user-developed trails, there are many ways to hike from the parking area at the Sandstone Bluffs Overlook. The same goes for reaching the bottom. From the parking area you might guess that nothing short of a rappelling line is required to reach the path 200 feet below. There are actually two practical ways to the bottom from the parking area.

The first and most precarious way down is to go to the south end of the parking area toward the picnic area. You might have to poke around the maze of rocks to find it, but you'll know it when you see it—a steep but manageable slope populated with tall pines. There's no discernible path in this short, scrubby section, but a few cairns offer helpful suggestions for picking your way down.

The second and definitely the easiest way down is to follow the braid of trails heading north from the parking lot. If you stay close to the top, you'll have fantastic views of the Zuni Mountains to west, the lava flows below, the sandstone formations around you, and Mount Taylor directly in front. Just this portion of the hike alone makes driving here more than worth the effort.

In a little over a mile, you'll reach an old fenceline (much of it fallen down). Depending on which braid of the trail you took, you might be on a small bluff. You'll

El Malpais National Monument: Sandstone Bluffs

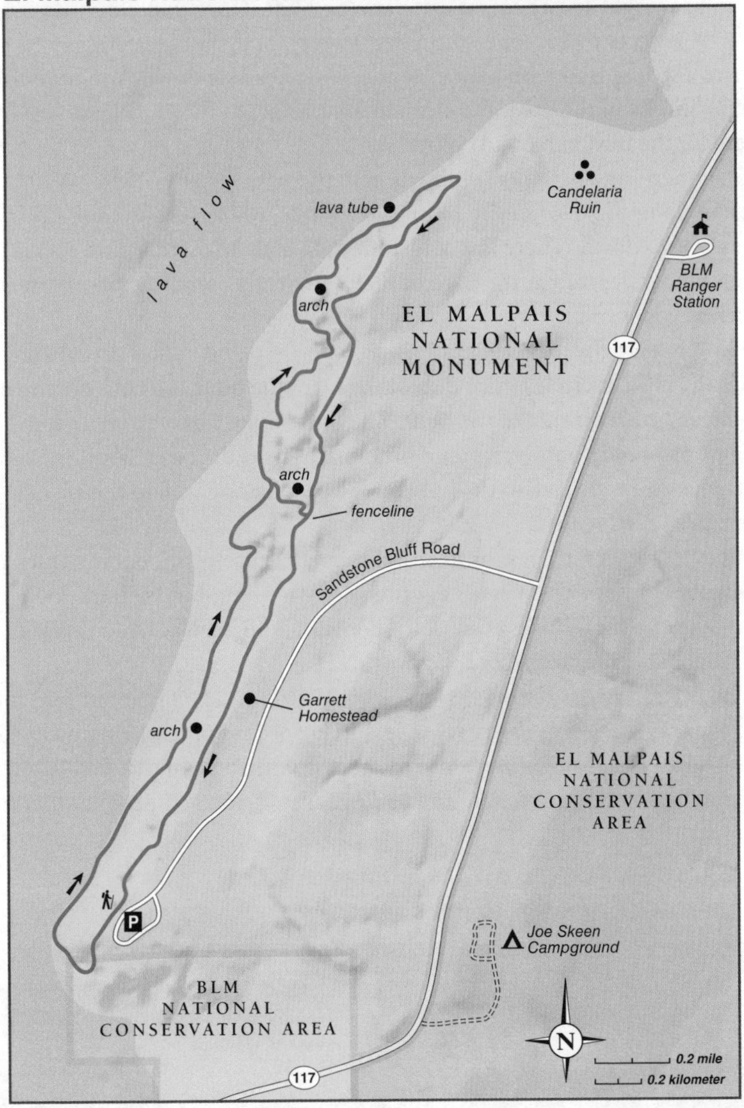

lava flow
lava tube
Candelaria
Ruin
arch
EL MALPAIS
NATIONAL
MONUMENT
BLM
Ranger
Station
117
arch
fenceline
Sandstone Bluff Road
Garrett
Homestead
arch
EL MALPAIS
NATIONAL
CONSERVATION
AREA
P
Joe Skeen
Campground
BLM
NATIONAL
CONSERVATION AREA
N
0.2 mile
0.2 kilometer
117

7,100 ft.
7,000 ft.
6,900 ft.
6,800 ft.
6,700 ft.
6,600 ft.
6,500 ft.
1 mi.
2 mi.
3 mi.
4 mi.
5 mi.

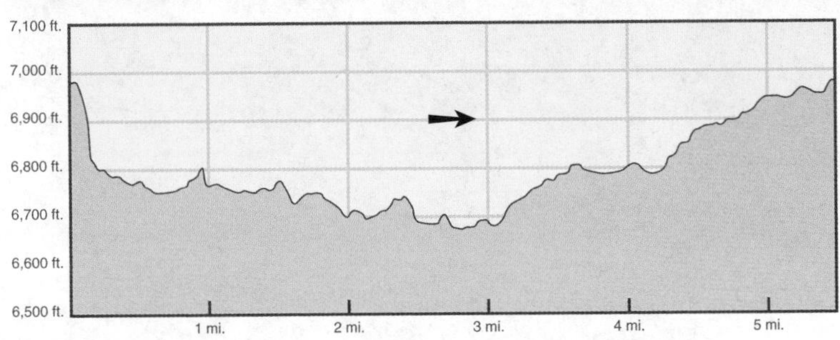

want to bear right (east) to navigate off the bluff. Once you clear the bluff (N34° 57.597' W107° 49.693'), look to the left (west). You should see a gap in the main bluff and a strong trail with a nice, gentle slope heading down. You may also notice some potsherds in the area. All of them are protected by law. Please leave them as they are for the next person to enjoy.

From here, the path downhill will join the path (N34° 57.720' W107° 49.846') that runs along the base of the bluff in 0.25 mile. Make sure to look up and to the right as you go down. There is a sandstone arch high up on the bluff. As for the hike, you can follow the trail at the base of the bluff in any combination of directions for as much as you want.

The path at the base begins where the first and more precarious descent reaches the base. It circles from the south end of the bluff and runs northwest into a fenceline on the west side of the bluff. The fence is very easy to go under. There are remnants of an old doubletrack and other paths near the base to follow. All of them squeeze between the lava to the west and the sandstone wall to the east. So there is no chance of getting lost.

Alcoves, towers, ridges, buttes, and spectacular sandstone formations multiply your exploratory options. Check out the ones you want, but keep track of your time because the overlook closes at sunset. There is no official way to do this hike, but the description here goes from south to north.

The first of three arches (N34° 57.097' W107° 50.111') is about 0.75 mile from where the trail started at the base. In less than another mile, the path catches up to the second arch and the other route to the bottom. You could, if you want, exit the base from here and head back to the parking area. If you go north another 0.75 mile

Take in the different textures of the landscape from the bluff.

or so, you'll reach the third arch (N34° 58.142' W107° 49.676') and an extraordinary gallery of petroglyphs depicting thunderbirds, scorpions, and other creatures.

Depending on how much time you have, you can continue north. In less than 0.4 mile there is a good place (N34° 58.316' W107° 49.425') for scrambling to the top of the bluff. From here, it's a little more than 2 miles back to the parking area. Stay above the rim, and you'll have no problem returning to the parking area.

With the spectacular sandstone formations to your right, it's easy to forget about the lava to your left. Sometimes it will be off in the distance and other times right on your shoulder. The different textures are amazing. And if you want to check out a lava tube (N34° 58.314' W107° 49.507') there's one near the exit at the north end.

With so many ways to get around and so much to check out, you can pick a different route the next time to see what you missed this time. No matter how many times you come out here, you won't be disappointed.

NEARBY ACTIVITIES

Garrett Homestead is a partially reconstructed residential structure from the mid-1930s. It stands roadside en route to the overlook.

Other nearby points of interest are listed below. (Driving distances are in approximate miles south of the Sandstone Bluffs Road/NM 117 junction.)

Zuni–Acoma Trail (6): This ancient trade route traverses four major lava flows in 7.5 miles, one way. It's a tough hike, and very hard on a dog's paws, but cairns make it easy to follow.

La Ventana (8): With a height of 80 feet and a span of 165 feet, this natural arch is the second-longest in New Mexico. (The state record goes to the inaccessible Snake Bridge in San Juan County.) A paved, wheelchair-accessible trail and picnic area are near the base of the arch.

Narrows Picnic Area (11): Facilities include wheelchair-accessible tables and restrooms. No water. The Narrows Rim Trail begins at the south end of the picnic area. This well-marked 6-mile out-and-back culminates with a view over La Ventana.

Lava Falls (26): A cairned 1-mile loop explores El Malpais's youngest lava flow. Facilities include a restroom and picnic area. No water.

• •

GPS TRAILHEAD COORDINATES N34° 56.651' W107° 50.298'

DIRECTIONS From I-40 West, take Exit 89 and turn left on NM 117. Go south 10 miles to the signed entrance for Sandstone Bluffs. Turn right and follow the gravel road 1.7 miles southwest to its end.

52 HERRERA MESA

Herrera Mesa offers many places to find adventure.

NEAR A LONELY corner of the Tohajiilee Navajo Reservation, a forgotten trail scraped into rocky ledges presents one of the few routes to the upper tiers of Herrera Mesa. Views along the way overlook equally impressive mesas, outcrops, and canyons. This hike, along with Hike 49, provides a good introduction to a wonderful tract of Bureau of Land Management (BLM) land north of Tohajiilee.

DESCRIPTION

Most of the approximately 12-square-mile Herrera Mesa stands on Navajo land. Formerly known as the Cañoncito, the Tohajiilee are one of three Navajo bands outside the Big Rez farther west. Their reclaimed name translates to "water dippers," referring to their ancestors' renowned survival strategy of harvesting water from catch basins in the rocks.

The ranch at the base of Herrera Mesa is privately owned and remains active. Even though the house and barn evoke a sense of hopeless abandonment, and ruts and cacti have rendered their long driveway impassible, the corrals and stock tanks are still in good use. Decades ago, the ranch was simply known as *Ojo,* and some 300 whiteface cattle roamed its 10 sections (6,400 acres). Estevan Herrera sold the ranch in 1985 and passed away three years later. You may have noticed the Herrera family cemetery on your drive in. It's in a fenced enclosure on the west side of the road.

DISTANCE & CONFIGURATION: 4- to 5-mile out-and-back

DIFFICULTY: Moderate

SCENERY: Jurassic rock formations, grasslands, homestead ruins, views

EXPOSURE: Mostly sunny, though shaded by midafternoon

TRAIL TRAFFIC: Low

TRAIL SURFACE: Rugged dirt roads, sand, loose rock

HIKING TIME: 2–3 hours

DRIVING DISTANCE: 44 miles from the Big I

ELEVATION GAIN: 5,924' at trailhead; 6,365' at high point

ACCESS: Year-round, no fees or permits required

WHEELCHAIR ACCESS: No

MAPS: USGS *Herrera*

FACILITIES: None

CONTACT: BLM–Rio Puerco Field Office, blm.gov/office/rio-puerco-field-office, 505-761-8700

LOCATION: North of Tohajiilee

COMMENTS: Driving on the dirt road can get tricky in wet conditions. Leashed dogs are allowed on trails.

LAST-CHANCE FOOD/GAS: Convenience store–gas station on TR-56, about 11.5 miles from the trailhead

Herrera Mesa displays the distinctive banding of the Morrison Formation, a group of sedimentary rock layers of the late Jurassic (161–145 million years ago). From a distance, the eastern face appears as an insurmountable wall. Closer inspection reveals that the wall is stepped. Think of it somewhat like a tiered cake. Old trails follow the edge of each tier, each leading to a point where you can easily walk up to the next level.

Information about these old roads is scant. They may have started as Indian trails, later used by ranchers leading livestock to mesa-top pastures, and perhaps still later enhanced by uranium prospectors. All that's certain is that someone put a tremendous amount of effort into clearing rocks and stacking them into walls to create a semblance of roads that don't seem to lead to anything but beautiful views.

The hike begins from where you parked near the fence. Walk 50 yards or so south along the road to a two-track going west (N35° 12.218' W107° 06.819'). Follow the two-track west as it curves south. In 0.5 mile you'll reach a green gate and a BLM sign that says CLOSED. The road is closed to vehicles not to hikers. You could, if you want, shorten the hike by driving to the gate.

The hike continues uphill along the road. In less than 0.5 mile there will be a fireplug-size cairn (N35° 12.162' W107° 07.276') on the left. This used to be a road and is our route to the top of the mesa. But before going to the top, take some time to go farther west on the road if only to plan future adventures in the area.

As the road begins to curve around an outcrop and lead into a wide canyon, fantastic vistas open up to the north. Unusual formations in the valley below might be described (albeit inadequately) as a series of small mesas tilted at a 45-degree angle. Some of those formations have geodes; others are full of marine fossils. Some of the land below you is State Trust Land, so you'll want to check with the State Land Office (nmstatelands.org) on their current policies before wandering onto state land. You can follow this road for about 0.5 mile to take in the views to the north.

Herrera Mesa

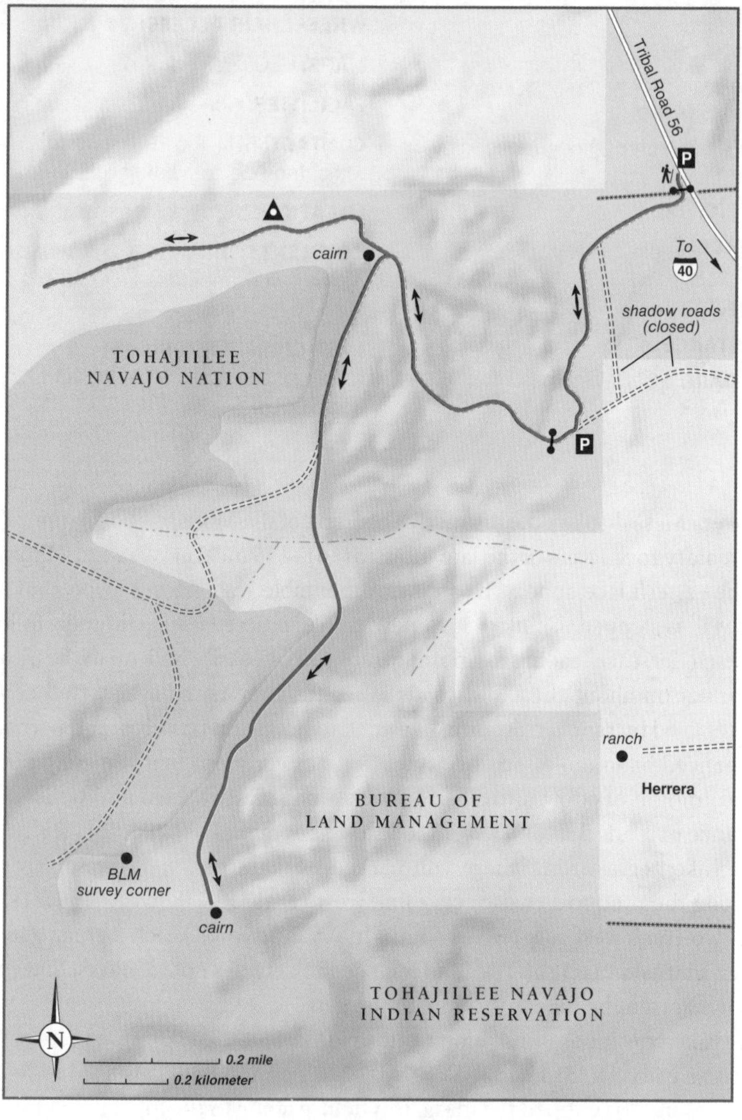

Tribal Road 56
P
To
40
cairn
shadow roads
(closed)
TOHAJIILEE
NAVAJO NATION
P
ranch
Herrera
BUREAU OF
LAND MANAGEMENT
BLM
survey corner
cairn
TOHAJIILEE NAVAJO
INDIAN RESERVATION
N
0.2 mile
0.2 kilometer

6,400 ft.
6,300 ft.
6,200 ft.
6,100 ft.
6,000 ft.
5,900 ft.
5,800 ft.
1 mi.
2 mi.
3 mi.
4 mi.
5 mi.

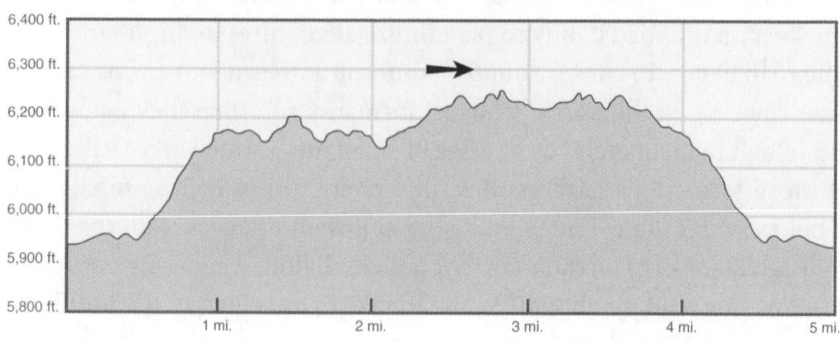

After you've taken in the view and possibilities, it's time to go back to the cairn and head south up the old trail. It may only be little more than a slight indentation right here. It becomes clearer as its rock edges stack up higher and it gradually climbs to the next tier. After 0.25 mile or so, the decrepit remains of a wire fence lean over the trail. The ranch can be seen far below to the left. At this point, you have little choice but to step up to the next level. A short climb to the right puts you in a sunken portion of the mesa top, a kind of triangular cove. The walls ahead and on your right delineate the boundary between public land and the Navajo reservation. From this perspective, it may seem as though only the top tiers of the mesa belong to the Navajo. Actually, aside from a few small bits of the northern and eastern sides, it's all theirs.

For this hike, continue south, keeping the mesa rim on your left. Cross the arroyo and pass the eastern end of the cove wall to pick up the old trail. It squeezes along a narrow ledge for about 0.25 mile before arriving at a fence much like the last one. Again, step up to a slightly higher level. This upper ledge soon widens, giving acrophobes a bit more breathing room. At this point you're directly behind the ranch on the old Herrera town site, and about 400 feet above it.

Continue south along the rim to a small cairn. It marks the Navajo boundary, as does a fence below, which stretches due east to the horizon. You're now in the southwesternmost corner of public land on Herrera Mesa. Accordingly, the route description ends here. A more natural terminus might be the mesa point in plain view just 0.25 mile ahead. Whether you proceed to that lovely overlook or turn back at the cairn is up to you.

NEARBY ACTIVITIES

If you're planning to stop for a bite to eat on your way home, you might want to consider a stop at **Laguna Burger** for a world-famous Laguna Burger. It's a very good New Mexico–style green chile cheeseburger made from fresh ground beef. You can find the restaurant at the Rio Puerco 66 Pit Stop on the north side of I-40 (across from the 66 Casino) at Exit 140. For more information, call 505-352-7848 or visit thelagunaburger.com.

• •

GPS TRAILHEAD COORDINATES N35° 12.253' W107° 06.818'

DIRECTIONS From I-40 West, take Exit 131 and go north toward Tohajiilee on Tribal Road 56/Cañoncito School Road. At 7.8 miles, TR 56 jogs right and becomes a dirt road heading north. In 3.3 miles there will be a Y. Bear to the right to continue north on TR 56. In 3.4 miles there will be a cattle guard marking the northern boundary of Tohajiilee. Continue 1.2 miles to the next fenceline and park just beyond the wire fence. (This is the same parking place as for Cañada del Ojo.)

53 HIDDEN MOUNTAIN

A ruin on top of Hidden Mountain

IT'S A TOUGH climb to the top, but the views and discoveries reveal there's a lot more to Hidden Mountain than the unsolved riddles inscribed in Mystery Rock, also known as the Decalogue Stone of Los Lunas. But if the stone is all you came to see, then your hike is a whole lot easier.

DESCRIPTION

Hidden Mountain isn't much of a mountain, nor is it very well hidden. The naked cone rises up in full view near the convergence of NM 6, the Rio Puerco, and the BNSF railroad. Aside from the occasional train, it's a quiet junction, and evidence of human activity is nearly absent from sight.

The volcano peaks at 5,507 feet, more than 400 feet above the riverbed, where water seldom flows. The crater on top sits tilted with a chipped rim, like a discarded bowl. A crack spreads down to the north, deepening into a gully cluttered with basalt. Tucked near the bottom of the steep chute is a boulder weighing around 90 tons. In this neighborhood, it looks like an average stone, not the kind that calls attention to itself, except maybe for the way it slumps over a dry wash as though attempting to conceal the one thing that makes it truly remarkable.

Pecked into its face is a strange message. Nine lines contain a total of 216 letters from the Old Hebrew alphabet, with a few Greek letters and maybe some Samaritan

DISTANCE & CONFIGURATION: 1.6-mile out-and-back to 3.3-mile out-and-back with extensions

DIFFICULTY: Easy to moderate with a tough climb for the extension

SCENERY: Basalt cliffs, petroglyphs, ruins, the Ten Commandments

EXPOSURE: Little shade

TRAIL TRAFFIC: Low

TRAIL SURFACE: Dirt road, rocky arroyos, sand

HIKING TIME: 1–2 hours (more if you wander)

DRIVING DISTANCE: 38 miles from the Big I

ELEVATION GAIN: 5,053' at trailhead; 5,430' on summit

ACCESS: State Trust Land Recreational Access Permit required

WHEELCHAIR ACCESS: No

MAPS: USGS *Rio Puerco*

FACILITIES: None

CONTACT: State Trust Land, nmstatelands.org, 505-827-5760

LOCATION: West of Los Lunas

COMMENTS: Leashed dogs are allowed on trails. State land policies are subject to change; check with the land office for the latest policies.

LAST-CHANCE FOOD/GAS: Full services at Exit 215. (If you're returning to Albuquerque via I-40, there are no services until you reach the Route 66 Casino on I-40 about 31 miles away.)

tossed into the mix. The earliest known documentation of the inscription came in 1936 from Professor Frank Hibben of the University of New Mexico. Since then, every savant with a penchant for cryptograms has attempted to crack the code of Mystery Rock.

If you do an internet search on Mystery Rock, you'll find many explanations, including hidden treasure, ancient Greeks, the lost tribes of Israel, crypto-Jews, the Mormon Battalion, and many more. The most commonly accepted explanation: it's a hoax or a prank. The likely culprits: Hobe and Eva, a couple of University of New Mexico students armed with chisels and Semitic-language reference books swiped from Zimmerman Library. The evidence: they left their names on another stone on the ground not 10 feet away, along with a date (3-19-30) that beats Hibben's initial discovery by three years.

In all the excitement to uncover the truth, the inscription has been scrubbed, chalked, re-etched, and ultimately rendered unsuitable for age-dating analysis. To add to the mystery someone gouged out the first line in November 2006. The bottom line is that if someone wants to believe that the rock has significance, they will. In the meantime it is a great place to explore.

The Mystery Rock is on State Trust Land and requires a State Trust Land Recreational Access Permit to visit. Because policies can change at any time, please check with the State Land Office (nmstatelands.org) for the most up to date information regarding permits.

The approach to this hike is a bit unusual, as the road to Hidden Mountain is also the access road for the Valencia Regional Landfill. So don't be surprised to see garbage trucks coming in and out. From NM 6, you'll cross the BNSF railroad tracks and go over a bridge to reach a landfill access gate. Park anywhere along the side of the road that isn't blocking a gate.

Hidden Mountain

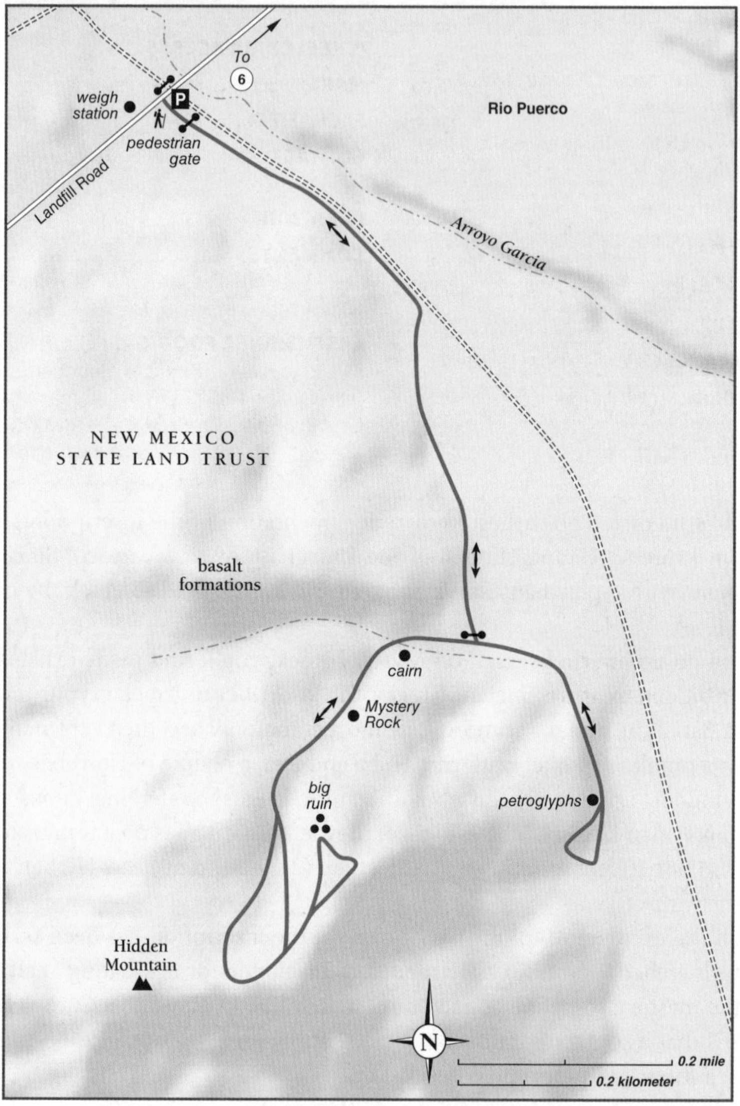

To
6
weigh station
P
pedestrian gate
Landfill Road
Rio Puerco
Arroyo Garcia
NEW MEXICO STATE LAND TRUST
basalt formations
cairn
Mystery Rock
big ruin
petroglyphs
Hidden Mountain
N
0.2 mile
0.2 kilometer

5,600 ft.
5,500 ft.
5,400 ft.
5,300 ft.
5,200 ft.
5,100 ft.
5,000 ft.
0.25 mi.
0.5 mi.
0.75 mi.
1 mi.
1.25 mi.
1.5 mi.

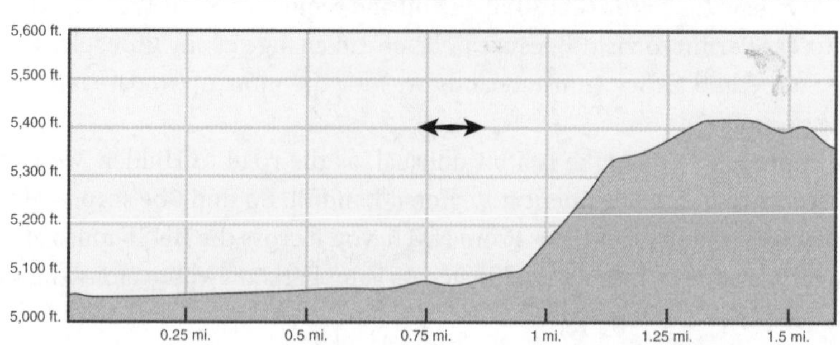

The eastbound *Southwest Chief* (Amtrak) heading to Albuquerque

The hike begins at the pedestrian gate on the left side of the road. Continue southeast on the dirt road toward Hidden Mountain. Soon after you clear the flank of the mountain in about 0.3 mile, there will be a wide path going off to your right (south). The path has arrows made out of stone pointing the way. Follow that path to the fenceline and pedestrian gate. Once on the other side of the fence, turn right (west) and follow the path along the fence. There is also a path going to the left. We'll be following that path later.

Follow the path as it veers to the left (south) away from the fenceline. The path will soon head uphill along a dry arroyo. There are some cairns and arrows scratched on rocks to keep you in the right direction. You are now very close to Mystery Rock (N34° 47.111' W106° 59.790'). It is on the left with the inscription facing the streambed at the base of the stone. At this point you have hiked 0.8 mile, and if you only want to check out the rock, you can head back to your car for a 1.6-mile out-and-back hike.

There is much more to see on this hike, and if you're ready to go to the top of the mountain, continue following the path uphill. This part of the path is much steeper and is generally on the left side of the arroyo. Keep an eye out for rock art and etchings as you go up, including another one by "Hobe and Eva" (N34° 46.991' W106° 59.869'). The chiseling on that etching looks very similar to Mystery Rock.

When you reach the top, try to stay to the north side of the mountain, as the south side is privately owned. Feel free to wander around. The views in all directions are amazing.

Look around and you'll start finding ruins of rooms and enclosures. The ruins were probably used as a defensive location by Pottery Mound pueblo a few miles to the east. These ruins are interesting, as archaeologists have found very few artifacts associated with them. This may suggest that the structures were never completed or rarely used.

If you walk around the edges of the mountain, you are likely to find rock art. If you wander to the north, you might find a cross on the ground made of stones. One thing you can't help noticing are the trains and their haunting horns from the tracks down below. The BNSF southern transcontinental line is a major rail corridor with over 90 freight trains a day.

The combination of all of this makes this a peaceful and perfect place to be. When you are ready to leave the top, you can go down the side of the mountain, but that choice is very steep and can be treacherous in places. If you are determined to go down the side, you'll find gentler grades to the west.

Our hike will go down the way we came up. When you reach the fenceline at the bottom, you can return to your car or continue walking along the fence to the east side of the mountain. There you will find several basalt boulders (N34° 47.029' W106° 59.544') covered with rock art. You don't want to venture too far south from here, as you'll be crossing into privately owned land.

When you are ready, you can retrace your steps back to your car.

NEARBY ACTIVITIES

If returning to Albuquerque, consider going north (left) on NM 6 for an 18-mile cruise through the southeastern corner of the **Laguna Indian Reservation.** It adds about 10 miles to your trip, but the scenery is spectacular. (The land is off-limits to the general public, so don't wander.) NM 6 comes out on I-40 near Correo, about 27 miles west of Albuquerque.

If you need another hill to climb, head back down NM 6 to **El Cerro de Los Lunas.** This 1,500-acre open-space preserve, donated by the Huning Land Trust in 2006, contains numerous rugged routes to the 5,955-foot peak. Trailheads on the south side of NM 6 are accessed at West Gate and Huning Ranch Loop.

• •

GPS TRAILHEAD COORDINATES N34° 47.578' W106° 59.985'

DIRECTIONS From I-25 South, take Exit 203 at Los Lunas. Turn right and follow NM 6 west and north 14.5 miles. About 0.20 mile after crossing the Rio Puerco, turn left on the landfill access road. Cross the railroad tracks and continue straight out 0.35 mile to the landfill check-in station. Park on the side of the road. Do not block any gates. The hike begins at the pedestrian gate on the left side of the road.

54 MONTE LARGO CANYON

Haze obscures the view west from Monte Largo Canyon.

THOUGH DESIGNATED AS a trailhead on U.S. Forest Service maps, Monte Largo lacks a designated trail. No problem—well-worn paths facilitate hiking along its primary drainage. The lush wooded corridor is a near-perfect environment for hikes throughout most of the year.

DESCRIPTION

Don't let the approach fool you. Though the Manzanos appear as barren scarps of granite and scrub, you'll find long stretches of shaded woodland hidden behind its stark facade. Also as you drive along NM 47 and the approach road you will see some houses, but most of it is a grass plain slowly rising all the way to the base of the mountains. This is how Albuquerque's Northeast Heights looked before World War II. And if you look at a map of the area, you'll see that there are dozens of streets that were platted but never built. They are from various 1960s land developments that sold residential building lots to out-of-towners as investments.

At the end of the approach, you'll enter a steel-pipe fence enclosure. Ahead of you is the trailhead for Monte Largo Canyon. Behind you to the west are fantastic views of the open plain sloping down to the Rio Grande and the Sierra Ladrones to the southwest. The canyon ahead of you has wonderful rocks to examine and a lush

DISTANCE & CONFIGURATION: 5-mile out-and-back

DIFFICULTY: Moderate

SCENERY: Broadleaf and pine forest, wildlife, caves

EXPOSURE: Mostly shade

TRAIL TRAFFIC: Very low

TRAIL SURFACE: Packed dirt, loose rock

HIKING TIME: 2–3 hours

DRIVING DISTANCE: 58 miles from the Big I

ELEVATION GAIN: 6,254' at trailhead; 7,003' at turnaround point

ACCESS: Year-round; no fees or permits required

WHEELCHAIR ACCESS: No

MAPS: USGS *Manzano Peak*

FACILITIES: None

CONTACT: Cibola National Forest–Mountainair Ranger District, fs.usda.gov/cibola, 505-847-2990; Manzano Mountain Wilderness

LOCATION: Southeast of Belen

COMMENTS: The last stretch of road can be rough and impossible in wet conditions. Leashed dogs are allowed on trails.

LAST-CHANCE FOOD/GAS: All services available in Belen, about 20 miles from the trailhead

mix of oak and pine. A good supply of acorns keeps squirrels and turkeys well fed, and summer bounties of currants attract birds and bears.

The state's only species of bear is *Ursus americanus,* the black bear, which often appears more a shade of cinnamon brown. Its predilection for verdant mountain forests keeps it confined (usually) to wooded "islands" throughout the American Southwest. Black bears may seem cute and clumsy but can charge at speeds up to 30 miles per hour. With that in mind, review the safety tips for hiking in bear country (page 14) before entering Monte Largo Canyon.

The hike begins at the gateway. Walk straight east along a path worn through rocky grassland. In about 0.25 mile, it bends downhill to the left. A black water line crosses the path here. Both the line and the path descend closer to the arroyo and then turn east into the canyon. You can follow the line for a more shaded path, though dense scrub ahead will eventually coax you to cross the arroyo. Or you can cross sooner to pick up a sunny doubletrack on the north bank.

Either way, you'll pass a water tower on the north bank. About 500 feet east of the water tower, the trail splits. For a great preview of the route ahead, veer right on the more prominent branch uphill. About 0.2 mile ahead, a steel sign marks the boundary of the Manzano Mountain Wilderness. Continue uphill another 200 yards or so. The object is to reach a rocky outcrop on the nearest ridge to your left, so just aim in that direction if the path fades or seems to stray elsewhere. When you reach the crest of the ridge, turn left and walk out to the point. Cuts in the exposed rock suggest minor quarrying or mining may have occurred up here.

Monte Largo Spring is directly below to the north, but it may be difficult to spot when foliage is full. Animals frequent the water source, making this overlook the perfect perch for watching birds and wildlife. Dense woods stretch for about 1 mile to the northeast before disappearing into the V of the canyon. Manzano Peak, the highest in the range, stands 2 miles to the southeast.

Monte Largo Canyon

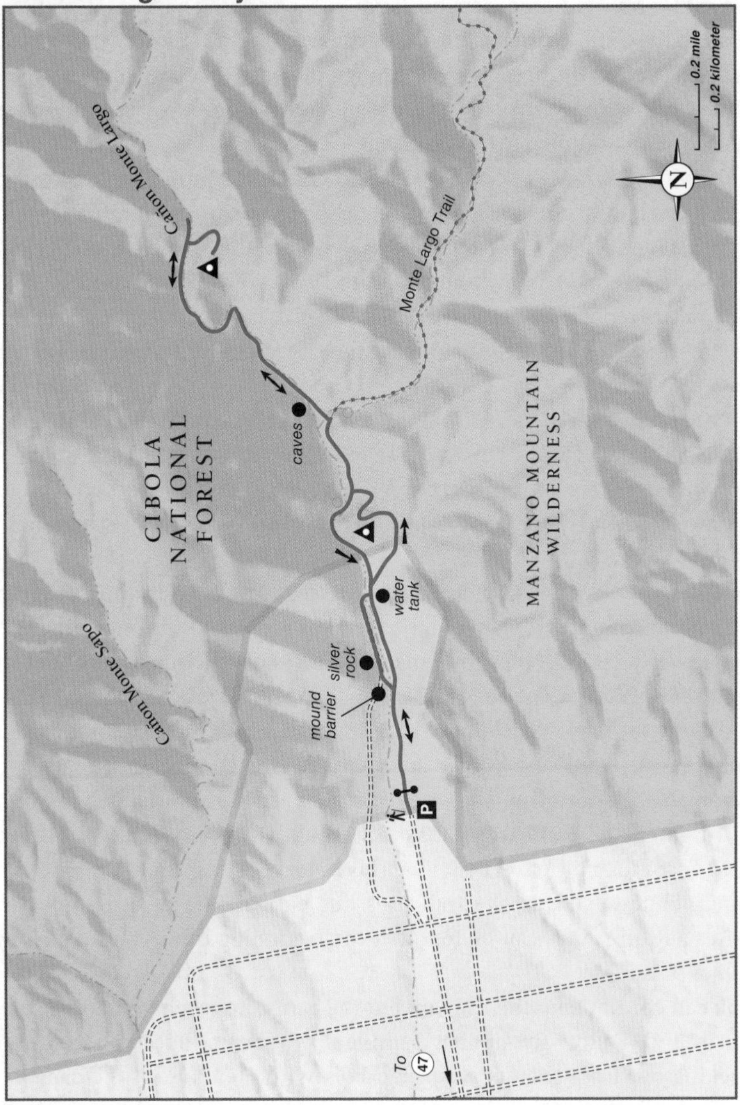

Cañon Monte Largo
Monte Largo Trail
CIBOLA NATIONAL FOREST
MANZANO MOUNTAIN WILDERNESS
caves
water tank
silver rock
mound barrier
Cañon Monte Sapo
To 47
P
N
0.2 mile
0.2 kilometer

7,200 ft.
7,000 ft.
6,800 ft.
6,600 ft.
6,400 ft.
6,200 ft.
6,000 ft.
0.5 mi.
1 mi.
1.5 mi.
2 mi.
2.5 mi.

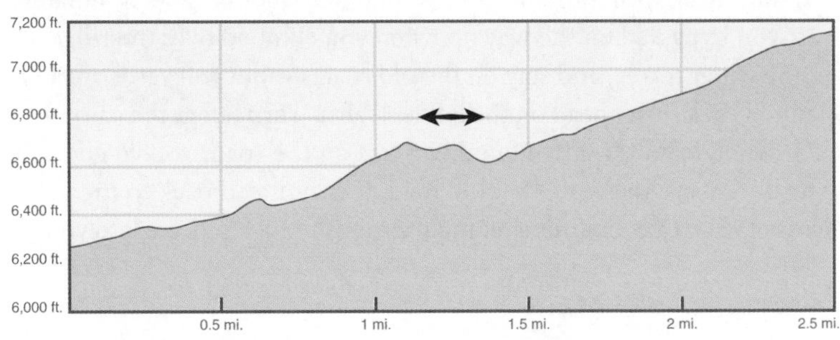

Note that Monte Largo Canyon is one of several in a basin that spans about 2.5 miles north to south. For navigational purposes, it helps to know that all waterways in this basin eventually merge to exit through the bottleneck to the west, the way you just came in. So as long as you don't cross any major ridges, you can follow any drainage downstream to return to the trailhead.

Return to the canyon floor by going down the side opposite the way you came up, then turn right to continue following the waterline upstream. In 0.25 mile, you'll arrive at a second fork. Stay left. (For reference: the waterline goes right to the Upper Monte Largo Spring, about a minute's walk south. From there the old Monte Largo Trail, a steeper, sunnier path marked with cairns, continues southeast, then climbs east on a strenuous route to meet the Crest Trail 170 about 0.5 mile north of Manzano Peak.)

As you continue northeast from the second fork, brown cliffs form vertical walls above to your left. Small caves can be seen in the sedimentary rock; pungent odors suggest that some are occupied and probably best left undisturbed. You can get a good view of them by reaching slightly higher ground on your right and looking across the arroyo.

The drainage deepens ahead, and the trail seems to split off in different directions. You may find traces of an old jeep road or a well-worn game path meandering through towering ponderosa. You can usually switch from one to another by running a short lateral. Either way, keep the main channel nearby, usually on your right. If you find yourself bushwhacking, wandering over a barren hill, or struggling up a ridiculously steep drainage, you've undoubtedly strayed off course.

About 2 miles into the hike, the drainage curves around a bulging outcrop on the left. Immediately afterward, it hooks around a towering outcrop on the right. The trail becomes a little steeper along this S-curve.

The incline lessens as the trail runs due east for the next 0.3 mile. Primitive campsites and fire rings can be found at the beginning of this stretch, along with a flourish of poison ivy.

You can continue up the canyon, but the campsites seem as good a place as any to turn around. Follow the drainage 1 mile downstream, until you locate the water line snaking out from the upper spring. Follow the line out of the canyon. As you approach the lower spring, the next 0.25 mile may suddenly seem unfamiliar; this is the part you bypassed on the way up when you climbed over the ridge. Continue down to the water tower, and stay on the old road. About 250 yards ahead is a large silver-painted rock. Just ahead on the left is a cairn. Turn left at the cairn to cross the arroyo. (If you encounter dirt-mound barriers on the road, you've gone about 100 yards past the cairn. Also note that the road does not lead back to the parking lot.) Once across the arroyo, continue on the trail another 0.4 mile back to your car.

NEARBY ACTIVITIES

For local history, and collections related to the Santa Fe Railroad, visit the Valencia County Historical Society's **Belen Harvey House Museum,** in the Harvey House Dining Room, which is listed on the National Register of Historic Places. En route back to I-25, after crossing the bridge over the railroad tracks, turn left on Third Street. Go two blocks south and turn left on Becker Street. Another two blocks and another left puts you on First Street. The museum is on the right at 104 N. First Street. Open Tuesday–Saturday, noon–5 p.m. (to be safe, call before you visit to make sure it's open). For more information, call 505-861-0581 or visit harveyhouse museum.org.

• •

GPS TRAILHEAD COORDINATES N34° 36.028' W106° 29.837'

DIRECTIONS From I-25 South, take Exit 195 toward Belen and go 4.6 miles on I-25 Bus/North Main Street. Turn left onto Reinken Avenue (NM 309). Go 2.4 miles east, crossing the railroad tracks and the river. Take a right onto Rio Communities Boulevard (NM 47). Go southeast 7.4 miles and turn left at Mallette Road and reset your odometer. (Mallette is just past mile marker 12 at the Tierra Grande entrance gate/arch.) Follow the wide unpaved road east 5.6 or 7 miles to the T intersection with Military Way. Turn left and follow Military north 0.7 mile (6.3 miles on your odometer). There will be a fenceline, a sign for Canyon del Rio, and a dirt road running on the north side of the fence. Turn right and follow the narrow road east for 4.1 miles. The rest of the drive has some very rough patches so please be careful. At 2.3 miles (8.7 miles on your odometer) the road will arc to the north. Turn right at the junction (10.4 miles on your odometer) and follow the rough dirt/rock road east 1.2 miles into the Monte Largo parking area.

55 MOUNT TAYLOR: Gooseberry Spring

Lush mountain meadows make this fantastic hike even better.

OFTEN SNOWCAPPED INTO midspring, Mount Taylor, at 11,301 feet, is the massive volcano on Albuquerque's sunset horizon. A classic hike on a designated trail with a nice, steady climb winds through woods and meadows to culminate at the very top of the mountain. It's unfortunate that this hike comes near the end of the book, as it is one of the best hikes in New Mexico and belongs on your must-do list.

DESCRIPTION

If you've looked to the west from much of Albuquerque, you've seen Mount Taylor. The Navajo know this volcanic peak as *Tsoodzil,* "turquoise mountain." According to their tradition, it's the mountain of the south, one of four sacred peaks that mark the boundaries of *Dinetah,* the Navajo homeland.

The mountains show up on early Spanish maps as *Sierra de la Zebolleta,* or "range of the little onion." Later settlers renamed them in honor of San Mateo. In 1849 an army lieutenant dubbed the central peak for President Zachary Taylor, who soon repaid the favor to New Mexicans by preventing Texas from expanding its state boundaries into the New Mexico Territory. The Anglo name stuck for the mountain, but the range is still referred to as both the Cebolleta Mountains and the San Mateo Mountains.

DISTANCE & CONFIGURATION: 6-mile out-and-back

DIFFICULTY: Moderate–strenuous

SCENERY: Ponderosa and aspen, meadows, volcanic crater, 100-mile views

EXPOSURE: Some forest shade

TRAIL TRAFFIC: Moderate

TRAIL SURFACE: Gravel, dirt, loose rock

HIKING TIME: 4–5 hours

DRIVING DISTANCE: 95 miles from the Big I

ELEVATION GAIN: 9,267' at trailhead; 11,301' at the top of Mount Taylor

ACCESS: Year-round, subject to road closures due to snow or fire; no fees or permit required

WHEELCHAIR ACCESS: No

MAPS: Brochure map available from Mount Taylor Ranger Station in Grants; USGS *Lobo Springs* and *Mount Taylor*

FACILITIES: None

CONTACT: Cibola National Forest–Mount Taylor Ranger District, fs.usda.gov/cibola, 505-287-8833

LOCATION: Grants

COMMENTS: Leashed dogs are allowed on trails. Pack your binoculars for the views and your snowshoes for winter hikes.

LAST-CHANCE FOOD/GAS: All services available in Grants

The area has an extensive history of logging, grazing, and mining, as evidenced by an endless web of roads. (For a driving guide, consult the 2011 Travel Management Decision for the Mount Taylor Ranger District, along with its supplementary map of open roads.)

The road (Forest Road 193) to the trailhead is well marked and has had recent improvements. It's still unpaved, but the bad spots have been filled in with gravel. Parking is on the right (south) side of the road across from the trailhead. You'll park in an aspen grove worthy of an Ansel Adams photograph.

The hike begins on the other side (north) of the road, in a patch of quintessential American woodland. Bluebirds, squirrels, and chipmunks frolic. Aspens bear the paired initials and heart-shaped scars of adolescent affections. To the south, runoff from Gooseberry Spring sometimes streams from the draw and tunnels under the road. You'll see this stream (or its dry bed) again often throughout the hike ahead. And if you miss a right turn on your way down from the peak, you'll end up following it back to the road.

The Gooseberry Trailhead is well marked and is just short of 9,300 feet in elevation. The path is very distinct and is also called Trail 77. Head north on the trail as it climbs quickly into denser woods. The path soon becomes a carpet of pine needles. The first 0.5 mile of the trail holds its form as it winds around rock formations near the edge of the draw, which by this point has assumed the proportions of a canyon. The trail then descends into an eroded meadow where trails and cow paths converge. A recent project of the New Mexico Youth Conservation Corps has improved the condition of the meadow and this part of the trail. After a short climb up to a closed forest road on the other side of the streambed, the trail turns south.

Mount Taylor: Gooseberry Spring

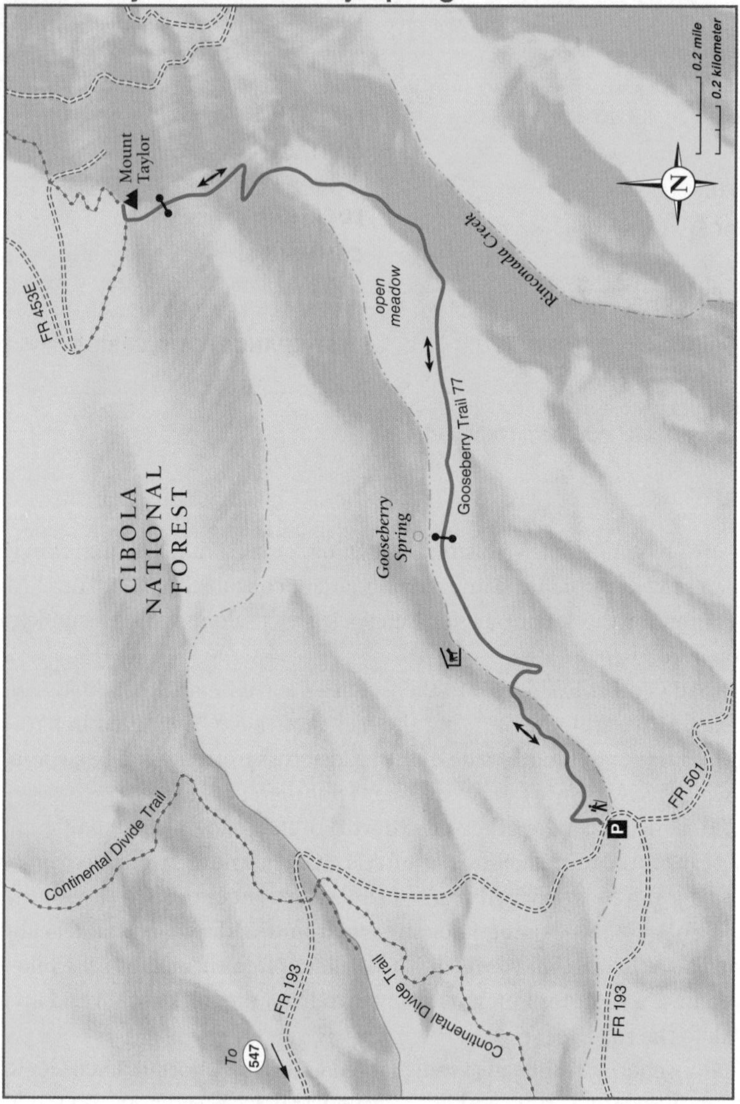

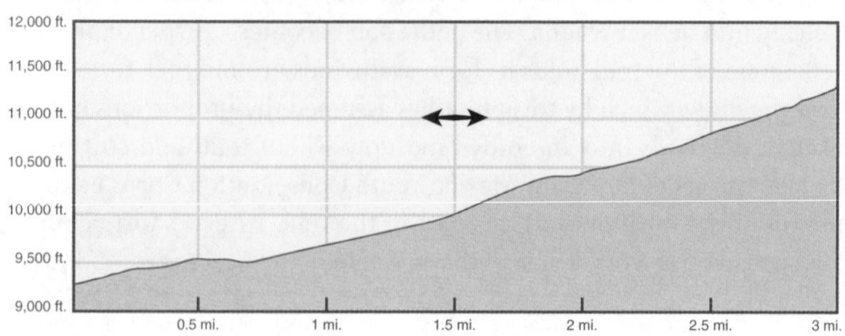

This hike begins in an aspen grove.

You'll soon reach a junction (N35° 13.352' W107° 37.809') with multiple cairns. You'll want to make a sharp left (north) turn here to continue going uphill. There are blue arrows to guide you through this junction. The trail from this point on is easy to follow.

In about 0.5 mile the trail will reach a fenceline with a pedestrian gate. Soon after the gate the trail will emerge from the woods and enter a wonderful meadow. You'll have incredible views that will remind you of the opening scene of *The Sound of Music*. At this point, you will have gone 1.4 miles and climbed 700 feet. So you're not quite halfway to the top.

As you follow the trail uphill, your destination peak will come into view on the left. At this point, you're about halfway there. The rest of the hike is high and exposed so keep an eye out for storm clouds.

At 1.8 miles, the trail slumps over a saddle on the ridge and curves left. Enjoy a brief stretch of flat terrain while it lasts. Far below to your right, Rinconada Creek begins its winding 14-mile course to the Rio San Jose. To your left, you might see cows grazing in the meadow near the trees. If you are hiking with dogs, now is a good time to grab their leash.

The trail eases back over the ridge and crosses the uppermost cut of the arroyo. Note the Z-shaped switchbacks ramping up the southern slope of the peak. Once you get through those, you'll arrive at the gateway in an old fence. From there it's less than 0.25 mile to the peak. You'll pass through tundralike sedges and continue to have fantastic views in all directions.

Upon the sacred summit of Tsoodzil, the head of Pogo the Possum is mounted on a steel pole, along with a sign reading MT. TAYLOR ELEV. 11,301 and a box containing a logbook and a thermometer. Take a moment to read past entries and enjoy the view. On a clear day, you can see into both Arizona and Colorado. If it's been a wet year, the valleys below will be filled with flowers.

You can extend your hike another mile on a steep, narrow path that winds down to FR 453 near La Mosca Lookout. Water Canyon Trail (76) starts from there and runs 4.5 miles to the east forest boundary, losing 1,500 feet in elevation along the way.

Otherwise, return the way you came up and enjoy the views. They are just as good going down as they were coming up. When you get back to your car, you will probably agree that this is one of the great hikes of New Mexico!

Note: Check with the Mount Taylor Ranger Station for road conditions and possible closures. The ranger station is en route at 1800 Lobo Canyon Road.

NEARBY ACTIVITIES

Continental Divide Trail (CDT): The parking area for Mount Taylor's section of the CDT is on the south side of NM 547 (Lobo Canyon Road) just beyond the forest boundary, about 3 miles past the ranger station. There is signage for the trailhead on the road. For a CDT hiker, this is the end of a long road walk through the Grants area. The trail begins with a fork. The right branch visits an overlook above water-sculpted (though usually dry) falls. The left branch is the actual CDT. The trail is marked and well defined. Casual hikers are content with the first 2 miles or so, which includes a strenuous climb up the west side of Horace Mesa. Views from the top seem endless.

GPS TRAILHEAD COORDINATES N35° 13.203' W107° 38.218'

DIRECTIONS From I-40 West, take Exit 85 and veer right toward Grants. About 2.5 miles from the exit, turn right on NM 547 and follow it about 13.4 miles up Mount Taylor. (NM 547 is also signed First Street, Roosevelt Avenue, and Lobo Canyon Road.) Do *not* turn at the Lobo Canyon Campground, which is about 4.5 miles too soon. And if you run out of paved road while still on NM 547, you've gone about 100 yards too far. Turn right on FR 193, a maintained dirt road, and follow it 5 miles. The trailhead is on the left. Park in a small lot on the right. (The signed junction of FR 193 and FR 501 is about 200 yards too far.)

56 SAN LORENZO CANYON

High walls flank a narrow path.

HERE'S THE CHALLENGE: hike 2 miles of San Lorenzo Canyon without getting lured into any caves, slots, or scrambles to the rim. To accomplish such a task would require a deadened sense of natural curiosity, or perhaps the unwavering determination of San Lorenzo (Saint Lawrence to the Anglos) himself.

DESCRIPTION

San Lorenzo Canyon is a primitive recreation area jointly managed by Sevilleta National Wildlife Refuge and the Bureau of Land Management. The hike in this book is as much about bringing you out to a wonderful area as it is a hike. For your trip you'll walk 2 miles up the canyon and return. Along the way you'll find plenty of detours to make this a longer walk or enough distractions to keep you from going the full 2 miles. There is no wrong way to hike San Lorenzo Canyon.

The adventure begins when you drive under I-25 through a one-lane tunnel. Very soon after clearing the tunnel the pavement will go off to the left. For San Lorenzo Canyon proceed ahead on the unpaved road. There are signs pointing the way to the canyon. At this point you'll be driving through the creosote bush and mesquite of the Chihuahuan Desert.

DISTANCE & CONFIGURATION: 4-mile out-and-back

DIFFICULTY: Easy

SCENERY: Sandstone canyon, slots, caves, hoodoos, springs

EXPOSURE: Some canyon shade

TRAIL TRAFFIC: Moderate

TRAIL SURFACE: Sand, rock

HIKING TIME: 2–4 hours

DRIVING DISTANCE: 70 miles from the Big I

ELEVATION GAIN: 5,234' at trailhead, with very little change in elevation on the canyon floor

ACCESS: Year-round; no fees or permits required

WHEELCHAIR ACCESSIBLE: No

MAPS: USGS *Lemitar* and *San Lorenzo Spring*

FACILITIES: None

CONTACT: BLM–Socorro Field Office, blm.gov/office/socorro-field-office; Sevilleta National Wildlife Refuge, fws.gov/refuge/Sevilleta

LOCATION: North of Socorro

COMMENTS: Do not attempt to drive the arroyo when heavy rains are expected. Leashed dogs are permitted on trails.

LAST-CHANCE FOOD/GAS: Exit 191 in Belen, 36 miles from trailhead

Two miles later the road will jog to the right (north). Just after completing the turn there is an information sign on the left side of the road describing the canyon. From here the road will enter San Lorenzo arroyo. At this point the arroyo is broad, flat, and usually very dry. Just follow the roadway in the arroyo west. Do not enter the arroyo if it is flowing.

In about 1.75 miles there will be another information sign on the right side of the arroyo describing the mesa off to the right. You won't miss it as it has an unusual angular unconformity. This is the first of many wonderful formations that you'll be seeing on this adventure. It only gets better from here.

After the mesa the arroyo will start to narrow and become a steep-walled canyon in less than a mile. Now is as good a time as any to park the car and start walking. It is possible to drive farther, but the road will end at a box 1 mile up; it's a lot more fun to get out of the car and start exploring.

Aside from the obvious route up the throat of the main canyon, there are many side canyons, slots, niches, and crevices begging for exploration. Possible detours are too numerous to list, so you may want to consider hiking the route as outlined here and then exploring the most alluring side options on your return. If you start by wandering into every crevice that catches your eye, you'll never make it halfway through this hike. But that's OK, too, since it will give you a reason to come back.

If you can't resist wandering off from the route keep in mind that the fenced land to the north is Sevilleta National Wildlife Refuge and closed to the public. (Sevilleta is featured in Hike 57, page 298.)

Start hiking up the canyon. Sculpted formations are nearby and impossible to miss. But look closely for the small details as well. You will find plenty of surprises. Please avoid climbing up the cliffs. Their composition is loose, and you can easily fall.

Depending on where you parked the car, there will be a narrow (almost a slot) canyon going off to the right within a few hundred feet of your starting point. It's

San Lorenzo Canyon

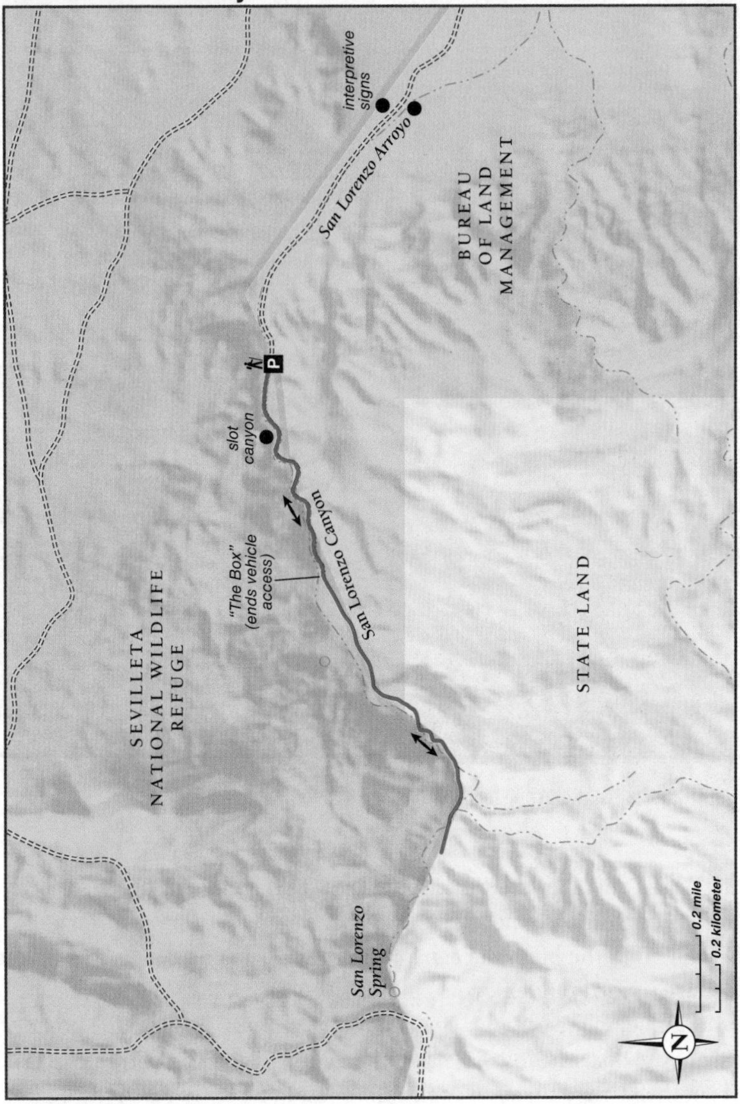

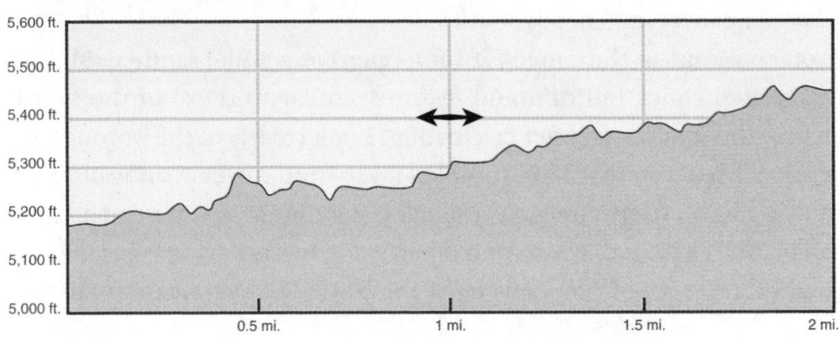

There is always another interesting landform to discover on this hike.

fantastic. A half mile into the hike, you'll see a trail going up to a small cave. Farther on there is another trail to the right that leads to a small spring with a wildlife camera.

At 1 mile into the hike, the canyon narrows again and seems to end in a box. If you get close to the boulders, you can hear water trickling through the rocks. If you wish to continue up the canyon, you can work your way through the boulders on the right side of the box. It's not that hard. If you don't want to continue up the canyon, there is another arroyo that you can explore just before you reach the box. It's on the left side of the canyon and heads south.

If you continue up the canyon it soon opens to a wide, sandy wash. The upper canyon ahead is chock-full of grand features similar to those in the first half, but here's where the small details get fascinating. Look closely at the porous basalt boulders, particularly those that have tumbled away from the canyon walls on the right side. At first glance, some appear as though caught in the crossfire of a multicolored paintball battle. These red, white, and green splotches are agate veins that have filled joints and other types of pore spaces in the basalt. Fine-crystalline forms of silica (quartz) mixed with various impurities show up in striking colors. Iron and copper impurities, for example, produce green colorations. Although it's obvious that amateur rock hounds have chipped away their own souvenirs, much still remains for other visitors to enjoy.

Continue following the spring's sinuous route. You might run into flowing water when the canyon narrows again. After the stream, at 1.4 miles into the hike, the canyon takes a right. A prominent arroyo opens up just past the outer corner of the turn. It flows from Red Mountain, about a 2.5-mile hike to the south. If you wish to follow that arroyo, check with the State Land Office (nmstatelands.org) for the latest information on hiking on state land. Much of the land south of the canyon is State Trust Land.

In a little more than 0.5 mile past the big arroyo opening on the left, you'll go through another narrow stretch with flowing water and then reach another box (or at least a place where the canyon is filled with boulders) with a spring. This is the end of the hike and where we turn around. Just before the turnaround point on the right side of the canyon is a huge boulder lying in the sand with a smooth flat side. That smooth side is called slickenside and is the result of the rock slipping on a fault. If the sun is right when you look at the canyon walls on your way back, you'll see more slickenside.

With so much more to check out than one can possibly do in one hike you'll need to come back for another hike to take it all in. You may even want to consider bringing a tent and spending the night.

NEARBY ACTIVITIES

For more sandstone cliffs, hoodoos and slickenside walls, visit **Cañoncito de las Cabras** ("little canyon of the goats"). To drive there, return to the Y and head 1.7 miles west to the mouth of the canyon. As before, you can continue driving up canyon, but again, it's far better on foot. Part of the Cañoncito is on private land, so the hike ends when you see a NO TRESPASSING sign. There are other similar canyons in the area that you might want to explore.

• •

GPS TRAILHEAD COORDINATES N34° 14.639' W106° 59.563'

DIRECTIONS From I-25 South, take Exit 163 at San Acacia. Turn left, cross over the interstate, then turn right and go 2.3 miles south on the frontage road. Turn right onto C94, or B90 on some maps. (Either way, it's unmarked, so just turn right and drive through a narrow underpass.) When the pavement ends, continue straight west 2 miles on the main dirt road. Bear right at the Y and follow the road up the streambed 2.5 miles northwest to the mouth of the canyon.

57 SEVILLETA NATIONAL WILDLIFE REFUGE

In winter, be sure to check out the cranes at nearby Bernardo Waterfowl Area.

AN OVERLOOKED JEWEL to the south, Sevilleta National Wildlife Refuge offers a very nice winter hiking option. With a trail starting at the visitor center, you'll get great views of this fascinating landscape. You can then wrap up the day by watching the birds at the nearby Bernardo Waterfowl Area.

DESCRIPTION

You've probably passed Sevilleta National Wildlife Refuge (NWR) many times as you drove south on I-25 without stopping. With its informative visitor center and wonderful 5.5-mile loop hike (with options for a shorter hike) it is well worth the stop.

The refuge gets its name from a military post established nearby in the 16th century. New Seville was later included in the Sevilleta de la Joya Land Grant, awarded to the community of Sevilleta in 1819. A century later, the state accepted the land from the community heirs in lieu of taxes. The land later served a 30-year stint as the Campbell Ranch before achieving national-refuge status in 1973.

Several major biotic zones meet within Sevilleta NWR, including piñon–juniper woodlands, Colorado Plateau shrub–steppe, Great Plains grassland, and Chihuahuan desert. There is also an extensive riparian zone along the Rio Grande. At the time of this writing the riparian zone was undergoing a massive restoration effort and was temporarily closed.

DISTANCE & CONFIGURATION: 5.5-mile loop

DIFFICULTY: Easy with some moderate sections

SCENERY: Wonderful landforms, desert grasslands, mountains, and a couple of surprises

EXPOSURE: Mostly sunny

TRAIL TRAFFIC: Low

TRAIL SURFACE: Dirt and rock

HIKING TIME: 3 hours

DRIVING DISTANCE: 60 miles from the Big I

ELEVATION GAIN: 4,839' at trailhead; 5,096' on mesa top

ACCESS: Year-round, sunrise–sunset; no fees or permits required

WHEELCHAIR ACCESS: No; there is a paved trail that is partially wheelchair accessible

MAPS: Brochure map at visitor center; USGS *San Acacia*

FACILITIES: Interpretive exhibits, restrooms, water at visitor center

CONTACT: U.S. Fish and Wildlife Service, 505-864-4021, fws.gov/refuge/sevilleta; NM Department of Fish and Game, 505-864-9187

LOCATION: South of Belen

COMMENTS: Leashed dogs are allowed on trails.

LAST-CHANCE FOOD/GAS: All services at Exit 191 in Belen, 26 miles from the trailhead

Sevilleta National Wildlife Refuge is primarily managed for scientific research and is probably best known for its role in the Mexican Gray Wolf Reintroduction Program. The University of New Mexico (UNM) has several facilities at the refuge to manage various research projects. A recent addition to the refuge has been a Long Wave Array radio telescope station. It is part of a developing network of coordinated radio telescope stations studying the cosmos.

With its many scientific projects, most of the 360-square-mile refuge is strictly off-limits. The refuge hosts monthly events open to the public that include tours to the far corners of the refuge.

Information on events can be found on the refuge's website: fws.gov/refuge/sevilleta. Also when you're at the website, look for Sheryl Mayfield's *Sevilleta National Wildlife Refuge Field Guide to Flowers*; it is an outstanding primer on local plant life and is available as a free download.

The Mesa View Trail begins behind the visitor center. While there you might want to spend a few minutes at the center to look at the various exhibits. They also have maps, brochures, and more information on the refuge, wildlife, and activities in the area. It is a very nice visitor center.

If the center is not open and the front gate closed, the trail is still open to hiking. Just park your car outside the gate and walk toward the visitor center. If the gate is closed while you are still hiking, the gate will still open when you leave. In short, this hike is open every day from sunrise to sunset.

The trail heads west from the visitor center toward the mesa and reaches a junction with a trail coming down from the mesa in 0.5 mile. Our hike continues north along the base of the mesa. The trail heading west from the junction to the mesa top can be used to shorten or vary your hike. The UNM facilities are off to your right.

The trail remains easy to follow as it passes many interesting rock formations and Chihuahuan desert plants (creosote, mesquite, and other shrubs) along the face

Sevilleta National Wildlife Refuge

SEVILLETA
NATIONAL
WILDLIFE
REFUGE
Old Highway 85
Mesa View Trail
UNM
facilities
interpretive
sign
Wildflower
Loop
P
visitor
center
Long Wave Array
radio telescope station
Nature Loop
25
N
0.2 mile
0.2 kilometer

5,200 ft.
5,100 ft.
5,000 ft.
4,900 ft.
4,800 ft.
4,700 ft.
4,600 ft.
1 mi.
2 mi.
3 mi.
4 mi.
5 mi.

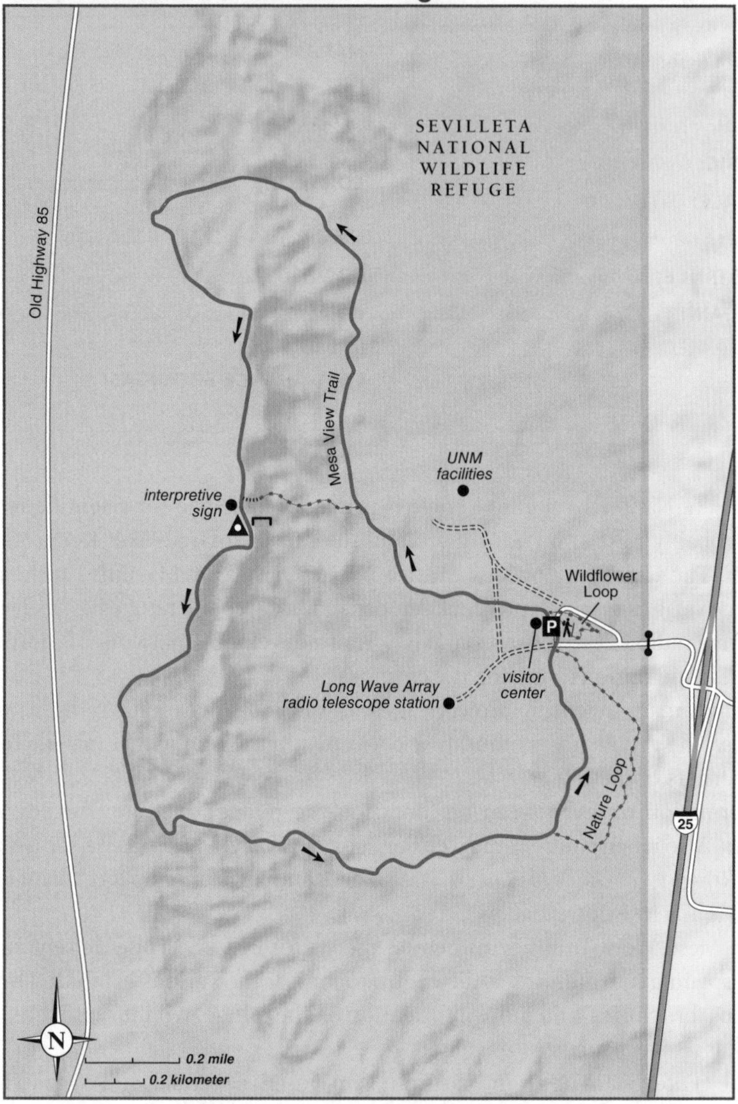

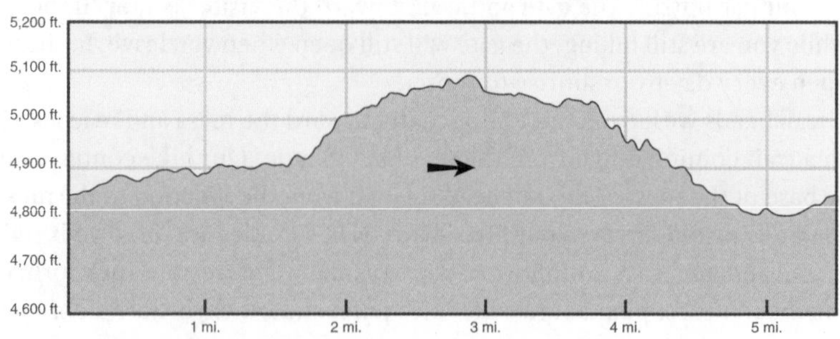

True to its name, the Mesa View Trail leads you to the mesa.

of the mesa. In less than a mile from the junction the trail turns west and enters a canyon. When you enter the canyon, you'll be able to see the Sierra Ladrones (Hike 58, page 303) off in the distance. When you reach the mesa top, the trail turns left to follow the mesa edge south.

As you look to the west, the Sierra Ladrones totally dominate the landscape. Between you and the mountains is a vast grassland plain. Before the interstate was built, the main north–south highway (US 85) travelled through this grassland a bit to the west. In April 1862, after losing their supplies at the Battle of Glorieta, the retreating Confederate army left the Rio Grande to escape the better-supplied Union army and headed across this plain to get to the other side of the mountains.

As you look to the east, you can see the visitor center, the interstate, the Rio Grande Valley, almost empty plains east of the valley, and the Manzano Mountains a bit to the northeast. As you continue south on the trail you'll have great views in all directions. You'll even run into a couple of information signs telling you about the area. There is something interesting the entire way.

In less than a mile you'll reach the trail that we saw earlier coming off the mesa. If you are pressed for time, you can follow it back to the visitor center for a 3.5-mile loop hike. Otherwise, keep on hiking and enjoy the view. In about 0.6 mile, the trail turns left again and heads east to follow a ridge down to the mesa base. As you get closer to the visitor center area, you'll see a large cluster of silver-colored metal objects at the base of the ridge. They are the Long Wave Array radio telescope station. You can get more information on the station at the visitor center.

When you get near the bottom of the ridge you'll join the Nature Loop Trail. The Nature Loop Trail has small signs identifying the various plants and shrubs in the area. It's a fantastic primer on desert plants and a good reminder on what a certain plant is if you've forgotten.

You can turn left now and head north directly to the visitor center, or continue east on the Nature Loop and return to the visitor center a little bit later. The first choice is 0.5 mile back to the visitor center; the second is about 0.7 mile.

NEARBY ACTIVITIES

The Bernardo Waterfowl Area (BWA) is very close to Sevilleta NWR and is the best place to see birds in the area. Bernardo is the second largest of the four wildlife management areas that make up the Ladd S. Gordon Waterfowl Complex. (The biggest is La Joya, which is adjacent to Sevilleta NWR.)

From November to February, about 15,000 sandhill cranes spend the winter along the Rio Grande from Albuquerque to Bosque del Apache. With cultivated fields managed by New Mexico Game and Fish, BWA has several thousand cranes, snow geese, and other birds feeding there every day during the season. The activity of birds swirling and clucking or quacking in every direction as they move from field to field is one of the most remarkable and joyful experiences that you will ever have. It is a perfect way to wrap up a day after a hike at Sevilleta NWR. If you're in need of a quick bird fix, BWA is a much shorter drive from Albuquerque than Bosque del Apache.

BWA features three observation decks along a 2.8-mile gravel road. It is OK to walk along the road, and dogs on leash are allowed. One of the observation decks has two short hiking paths to give you a closer look at the wetlands. You may even want to drive east along US 60 for a little bit, as you can see considerable bird activity from the road.

To get to BWA from Exit 175 (the first exit north of Sevilleta NWR), turn left on the frontage road (NM 116) immediately after the northbound ramp (if you're coming from Albuquerque). If you're coming from Sevilleta NWR, just cross US 60 and you'll be on NM 116. Drive north 1.7 miles and turn right at the sign for the Bernardo unit. For more information, call 505-864-9187 or visit wildlife.state.nm.us.

• •

GPS TRAILHEAD COORDINATES N34° 21.073' W106° 52.952'

DIRECTIONS From I-25 South, take Exit 169. At the bottom of the off-ramp, pull a U-turn around the fence to the right and proceed 0.4 mile, following signs to the Sevilleta NWR Visitor Center.

58 SIERRA LADRONES

Looming on Albuquerque's southwest horizon, the isolated Sierra Ladrones appear remote and forbidding.

FOLLOWING A GAME path on a long, undulating uplift, this straightforward route provides a friendly introduction to an isolated mountain range with a mean reputation. Peaks along the way allow for great views down to the foothills and canyons, up to the toothy ridges of the Sierra Ladrones, and of great emptiness.

DESCRIPTION

The Sierra Ladrones, or "thieves mountains," earned their name as a hideout for Navajo raiders who, having relieved local ranches of their stock, spirited them across the *jaral* (chaparral or scrubland) to untraceable retreats. Later banditos and rustlers continued the tradition by holing up in the range's deep canyons. Few were known to reemerge, and speculation of lost loot continues to this day.

The granite massif rises 4,500 feet above the Rio Puerco. It stands alone on a plain too prone to erosion to sustain reliable roads. A checkerboard of private ranchland further complicates the approach from the northeast, whereas its southeast quadrant falls in the strictly off-limits Sevilleta National Wildlife Refuge.

More than 45,300 acres in the Ladrones have been designated as a Bureau of Land Management Wilderness Study Area. The local wildlife population includes mule deer, black bear, mountain lion, and pronghorn. Desert bighorn sheep were

DISTANCE & CONFIGURATION: 7-mile or less out-and-back

DIFFICULTY: Moderate–strenuous

SCENERY: Desert scrub, cacti, expansive views

EXPOSURE: Full sun

TRAIL TRAFFIC: Low

TRAIL SURFACE: Sand, limestone, loose rock

HIKING TIME: 3–4 hours

DRIVING DISTANCE: 72 miles from the Big I

ELEVATION GAIN: 5,791' at trailhead; 7,155' at turnaround point

ACCESS: Year-round; no fees or permits required

MAPS: USGS *Riley* and *Ladron Peak*

FACILITIES: None

CONTACT: BLM–Socorro, blm.gov/office/socorro-field-office, 575-835-0412

LOCATION: Southwest of Belen

COMMENTS: The hike featured here does not reach Ladron Peak. Leashed dogs are allowed on trails.

LAST-CHANCE FOOD/GAS: All services available at Exit 191 in Belen, 38 miles from the trailhead

reintroduced in 1992. Grasses and scrub sum up the vegetation on the lower slopes; ponderosa pine, aspen, and Douglas-fir grow near the twin summits. The eastern summit, Ladron Peak, is the only named peak in the range, but the summit less than 0.5 mile to its west is the taller of the two.

From a distance the range appears monolithic. Its complexity becomes more apparent up close. Because there are no developed trails, campgrounds, or trailheads the Ladrones have a longstanding reputation as one of the last places you'd want to hike alone. A local fireman who knows the peak well summed it up best: "It will kick your butt."

Don't let that deter you. Navigationally, this route is foolproof. You just follow a ridgeline from bottom to top or however far you want to go. Climbing becomes more difficult with distance. Each new mile begins with an incremental challenge. How far you get depends entirely on how hard you want to hike. Elevation enhances the views, of course, but you don't have to go far for wide-open vistas in all directions. So pack a lunch and plenty to drink. Above all, remember the sunscreen.

Start the hike at the side of the road by climbing south up the point of the ridge. This elongated uplift runs parallel to Cañon del Norte, but like most features in the Ladrones, lacks a name for itself. Creative christening suggestions include El Cuchillo de la Viuda, Lomo del Vaquero, and Rustlers' Ramp—each appropriate in its own way. For now it remains unnamed.

Juniper, creosote, Mormon tea, and cacti do their best to green the otherwise barren slopes. Limestone pavements keep the vegetation spread out, and narrow paths seem to show up wherever grasses take hold. Your only obstacles in the first 2 miles are a few barbwire fences, all easily crossed or circumvented.

The limestone surface is very rough, so getting good traction is not a problem. Keep an eye on your dogs to make sure the rough surface isn't chewing up their paws. As you go along the ridge, the views in all directions will be fantastic, but don't forget to look down at the limestone. It is loaded with marine fossils. There are shells,

Sierra Ladrones

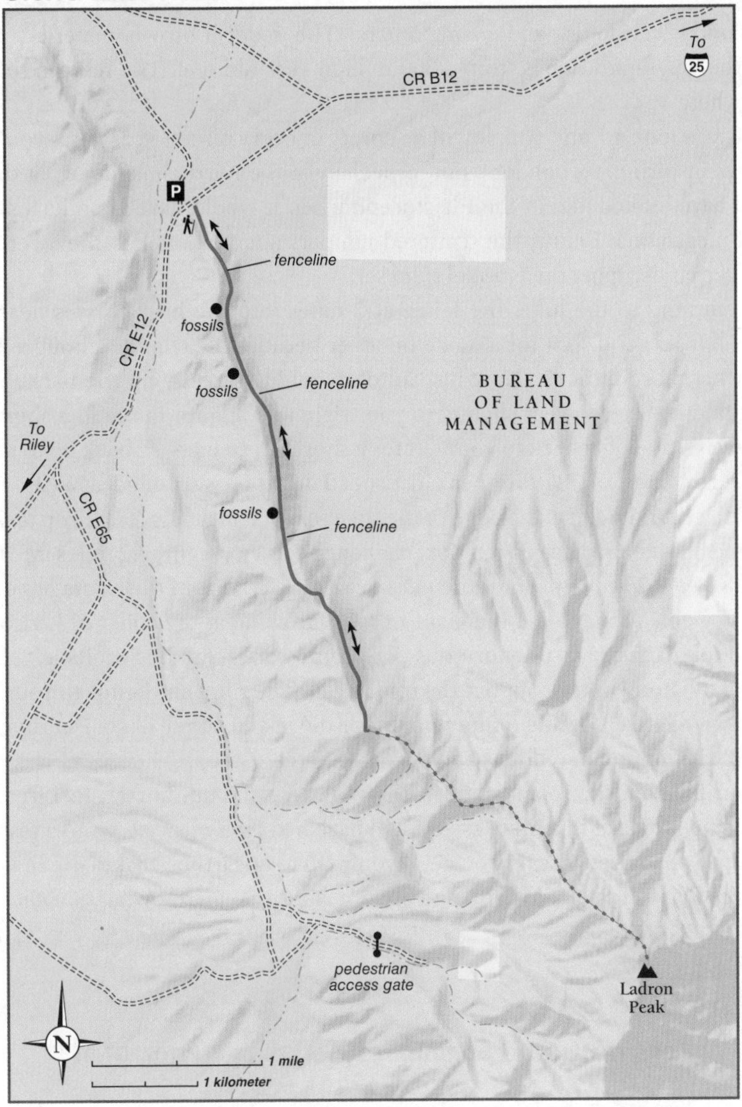

To
25
CR B12
P
fenceline
fossils
CR E12
fossils
fenceline
BUREAU
OF LAND
MANAGEMENT
To
Riley
fossils
fenceline
CR E65
pedestrian
access gate
Ladron
Peak
N
1 mile
1 kilometer

8,000 ft.
7,500 ft.
7,000 ft.
6,500 ft.
6,000 ft.
5,500 ft.
5,000 ft.
0.5 mi.
1 mi.
1.5 mi.
2 mi.
2.5 mi.
3 mi.
3.5 mi.

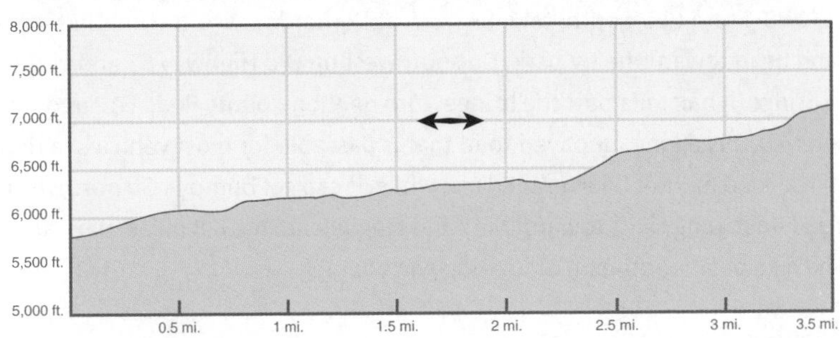

brachiopods, crinoids, and many others. The reddish-brown material emerging from the gray limestone is from a 300-million-year-old reef. The reddish material is everywhere.

As you look around you, it will be empty in every direction as far as you can see. It is awe inspiring. As you look out, especially to the north, imagine what the valley would have looked like in the Pleistocene when it would have been lush grassland full of megafauna. Below, the scattered junipers almost look like they were placed there like landscaping on a model train set.

Returning to the hike, the fence at 2 miles into the hike crosses near a peak (6,398'). It's a good spot for a quick breather because the climb is about to become somewhat more difficult. Now instead of marching directly up the backbone, you might find it easier to veer slightly to your right and aim for the saddle ahead. Once you reach that, angle back to your left for a short but steep push back up to the crest. A short rest on the 6,780-foot peak just ahead might be warranted as well.

The next mile skirts the edge of the sheer east-facing cliffs. The drop to your left is a good 300 feet in places. Your next challenge comes roughly 3.2 miles into the hike with a steep 0.25-mile push to the next peak (7,155'). From this vantage point, you should be able to make out the giant fir trees growing at the collar of Ladron Peak, in addition to the rows of enormous tiger-tooth rocks standing on its left shoulder. Also take a moment to scout out the trail ahead. The ridgeline bends to your left and assumes a relatively gentle temperament for the next 0.5 mile or so. But then, as you can see, the mountain reddens and becomes fiercely steep.

Our hike ends here and returns the way we came up. In fact, feel free to turn back at any point of this hike, as you will have had fabulous views and a taste of the big empty no matter how far you go. If you wish to go farther, make sure that you are prepared, have enough daylight, and are not alone. No matter what you choose, you will have a great hike.

• •

GPS TRAILHEAD COORDINATES N34° 29.740' W107° 07.924'

DIRECTIONS From I-25 South, take Exit 175 at Bernardo. Take the first left off the exit ramp and head toward the RV park. Go southwest on Old Highway 85 and cross the Rio Puerco Bridge. A half mile past the bridge, turn right on County Road B12 and reset your odometer. (B12 is a long, unpaved road that is passable for most vehicles in dry conditions. If the road has not been graded in a while, it can get bumpy.) Go northwest on the main road, following signs toward Riley and Magdalena. At 18.8 miles, park at the junction. The hike begins at the tip of the ridge on your left.

59 TRIGO CANYON

Trigo Canyon is one of only two public-access points to the west face of the Manzano Mountains.

WITH ITS CAMPGROUND removed, its trails no longer officially maintained, and its access road closed for many years, Trigo Canyon is a seldom-visited gem on the west face of the Manzanos. If you're willing to make the trek on a rough road, you'll be rewarded with a challenging hike in an absolutely gorgeous canyon full of surprises.

DESCRIPTION

Trigo Canyon is a beautiful canyon with wonderful hiking potential that is a true enigma. At one time its trailhead hosted an active campground (John F. Kennedy Campground) and had three trails (Trigo Canyon, Comanche Canyon, and Salas) radiating from it.

Over time the campground was vandalized and finally closed. Other than a rutted loop road and some old foundations there is little to remind you of what was once there. Along with the campground closure, the trails have not been officially maintained for years. And to add insult to injury, the rutted access road to the canyon was closed for several years by local landowners.

Because of access issues Trigo Canyon was removed from the second edition of this book. The road is now open, though, and Trigo Canyon is back in the book. The

DISTANCE & CONFIGURATION: 5.2-mile out-and-back

DIFFICULTY: Moderate with some strenuous sections

SCENERY: Wooded canyon, rock formations, running water, waterfalls, caves

EXPOSURE: Mostly shade

TRAIL TRAFFIC: Very low

TRAIL SURFACE: Dirt, rock

HIKING TIME: 4–5 hours

DRIVING DISTANCE: 58 miles from the Big I

ELEVATION GAIN: 6,263' at trailhead; 7,667' at turnaround point

ACCESS: Year-round, no fees or permits required

WHEELCHAIR ACCESS: No

MAPS: Manzano Mountain Wilderness; USGS *Capilla Peak*

FACILITIES: None

CONTACT: Cibola National Forest–Mountainair Ranger District, fs.usda.gov/cibola, 505-847-2990

LOCATION: East of Belen

COMMENTS: The last stretch of road is very rough and impossible in wet conditions. Leashed dogs are allowed on trails.

LAST-CHANCE FOOD/GAS: All services in Belen

access road is still difficult to drive, and the overall feeling of the trailhead area is still one of abandonment. But the canyon is still beautiful, and the trail is still walkable.

This is a good hike that will leave you thinking of "if." If the road access were easier, if the trail had some maintenance, and if the trailhead were a bit closer to Albuquerque, this would be a fantastic hike to do again and again. As it is today, the beauty of the canyon makes it worthwhile to overcome the obstacles to check it out at least once.

The adventure begins with an 18-mile drive on unpaved roads. Most of the roads are fine, but the last few miles are rough. You'll have to go slow to navigate some of the ruts. Although most of the land you're driving through is empty, it is all owned. The land was part of the original Tomé Land Grant and was sold by land grant heirs in the 1960s to an out-of-state land developer. The developer subdivided the land into individual building lots and sold them to out-of-state buyers as an investment in the upcoming Sunbelt boom. As you can see the boom hasn't quite reached this part of the Sunbelt.

When you get closer to the mountains and near the trailhead, you'll pass through a gate that should be open. If not, you can start the hike from here. It's 0.6 mile to the trailhead. When you reach the old campground bear left and drive counterclockwise through the remains to a steel-pipe fence parking area. The trail starts on the other side of the fence in the Manzano Mountain Wilderness.

The trail at this point is very wide and obvious, as it used to be a road. The trail becomes a footpath farther up the canyon. If there has been sufficient rainfall there is also a stream flowing through the entire canyon. Otherwise, the stream will appear in some places and run underground in other places. Very few canyons have this much water, and it is one of the things that makes Trigo Canyon so special. Even in a dry year, you should find water somewhere in the canyon. The trail will cross the stream more times than you can count during the entire hike.

Trigo Canyon

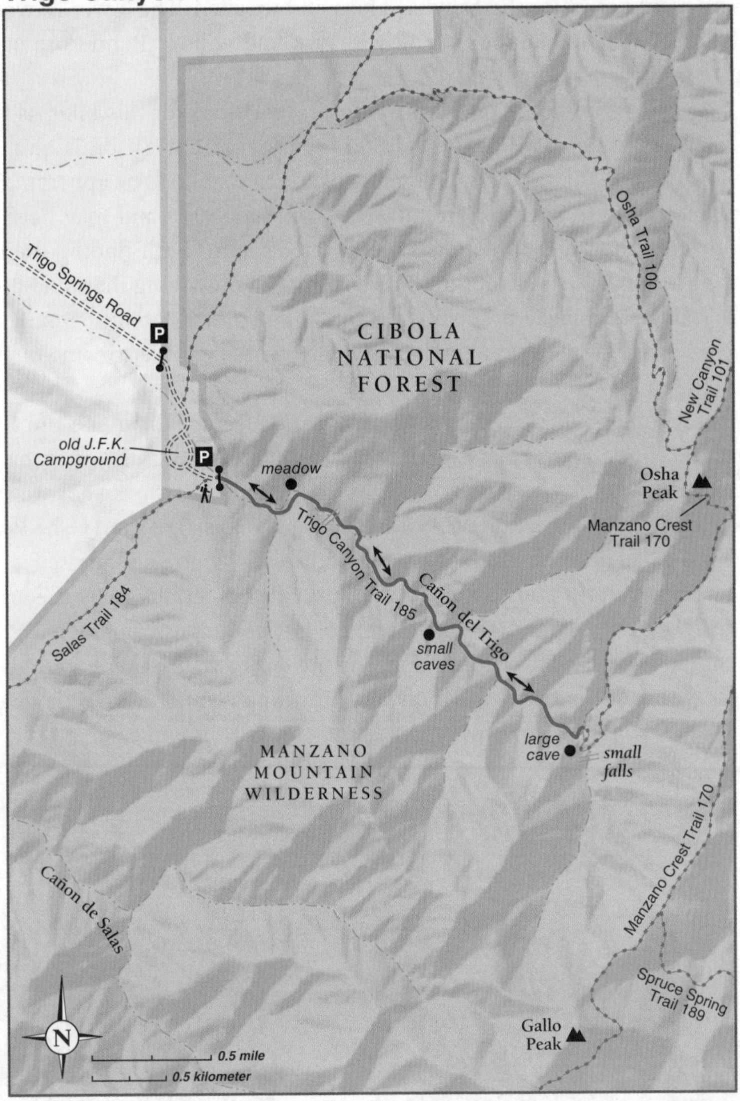

Trigo Springs Road
P
old J.F.K. Campground
P
meadow
CIBOLA NATIONAL FOREST
Osha Trail 100
New Canyon Trail 101
Osha Peak
Manzano Crest Trail 170
Trigo Canyon Trail 185
Cañon del Trigo
Salas Trail 184
small caves
large cave
small falls
MANZANO MOUNTAIN WILDERNESS
Cañon de Salas
Manzano Crest Trail 170
Spruce Spring Trail 189
Gallo Peak
N
0.5 mile
0.5 kilometer

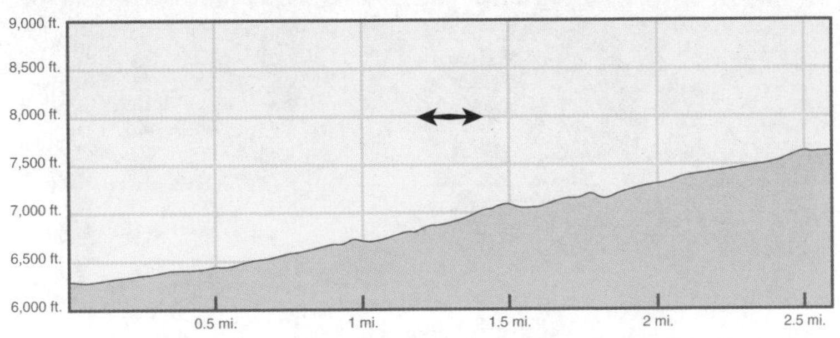

With plenty of water the canyon is lush and wooded. The lower canyon has an abundance of alligator juniper, along with oak and willow. Ponderosa and aspen dominate farther up the canyon.

There is no point in giving turn-by-turn instructions for this hike, as there are as many twists in the trails as there are in the canyon. Navigation is quite simple: just follow the trail up the canyon. In most places the trail will be apparent. In other places, you'll have to navigate around rocks and blockages and may have to poke around to find the trail. Blowdowns will be an issue for both finding the trail and for getting around them farther up the canyon. The only thing that might look like another trail is a drainage branching off to the left (north) about 0.8 mile into the hike. Just stay with the canyon, and as long as you are near the stream you won't be far from the trail.

After 2.5 miles of hiking, the blowdowns really become too much and almost fill the canyon. This is a good place to end the hike and turn around. You've had a good hike and have seen plenty. If you're very patient, you could work your way through the blockages and climb all the way to the Manzano Crest Trail and Osha Peak.

With the bad news about this hike out of the way, Trigo Canyon itself is wonderful and worth visiting. The abundant water provides waterfalls along the way; some very small and others larger. The canyon's geology is fabulous. You'll see white quartz seams and massive quartzite formations for the entire walk. There are huge quartz boulders with wavy patterns that only a contortionist could make. It is rare to find

Consider camping at this cave.

such unusual geology, and it is so different from what we find in the Sandias. It's hard to believe that two mountain ranges, so close to each other, could be so different. In addition to the rock formations, the canyon has caves. There is a very large cave with a campfire ring right on the trail. With the woods so thick and the canyon so narrow at this point, this might be a very dark and spooky place to spend the night.

Since the canyon was the site of a catastrophic fire in 2008, you also have the opportunity to see how a mountain recovers from a fire. You'll see some burned trees on this hike, but you'll also see where the fire has opened vistas and exposed many quartz formations. Even better, you'll see how quickly new growth is replacing the old growth. In many places young aspens are replacing the burned-out ponderosa.

When you do decide to turn around, you'll be surprised at how much you have climbed. You've gained 1,400 feet in 2.5 miles. You probably didn't notice the climbing because you were so focused on working around obstacles and blowdowns and checking out all the features along the trail. The good news is that you'll get to see them all again from a different angle in a different light on the way back. You might even spot something you missed on the way up. When you return to the trailhead, you'll have a sense that you just completed an adventure in a very wild part of our 60-mile hike radius. Because of the obstacles, the hike will take longer than a comparable hike at another location. And again if this trip were more convenient, it might become one of your regular outings.

• •

GPS TRAILHEAD COORDINATES N34° 40.210' W106° 27.917'

DIRECTIONS From I-25 South, take Exit 195 toward Belen and go 4.6 miles on I-25 Bus/North Main Street. Turn left onto Reinken Avenue (NM 309). Go 2.4 miles east, crossing the railroad tracks and the river. Take a right onto Rio Communities Boulevard (NM 47). Go southeast 2 miles to North Navajo Road (N34° 37.691' W106° 42.887'). There's no street sign (at this time) identifying the road; there is a white gate structure on the left and a green gate on the right. (If you reach mile marker 17 or the Mennonite church, you've gone too far.) Follow the road east for 8.4 miles to a T-junction with another unmarked dirt road. Turn left and go north 3 miles. (Again, there is no sign identifying the road, but some maps name it as Trigo Springs Road.) Turn right (N34° 40.957' W106° 34.315'). (The eastbound road is also called Trigo Springs Road.) Follow the road 7.1 miles east to the trailhead. The road will turn left (north) and then right (east) before reaching the destination. This road can be very rough, so be careful. The trail starts at the pedestrian gate on the east side of the parking area.

60 WATER CANYON WILDLIFE AREA

Awe-inspiring views of tent rock formations occur all along this hike.

IN AN AREA with breathtaking sights and gorgeous landforms that for all practical purposes is off-limits to exploring, Water Canyon Wildlife Area is a welcome oasis of land open to hiking. With no formal trails, there are plenty of options to wander and to discover spectacular views that go on forever.

DESCRIPTION

Water Canyon Wildlife Area (WCWA) on the eastern flank of Mount Taylor is a narrow 2,840-acre property of the New Mexico Department of Game and Fish. Completely surrounded by tribal and land-grant communities, Water Canyon offers a small island of beautiful land open to hiking. The drive alone is both educational and gorgeous.

When you leave the interstate, you'll drive along a small stretch of old Route 66. The route leaves Route 66 at Budville for an older version of 66 to pass by the old land grant community of Cubero. From there you'll go through Cubero Land Grant farms and pastures. You'll also have uninterrupted and magnificent views of Mount Taylor. A bit farther on you'll leave the pavement and be in the midst of sandstone mesas and canyons. The unpaved road can be rough, so you won't want to take this drive in bad weather. In dry weather you should be OK if you're careful. Eventually, you'll see a small stream flowing from Water Canyon. And when you enter the canyon, you'll be in a ponderosa forest. There are several places along the road where you can park.

DISTANCE & CONFIGURATION: 2.5- to 3.5-mile out-and-back

DIFFICULTY: Moderate–strenuous

SCENERY: Forest, stream, canyon, grassland, expansive views

EXPOSURE: Shaded along the stream; full sun at higher elevations

TRAIL TRAFFIC: Low

TRAIL SURFACE: Pine straw, rock, scree

HIKING TIME: 1.5–2.5 hours

DRIVING DISTANCE: 64 miles from the Big I

ELEVATION GAIN: 7,172' at trailhead; 7,680' at overlook

ACCESS: Habitat Management and Access Validation required for access (see Description for details)

WHEELCHAIR ACCESS: No

MAPS: USGS *Mount Taylor*

FACILITIES: None

CONTACT: New Mexico Department of Game and Fish, wildlife.state.nm.us, 505-476-8000

LOCATION: North of Acoma

COMMENTS: The access validation only costs $4 and can be bought online (it's good for 4 people). Leashed dogs are allowed on trails.

LAST-CHANCE FOOD/GAS: All services at Exit 108, 13 miles from the trailhead

Water Canyon is a major drainage that spills east from Mount Taylor's caldera and turns south to flow down to the Cubero Land Grant. Its total length runs about 8 miles, 7 of which cross strictly off-limits pueblo and private lands. In 1953 the state purchased the property that would become the Water Canyon Wildlife Area (WCWA) to provide public access to big-game hunting. Deer, elk, and turkey are the most common game.

Although the land was acquired for hunting, hikers are also welcome now that the Department of Game and Fish added WCWA to its Gaining Access Into Nature (GAIN) inventory. The GAIN program allows for wildlife viewing and other activities on State Game Commission–owned Wildlife Management Areas (that is, lands that normally are open mainly for hunting and fishing).

You'll need a New Mexico Department of Game and Fish Habitat Management and Access Validation to hike in WCWA. At the time of this writing the validation only costs $4 and allows up to four people to hike at WCWA. You can buy the validation online at wildlife.state.nm.us. The fee goes toward improving wildlife habitat.

Several old roads and trails cross the property, but they're not easy to come by. You'll quickly notice the obstacles to long hikes here. The road section through the WCWA is a mere mile long, terminating at a hefty gate to Mount Taylor Ranch. To complicate east–west exploration, canyon walls escalate 700 feet within 0.3 mile of the stream banks.

Since there are no formal trails at WCWA, our hike follows paths made by local cows. The paths lead to incredible views. Begin the hike by following the road or stream (your choice) north. Depending upon where you parked, you'll reach the northern boundary of WCWA at the gate to Mount Taylor Ranch very soon.

Turn left (west) at the boundary and start following the fence uphill. Keep an eye out for a cow path coming in from the left. When you see it, follow it uphill into the woods. In a few hundred feet, the cow path will angle off to the left. There should

Water Canyon Wildlife Area

Water Canyon

CR 8

WATER CANYON WILDLIFE AREA

N

0.2 mile

0.2 kilometer

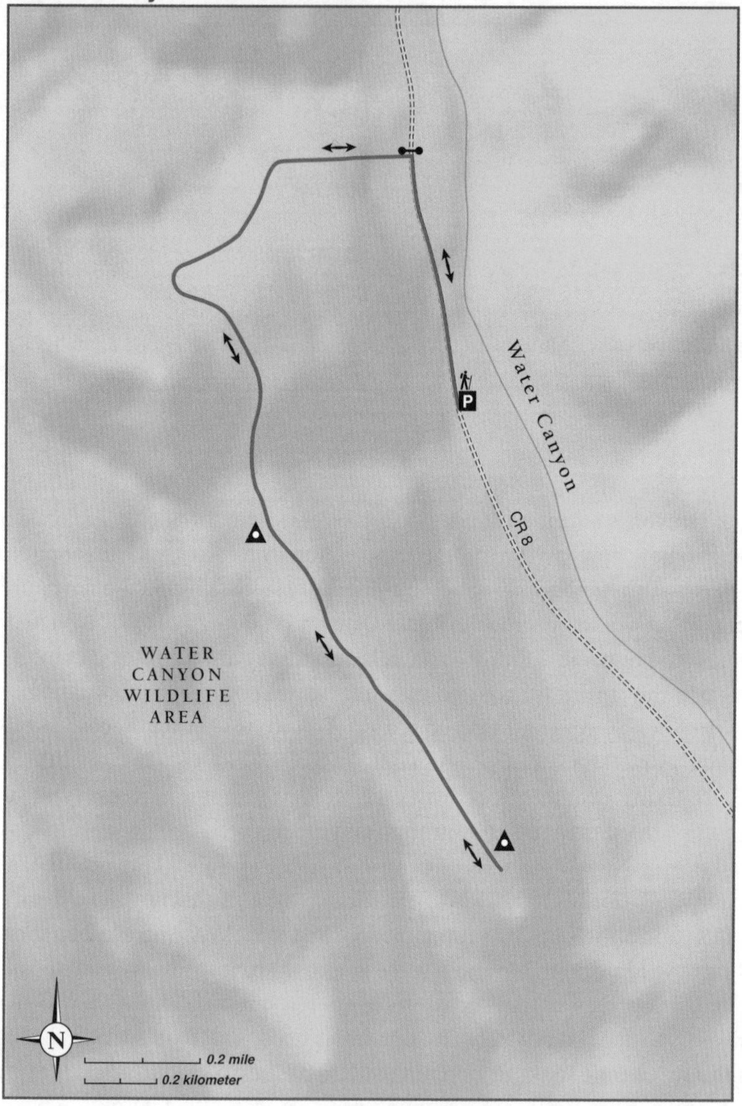

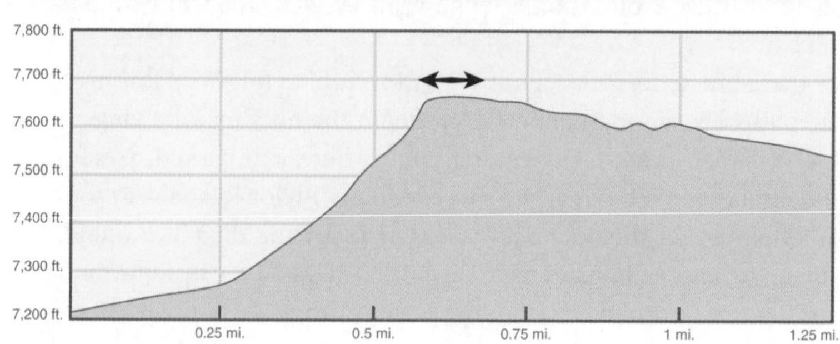

be a cairn marking the change of direction. Keep following the path and watch out for branches. (Remember this is a cow path.) You'll be going through a mixture of piñon, juniper, alligator juniper, ponderosa, and scrub oak.

The path soon levels and begins heading south. At this point you have climbed 450 feet in a little more than 0.3 mile. The path soon emerges from the woods (N35° 10.586' W107° 30.834') and you'll be on a mesa top with open views. The ground on the mesa top is a mixture of volcanic rock, ash, and sandstone. You'll have fabulous views of sandstone cliffs and tent rock–like formations in the ash. Keep walking south to the tip of the mesa for amazing views that go on forever. You can see the sandstone formations across Laguna and Acoma lands, the volcanic fields of Malpais, and mountains far to the south. This view alone makes this hike worthwhile.

To return to the bottom, just go down the way you came up. When you reach the bottom, take some time to explore the creek. And one final note, you're likely to see cows running through the canyon, so you might want to keep your dogs leashed.

NEARBY ACTIVITIES

Bibo is a small community in the Cebolleta Land Grant on the east side of Mount Taylor. As the crow flies, Bibo is only 7.5 miles from Water Canyon. With mountains and broken country in between it's about a 30-mile drive. But a drive to Bibo and its sister community of Seboyeta is a good way to complete your exploration of the area.

When you reach Bibo, get a "world-famous Bibo burger" at the historic **Bibo Bar,** established in 1913. The fresh half-pound patties are handmade daily. Friendly staff there can best advise on how to enjoy the local sights. Call 505-552-9428 or visit bibobar.com. To get there, take Exit 114 at Laguna and go west about 1.2 miles to the turnoff for Paguate and Seboyeta. Turn right and drive about 11 miles north to Bibo.

After having a burger, you might consider driving 2 more miles north to Seboyeta to visit **Los Portales Shrine.** The shrine is tucked into a cavelike sandstone alcove about a mile north of the town and requires a short walk to get there. It is definitely an only-in-New Mexico experience and part of what makes this state so special.

• •

GPS TRAILHEAD COORDINATES N35° 10.615' W107° 30.634'

DIRECTIONS From I-40 West, take Exit 104. Turn right off the ramp, then left onto NM 124, and go about a mile northwest toward Budville. (Heed the notice regarding the Cubero Land Grant.) Bear to the right on "Old" Route 66 toward Cubero and go 1 mile north. Turn right onto Water Canyon Road and go 0.2 mile northeast. Bear left onto CR 8 and go 2.1 miles to a Y-junction. Bear left onto Picaco Peak Road and go 5 miles north. Park in the pulloff by the stream.

APPENDIX A: Public Lands

STATE AND LOCAL AGENCIES

ALBUQUERQUE OPEN SPACE DIVISION

www.cabq.gov/openspace
6500 Coors Blvd. NW
Albuquerque, NM 87120
505-897-8831

The OSD manages 28,000-plus acres in and around Albuquerque to conserve natural and archaeological resources, provide opportunities for outdoor education and places for high- and low-impact recreation, and define the edges of the urban environment.

BERNALILLO COUNTY OPEN SPACE

bernco.gov/openspace
111 Union Square SE, Suite 200
Albuquerque, NM 87102
505-314-0400

With a mission to provide opportunities for education and recreation, BernCo Open Space manages a dozen properties in the East Mountains and in Albuquerque's North and South Valleys.

MIDDLE RIO GRANDE CONSERVANCY DISTRICT (MRGCD)

mrgcd.com
1931 2nd St. SW
Albuquerque, NM 87103
505-247-0234

The MRGCD oversees 1,200 miles of ditches and canals to ensure that the Middle Rio Grande Valley is full of farmlands, wildlife, and recreational opportunities.

NEW MEXICO DEPARTMENT OF GAME AND FISH (NMDGF)

wildlife.state.nm.us
3841 Midway Place NE
Albuquerque, NM 87109
505-222-4700

The NMDGF manages 56 areas that provide primarily for fishing and hunting, though many include camping, picnicking areas, and trails for hiking and wildlife viewing.

NEW MEXICO STATE LAND OFFICE

nmstatelands.org
310 Old Santa Fe Trail
Santa Fe, NM 87501
505-827-5760

The New Mexico State Land Office manages some nine million surface acres. Hiking, hunting, and horseback riding is allowed by permit on publicly accessible and non-commercial land. Permit applications can be downloaded from the office's website.

NEW MEXICO STATE PARKS

nmparks.com
1220 S. St. Francis Drive
Santa Fe, NM 87505
505-476-3355

With 34 parks throughout the state, the New Mexico State Parks Division manages more than 118,000 acres, not including water-surface area in 17 reservoirs. Annual day-use passes and camping permits are available to purchase online.

FEDERAL AGENCIES

BUREAU OF LAND MANAGEMENT (BLM)

blm.gov

The BLM manages 13.4 million surface acres in New Mexico, most of which are open to outdoor recreational activities, including backpacking, hiking, biking, whitewater boating, fishing, caving, wildlife viewing, and cultural-site touring.

Rio Puerco Field Office
100 Sun Ave. NE
Pan American Building, Suite 300
Albuquerque, NM 87109
505-761-8700

Taos Field Office
226 Cruz Alta Road
Taos, NM 87571
505-758-8851

Socorro Field Office
901 S. Highway 85
Socorro, NM 87801
575-835-0412

NATIONAL PARK SERVICE (NPS)

nps.gov

NPS boasts more than 1.6 million visitors to the 13 national parks in New Mexico. Also included in the NPS New Mexico inventory are 1,085 National Register of Historic Places listings, 12 National Natural Landmarks, and three World Heritage Sites.

U.S. FISH AND WILDLIFE SERVICE (USFWS)

fws.gov

USFWS manages seven National Wildlife Refuges that are open for wildlife viewing.

U.S. FOREST SERVICE (USFS)

fs.usda.gov

The USFS manages about 9 million acres of New Mexico's most ecologically diverse lands ranging in elevation from 4,000 to more than 13,000 feet.

Cibola National Forest

fs.usda.gov/cibola
2113 Osuna Road NE, Suite A
Albuquerque, NM 87113
505-346-3900

Mountainair Ranger District
40 Ranger Station Road
Mountainair, New Mexico 87036
505-847-2990

Mount Taylor Ranger District
1800 Lobo Canyon Road
Grants, NM 87020
505-287-8833

Sandia Ranger District
11776 NM 337
Tijeras, NM 87059
505-281-3304

Santa Fe National Forest

fs.usda.gov/santafe
11 Forest Lane
Santa Fe, NM 87508
505-438-5300

Española Ranger District
1710 N. Riverside Drive
Española, NM 87532
505-753-7331

Jemez Ranger District
NM 4
Jemez Springs, NM 87025
575-829-3535

OTHER AGENCIES

PUBLIC LANDS INFORMATION CENTER (PLIC)

publiclands.org
301 Dinosaur Trail
Santa Fe, NM 87508
505-954-2002, 877-276-9404

Billing itself as "Your One-Stop Source for Recreation Information," the PLIC is a handy resource for planning outdoor activities in the western states. Their site includes links to road conditions, weather, fire alerts, and an online store for books and maps.

APPENDIX B: Everything Else You Need to Know About New Mexico

GET INVOLVED

ALBUQUERQUE WILDLIFE FEDERATION (AWF)

abq.nmwildlife.org

Albuquerque Wildlife Federation is an all-volunteer nonprofit organization focused on New Mexico's wildlife and habitat resources. AWF offers monthly meetings featuring guest speakers, and opportunities to participate in restoration projects.

AUDUBON NEW MEXICO

nm.audubon.org; 505-983-4609

Four chapters of the New Mexico Audubon Council offer programs and field trips throughout the year. Visit the scenic headquarters and hiking trails at the Randall Davey Audubon Center at 1800 Upper Canyon Road in Santa Fe.

NEW MEXICO WILDERNESS ALLIANCE

nmwild.org; 505-843-8696

The New Mexico Wilderness Alliance is a grassroots environmental organization dedicated to the protection, restoration, and continued enjoyment of New Mexico's wildlands and wilderness areas. Check their events calendar for hikes and other outings.

SIERRA CLUB

riograndesierraclub.org; 505-243-7767 (Albuquerque Office)

With a mission to "explore, enjoy and protect the planet," the Sierra Club offers numerous opportunities for activism, volunteer programs, and organized hikes throughout New Mexico.

GEAR UP

ALBUQUERQUE

Cabela's

cabelas.com
5151 Lang Ave. NE
505-326-2700

Charlie's Hunting and Fishing Specialist

charliessportinggoods.net
7600 Menaul Blvd. NE
505-293-5290
This is the spot for topo maps.

The North Face

thenorthface.com
2240 Q Street NE
505-872-0134

REI

rei.com
1550 Mercantile Ave. NE
505-247-1191

Sportsman's Warehouse

sportsmanswarehouse.com
1450 Renaissance Blvd. NE
505-761-9900

Sport Systems

nmsportsystems.com
6915 Montgomery NE
505-837-9400

SANTA FE

Alpine Sports
alpinesportsonline.com
121 Sandoval St.
505-983-5155

REI
rei.com
500 Market St.
505-982-3557

Travel Bug
mapsofnewmexico.com
839 Paseo de Peralta
866-992-0418

VISITOR INFORMATION

ALBUQUERQUE CONVENTION AND VISITORS BUREAU

visitalbuquerque.org
800-284-2282

NEW MEXICO TOURISM DEPARTMENT

newmexico.org
505-827-7336

SANTA FE CONVENTION AND VISITORS BUREAU

santafe.org
800-777-2489

For information on just about everything else in Albuquerque, dial 311 from any local phone or visit cabq.gov/a-z.

Aspens cover the hillside seen at Del Agua Overlook (Hike 15, page 91).

INDEX

A

Abbey, Edward, 62
Abert's squirrels, 95–96
Abó Pass Area, 254–258
Abó Ruins–Salinas Pueblo Missions National Monument, 258
Access (hike profiles), 5
Acequias, 36–37
agencies, federal, state, local, 316–318
Albert G. Simms Park, 64
Albuquerque
  and environs map, viii
  Greater. *See* Greater Albuquerque
  northwest of. *See* Northwest of Albuquerque
  south, west. *See* South and West of Albuquerque
Albuquerque Riverside Drain, 70
Aldo Leopold Forest, 72
Aldo Leopold Trail, 70
Alpine Sports (Santa Fe), 320
altitude sickness, 13
Alvarez, Armando, 267
Anaya, Rudolfo, 227
Ancestral Puebloan cliff dwellings, 133
Ancho Springs Trail, 169
animal encounters, 18
animals and plants, 18
Armijo Trail–Cienega Spring, 86–90
aspen trees, 91–92
Ausherman, Stephen, xi, 327

B

Ball Ranch, 22–25
Bandelier National Monument, 166
Bandelier National Monument, Falls Trail, 132–136
Battle of Glorieta (Civil War), 301
Battleship Rock picnic area, 213, 214
Bear Wallow Trail, 138, 140
bears, 14, 284
Belen Cutoff, 254–255
Belen Harvey House Museum, 287
Bernalillito Mesa, 219
Bernalillo, 221
Bernalillo Open Space, 30, 31
Bernardo Waterfowl Area (BWA), 302
Big Block Climbing Area, 109
black bears, 14, 284
Black Volcano, 55, 57
Bond Volcano, 57–58
book, this
  about, 1–3
  how to use, 3–7
boots, hiking, 9
Borrego Trail, 137–140
Bosque Preserve, 38–40
Bosque Preserve and Corrales Acequias, 36–40
Bosque/Ditch Walk–Rio Grande Nature Center, 69–73
Box Spring Trail, Red Canyon, 110–111
Brave Cowboy, The (Abbey), 62
Broken Mesa Trail, 169–170
bubonic plague, 16
Buckman–Diablo Canyon, 151–155

C

Cabelas (Albuquerque), 319
Cabeza de Baca family, 242
Cabezon Peak, 192–195
cacti and yucca, 17
Caja del Rio, 180
Camino Real, 155, 161
Cañada de la Cueva, 141–145
Cañada del Ojo, 259–263
Candela, Gregory, 265
Candelaria Farm, 73
Cañon, 162
Cañon de San Diego Land Grant, 205
Cañon del Agua, 121
Cañoncito de las Cabras, 297
Cañoncito Trails, 89
Canyon Estates–Faulty Trails, 26–30
Carlito Springs, 31–35
Casa Grande Trading Post & Mining Museum, 150
Casa San Ysidro, 37
category, hikes by, xiii–xvi
Cebolleta Mountains, 288
cell phones, 13
Cerrillos Hills State Park, 146–150
Cerro Blanco–Fourth of July Canyon, 95–99
Cerro Columbo, 124
Cerro Guadalupe, 201
Cerros Colorados, 199
Cerros del Rio volcanic field, 180
Chaco Canyon, 200
Chamisa Trail, 159
Charlie's Hunting and Fishing Specialist (Albuquerque), 319
Cibola National Forest, 116
Cienega Spring–Armijo Trail, 86–90
Cienega Trail, 66

clothing, 9
Cochiti Lake, Cochiti Dam, 44
Cochiti Pueblo, 133
Comments (hike profiles), 5
Contact (hike profiles), 5
Continental Divide Trail (CDT), 292
Continental Divide Trail (CDT), Deadman Peaks, 196–199
Coronado, Francisco Vasquez de, 50
Coronado State Monument, 221
Corrales, 36
Corrales Acequias and Bosque Preserve, 36–40
Corrales Bosque Preserve, 38–40
Corrales Winery, 37, 40
cougars, 15
cows, 14
Coyote Call Trail, 245–246
Crest Spur Trail, 94
Crest Trail, 26, 29, 94, 98
Crest Trail–Tree Spring, 125–129
Cubero Land Grant, 312, 313

D

David Canyon–Mars Court Trailhead, 105–109
Deadman Peaks, Continental Divide Trail (CDT), 196–199
deer mice, 16
dehydration, 13
Del Agua Overlook, 91–94
Description (hike profiles), 6
Devils Tower, 193
Diablo Canyon–Buckman, 151–155
Difficulty (hike profiles), 4
Diplodocus dinosaur, 223
Directions (hike profiles), 6
Distance & Configuration (hike profiles), 4
Dominguez, Fray Francisco, 265
Dominguez, Tomé, 264
drinking water, 8–9, 13
Driving Distance (hike profiles), 5
Dry Rivers and Standing Rocks (Thybony), 228
Dunigan, James "Pat," 243

E

East Fork Trail, 217
East of the Mountains
  described, 1–2
  featured hikes, 85–129
  hikes by category, xiii, xv
  map, 84
El Cerro de Los Lunas, 282
El Cerro Tomé, 264–268
El Malpais National Monument, Sandstone Bluffs, 269–273
El Modelo, Albuquerque, 83
El Rancho de las Golondrinas, 165
Elena Gallegos Picnic Area, Albert G. Simms Park, 64, 66
Elevation Gain (hike profiles), 5
elevation profiles, 4
equipment, gear, 10–11
Espinosa, Aurelio Macedonio, 101
etiquette, trail, 18
Exploring the Jemez Country (Pettitt), 227
Exposure (hike profiles), 5
exposure to sun, heat, 13

F

Facilities (hike profiles), 5
Falls Trail, Bandelier National Monument, 132–136
Faulty Trails–Canyon Estates, 26–30
fauna and flora, 14–17
federal agencies, 317–318
first aid kits, 10–11
Fletcher Trail, 62
flora and fauna, 14–17
food, 13
footwear, 9
Four Seasons Visitor Center, 129
Fourth of July Canyon–Cerro Blanco, 95–99
Frijoles Canyon, 132

G

Gaining Access Into Nature (GAIN) inventory, 313
Galisteo Basin, 141–142
Garrett Homestead, 273
gear
  essential, 10–11
  stores, 319–320
Golden Open Space, 100–104
GPS Trailhead Coordinates (hike profiles), 6
Greater Albuquerque
  described, 1
  featured hikes, 21–83
  hikes by category, xiii, xv
  map, 20
Greater Santa Fe
  described, 2
  featured hikes, 131–189
  hikes by category, xiii–xiv, xv–xvi
  map, 130

Guadalupe ghost town, 203
Guadalupe Outlier, 200–203
Guadalupe Ruin, 200, 201
Guide to the Jemez Mountains (Isaacs), 227
guidebook, how to use this, 3–7
Gutiérrez-Minge House, 37
gypsum crystals, 263

H

Hagan, 104
hantavirus, 16
Harvey House Dining Room, 287
hats, 9
hazard trees, 14
heat exhaustion, 13
Herrera Mesa, 260, 274–277
Hibben, Frank, 279
Hidden Mountain, 278–282
hike profiles, 4
hikes
  by category, xiii–xvi
  East of the Mountains, xiii, xv, 84–129
  Greater Albuquerque, xiii, xv, 20–83
  Greater Santa Fe, xiii–xiv, xv–xvi, 130–189
  Northwest of Albuquerque, xiv, xvi, 190–251
  South and West of Albuquerque, xvi, 252–315
hiking boots, 9
Hiking Time (hike profiles), 5
Holiday Mesa, 204–208
Hoodoo Trail, Ojito Wilderness, 218–221
hoodoos, 228, 230
Horse Trail, 251
hunting, 18
Hyde, Benjamin, 159
Hyde Memorial State Park, 138, 156–160
Hyde Park Lodge, 159
hypothermia, 13

I

Immaculate Church and Museum, 268
In Brief (hike profiles), 5
Isaacs, Judith Ann, 227

J

JA Volcano, 55, 57
Jemez, 227
Jemez Falls, 216, 217
Jemez Mountains, 213, 216
Jemez Pueblo, 204, 232
Jemez River, 214
Jemez Spring (Anaya), 227
Jemez Spring Bath House, 217
Juan Tomas Open Space, 115–119

K

Kasha-Katuwe Tent Rocks National Monument, 41–44
key information, 4–5

L

La Bajada Road, 165
La Cieneguilla Petroglyph Site and Cañon, 161–165
La Leña WSA: Empedrado Ridge–CDT, 209–212
La Luz Trail to the Crest and Tram, 45–49
La Madera, 104
La Madera Ski Area, 125
La Puerta del Sol sculpture, 267
La Ventana, 273
Ladron Peak, 304
Laguna Burger, 277
Laguna Indian Reservation, 282
Las Conchas, 217
Last-Chance Food/Gas (hike profiles), 5
latitude and longitude, 6
Lava Falls, 273
legend, map, vii, 3
Leonora Curtin Wetland Preserve, 165
Leopold, Aldo, 72
lightning, 13–14
Lion Cave Trails–Lower Water Canyon, 166–170
livestock, 14–15
Location (hike profiles), 5
Lonely Are the Brave (movie), 62
longitude and latitude, 6
Los Alamos National Laboratory (LANL), 166
los duendes (elves or dwarfs), 101
Lower Water Canyon–Lion Cave Trails, 166–170

M

Madrid, 150
Manzano Crest Trail, Red Canyon, 113, 310
Manzano Mountain Wilderness, 284, 308
Manzano Mountains, 32, 105, 115, 254, 283, 307
maps
  See also specific hike
  Albuquerque and environs, iv
  East of the Mountains, 84
  Greater Albuquerque, 20
  Greater Santa Fe, 130

maps *(continued)*
Northwest of Albuquerque, 190
overview and legend, 3
regional, 3
South and West of Albuquerque, 252
topographic, 7
trail, 3–4
Maps (hike profiles), 5
Mars Court Trailhead–David Canyon, 105–109
Mayfield, Sheryl, 299
McCauley Hot Springs, 213–217
Medallion Trees, 30, 87, 89
Mendoza, Eleña Ramirez de, 264
meridians and parallels, 6
Mexican Gray Wolf Reintroduction Program, 299
Middle Rio Grande, 69
Montaño, 73
Monte Largo Canyon, 283–287
Monte Largo Spring, 284
Morrison Formation, 275
Mount Taylor, 54, 193, 201, 270
Mount Taylor: Gooseberry Spring, 288–292
Mount Taylor Ranch, 315
mountain lions, 15
Movie Trail, 62
Museum of Indian Arts and Culture, 145
Museum of New Mexico Foundation (MNMF), 145
Musical Highway, the, 35
Mystery Rock, Hidden Mountain, 279, 281

N

Nambe Lake, 171–175, 179
Narrows Picnic Area, 273
National Hispanic Cultural Center, 83
National Recreation Trail, 41
Navajo Indians, 274
Nearby Activities (hike profiles), 6
New Mexico, public involvement, 319
New Mexico Trials Association (NMTA), 232, 233
North Face, the (Albuquerque), 319
Northwest of Albuquerque
described, 2
featured hikes, 191–251
hikes by category, xiv, xvi
map, 190

O

Ojito de San Antonio Open Space, 30
Ojito Wilderness
Hoodoo Trail, 218–221
Seismosaurus Trail, 222–226
Ojo del Espirita Santo Grant, 192, 193, 195
Old Monte Largo Trail, 286
Open Space Visitor Center, 53
Osha Peak, 310
Oso Corredor, 126
Otero Canyon Trail, 115
Overlook Park, White Rock, 186, 189
Ox Canyon Trail, Red Canyon, 111, 113

P

Paliza Canyon Goblin Colony, 227–231
panthers, 15
parallels and meridians, 6
Paseo de la Mesa Trail, 58
Paseo del Bosque, 70
Pecos Wilderness, 171, 172, 176
Penitente Brotherhood, 264
Perea Nature Trail, 236
Petroglyph National Monument
Piedras Marcadas, 50–53
the Volcanoes, 54–58
Petroglyph National Monument Visitor Center, Las Imágenes, 53
Pettitt, Roland A., 227
Piedra Lisa Trail, 60
Piedra Lisa Trailhead Options, 59–63
Piedras Marcadas, Petroglyph National Monument, 50–53
Piedras Marcadas Pueblo ruins, 53
Pino Trail, 64–68
plague, 16
plants and animals, 14–17
poison ivy, 16
Ponderosa Family Restaurant & Grill, 99
Porter, 237, 238
Pottery Mound pueblo, 282
Powerline Point Trail, 169
precipitation, monthly averages, 8
public lands agencies, 316–318
Public Lands Information Center (PLIC), 318
Pueblo Indians, 54–55, 237
Pueblo Revolt, 264
Puerto Nambe–Santa Fe Baldy, 176–179

R

rattlesnakes, 17
Red Canyon, 110–114
Red Mountain, 297
regional maps, 3
REI (Albuquerque), 319

REI (Santa Fe), 320
Riedling, Alexander, 116
Rio Grande Nature Center–Bosque/Ditch Walk, 69–73
Rio Grande River, 69, 135, 151, 152, 185, 221, 301
Rio Grande Valley State Park, 80
Rio Guadalupe, 205
Rio Puerco, 303
Route 66, 312
Ryan, David, 327

S

Sabino Canyon and Juan Tomas Open Spaces, 115–119
safety
  advice for hikers in the Southwest, 13–14
  general, 11–12
Salinas Pueblo Missions National Monument, 114
San Antonio Hot Springs, 213–214
San Lorenzo Canyon, 293–297
San Luis, 199
San Mateo Mountains, 288
San Pedro Mountains Mining Area, 120–124
San Ysidro Church, 37
San Ysidro Trials Area, 232–236
sandhill cranes, 302
Sandia Crest, 45, 49, 92
Sandia Mountain Medallion Trees, 30, 87, 89
Sandia Mountain Wilderness, 75, 87, 128
Sandia Mountains, 59, 64–65
Sandia Peak Ski Area, 125
Sandia Peak Tramway, 129
Sandia Pueblo, 94
Sandia View Adventist Academy, 37
Sandiago's Grill, Albuquerque, 49
Sandstone Bluffs, El Malpais National Monument, 269–273
Sangre de Cristo Mountains, 137, 138, 171, 186
Santa Fe, Greater. *See* Greater Santa Fe
Santa Fe Baldy–Puerto Nambe, 176–179
Santa Fe Botanical Gardens, 165
Santa Fe National Forest, 137
Santa Fe Northwestern railroad, 237
Santa Fe River, 164
Scenery (hike profiles), 4
scorpions, 16–17
Second Street, Albuquerque, 83
Seismosaurus Trail, Ojito Wilderness, 222–226
Sevilleta de la Joya Land Grant, 298
Sevilleta National Wildlife Refuge, 254, 293, 298–302
Sevilleta National Wildlife Refuge Field Guide to Flowers (Mayfield), 299
Shinrin-yoku (forest bathing), 86
Shooting Range Park, 58
Sierra Ladrones, 301, 303–306
Sierra Nacimiento, 232
Silvery Minnow Channel, 71
snakes, 17
Soda Dam, 213
Soda Springs Trail, 154
South and West of Albuquerque
  described, 3
  featured hikes, 253–315
  hikes by category, xiv, xvi
  map, 252
South Sandia Peak, 74
Spence Hot Springs, 213
Spirit Lake, 176
Sport Systems (Albuquerque), 319
Sportsman's Warehouse (Albuquerque), 319
Spruce Spring Trail, 110
Stable Mesa, 237–241
state, local agencies, 316–317
Station San Marcos, 144
Sulfur Canyon, 86, 87, 90
Surfing New Mexico (Candela), 265

T

Taylor, President Zachary, 288
Tecolote Trail, 129
temperatures, average daily, 8
Tent Rocks, 41–44, 242
Thorton Ranch, 142
Three Gun–Embudo Trails, Up-and-Over-the-Sandias Adventure, 74–78
thunderstorms, 13–14
Thybony, Scott, 227–228
ticks, 17
Tierra Amarilla Anticline, 218, 223, 247
Tijeras, 31
Tijeras Pueblo Archaeological Site, 119
Tinkertown Museum, 90
Tiwa pueblo of Kuaua, 221
Tomé Hill Park, 265, 267, 268
Tomé Land Grant, 264, 308
Tomé Plaza, 268
topographic maps, 7
trail etiquette, 18
trail maps, 3–4
Trail Surface (hike profiles), 5
Trail Traffic (hike profiles), 5
Travel Bug, Santa Fe, 320

Travertine Falls, 27
Tree Spring–Crest Trail, 125–129
trees, hazard, 14
Trigo Canyon, 307–311
Truchas Peaks, 177
Trumbo, Dalton, 62
Tunnel Canyon, 115
Twin Hills, 180–184

U

University of New Mexico (UNM), 299
Up-and-Over-the-Sandias Adventure, Three Gun–Embudo Trails, 74–78
Upper Frijoles Falls, 133
Upper Rio Puerco, 209

V

Valle de Oro National Wildlife Refuge, 79–83
Valle Grande Trail, 246
Valles Caldera, 270
Valles Caldera National Preserve, 242–246
Valles Caldera Trust, 243
visitor information, 320
Volcanoes, Petroglyph National Monument, 54–58
Vulcan Volcano, 55, 57, 58

W

Walatowa Visitor Center, 208
water, drinking, 8–9, 13
Water Canyon Trail, 292
Water Canyon Wildlife Area (WCWA), 312–315
Waterfall Canyon, 62
weather, 7–8
West of Albuquerque. *See* South and West of Albuquerque
Wheelchair Access (hike profiles), 5
White Ridge Bike Trails Area, 247–251
White Rock, 185
White Rock Canyon, 151, 154
White Rock Canyon: Red Dot/Blue Dot Trails, 185–189
White Rock visitor center, 189
wilderness study areas (WSAs), 209
Winsor Trail, 140, 172, 177, 179
Woodruff, Michael, 209

Y

yucca and cacti, 17

Z

Zia Pueblo, 225
Zuni-Acoma Trail, 273

ABOUT THE AUTHORS

David Ryan left his conventional job in the business world at the age of 49 to rearrange his life into a mixture of income-producing and personal activities. Since making that change, he has found time to walk the 2,180-mile Appalachian Trail from end to end, walk the Camino de Santiago from France to Santiago de Compostela in the west of Spain, become involved in archaeology, earn a black belt in aikido, and pursue several other outdoor and walking activities. For the past 18 years he has explored the New Mexico backcountry, looking for previously unknown archaeology sites as a volunteer for the Bureau of Land Management. He is the author of *Long Distance Hiking on the Appalachian Trail for the Older Adventurer, The Gentle Art of Wandering, The Bisbee Stairs,* and a blog on walking and wandering at gentleartofwandering.com. David lives in Albuquerque with his wife, Claudia, and his three dogs, Paddy, Petey, and Sparky. To contact David Ryan or receive hike updates, please visit 60hikesabq.com.

Stephen Ausherman has worked as a public-health assistant in Iraq, Nigeria, Kenya, and Tanzania; a teacher in Korea and China; and a journalist in India and the United States. He was a writer-in-residence at Buffalo National River in Arkansas, Devils Tower National Monument in Wyoming, and Bernheim Forest in Kentucky, and an artist-in-residence for Cornucopia Art Center in Minnesota, Blue Sky Project in Illinois, and Cape Cod National Seashore in Massachusetts. Born in China and raised in North Carolina, Stephen took an unscheduled detour to Albuquerque in 1996. He has lived there ever since.

DEAR CUSTOMERS AND FRIENDS,

SUPPORTING YOUR INTEREST IN OUTDOOR ADVENTURE, travel, and an active lifestyle is central to our operations, from the authors we choose to the locations we detail to the way we design our books. Menasha Ridge Press was incorporated in 1982 by a group of veteran outdoorsmen and professional outfitters. For many years now, we've specialized in creating books that benefit the outdoors enthusiast.

Almost immediately, Menasha Ridge Press earned a reputation for revolutionizing outdoors- and travel-guidebook publishing. For such activities as canoeing, kayaking, hiking, backpacking, and mountain biking, we established new standards of quality that transformed the whole genre, resulting in outdoor-recreation guides of great sophistication and solid content. Menasha Ridge Press continues to be outdoor publishing's greatest innovator.

The folks at Menasha Ridge Press are as at home on a whitewater river or mountain trail as they are editing a manuscript. The books we build for you are the best they can be, because we're responding to your needs. Plus, we use and depend on them ourselves.

We look forward to seeing you on the river or the trail. If you'd like to contact us directly, visit us at menasharidge.com. We thank you for your interest in our books and the natural world around us all.

SAFE TRAVELS,

Bob Sehlinger

BOB SEHLINGER
PUBLISHER